Dirk Alvermann

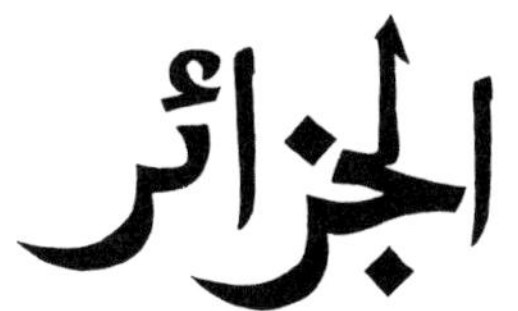

DIRK ALVERMANN

ALGERIA

Steidl

In Fall 2011, Steidl Verlag published *The Protest Box* edited by Martin Parr. It contains facsimile editions of five classic photo books, which until then had been out of stock, and which in different ways address the topic of political resistance. Dirk Alvermann's *Algerien* (Algeria) is one of these books.

For *The Protest Box* a facsimile edition of *Algerien*, which Rütten & Loening had published in 1960 in East Berlin, had been printed. When Gerhard Steidl visited the photographer in his studio to discuss the details of the reprint, he learned of the fascinating history of the book's publication, which convinced him to bring out another edition of *Algerien*.

Dirk Alvermann was twenty, a rebellious young man impressed by the Algerian people's struggle for freedom when, in the early 1950s, together with a unit of the Algerian National Liberation Front (FLN), he crossed the hermetically sealed border from Tunisia into the east Algerian war zone, determined to keep a photographic record of the events that were unfolding there. On his return to West Germany he endeavored to have his photos published by Rowohlt Verlag. Ernst Rowohlt, the aged founder of the company, inspected the dummy and promised Alvermann he would publish the book.

By the time Alvermann had completed the layout, management of the company had devolved into the hands of Heinrich Maria Ledig-Rowohlt, with whom the photographer now discussed the publication. Alvermann had designed a paperback book, as he wanted to reach as broad an audience as possible. The book was intended to be handed on from one person to another, like a political manifesto, for which the format of the "rowohlts-rotations-romane"[1], which had been appearing since 1950, was ideal.

Just at this time an unofficial delegation of the FLN journeyed to Bonn, then the capital of the Federal Republic of Germany. It negotiated with Hans-Jürgen Wischnewski, a member of the opposition Social Democrat party in the German parliament. While these political discussions were still taking place, the terrorist organization *La Main Rouge*[2] detonated a car bomb, which killed numerous people. As a result of the tense political situation and the fear of alienating Francophile readers and authors by siding with the Algerian resistance, Ledig-Rowohlt removed the book from the list of the publishing house.

The Algerian War and the struggle of the FLN was clearly too hot a potato for West Germany under Chancellor Adenauer, which had made Franco-German reconciliation a key issue. In East Germany, in the German Democratic Republic (GDR), Alvermann met with greater acceptance of his political photo and book project. The East Berlin publishing house Rütten & Loening was in principle willing to publish the book, but as a large-format illustrated hardcover edition. Alvermann, however, insisted on his idea for a pocketbook because the layout had been conceived for that format. Ultimately a compromise was agreed whereby the book was published in a pocketbook format but with a hard cover.

This new edition of *Algerien* can be traced back to the photographer's original idea: The book is designed in the traditional "rororo" format, has the desired cardboard cover and, with regard to content, corresponds down to the very last detail with the initial design. The photographs are accompanied by political documents of the time, quotations from French military sources, from pamphlets, newspapers, and magazines.

More than fifty years after it was first published, the book is more topical than ever, as it tells of a people's uprising against suppression and despotism, be it against European colonialism or, like today, against a home-grown dictatorial regime.

Translation: Jeremy Gaines

---

[1] "Rowohlt's rotation novels": the famous "rororo" books, the first German paperbacks.
[2] Red Hand. In the 1950s the organization was led by the foreign section of the French secret service, its task, to liquidate supporters of the Algerian fight for independence as well as leading members of the FLN at the time of the Algerian War.

FACTS

1.

"… colonisation knows neither humanity nor justice, neither civilisation nor progress."

2.

"They respect the rights of all peoples …"

3.

"Who have dared to rise up …"

4.

"… an organised revolution and not an anarchistic revolt."

5.

"The liberation of Algeria will be the shared achievement of all Algerians …"

6.

"… by the people and for the people."

On June 14, 1830, a 30,000-man French army landed in Algeria. In struggling for their freedom, the population put up fierce resistance to the intruders. It took half a century for the French to complete the conquest.

> "The conquest is based on the most important requirements that are closely bound to the maintenance of public order in France and even in Europe: opening a spacious realm for our surplus population and for the sale of the products of our manufacturing in exchange for goods that are foreign to our soil and our climes." General Gérard, French Minister of War, 1832

And how was this carried out?

> "We defiled temples and graves as well as the interiors of their houses — the sacred refuge of the Muslims — we have massacred people who had been guaranteed safe passage, we have had entire segments of the population slaughtered on mere suspicion and whose innocence was later proven. We have placed respected persons before trial, honourable men admired for having the valour to subject themselves to our rage, to stand up for their despondent countrymen."
> From a report of a French parliamentary commission, 1833

> "The bloodbath was horrifying. Their dwellings, the tents of the natives, found on the squares, streets, and courtyards, were strewn with corpses. One statistic from after the conquest established that 2,300 women and children had been killed." Pain, *Lettres familières sur l'Algérie*

This was "opening a spacious realm for our surplus population" according to the principle:

> "We must place our settlers wherever there is good and fertile land, without asking to whom the estates belong."
> General Bugeaud, Supreme Commander in Algeria, May 14, 1840

In 1850, the settlers had appropriated 115,000 hectares of land; by 1900, 1,682,000 hectares; by 1940, 2,720,000 hectares.

In 1950, the Muslim population possessed only 7,133,000 hectares in northern Algeria, which has a total surface area of 21 million hectares, while European and French subjects held 13,703,000 hectares. At this time, only 20 percent was in the hands of the smaller settlers. The rest was divided among large estate owners and large capitalist corporations. European colonisation in northern Algeria possesses not only two thirds of the soil; it also holds the estates with the best water resources. As early as 1925, it was estimated that the value per hectare of the European land holdings was three times that of the Muslim fields.

But only every tenth resident of Northern Algeria is of European descent.

The Mohammedan peasant has an average annual income of 180 new francs.

In France, an ordinary table costs 180 new francs.

In 1870, the Mohammedan peasant used an average of 5.9 hundredweights of grain per year.

In 1936, only 2.8 hundredweights.

In 1950, less then 2, including both seed and feed.

> "Around half a million families have no land at all, and earn their living as semi-tenants, full tenants, or as paid farm workers. The current distribution of property and land has led to the emergence of a huge rural proletariat whose life conditions are difficult and precarious."

"Documents algériens," May 17, 1956

With the natural resources at hand, the country could completely satisfy the needs of its population. In northern Algeria, there are luscious vineyards and orchards, large olive and cork groves, fertile grain and alfalfa fields. There is sheepherding in the steppes of southern Algeria, and the esparto grass that grows there is also an important raw material for papermaking.

Algeria is not a poor country. Its resources are considerable: iron, phosphate, zinc, lead, coal, manganese, natural gas, and oil.

The prerequisites are there, but there is almost no heavy or light industry in this country.

What again was the logic behind General Gérard's claim for the need to conquer Algeria? "For the sale of the products of our manufacturing in exchange for goods that are foreign to our soil and our climes." This is why there is only an insignificant food and textile industry, other than the remnants of local craftsmanship.

> "Almost a million people are without occupation, or not fully employed; the majority of the 350,000 young men who will have reached employment age in the next five years are left with the sole perspective of emigrating to a major city."
>
> *Quelques données du problème algérien*, June 1957

In Algeria, more than half of the Muslim population is under age 20, and only 5.5 percent is older than 60. Of 1,000 newborns, 181 have to die.

> "When considering the topographical distribution of doctors, it becomes clear that the cities of Algiers, Oran, and Constantine together have 1145 doctors, and that for the seven other larger cities, there are only 50. This means that for the rest of Algeria there are only approximately 350 doctors available, that is, four to eight for every 100,000 residents."
>
> C.-H. Favrod, *La Révolution Algérienne*

Before conquest, Algeria possessed 100 public and private schools. There were four universities: today there is only one, where 4,548 students of European background study, and only 557 of Arab-Berber background.

> "Only every sixth Mohammedan child of schooling age attends school, but all children of European origin; every third child of European origin attends secondary school, in contrast, only every 175th Mohammedan child."
>
> C.-H. Favrod, *La Révolution Algérienne*

And Arabic, the mother tongue of 92 percent of the population, is officially a foreign language.

> "Colonisation knows neither humanity nor justice, neither civilization nor progress. It is at its core an imperialist phenomenon. It thus requires for its development and mainte-

nance the simultaneous existence of two societies, where one
is suppressed by the other."

From the Manifesto of the Algerian People, submitted on
May 31, 1943 to French Governor General Peyrouton

*

"They respect the right of all peoples to choose the form of
government under which they will live; and they wish to see
sovereign rights and self government restored to those who
have been forcibly deprived of them."

Point 3, Atlantic Charta, signed on December 26, 1944 by France

When on the day of victory against fascism the Algerian people –
who had helped in the war effort – announced their desire for independence, the colonists in the city of Setif had 15,000 unarmed
demonstrators shot down. In a ten-day, gruesome massacre, tens
of thousands Muslims were killed.

On November 1, 1954, the Algerian people took up the armed struggle for its national demands. To crush the liberation movement,
French imperialism mobilised the largest colonial army in its history.
In 1955, the French troops in Algeria numbered 80,000. Today,
800,000 men stand on Algerian soil: one soldier for every European civilian.

"Our soldiers risk their lives
fighting against the unbelievers
who have dared to rise up.
The cross will know to protect them."

From a song sung by French settlers in the churches of
Algeria, "Free Algeria," October 1959

French taxpayers' money is being spent on this endeavour. As
a result, bread and wine in France is becoming more expensive,
the rents are rising, and social achievements are being dismantled.

"Fathers and sons are being stabbed to death as the French
soldiers occupy the villages. Mothers and daughters raped,
and then killed. Girls are being assembled and then taken
away, nobody knows where to ..."

Vecko Journalen, Stockholm, March 21, 1958

"In the hospital rooms, they ripped the clothes of the Muslims from their bodies, poured water on them, and attached the electrodes of a strong light machine to various body parts. After hours of such maltreatment, the tortured were awakened with a camphor injection, and hung from their thumbs with wires. They were whipped, and then, their bodies covered with wounds, were released, and they died soon thereafter or were beaten to death in cold blood."

Paul Lefèvre, soldier of the 3/94th Infantry Regiment, to the
President of the French Republic, September 1958

"45 dead, 74 disappeared, 27 villages, 1,000 huts, and 80 dugouts for the population, 1,000 tons of food, and 5,000 liters of oil destroyed or made inedible, 500 livestock confiscated."

Communiqué of the French Superior Command, from near El Milia, November 1958

But neither the military destruction machine of an army equipped with the most modern weapons and overwhelming numbers, nor its terror can break the resistant will of the Algerian people. This is why the colonialists are trying to prevent all contact between the fighters of the liberation movement and the Muslim population.

"One needs to realise what measures are used toward 'pacification.' The Algerians in the larger cities were banned to ghettos, the cities isolated on the flat countryside, the borders to Morocco and Tunisia installed with huge electric barriers. 365,000 people were forced to flee from the no man's land along the border fortifications."

Stimme der Gemeinde, Darmstadt, April 1, 1960

The villages were violently cleared or destroyed – or also simply bombed without warning and then combed through – the surviving residents settled in camps. One and a half million people vegetate between beating and watchtowers, usually the elderly, women, and children.

"The food situation is alarming in almost all the settlement centres: means of sustenance must be supplied for the people at any price to keep the experiment from ending in a catastrophe."

From the report of the official French Examination
Commission, April 1959

"According to estimates of French experts, the mortality of those interned at the resettlement centers runs to 30 percent."

"Free Algeria," October 1959

In five years, the Algerian people have lost 600,000 civilians through war and terror. How many are to be annihilated in this "experiment"?

*

"The overseas territories have reached a historical state of development as a result of which the colonial system has become economically useless, but socially and politically dangerous. Whether those that live from it like it or not – and whatever their rights might be – the time of presumptions has passed."

Capitaine Méric, *Révue militaire d'Information*, March 25, 1956

As the French expedition carried out their *sale guerre*, the dirty war in Vietnam, they also worked with Algerian units. The example and lessons of the victorious Vietminh and the success of national efforts in other formerly colonial or semi-colonial countries promoted the development of the Algerian liberation movement.

1954, the last year of the French colonial war in Indochina, would become the first year of the French colonial war in Algeria.

"France chose war to destroy Algerian national consciousness, and to maintain a state of affairs whose time had passed. In so doing, France made a decisive contribution to its own ruin."

El Moudjahid, November 1, 1959

Algerian parties and unions have joined to form the national liberation movement, the FLN. The military formation of the liberation movement is the national liberation army, the ALN, with up to 150,000 men. Although the Communist Party of Algeria maintains its political and organisational independence, it shares the movement's demands. Many of their members have been awarded medals in their struggle against the French colonial leaders.

In the summer of 1956, the FLN formulated their program:

"The Algerian Revolution has the historical task of destroying
the hated, decadent colonial system, anti-progress and
peace, and without reservation ... This is an organised revolution and not an anarchistic revolt. It is a national struggle
for the destruction of the anarchic colonial system and not a
religious war. It is an historical step forward for humanity and
not a return to feudalism. Finally, it is a struggle for the re-
birth of an Algerian state in the form of a democratic and social republic and not the restoration of outdated monarchies
or theocracies ... The liberation of Algeria will be the achievement of Algerians, and not of a part of the Algerian people,
regardless of how important it might be."

From the Charte de la Soumam, August 20, 1956

The National Liberation Front turns to the peasants and declares
its solidarity with their demands for land reform.
It appeals to the working class to organise Muslim and European
workers in a joint struggle against the collective enemy.
It appeals to intellectuals, merchants, and craftsmen, to women
and youth, to all segments of the population, to all ethnic groups.
It knows no racial discrimination, no religious persecution, and
no national superiority.
In the banner of its newspaper, *El Moudjahid* (the Fighter) it pres-
ents the demand: "Revolution by the people for the people."
The National Liberation Army is the army of the Algerian people.
The people have faith in this army, they join its ranks, they feed
the soldiers, clothe them, arm them, and invite them to their
hearth. The army liberates, protects, builds.
It cares for those left behind by acts of colonial terror and for the
refugees, in the liberated territories it helps with the establish-
ment of local self-administration and schooling. Their doctors and
nurses care for the ill among the civilian population. The army is
the hope of the people.

*

"On the Tenth Anniversary of NATO, Admiral Auboyneau,
Commander of the French Army of the Mediterranean and
Inter-Allied Commander in the Western Mediterranean, gave
a speech in which he claimed that the French army in Alge-

ria was fulfilling the 'traditional mission of protecting the population' by, 'whilst suffering great loss of life for four years, struggling against the most violent form of subversion that has ever been undertaken against NATO'... Among all NATO partners, the West German government has been most unabashed in their support."

Stimme der Gemeinde, Darmstadt, April 1, 1960

*

"Confident of the support of the People's Republic of China and other anti-imperialist countries, the Algerian people is more determined than ever to achieve its national independence.

Neither with fire nor with the sword, nor with military manoeuvers, nor the contribution of a dying colonialism, will the French imperialists and their Western allies vanquish our people.

The Algerian race is peace loving. But it also knows that this freedom can only be achieved through the decisive and uninterrupted struggle that it carries out against imperialism and for liberation and national independence."

Benjussef Benkhedda, before the Chinese People's Congress,
El Moudjahid, November 1, 1959

1.

" ... colonisation knows neither humanity nor justice, neither civilisation nor progress."

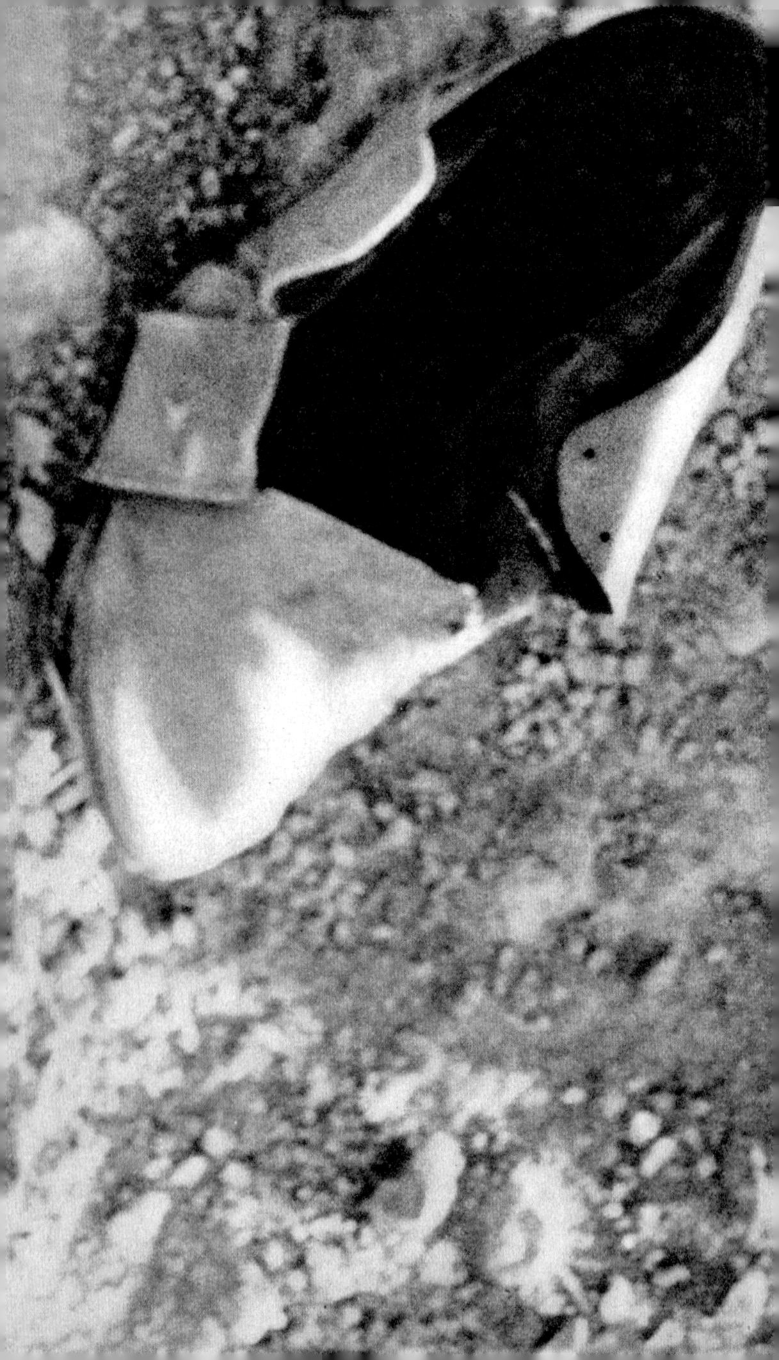

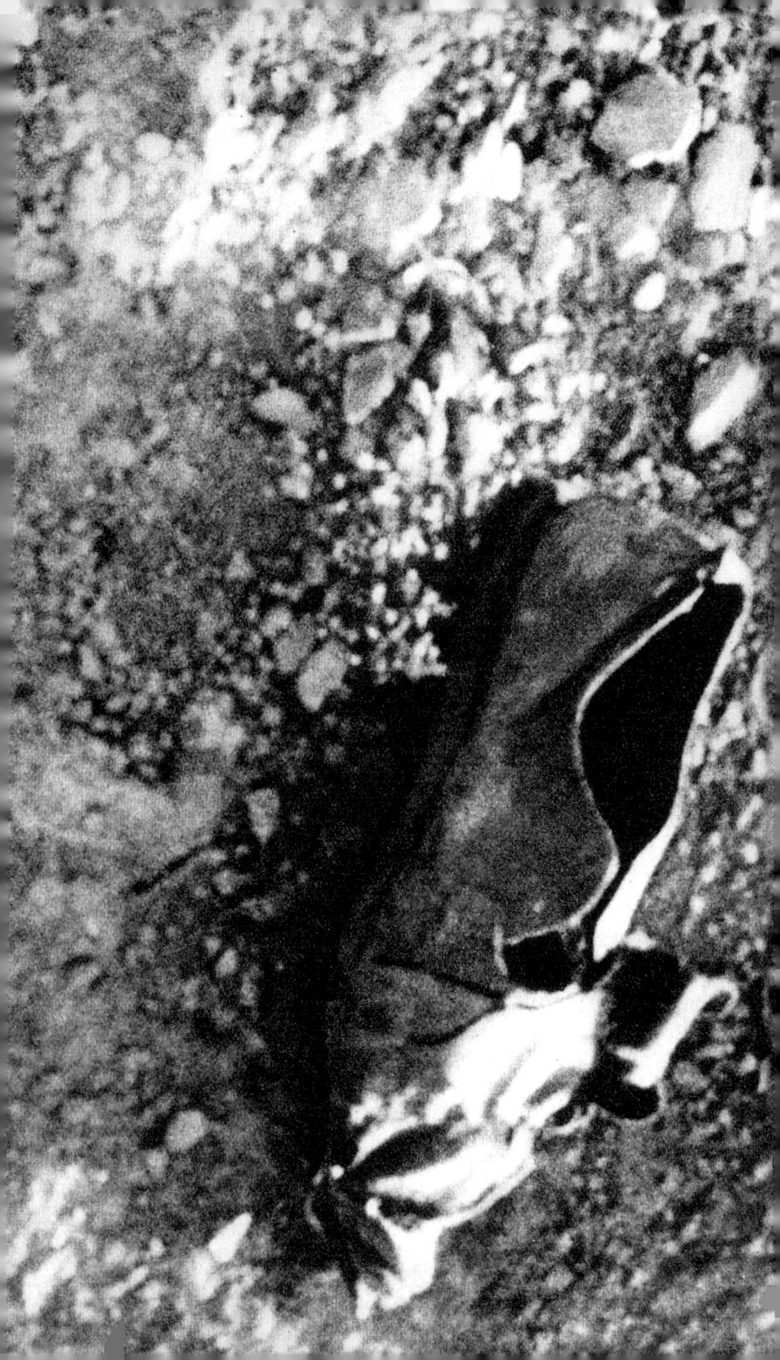

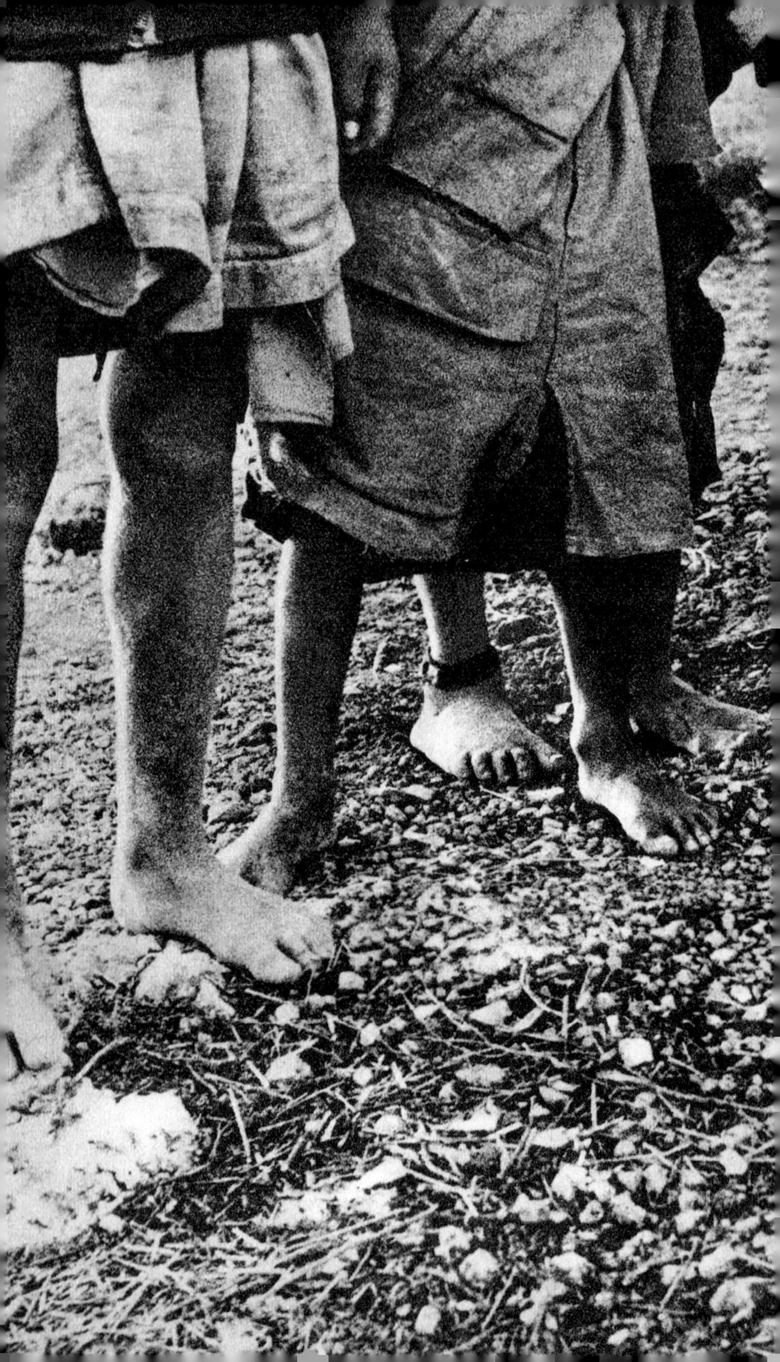

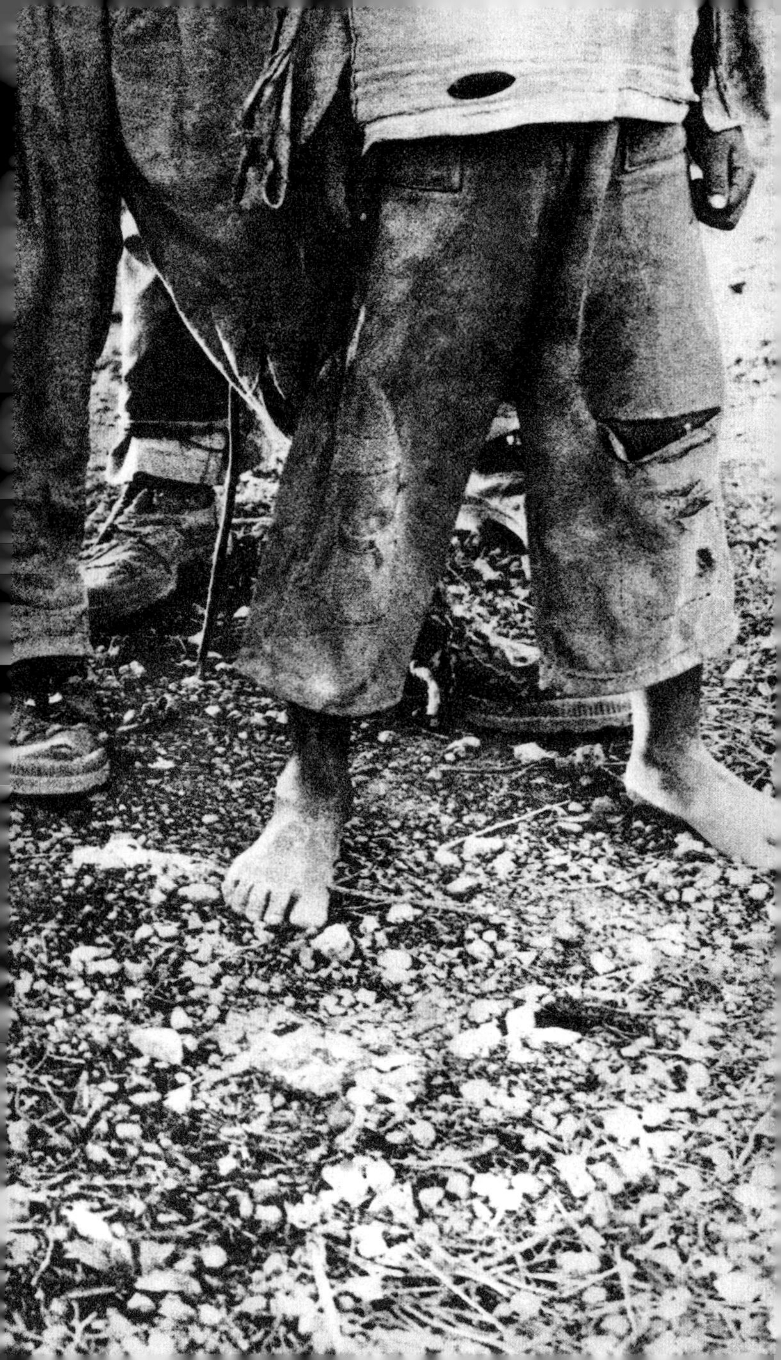

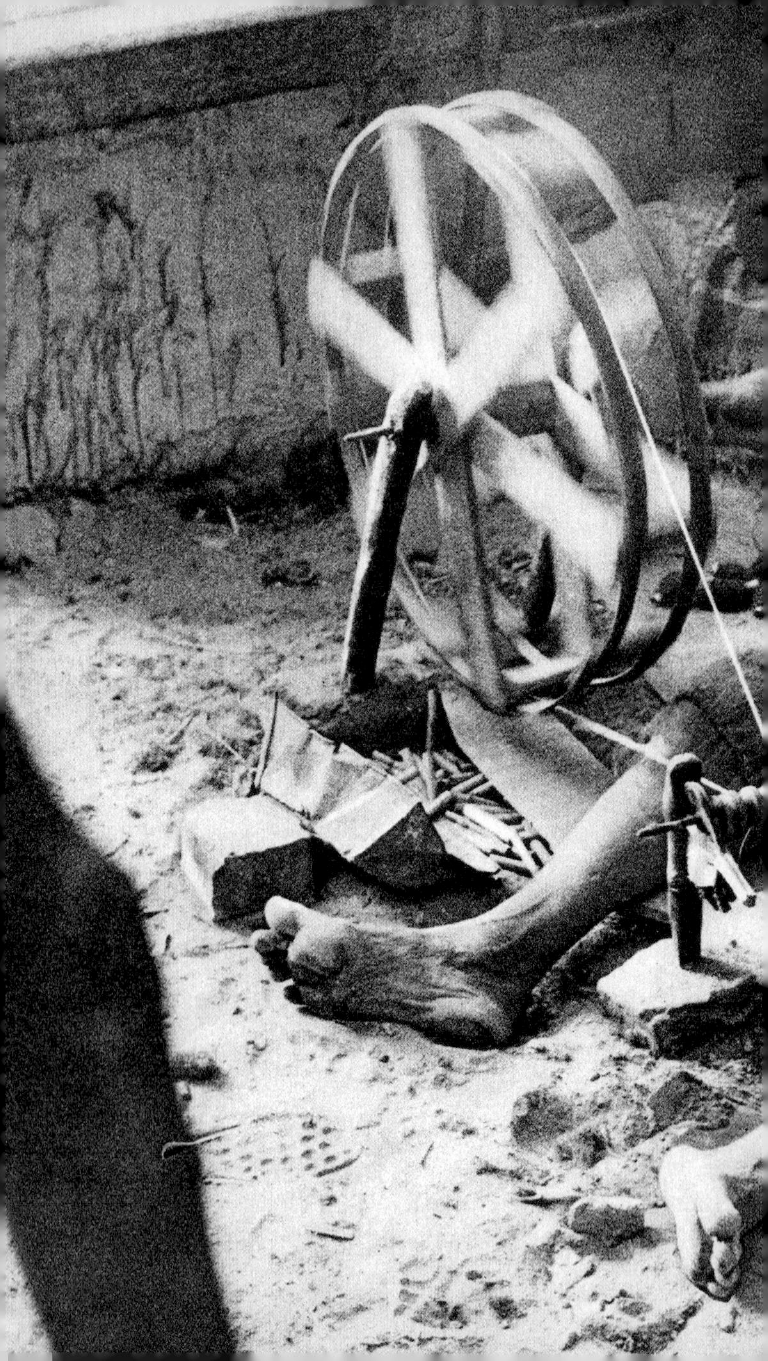

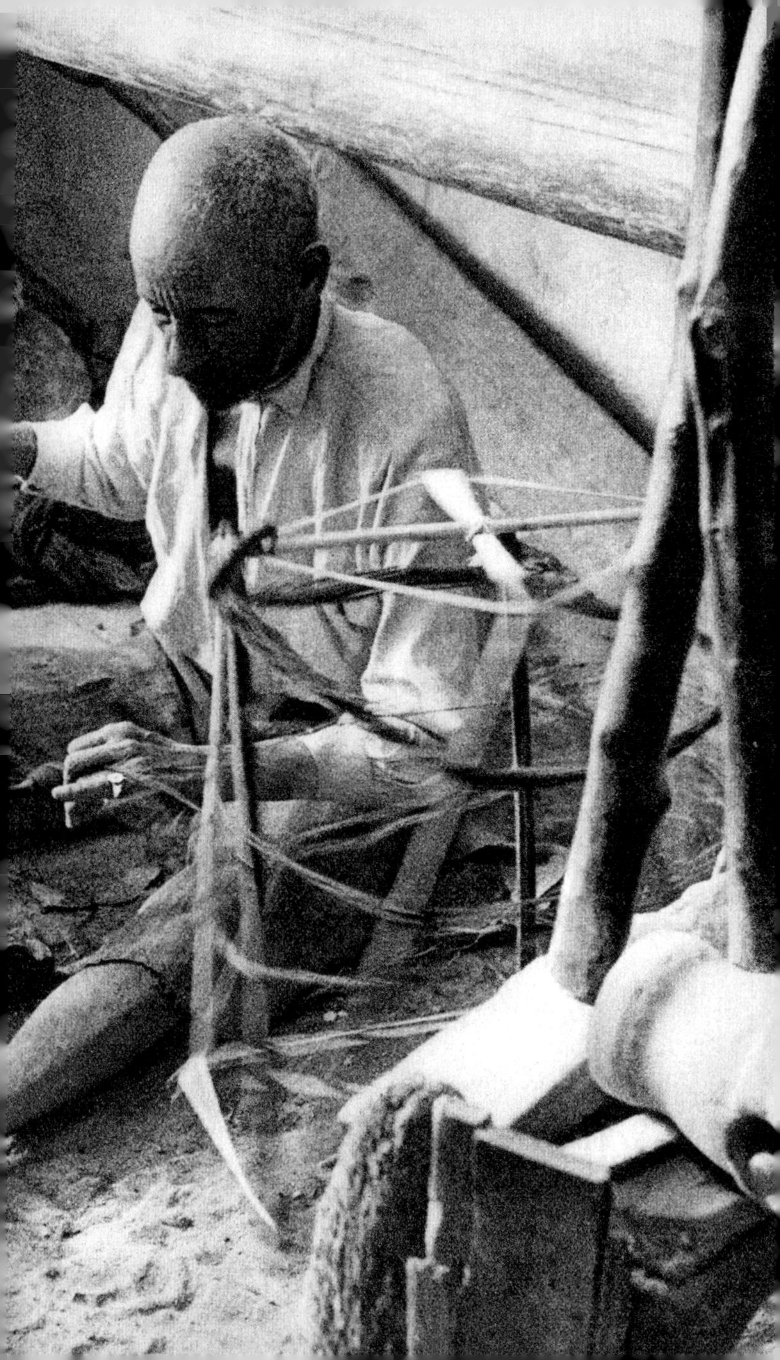

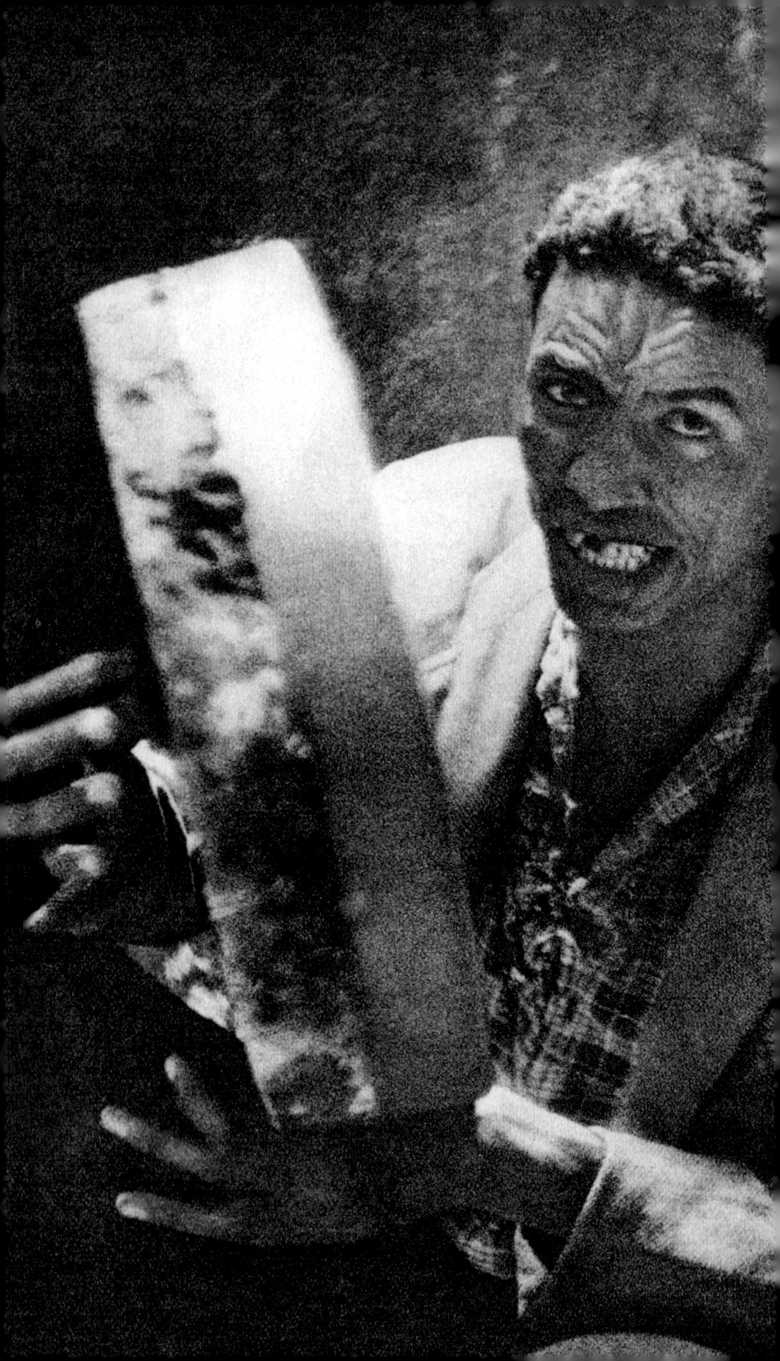

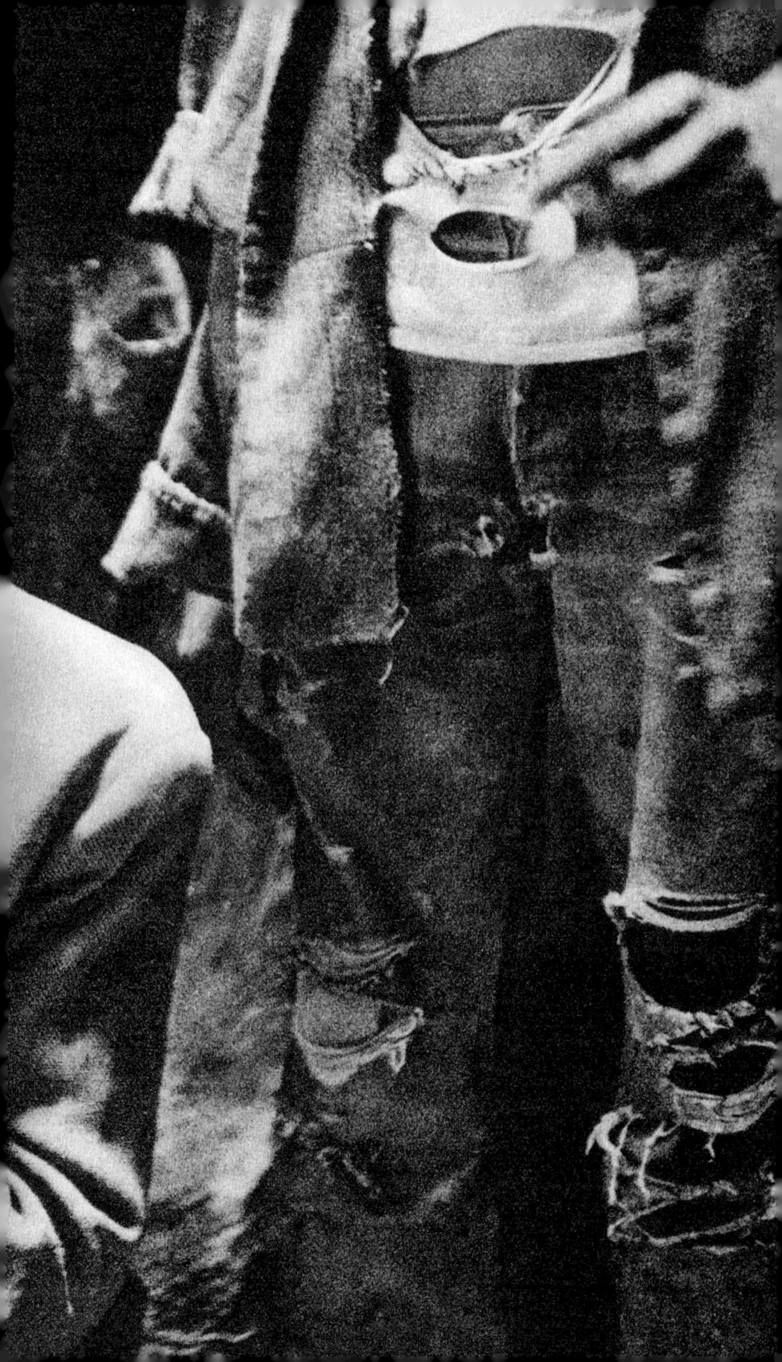

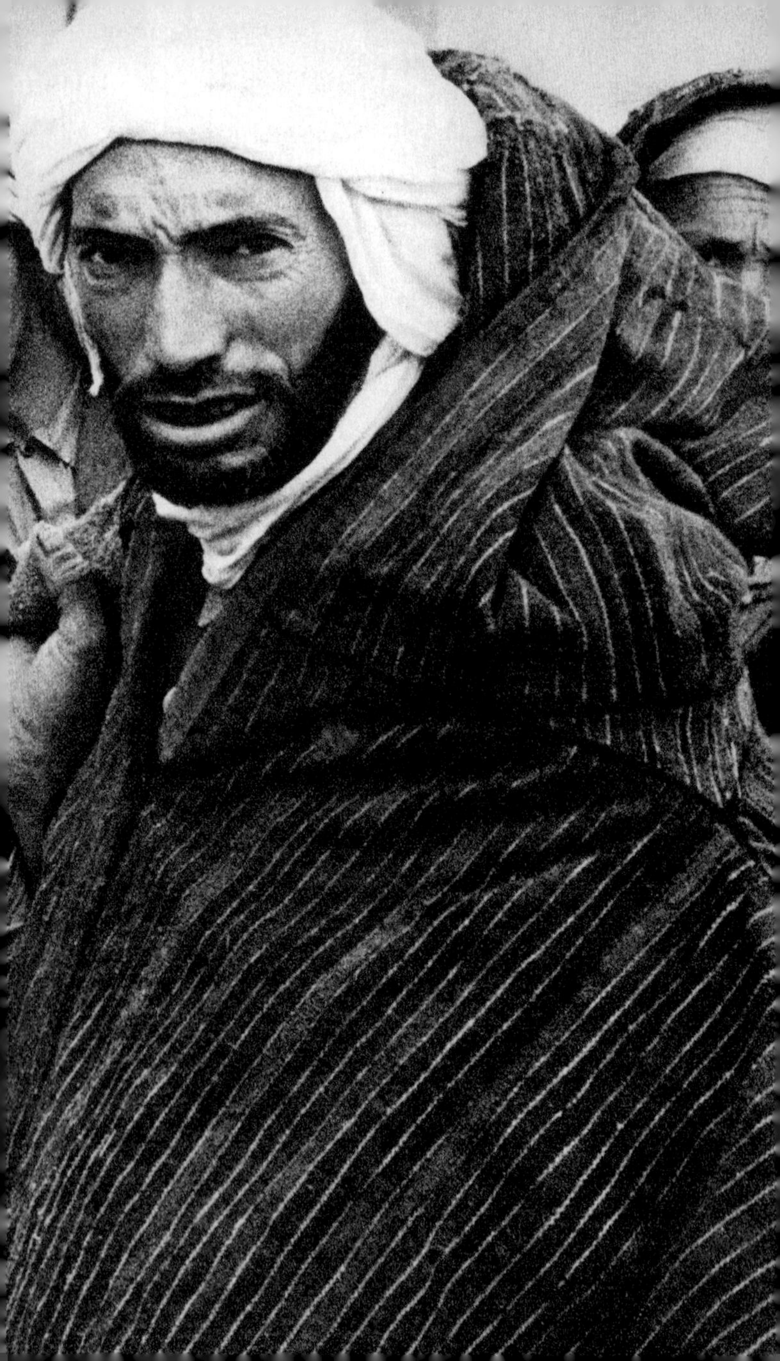

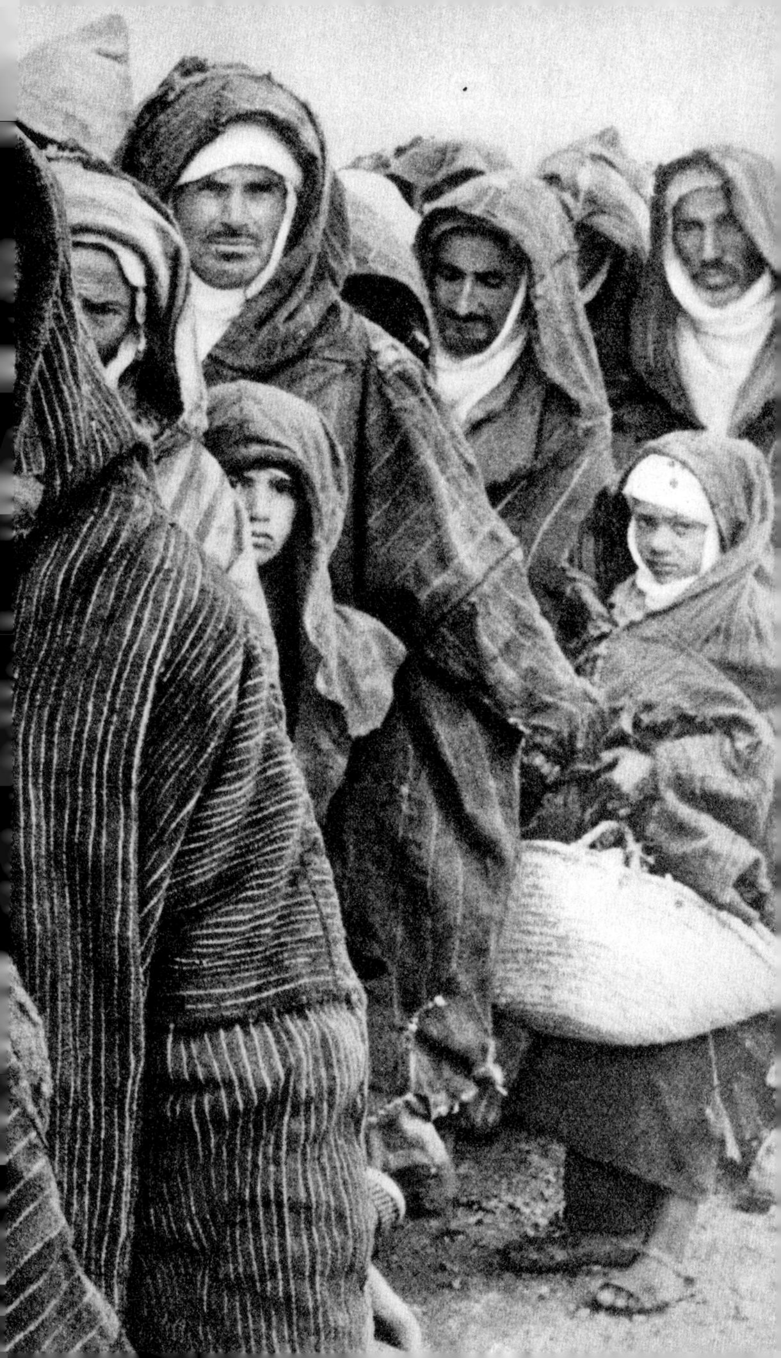

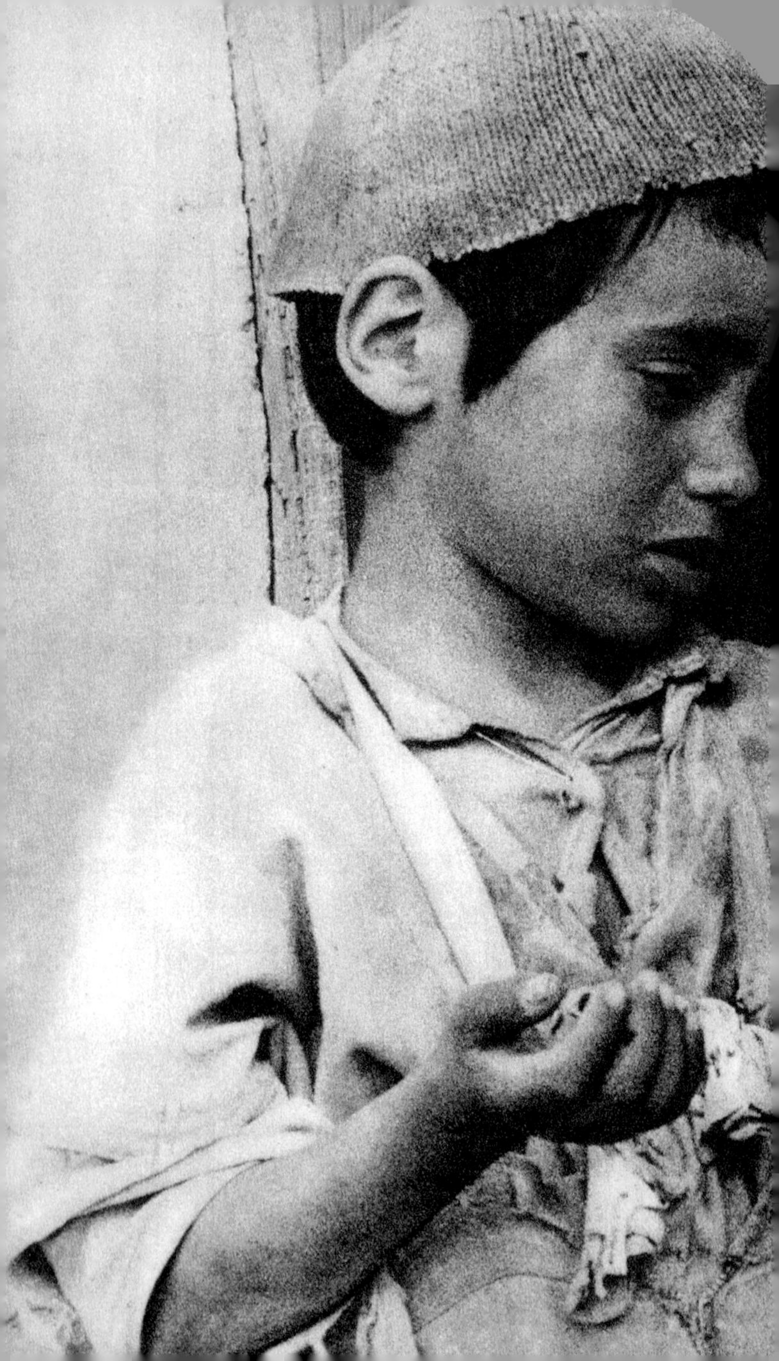

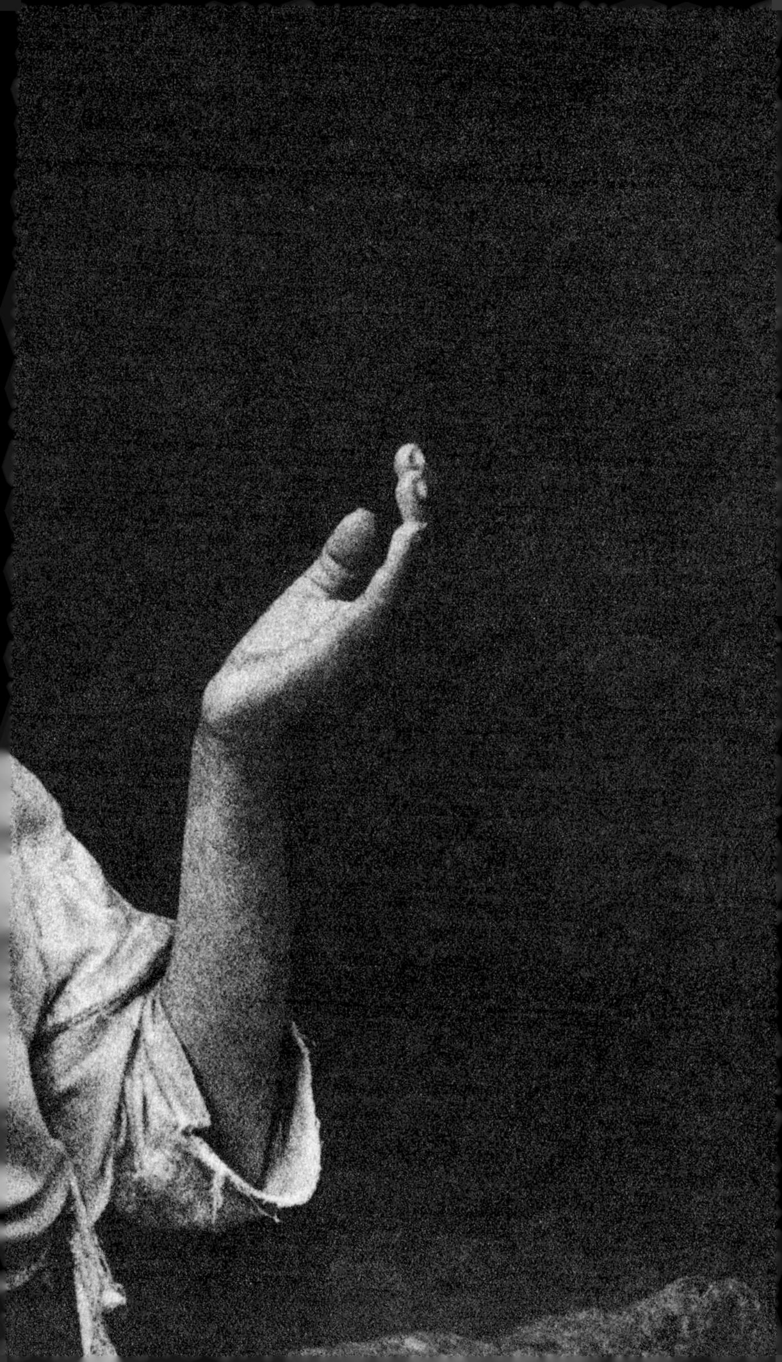

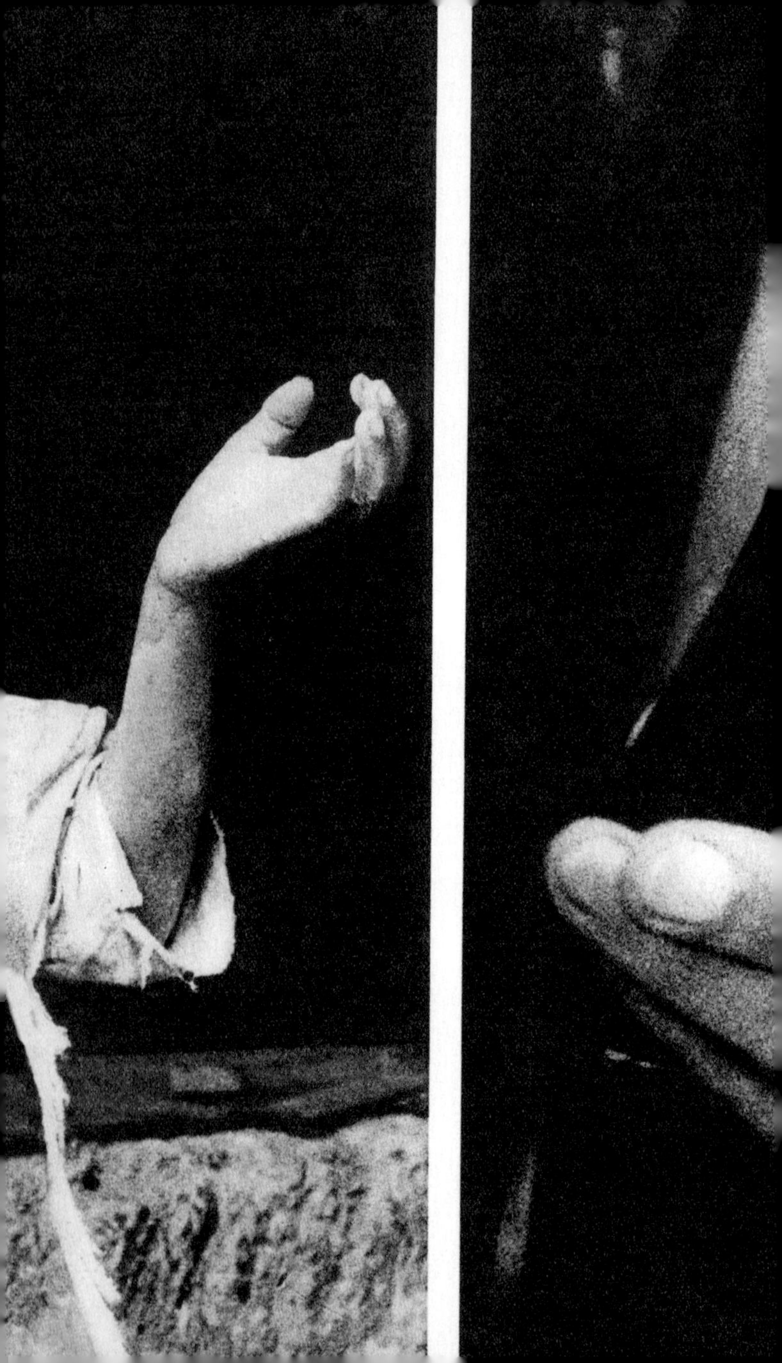

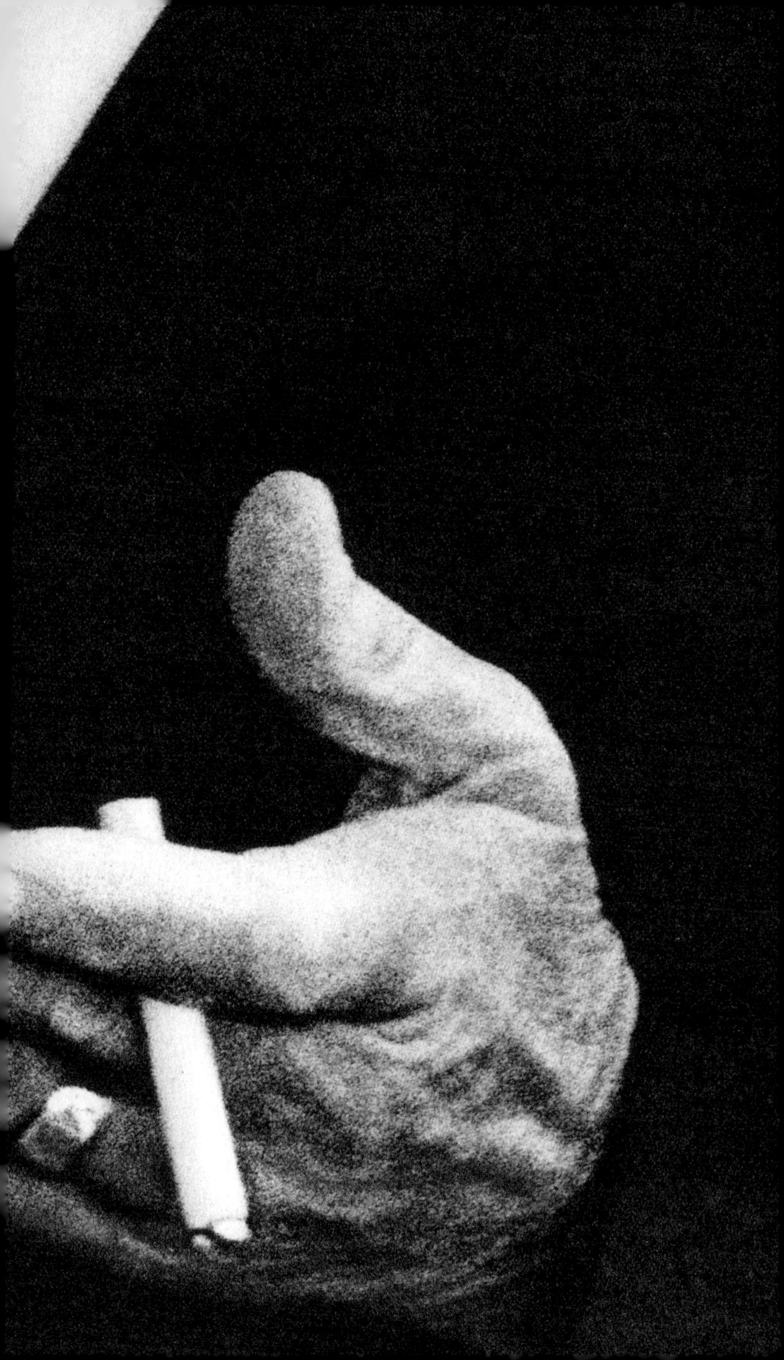

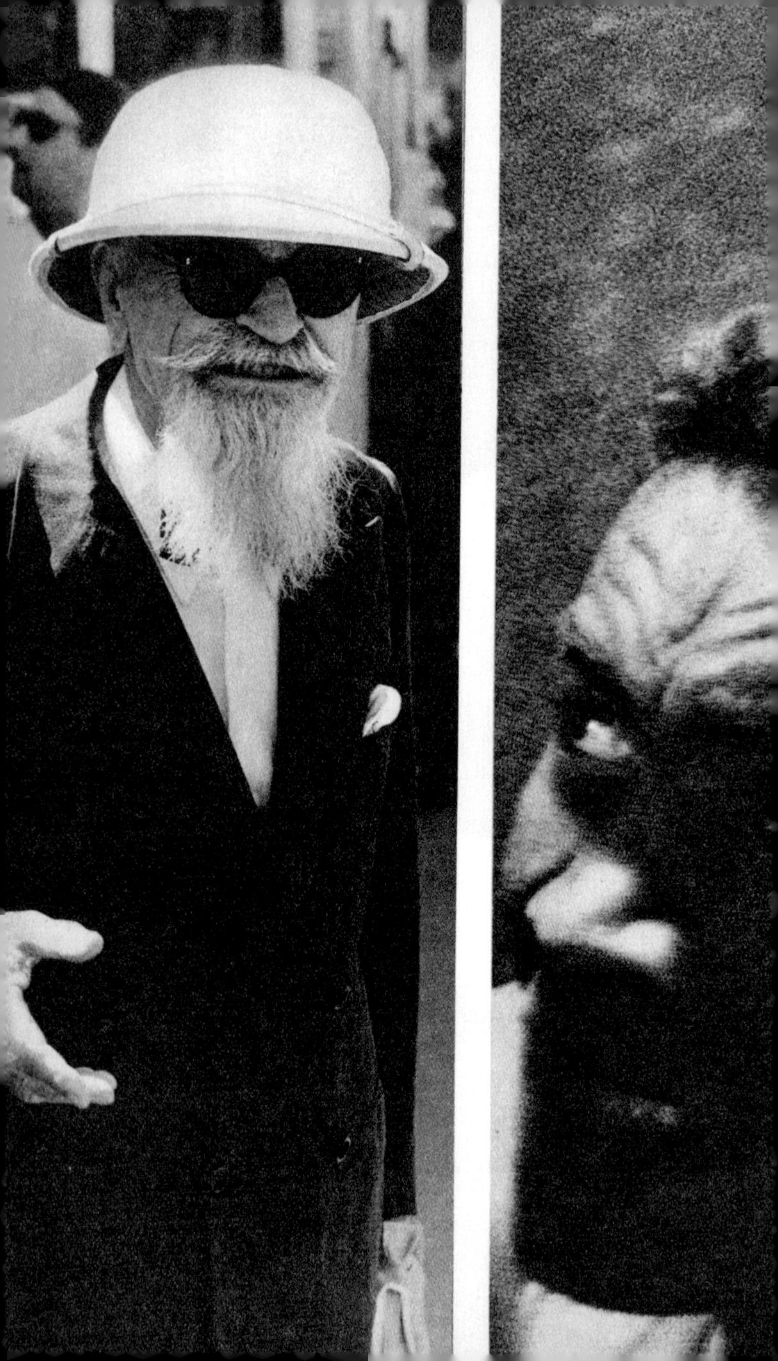

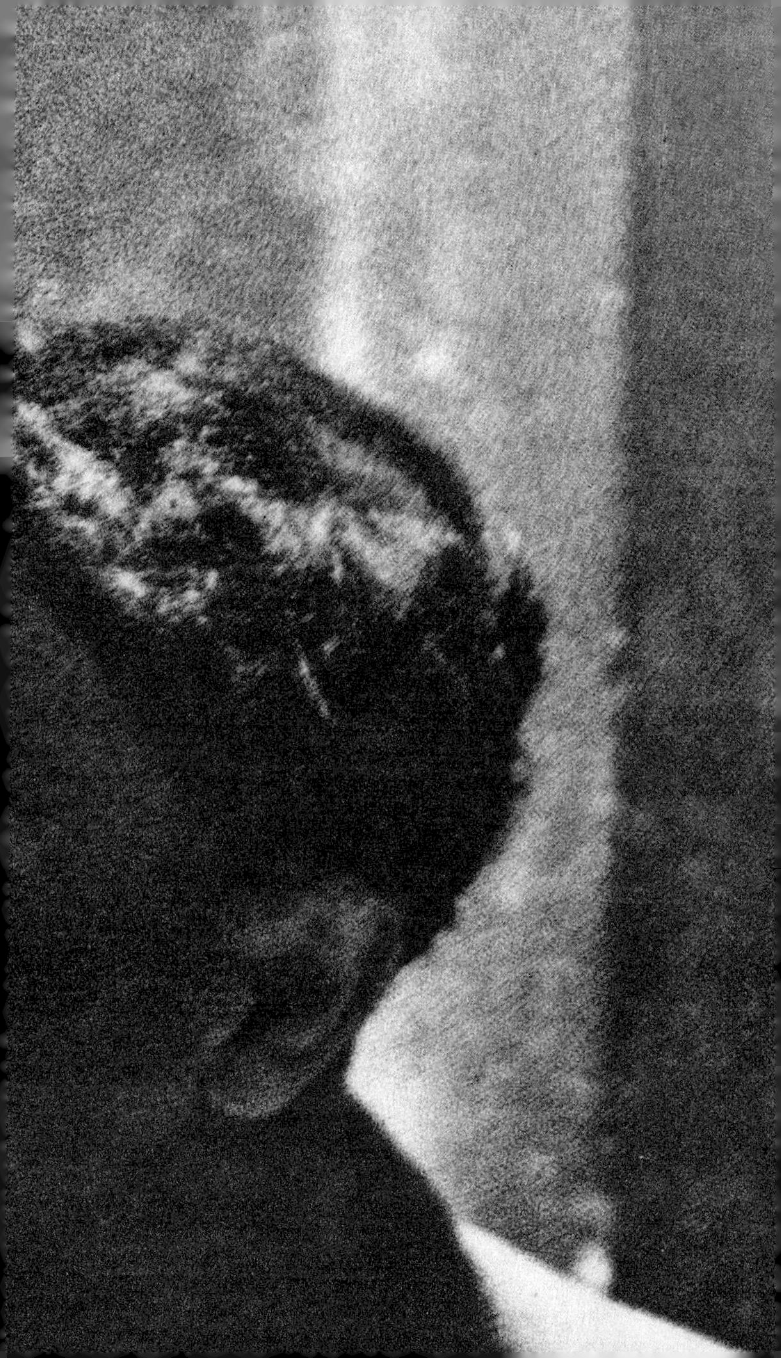

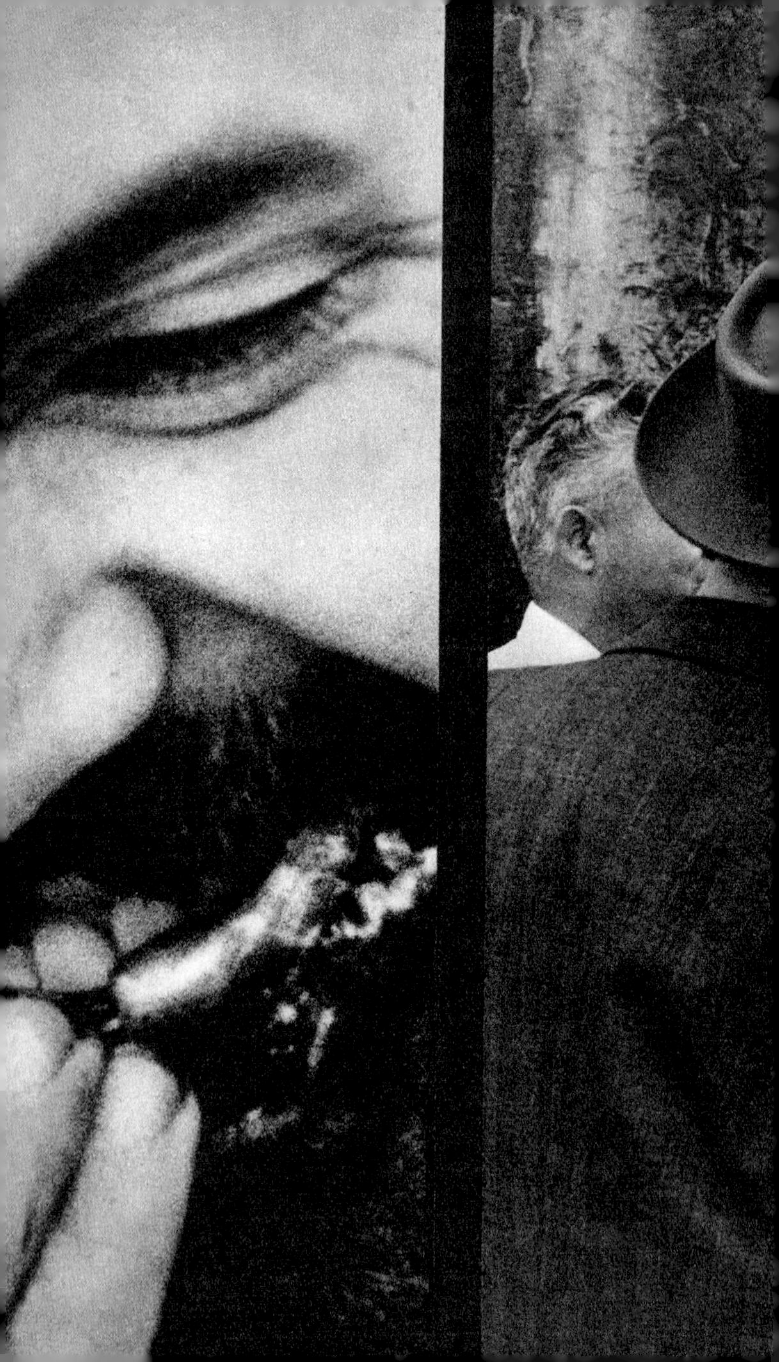

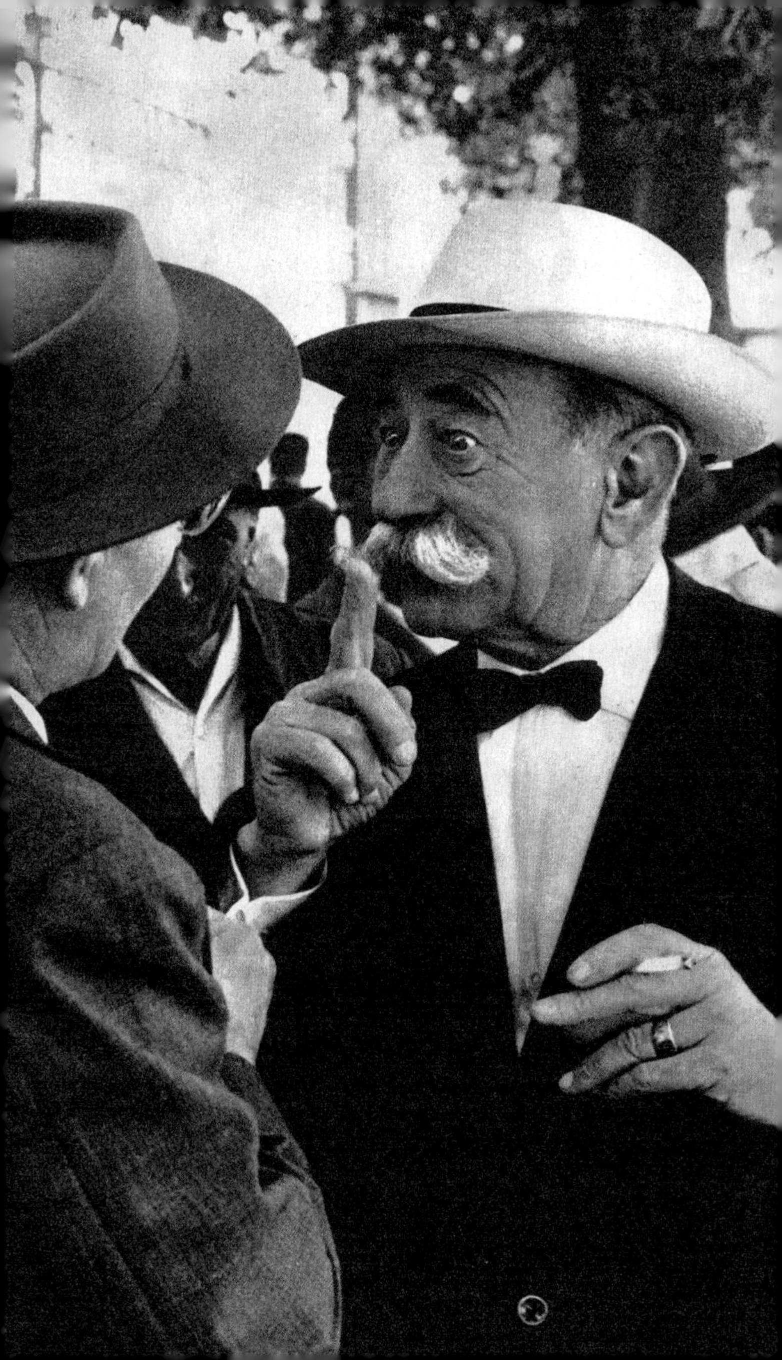

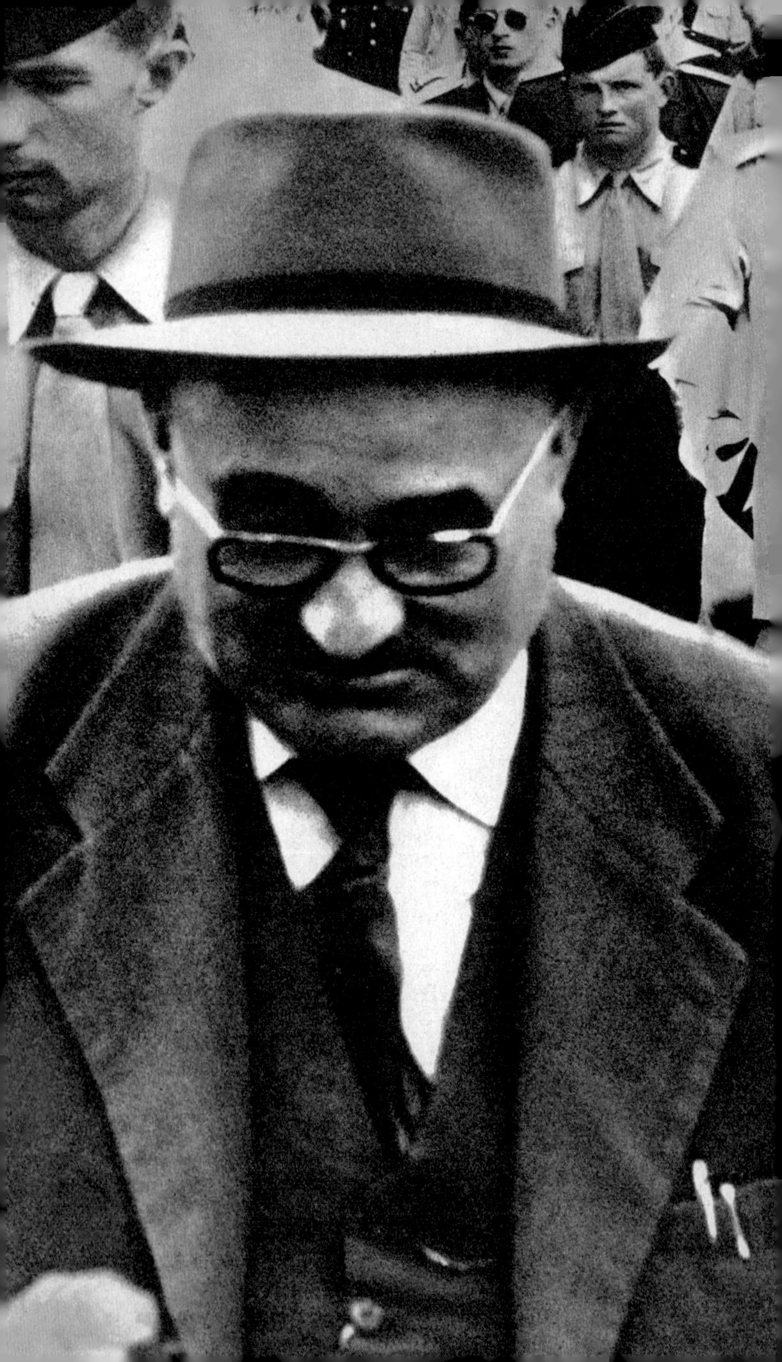

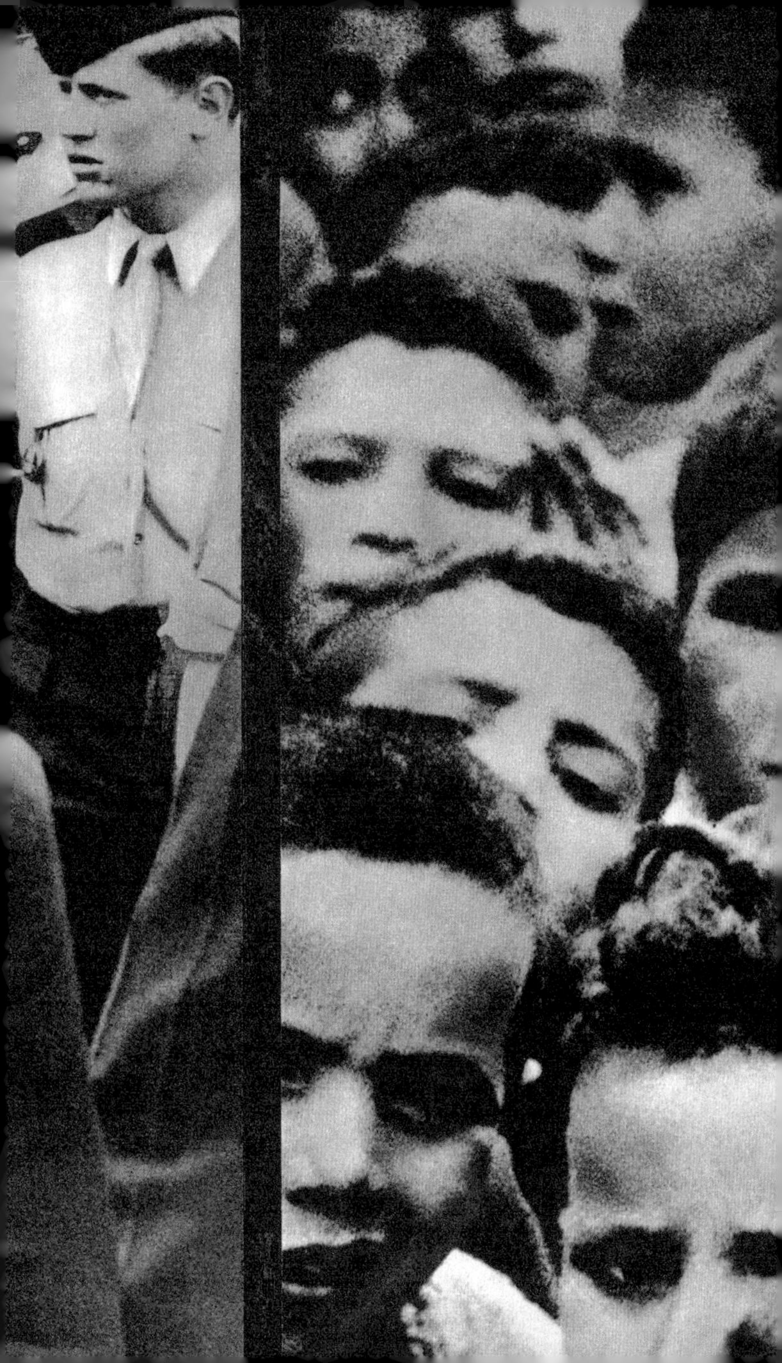

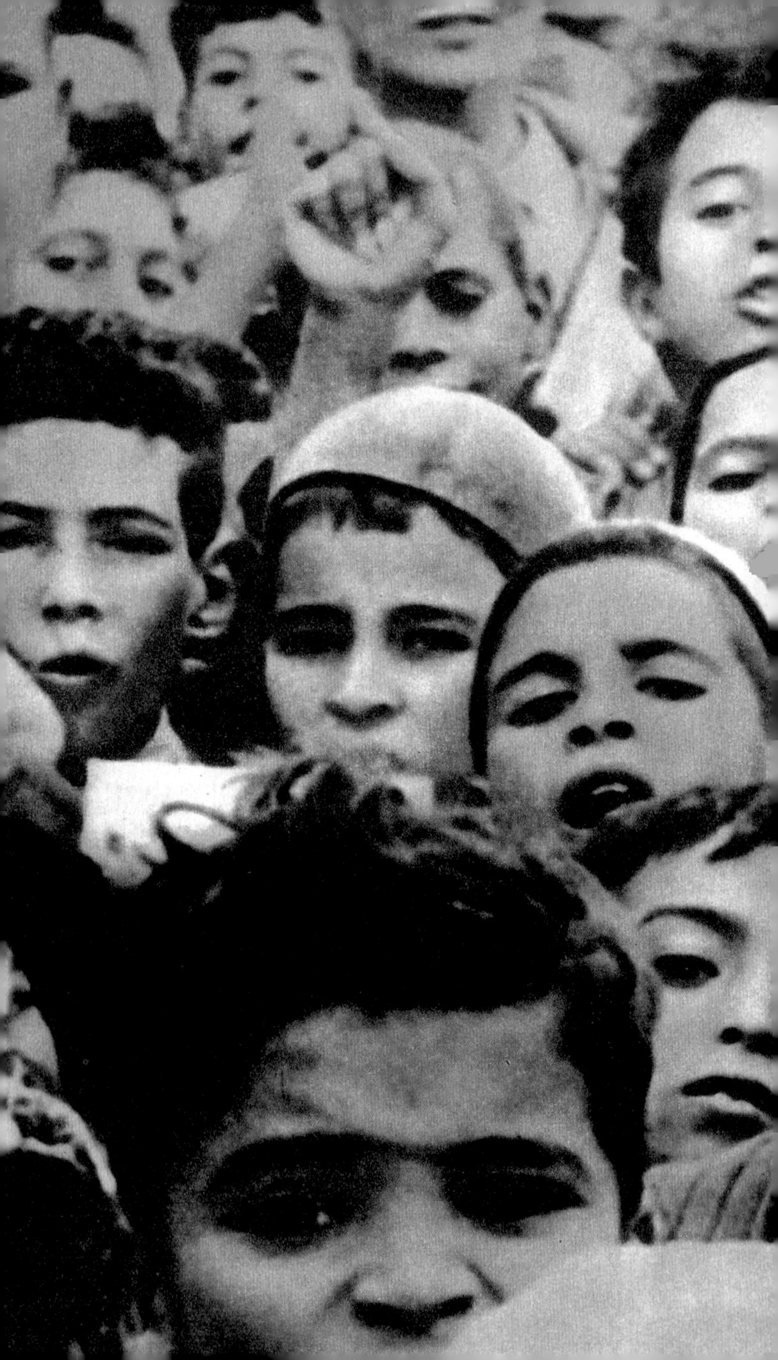

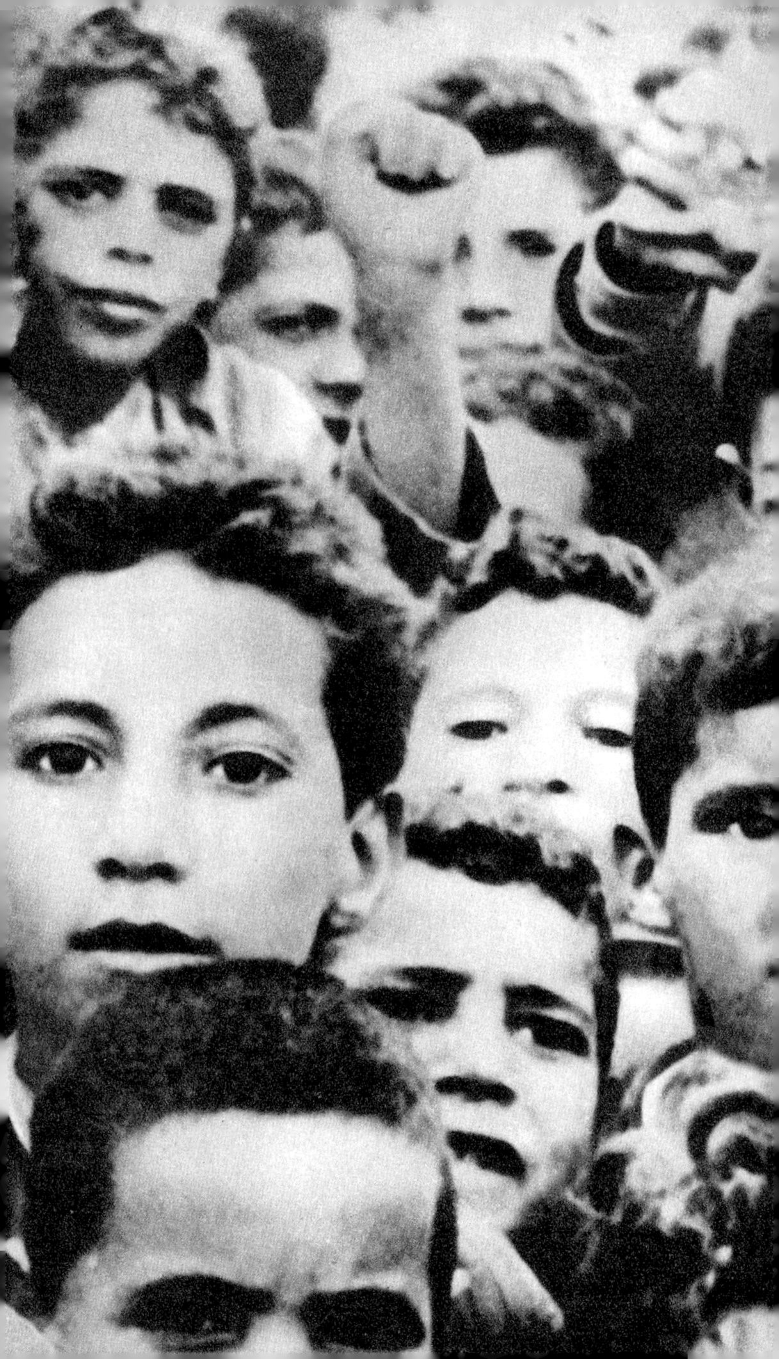

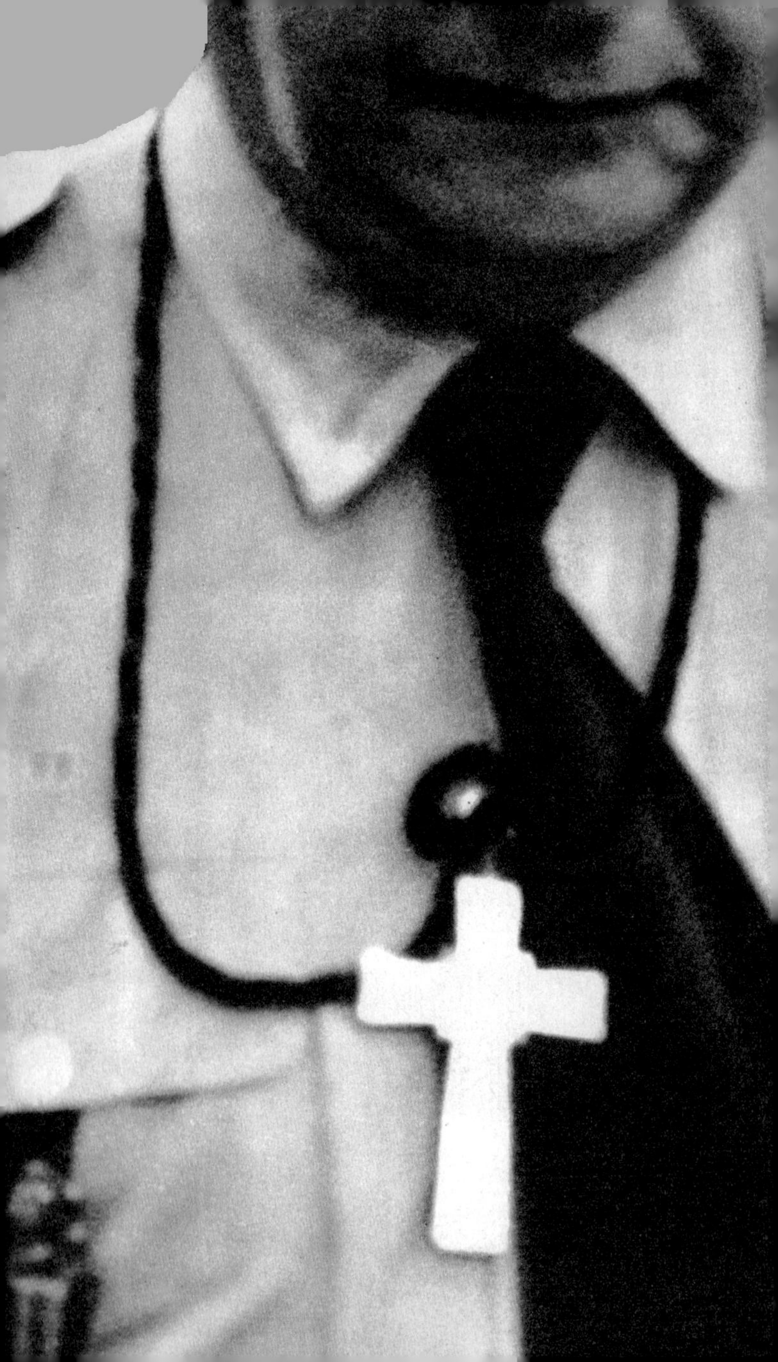

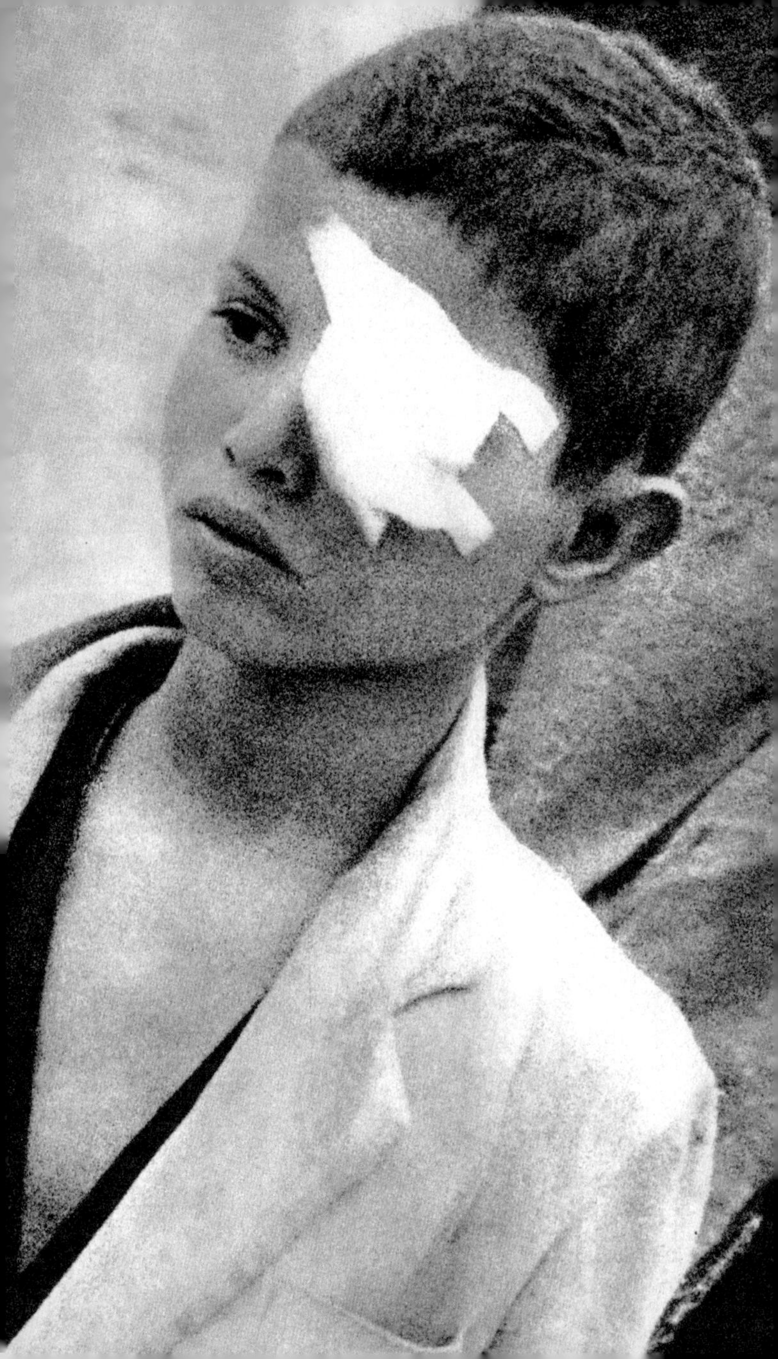

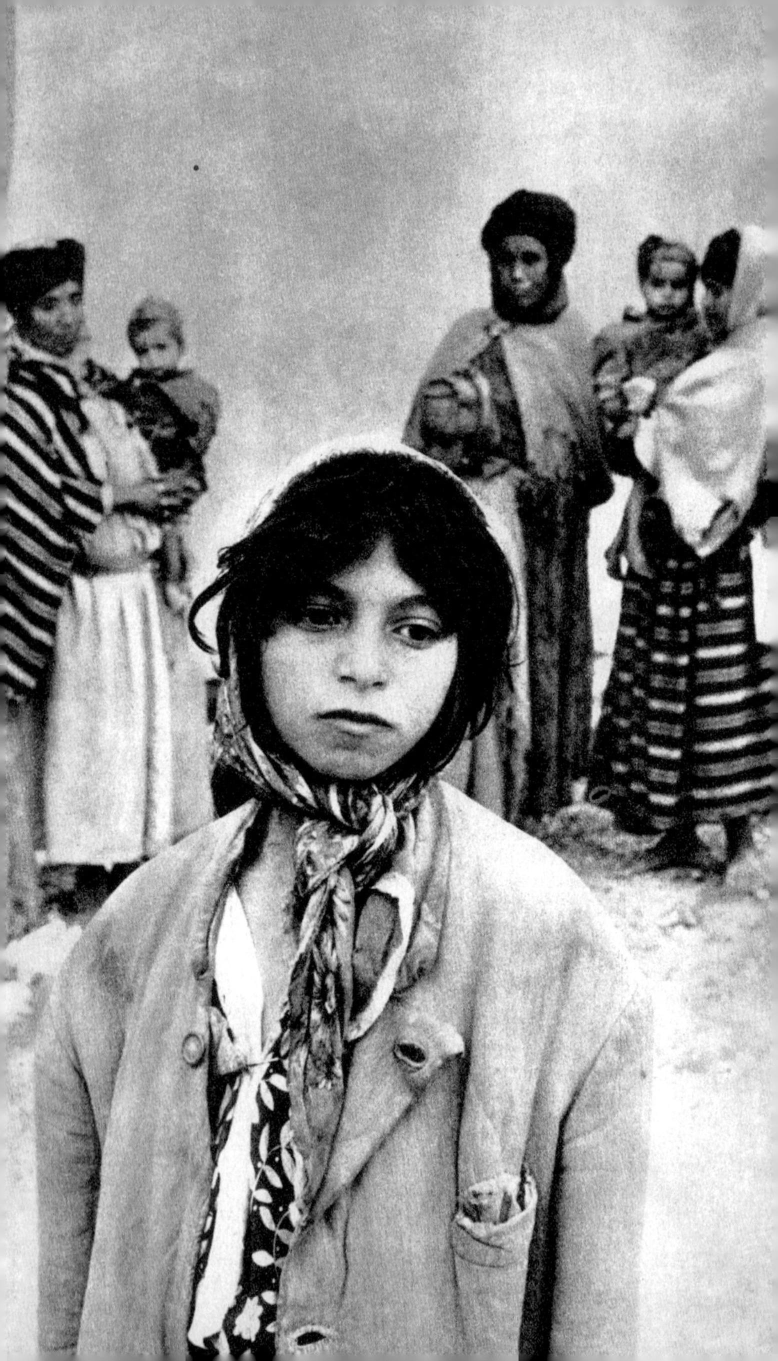

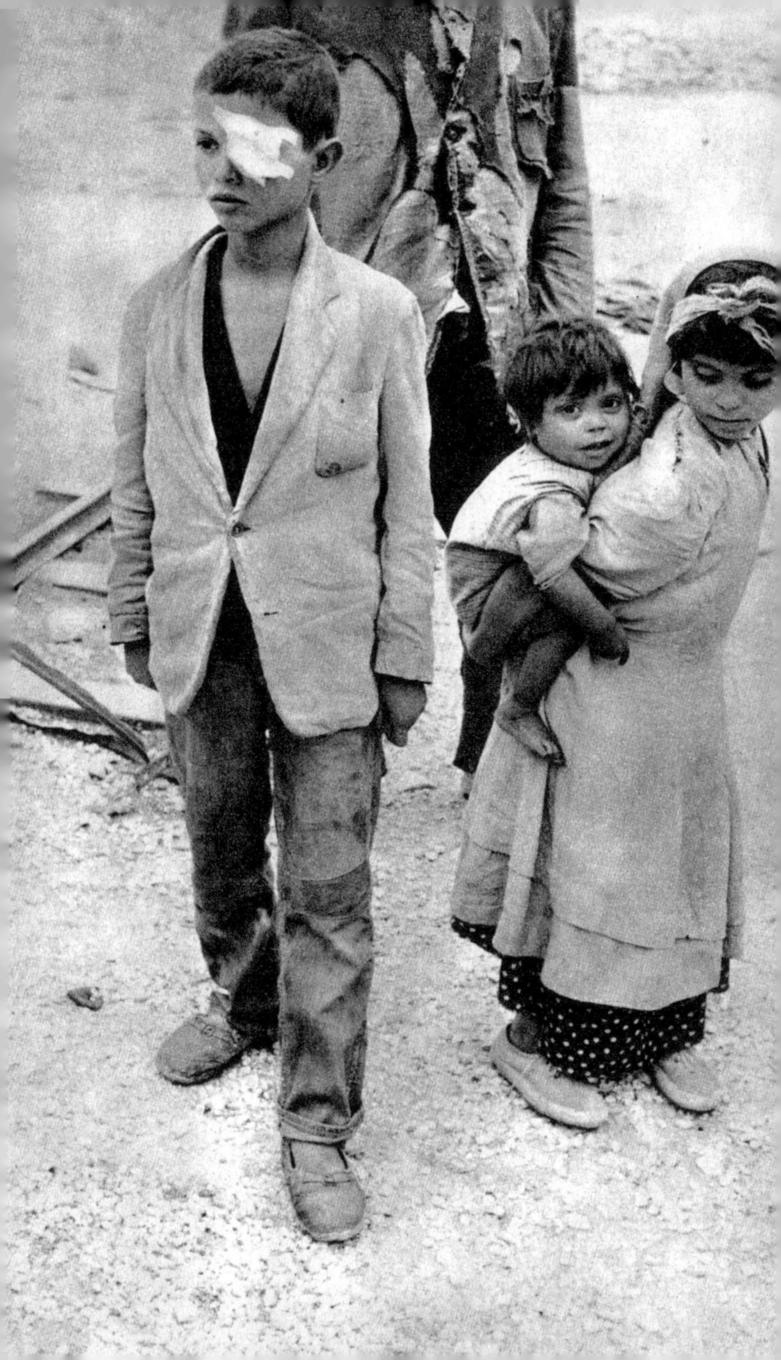

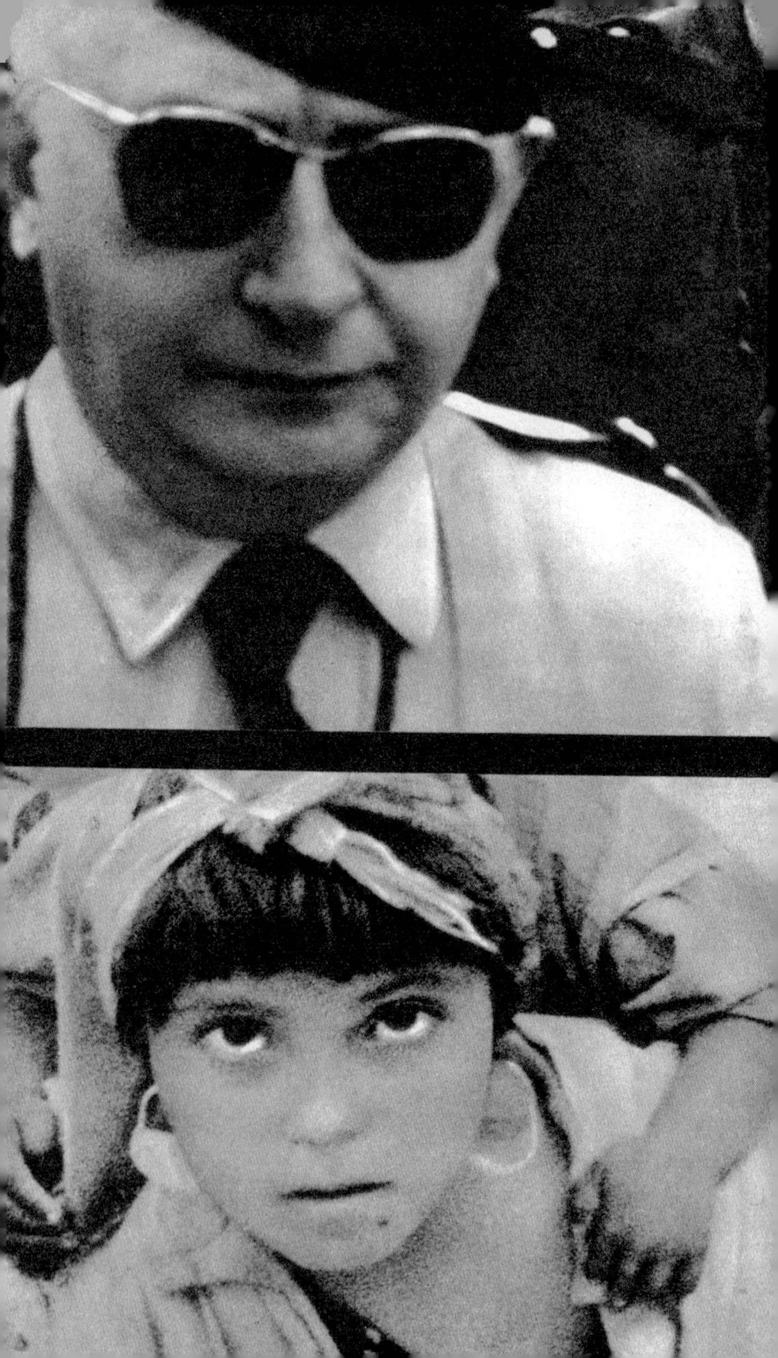

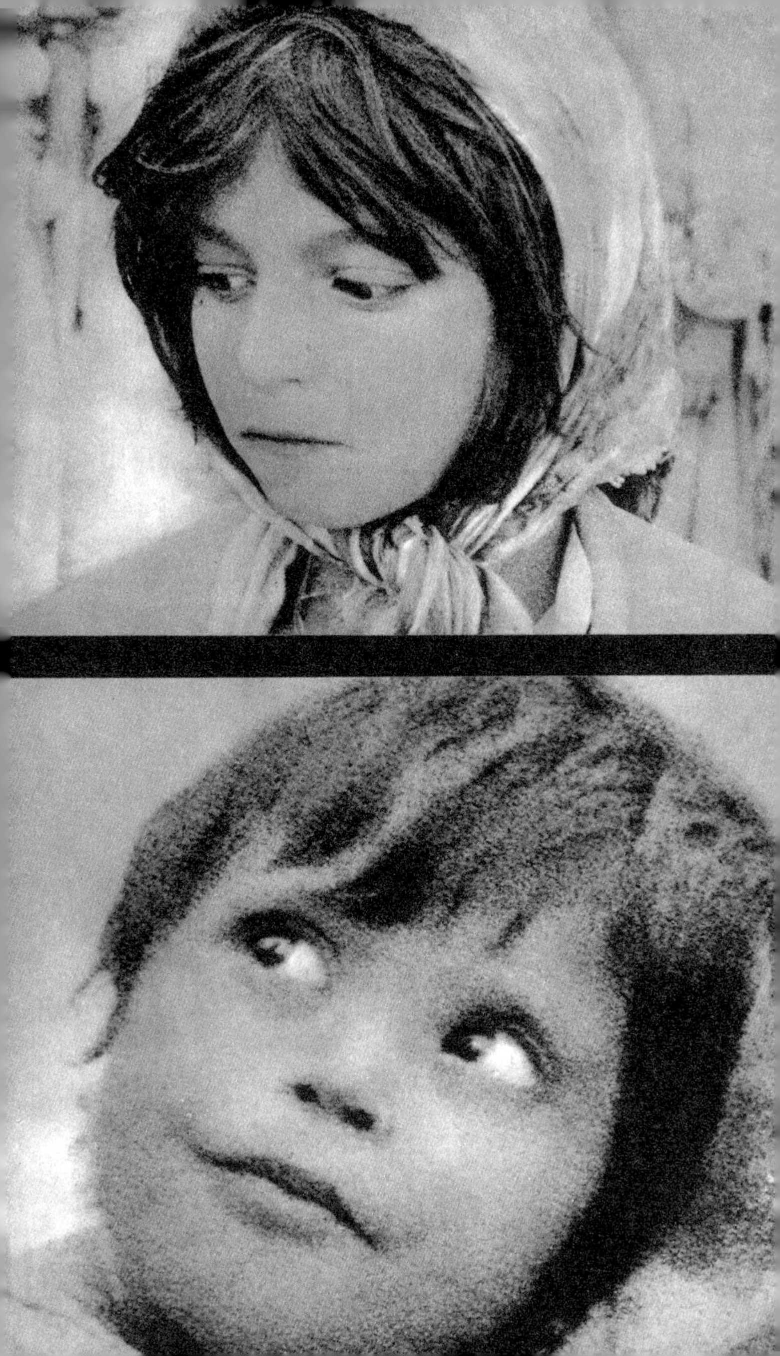

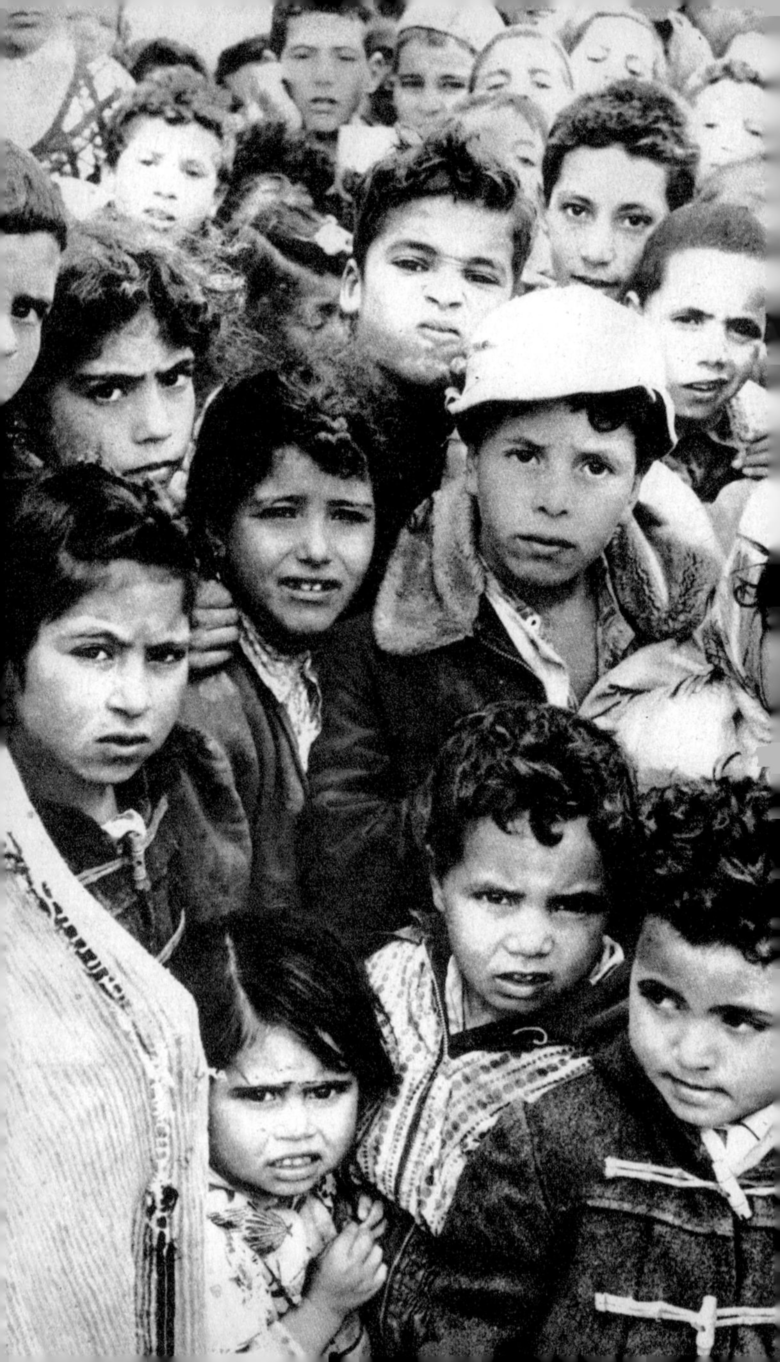

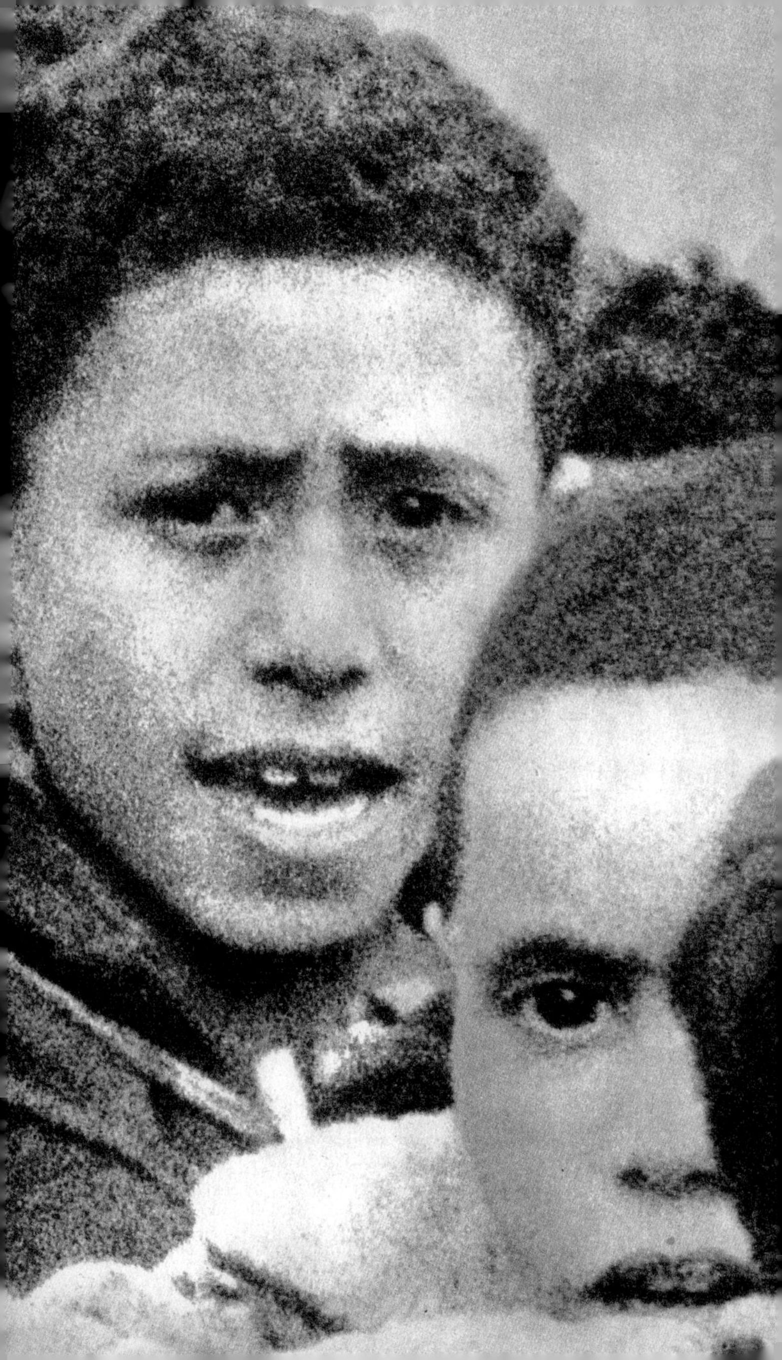

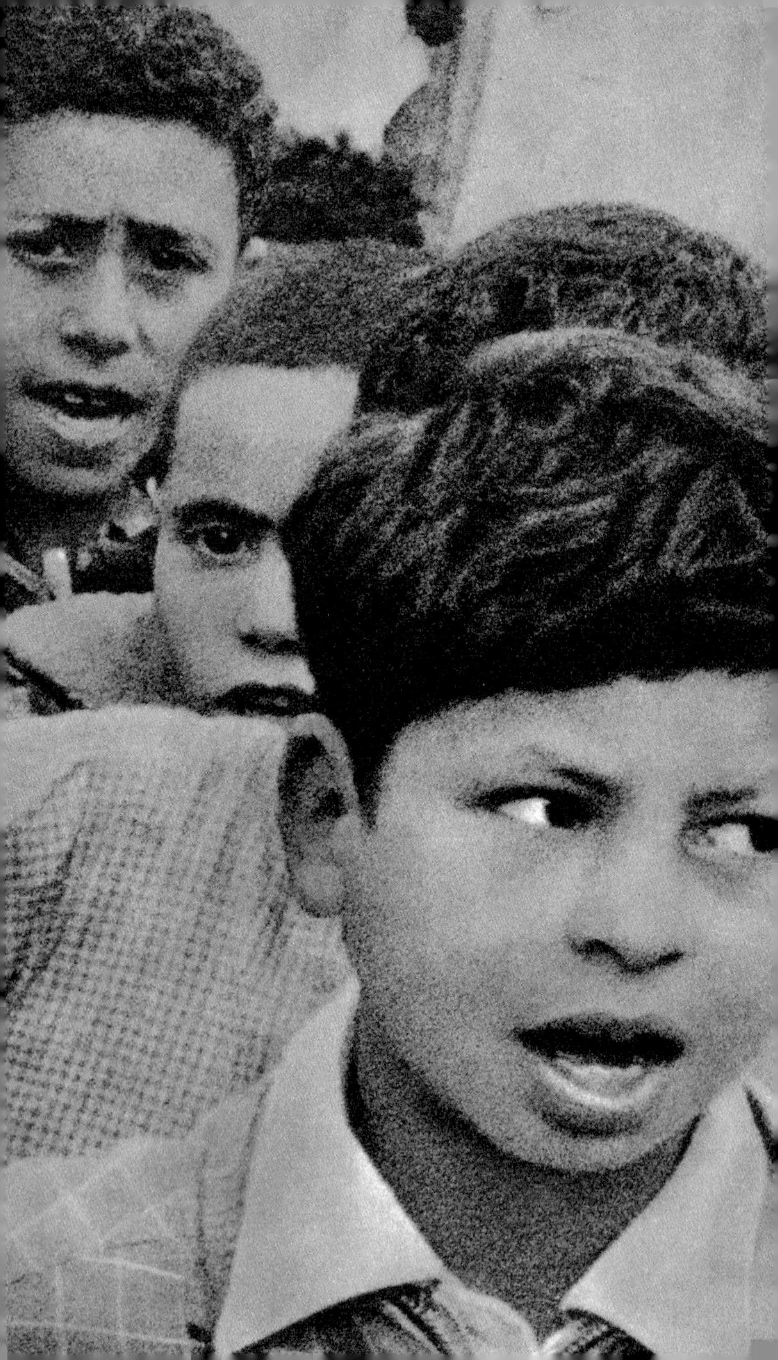

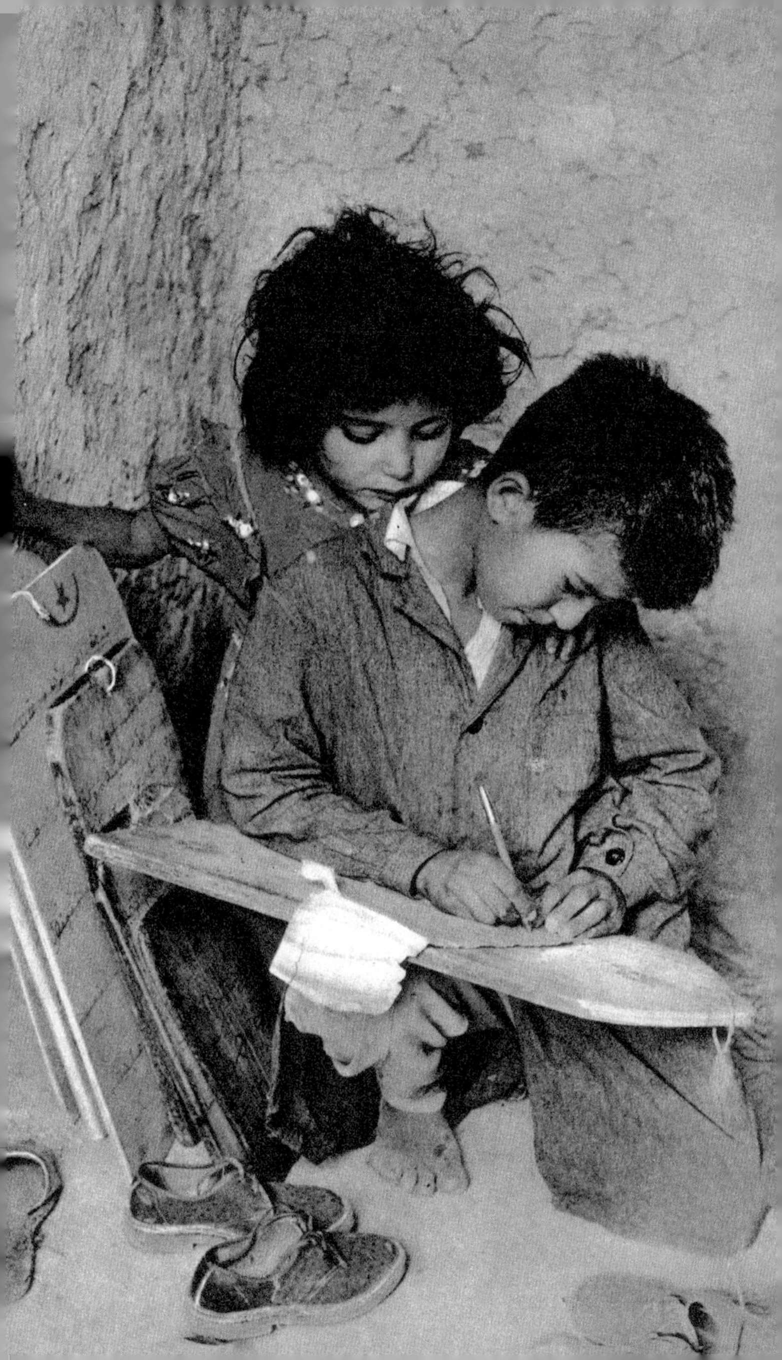

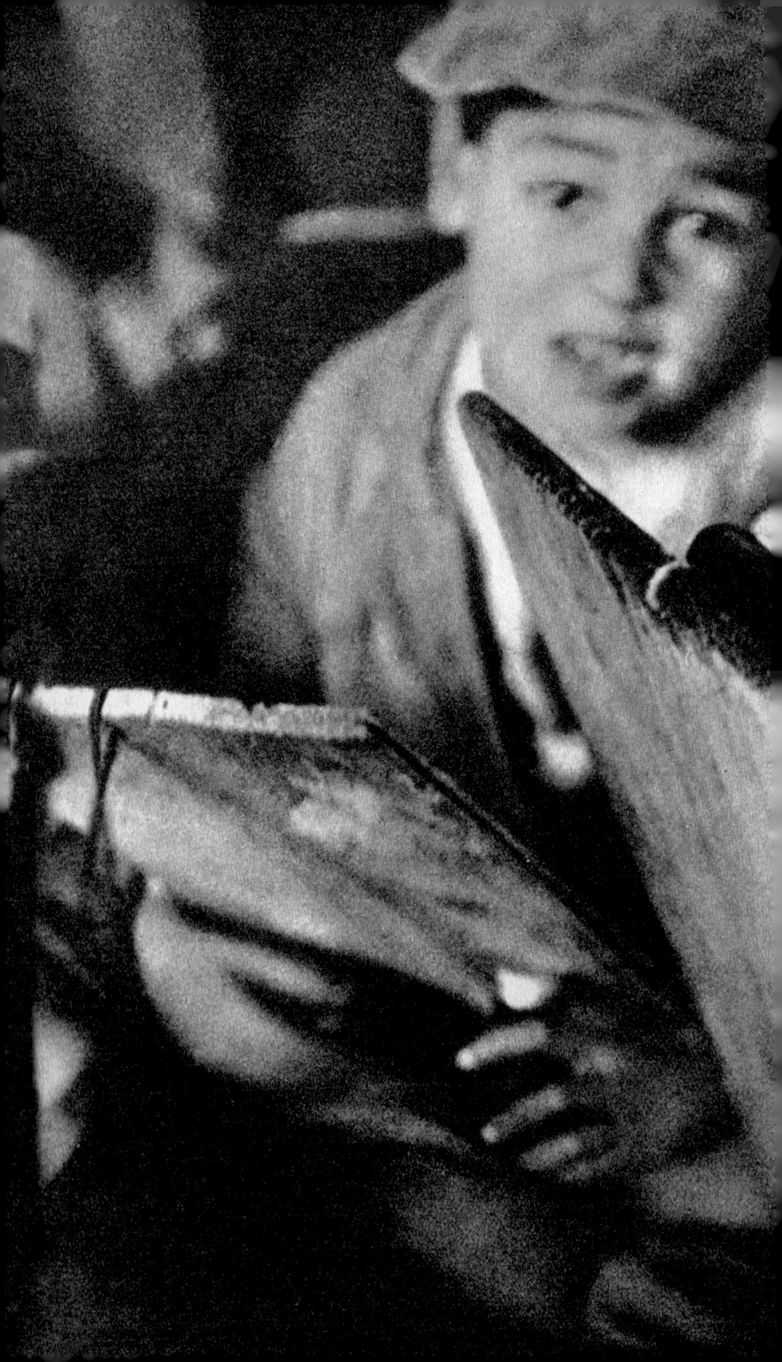

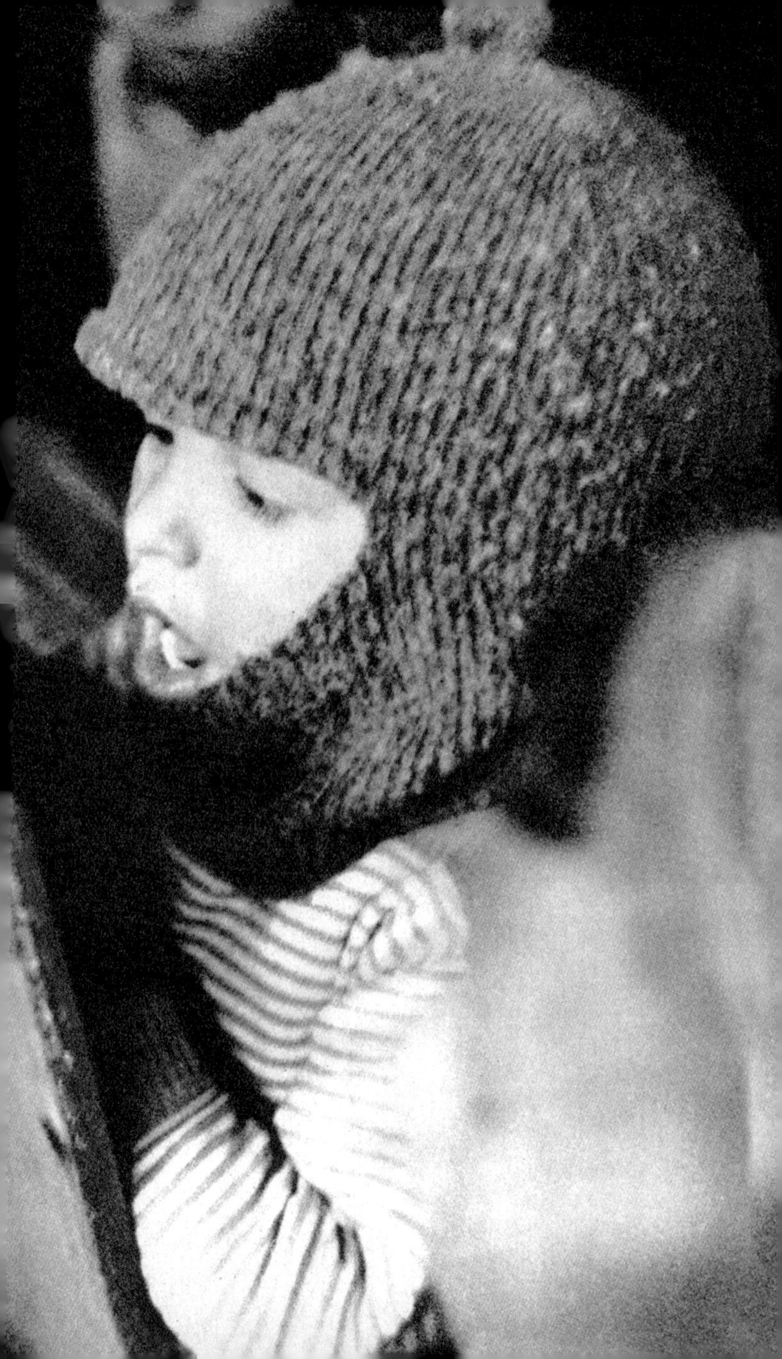

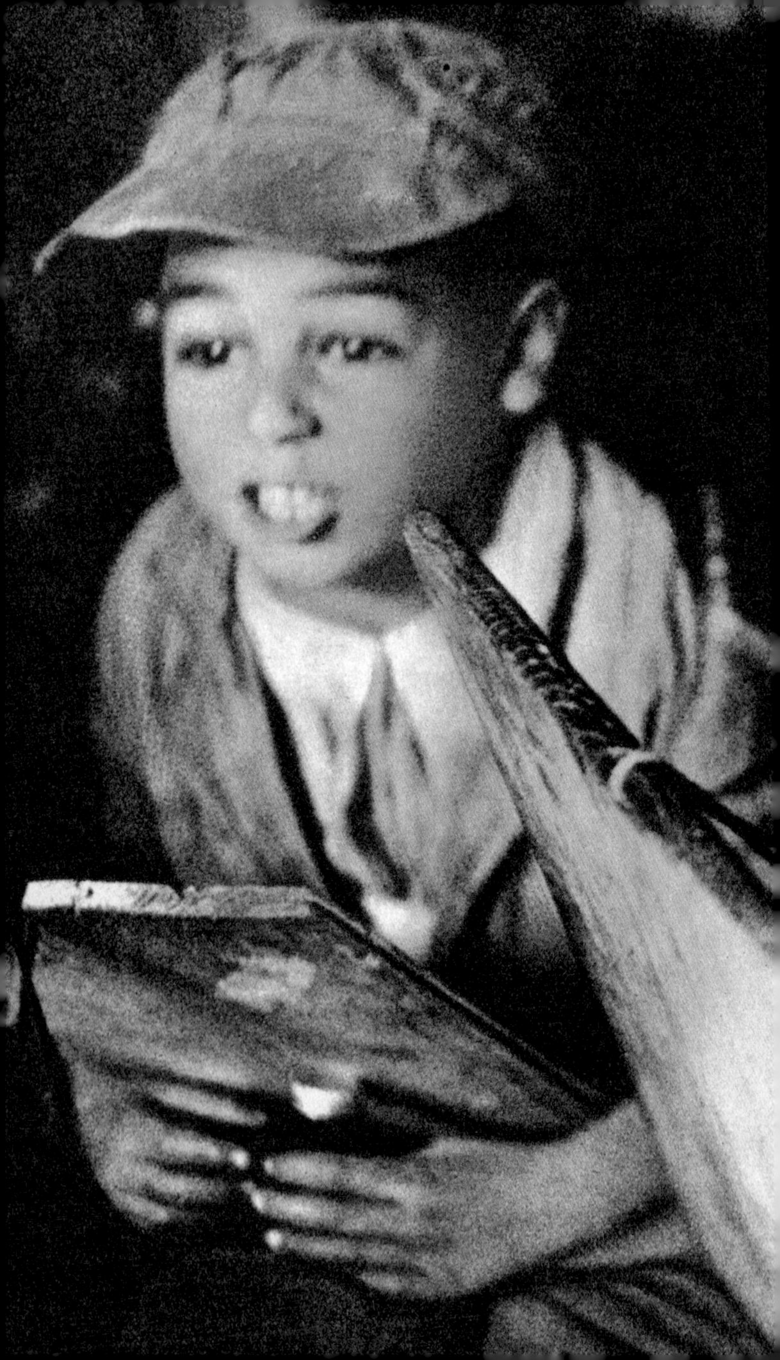

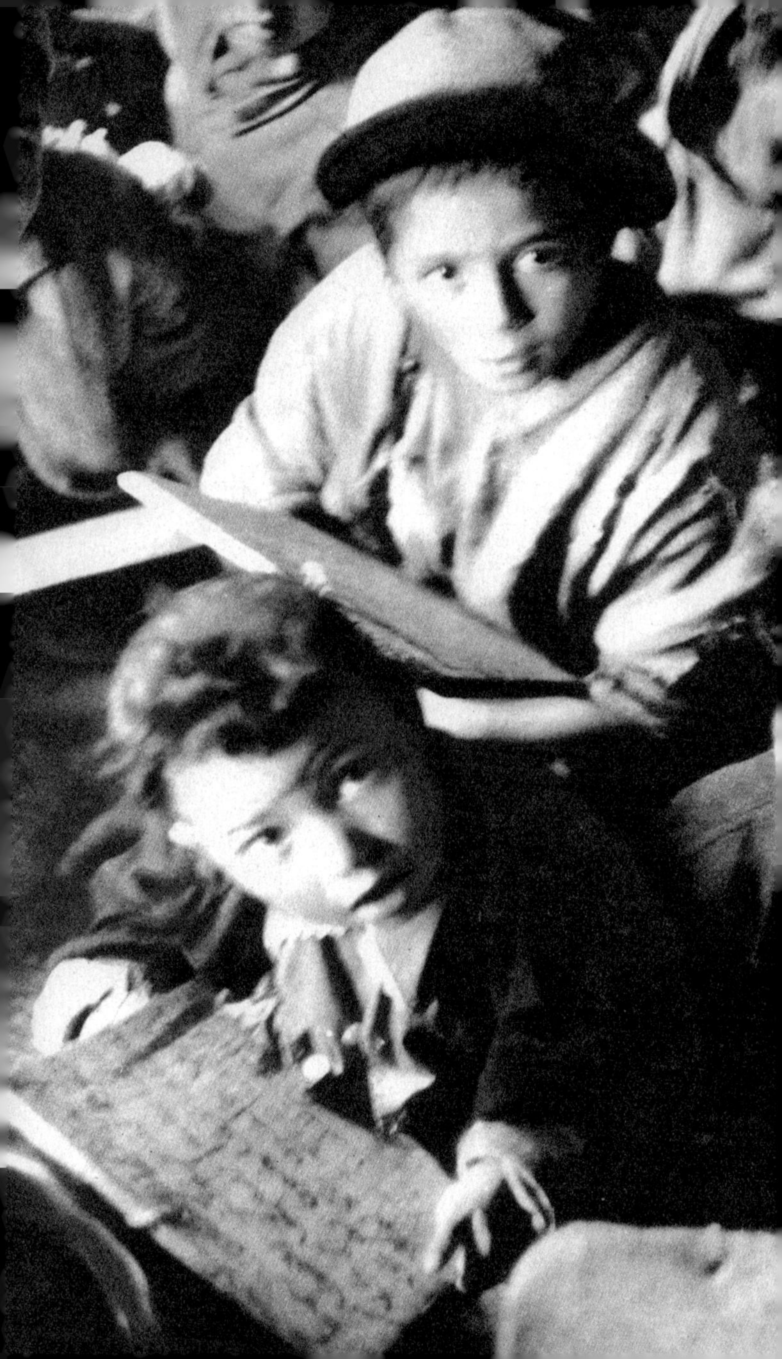

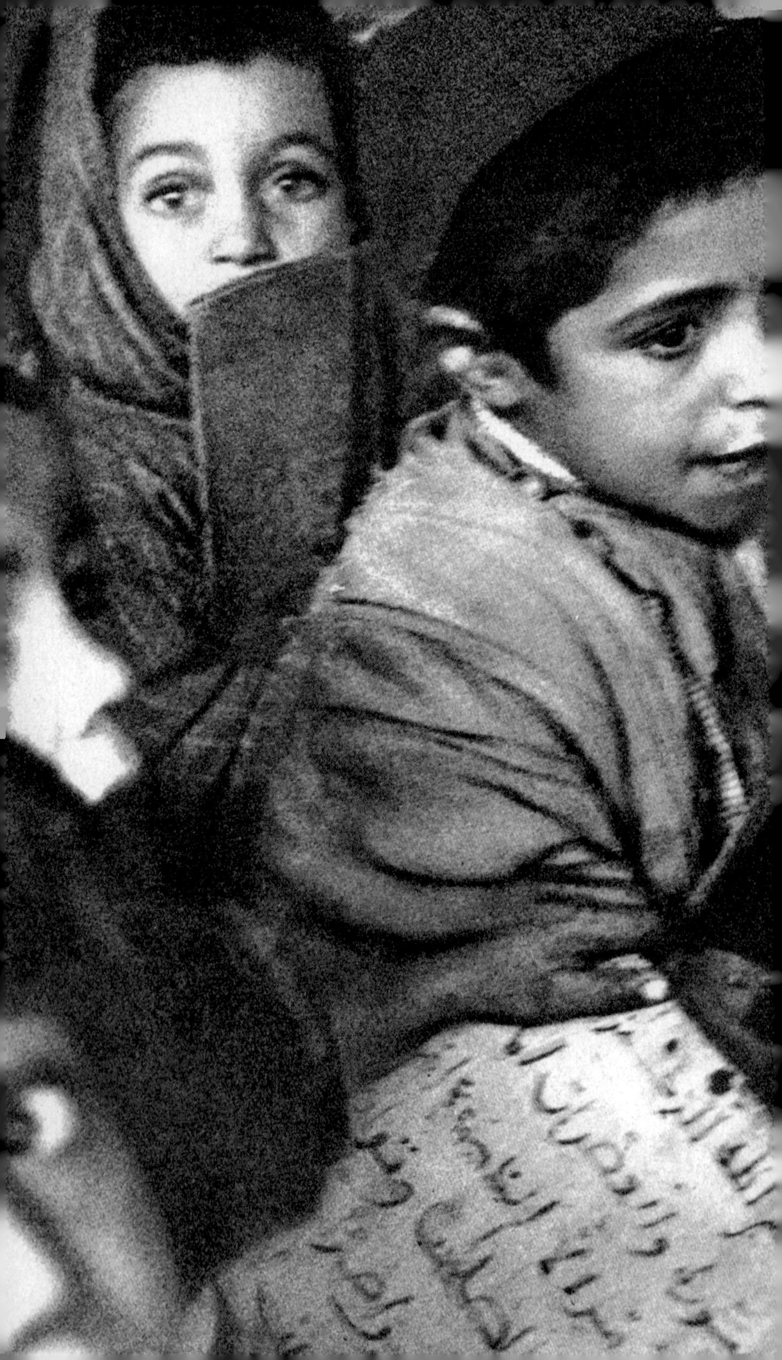

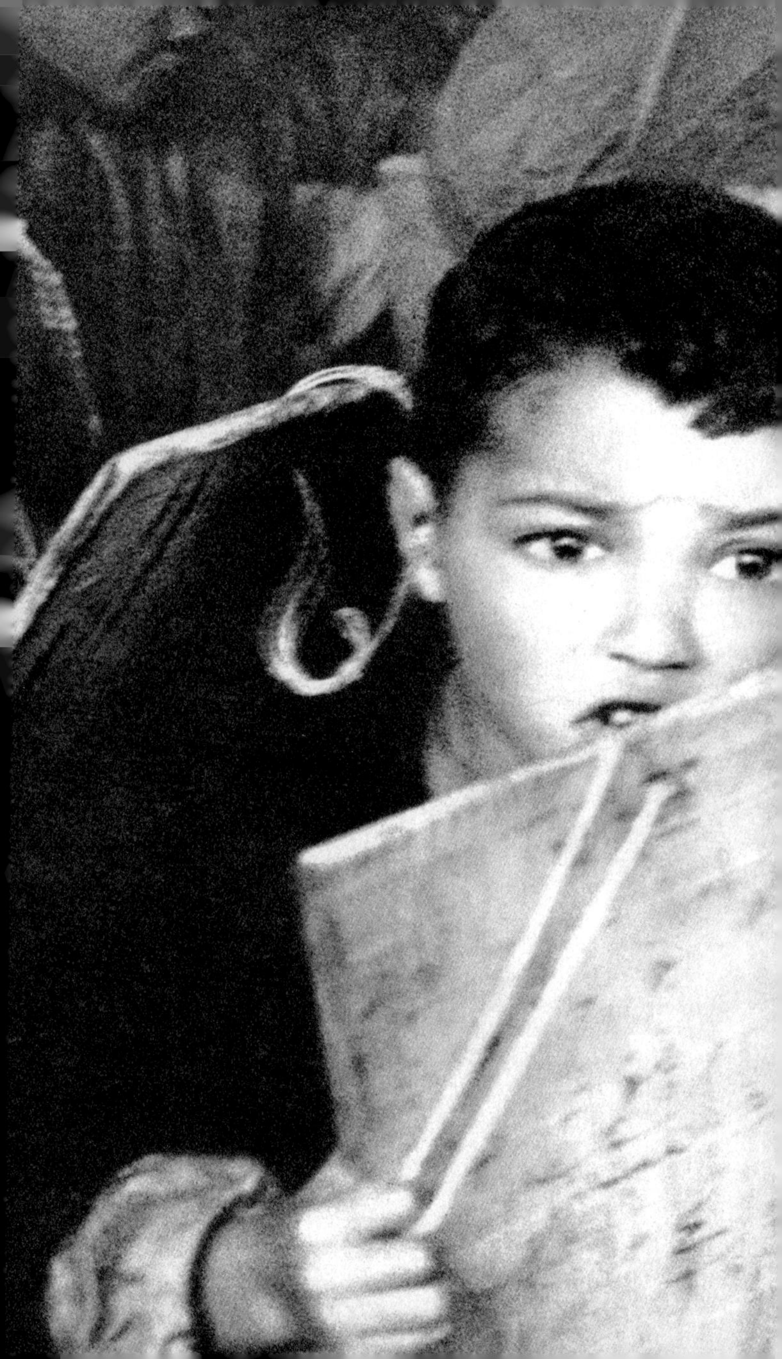

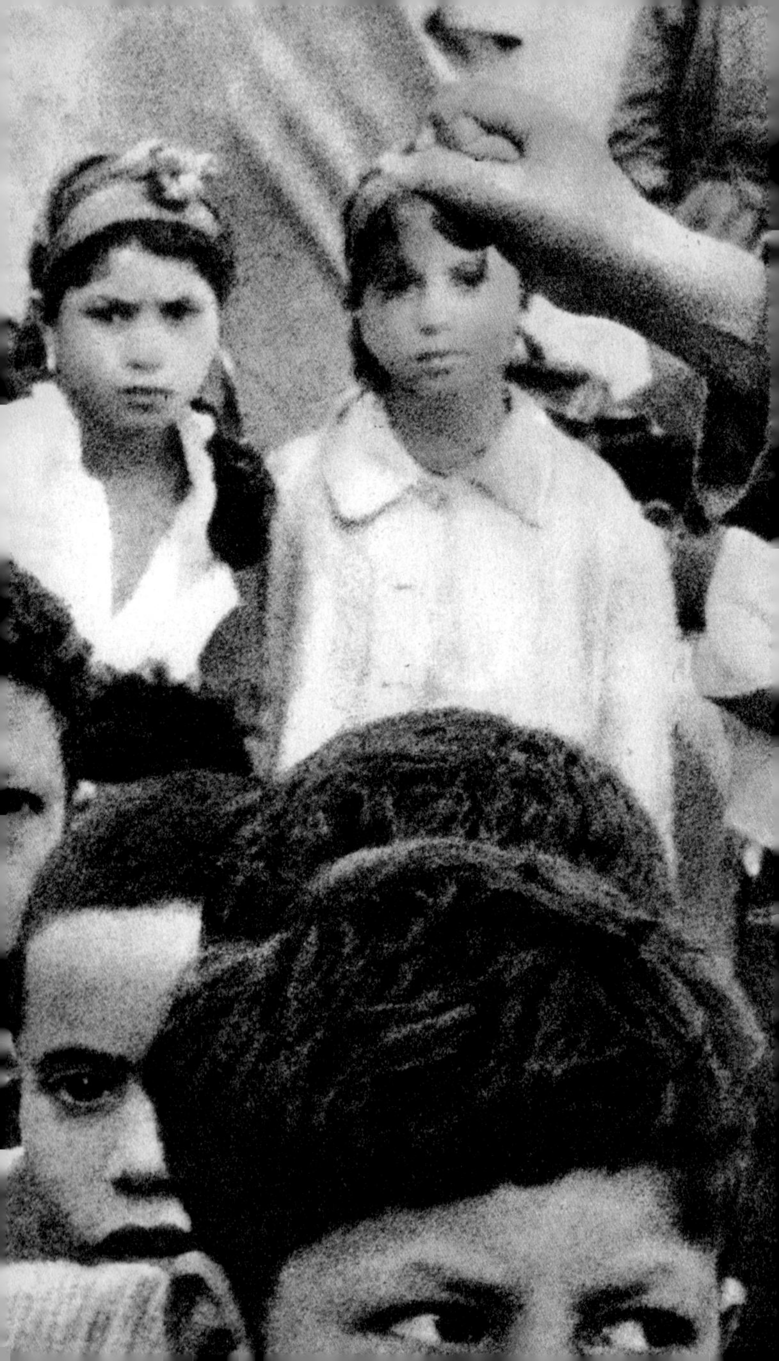

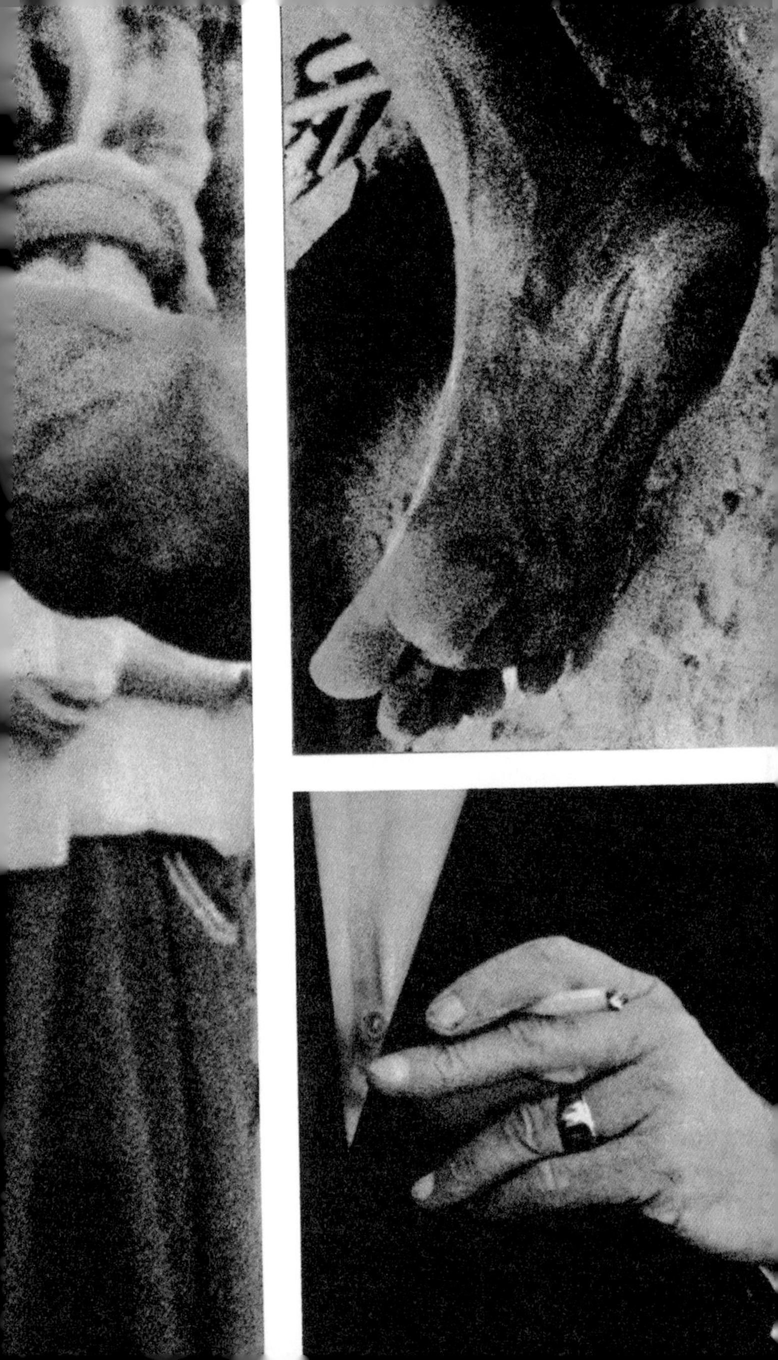

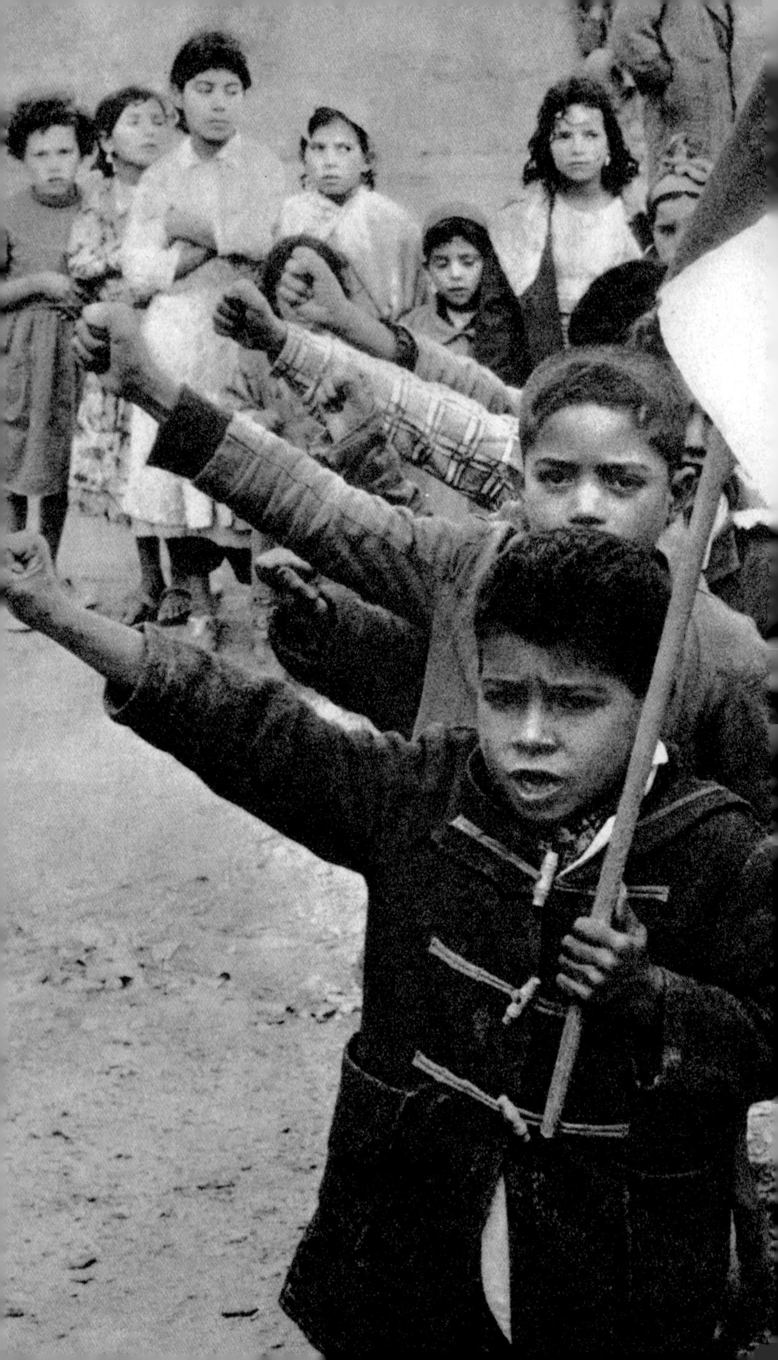

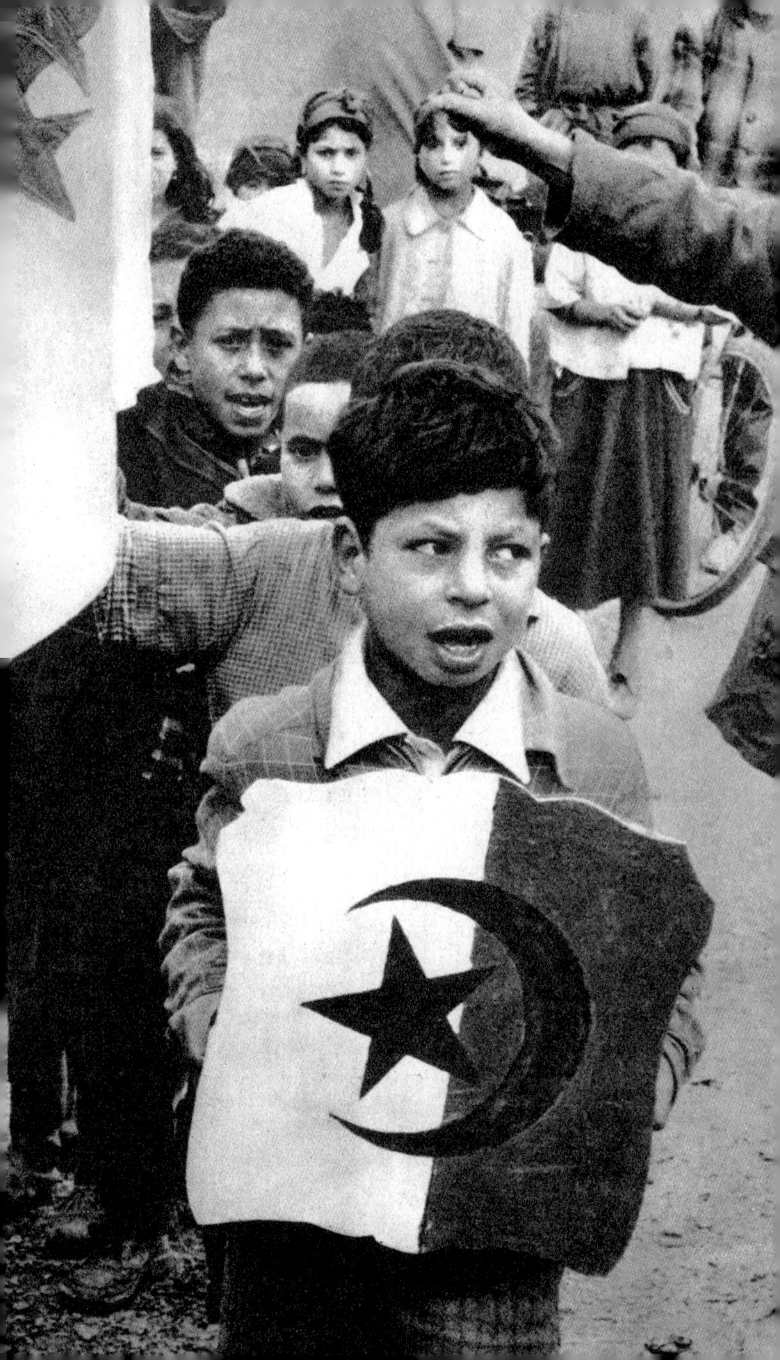

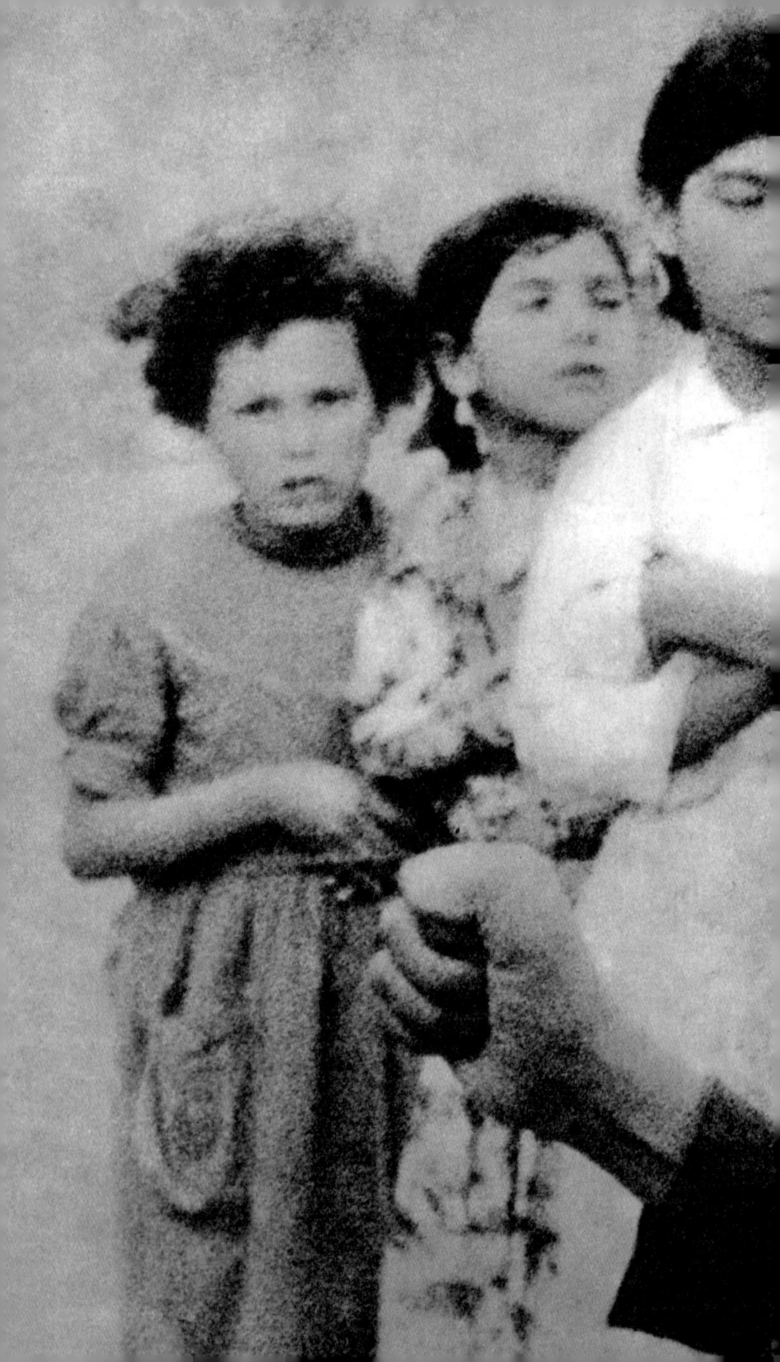

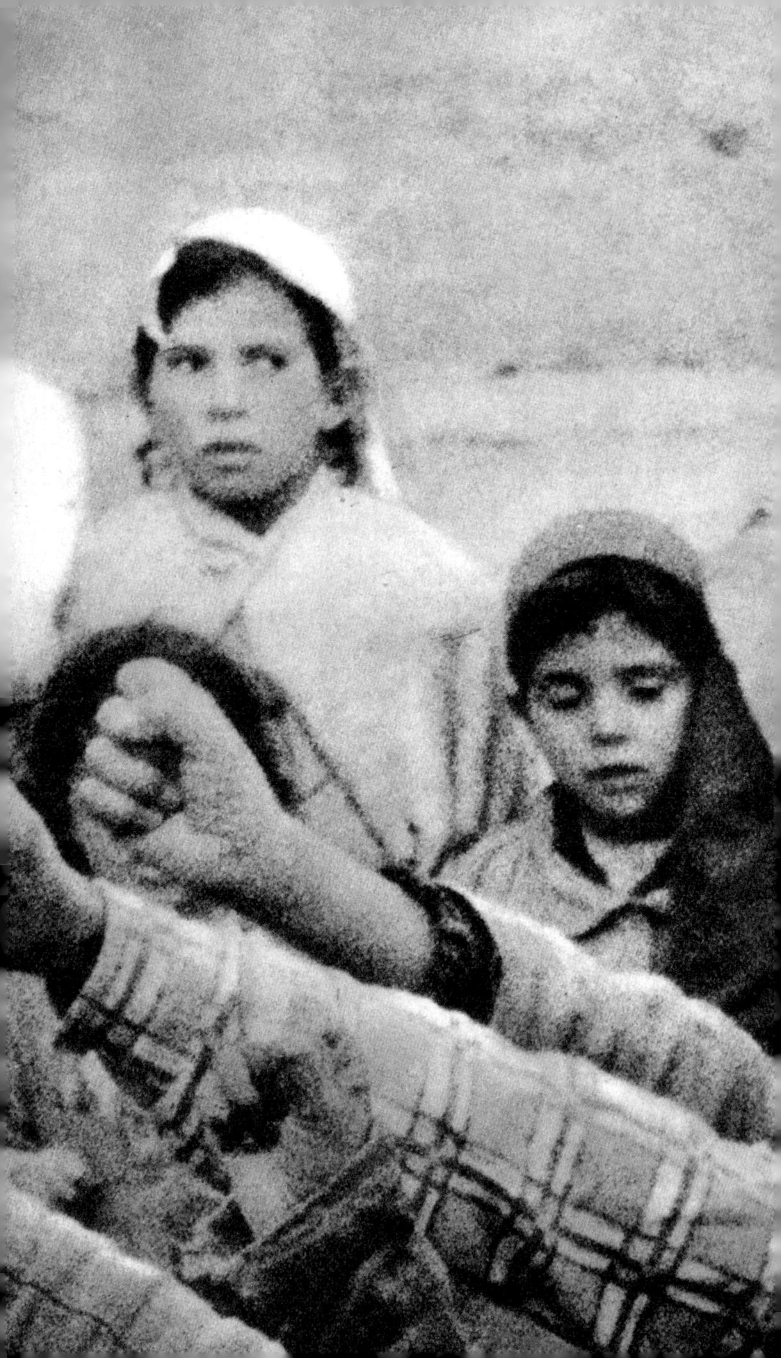

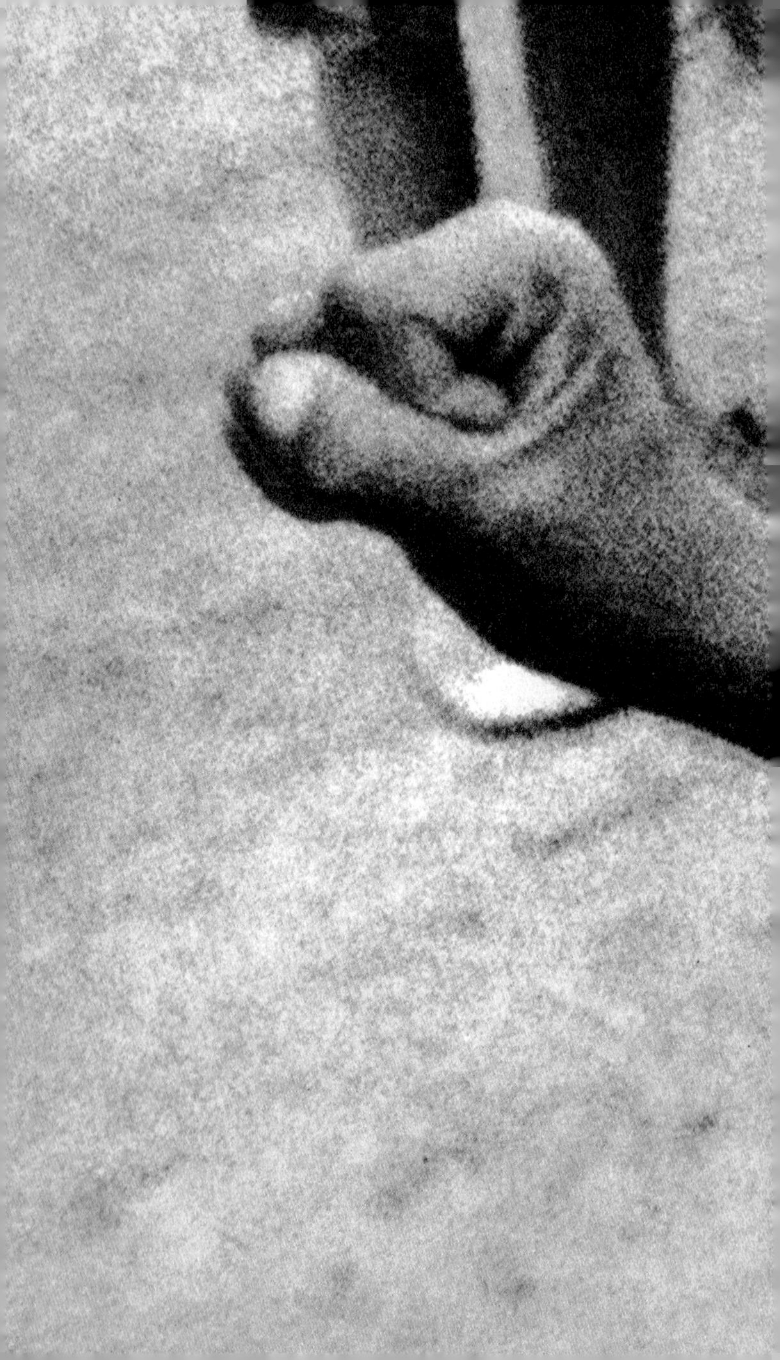

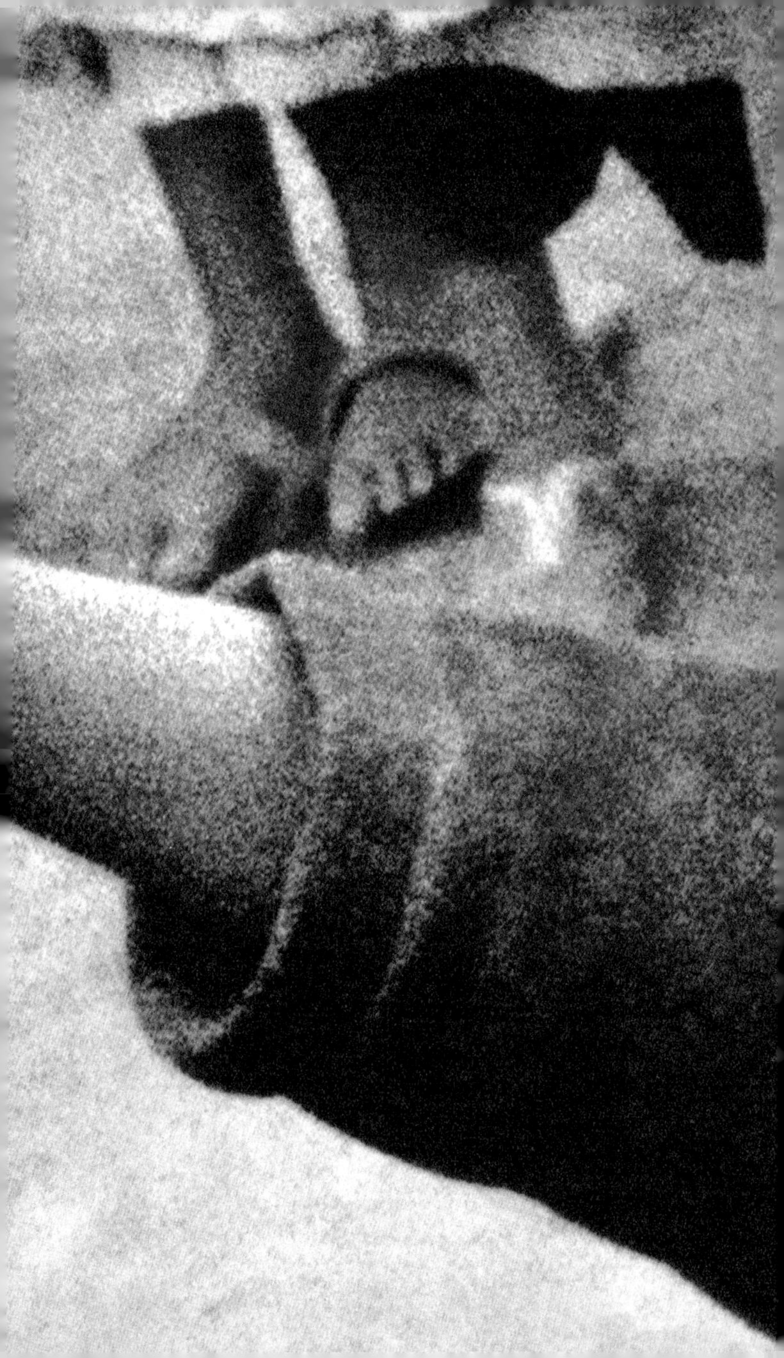

2.

" They respect the rights of all peoples ..."

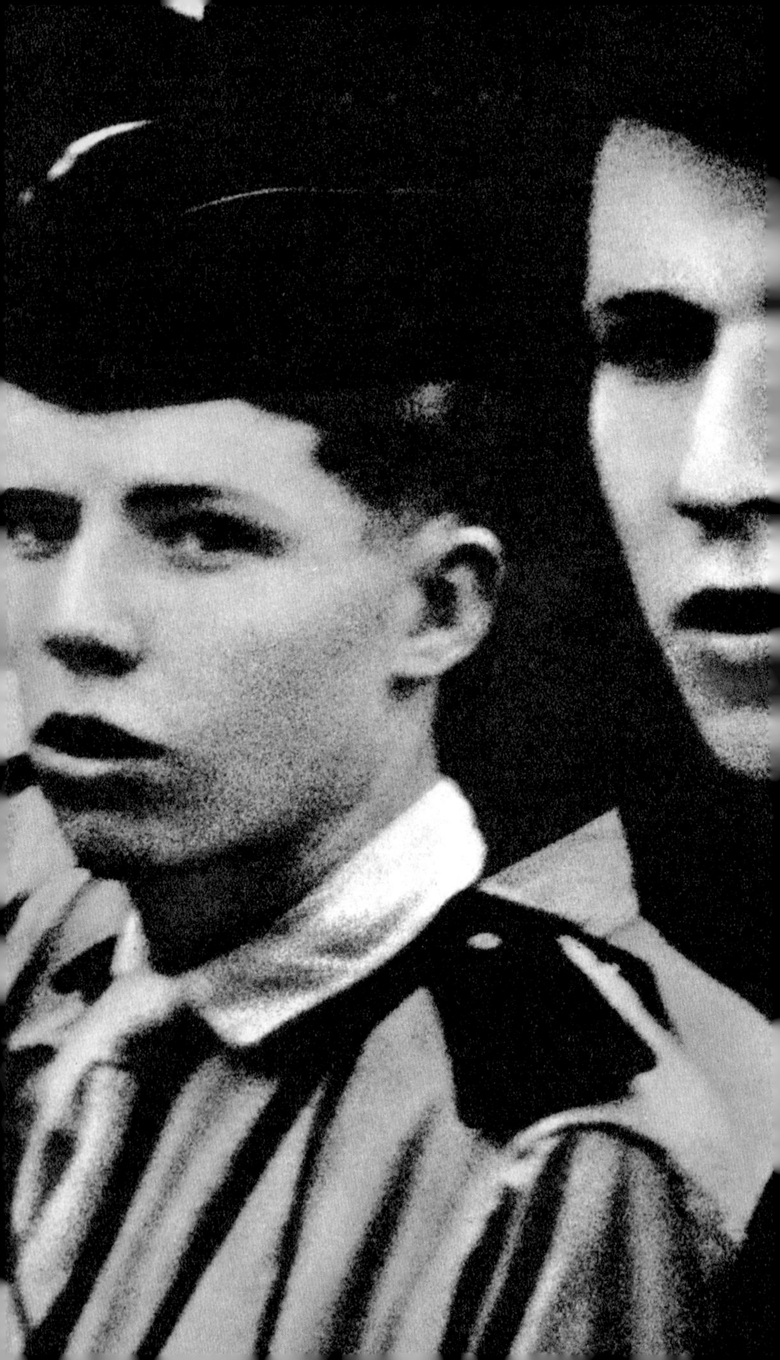

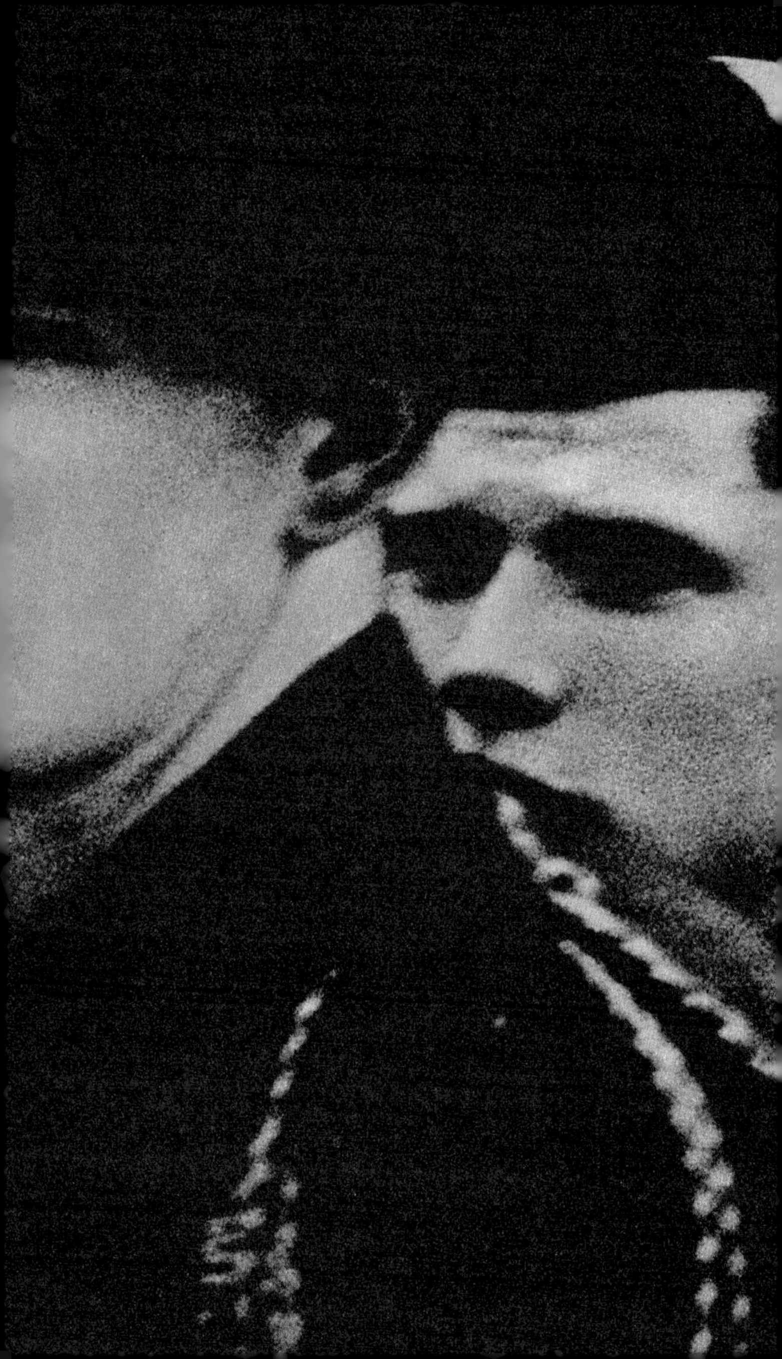

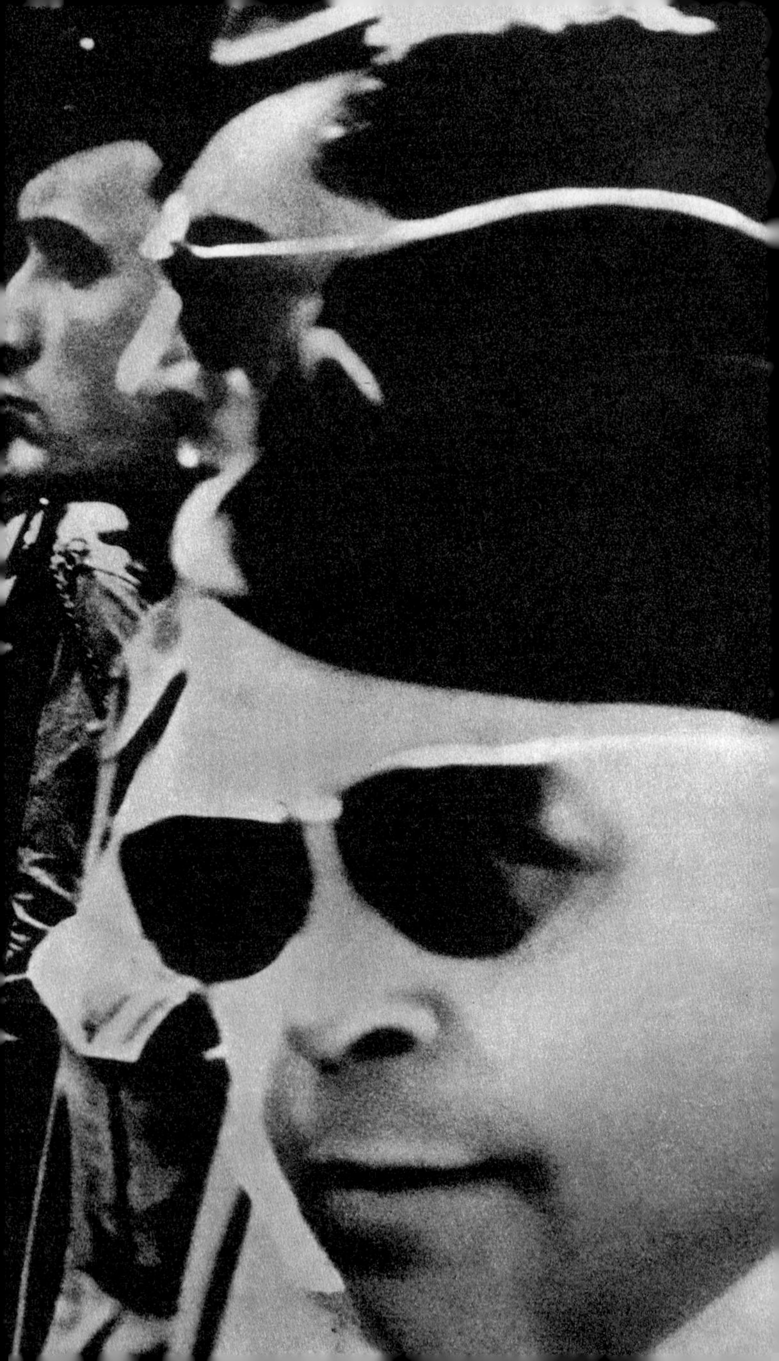

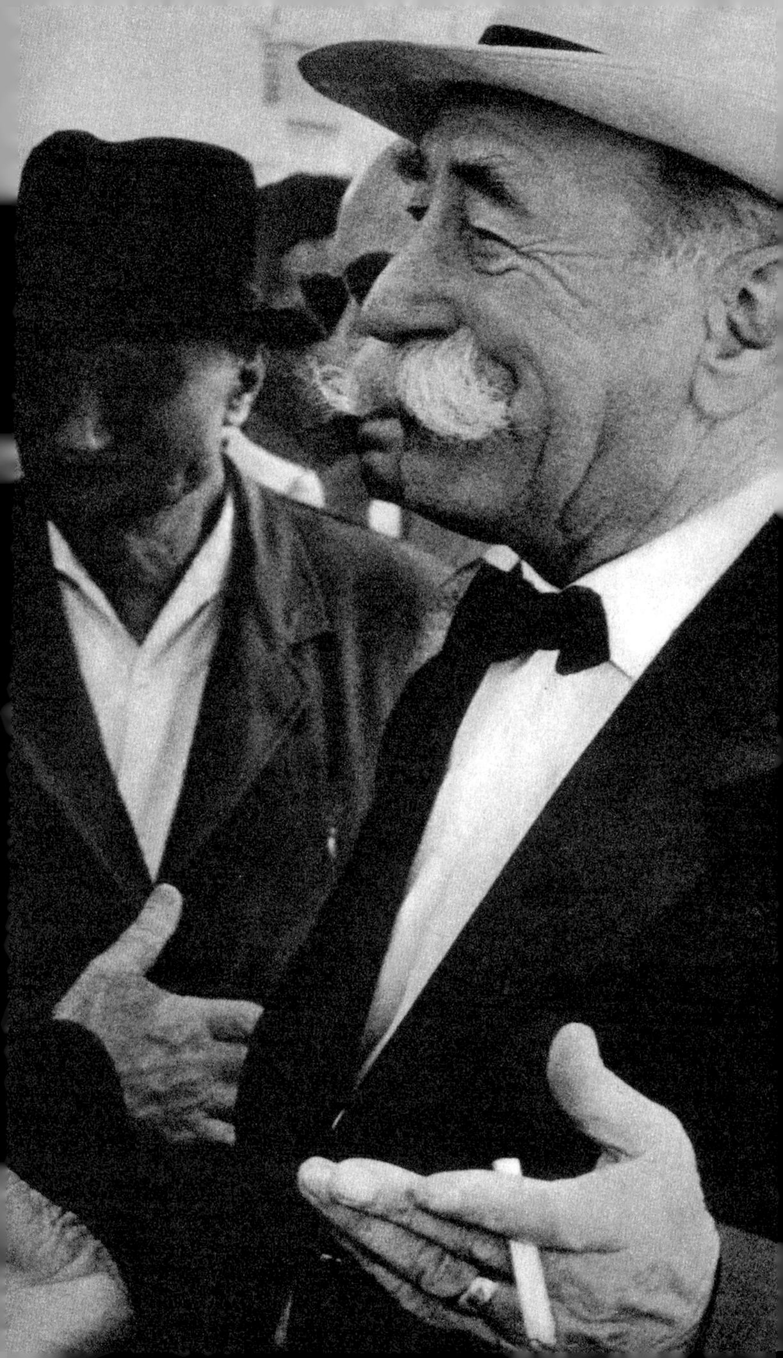

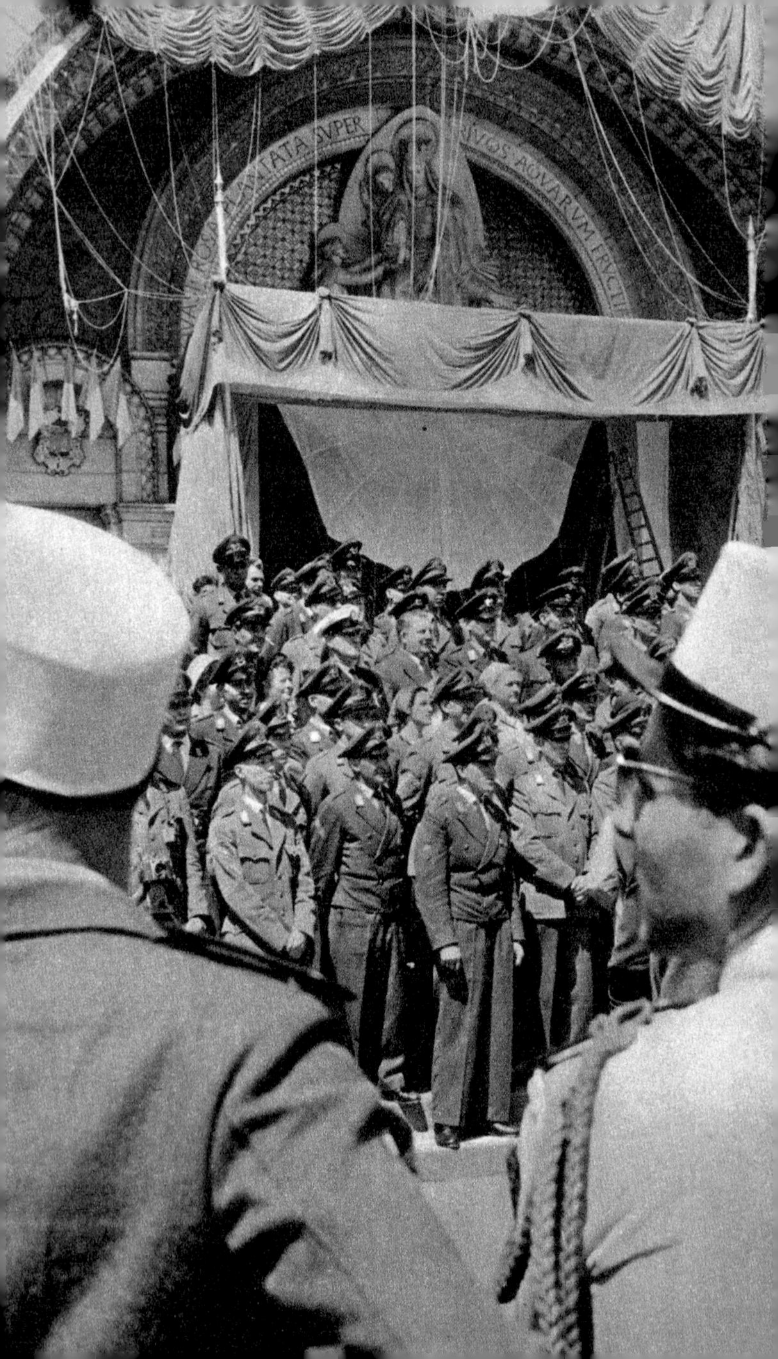

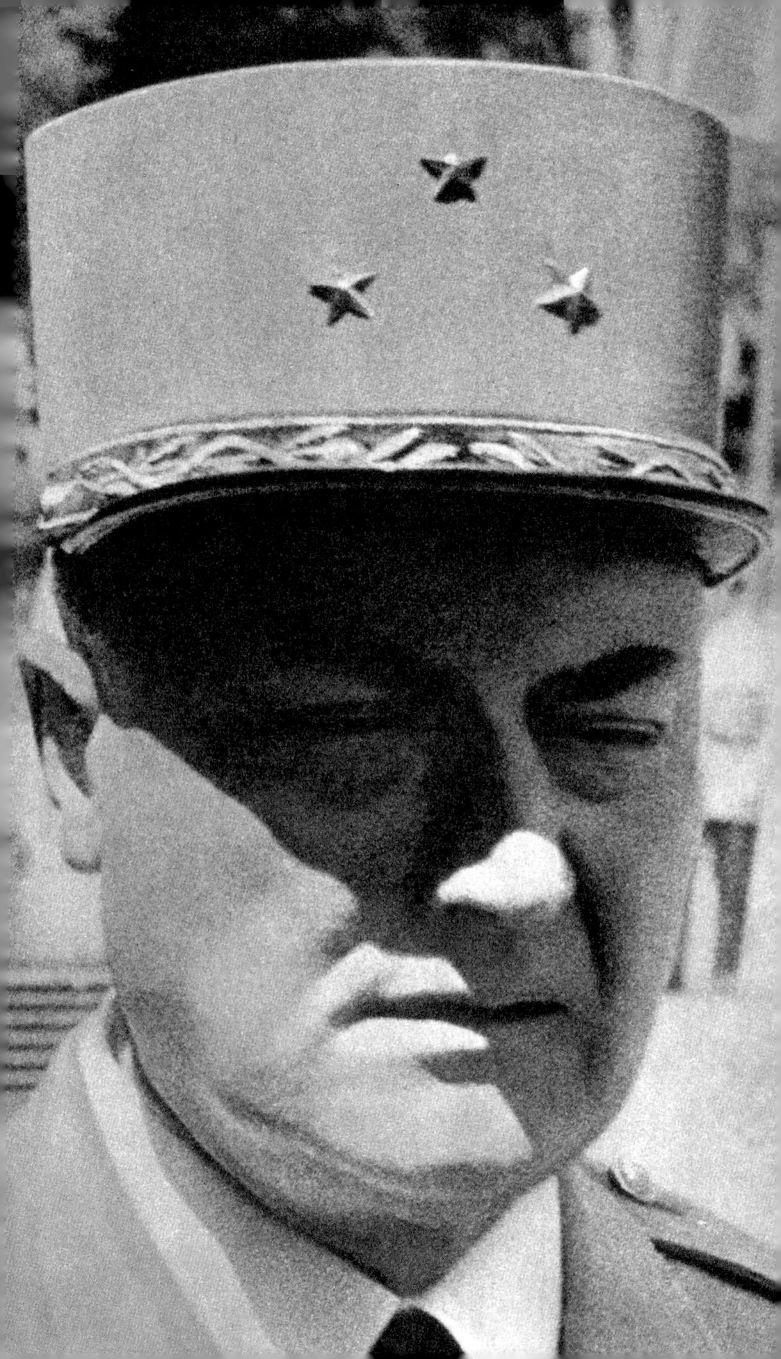

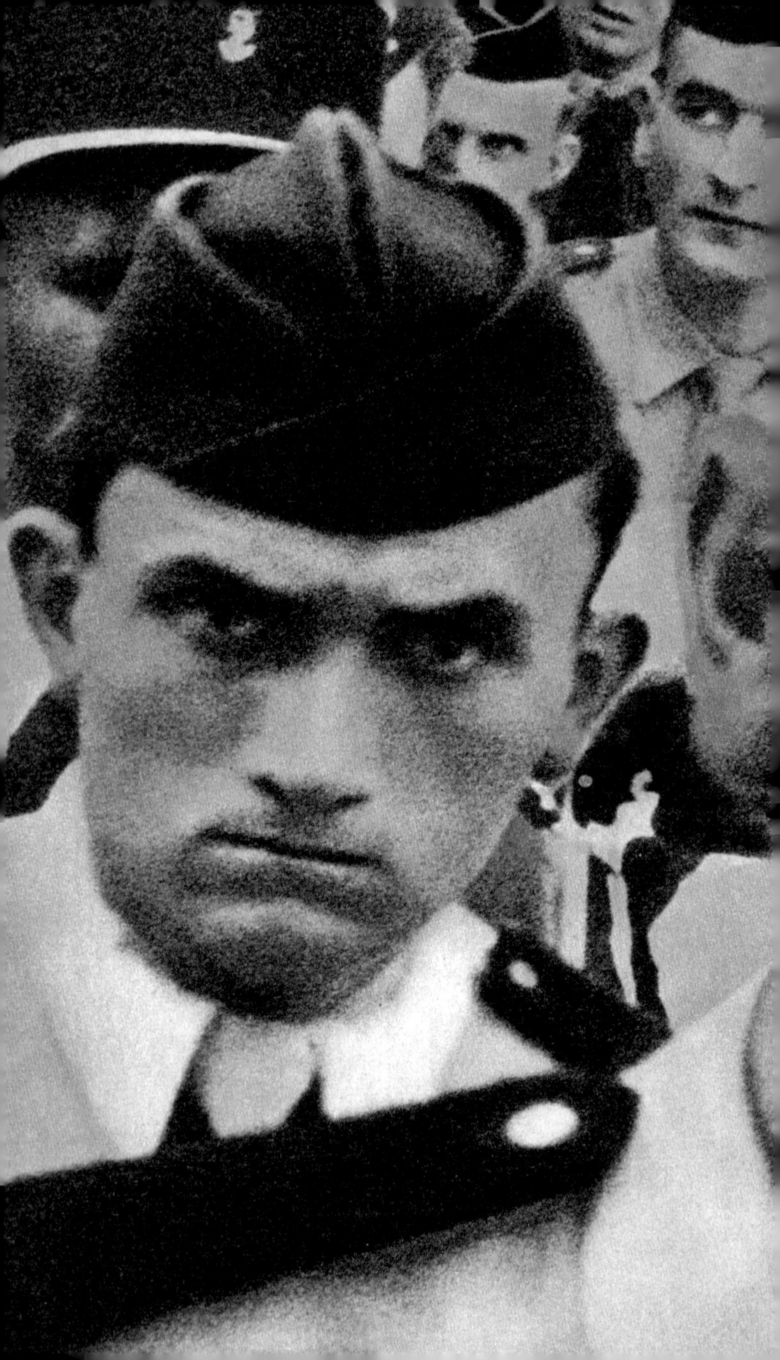

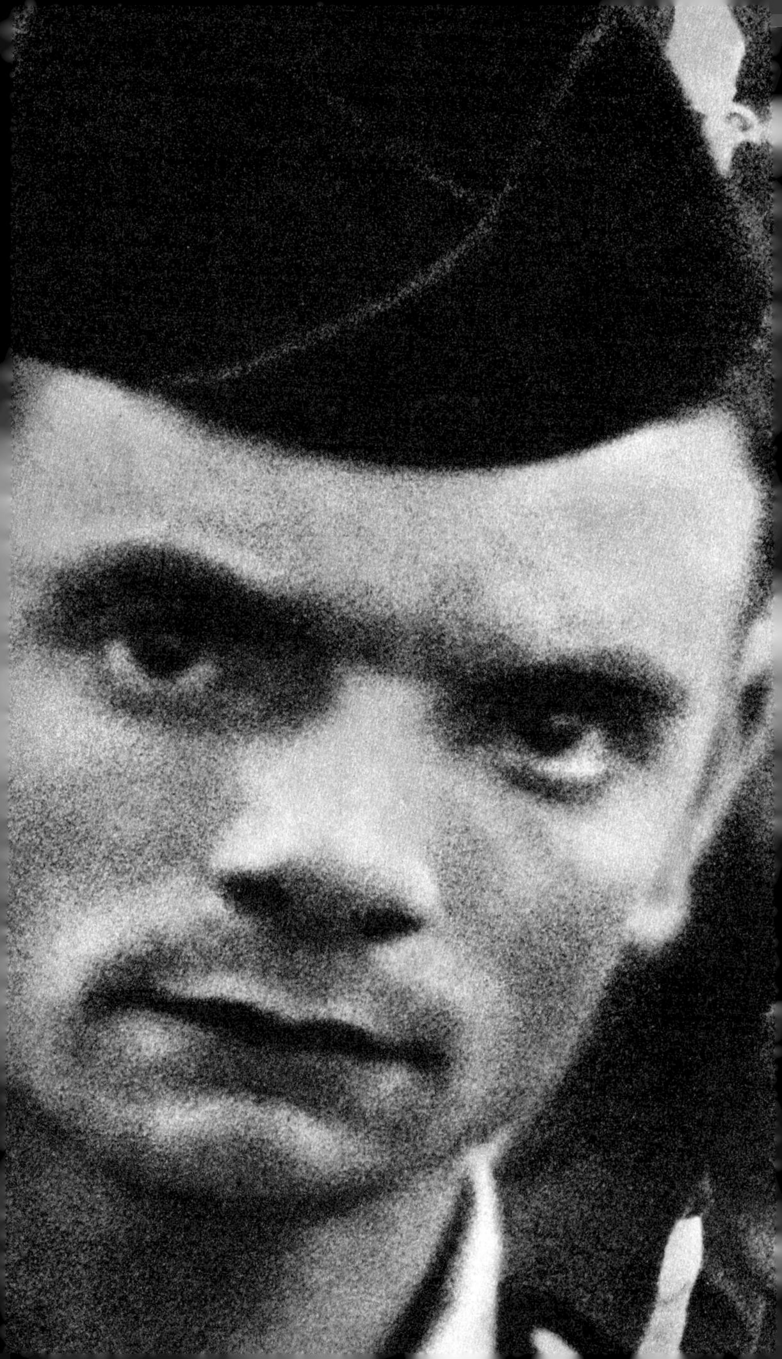

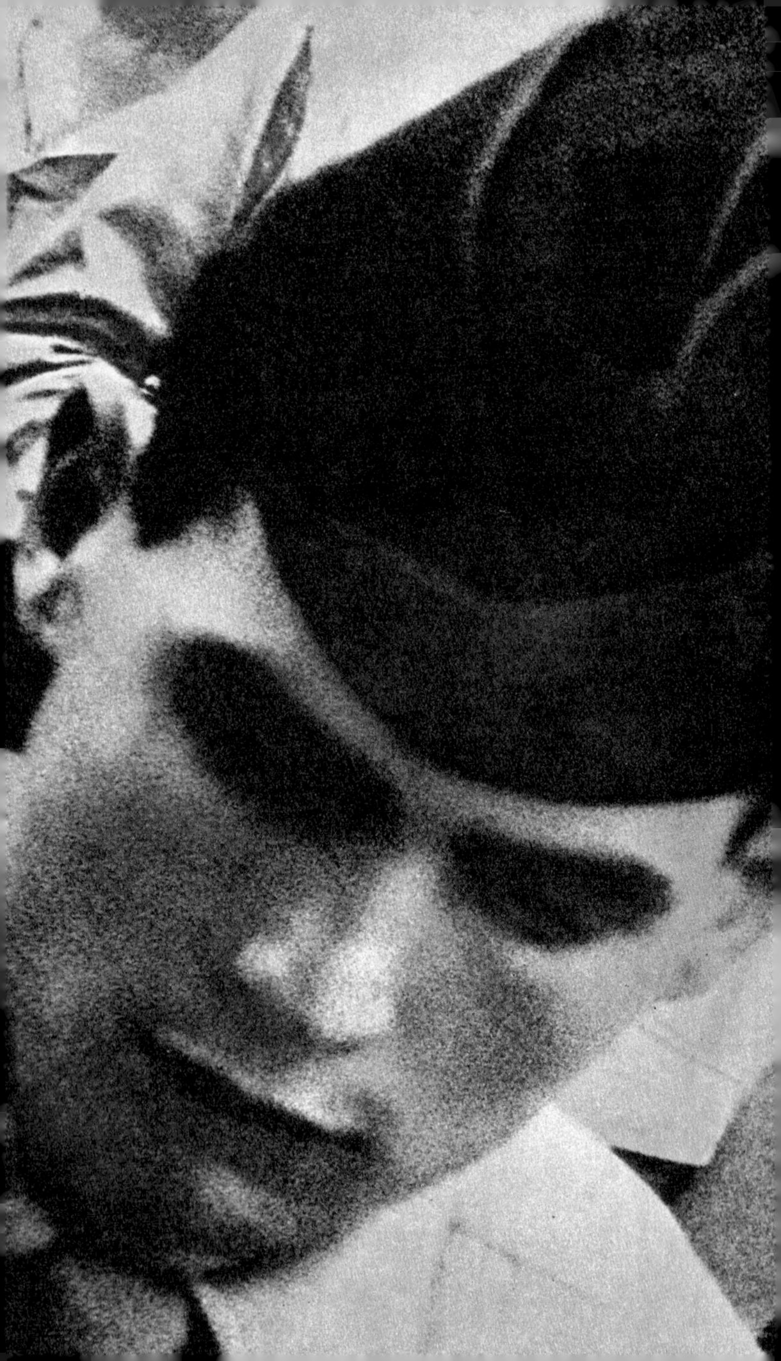

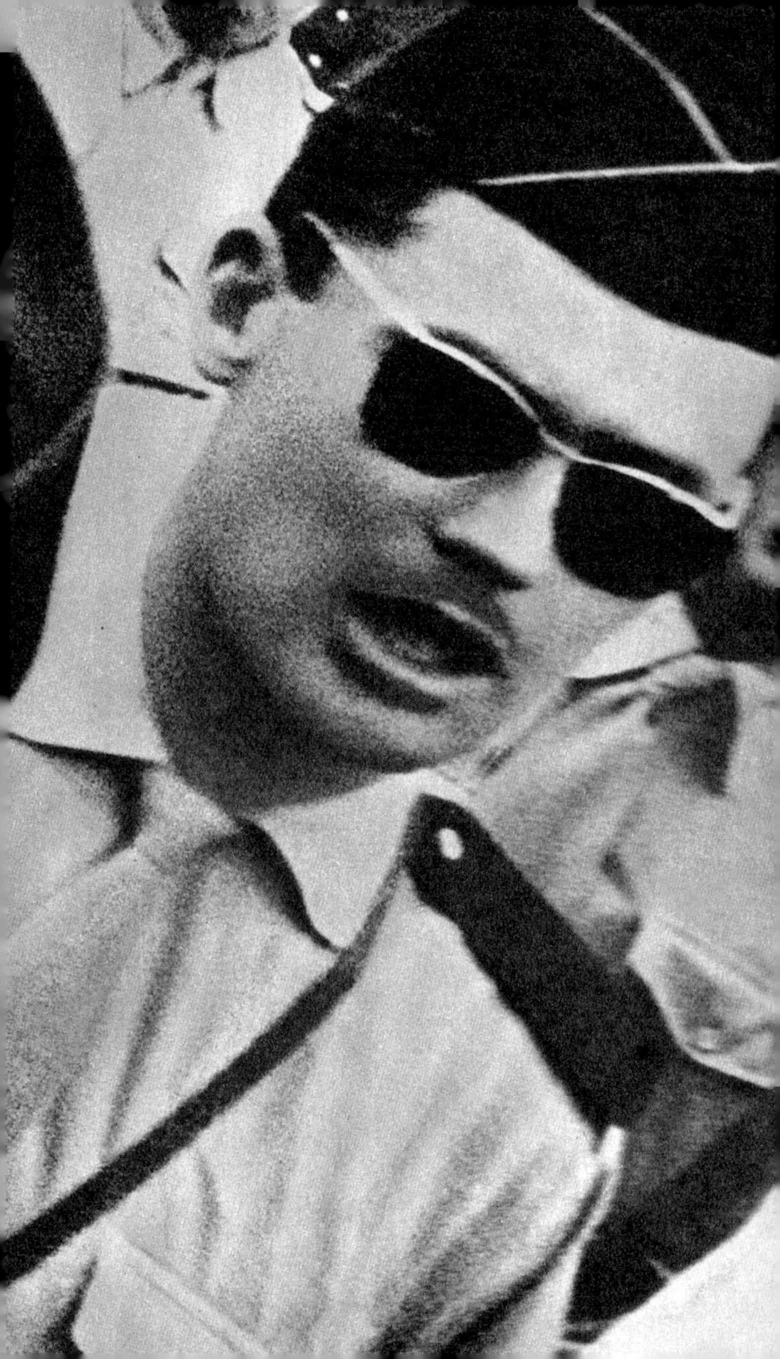

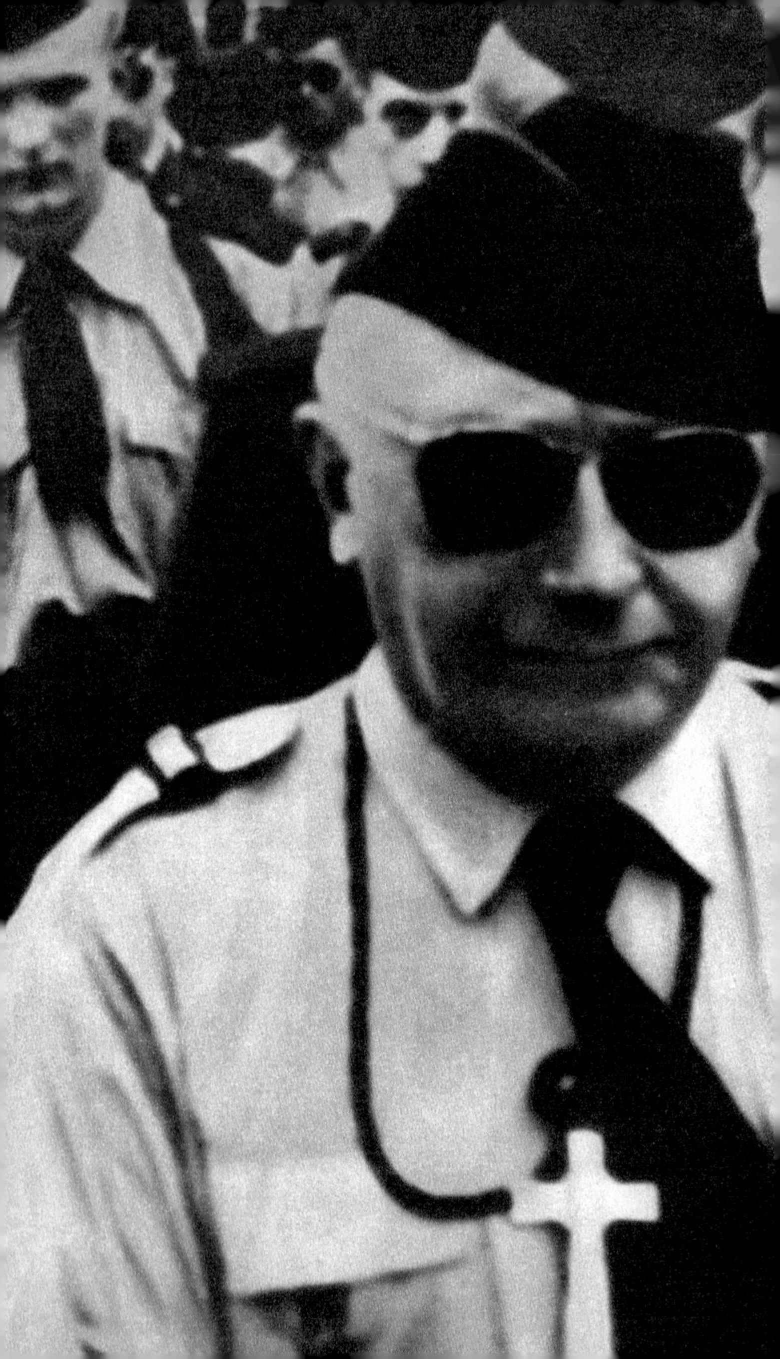

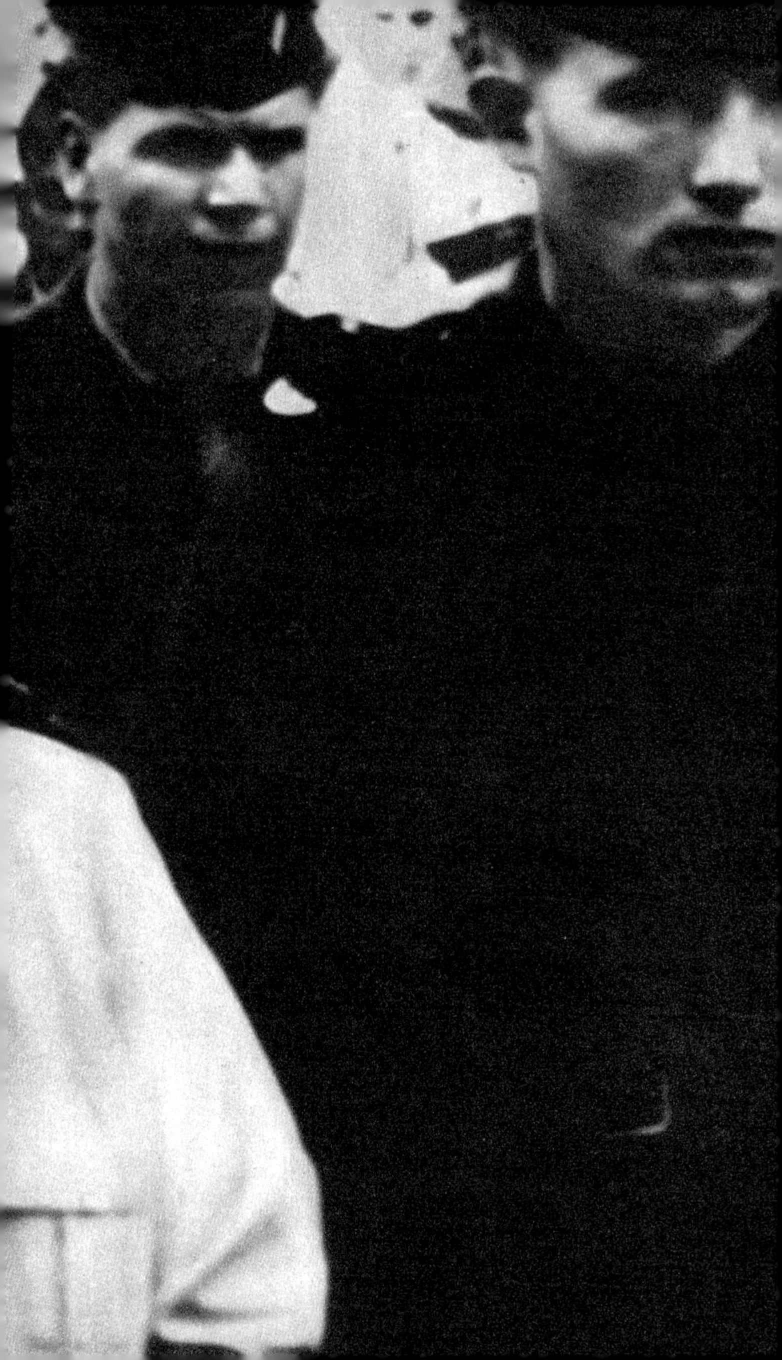

3.

"Who have dared to rise up ..."

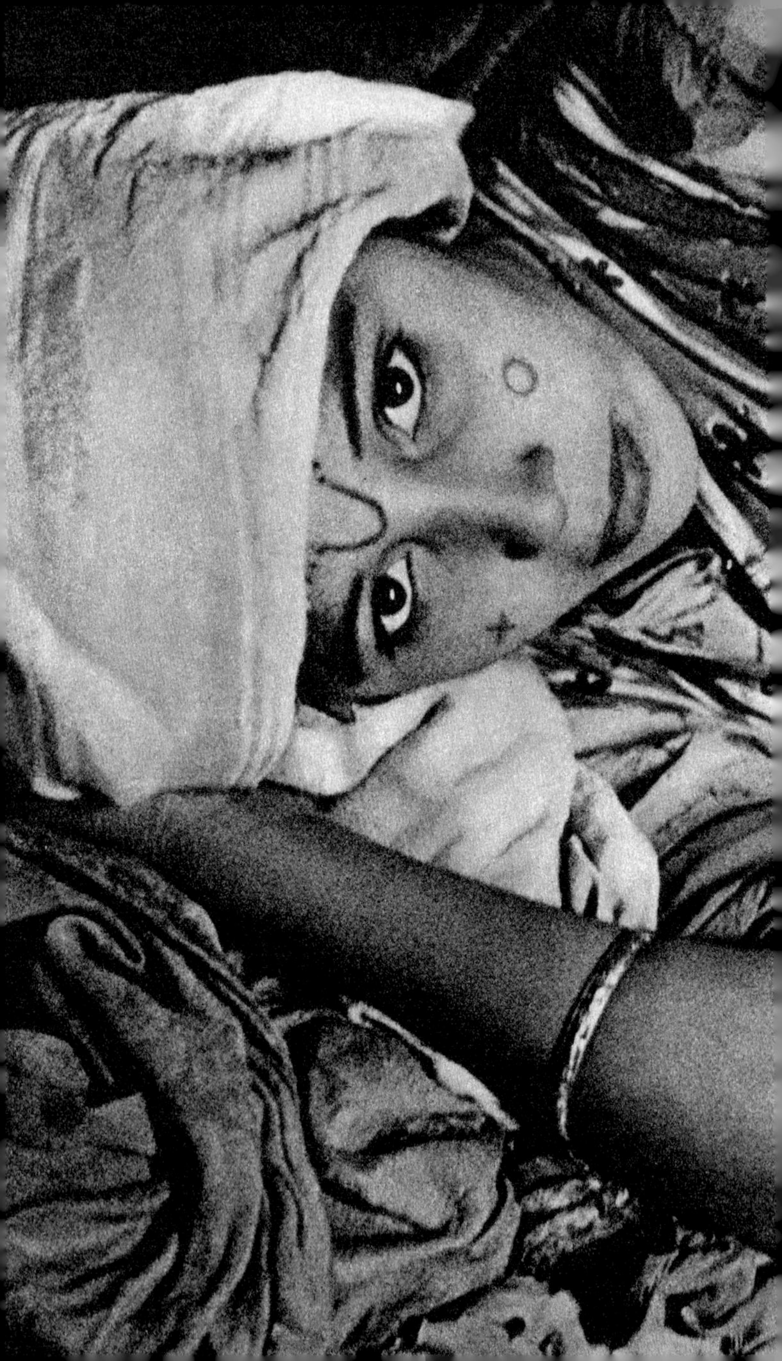

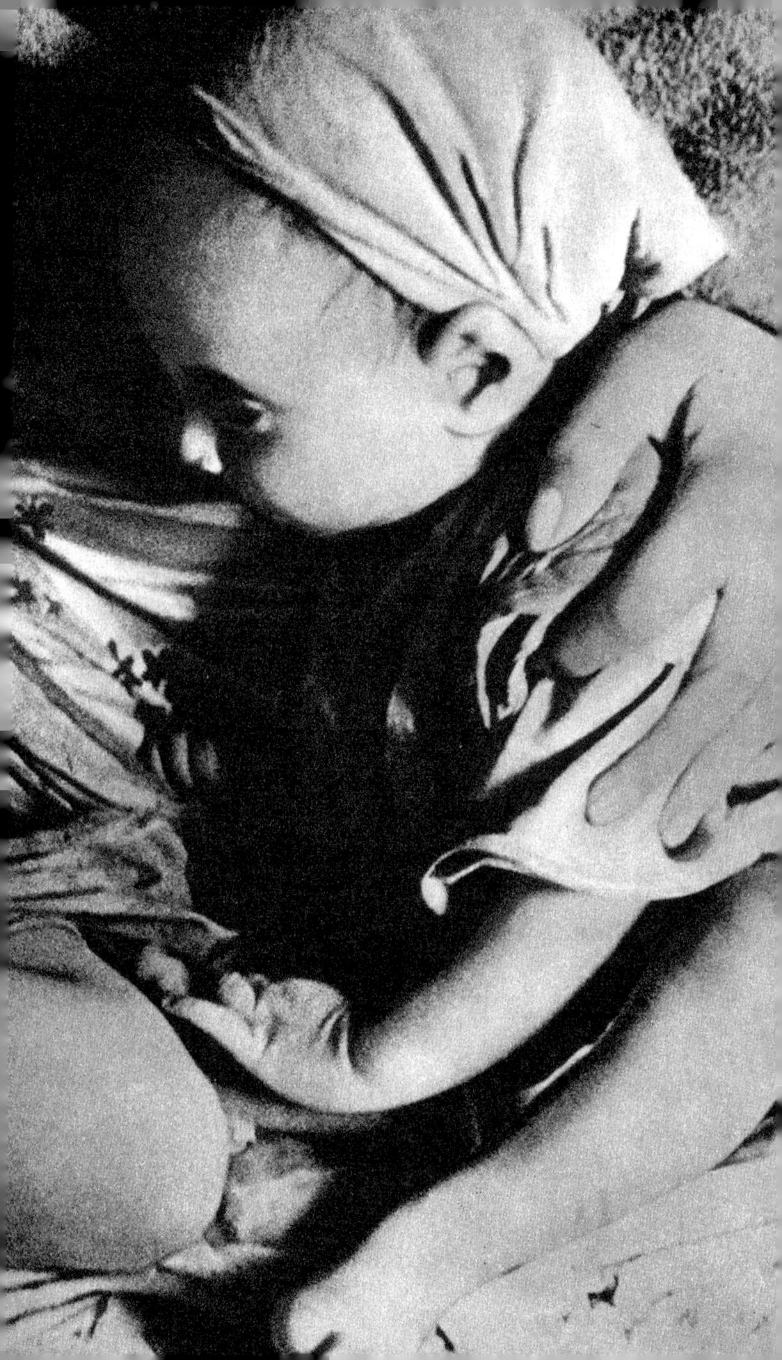

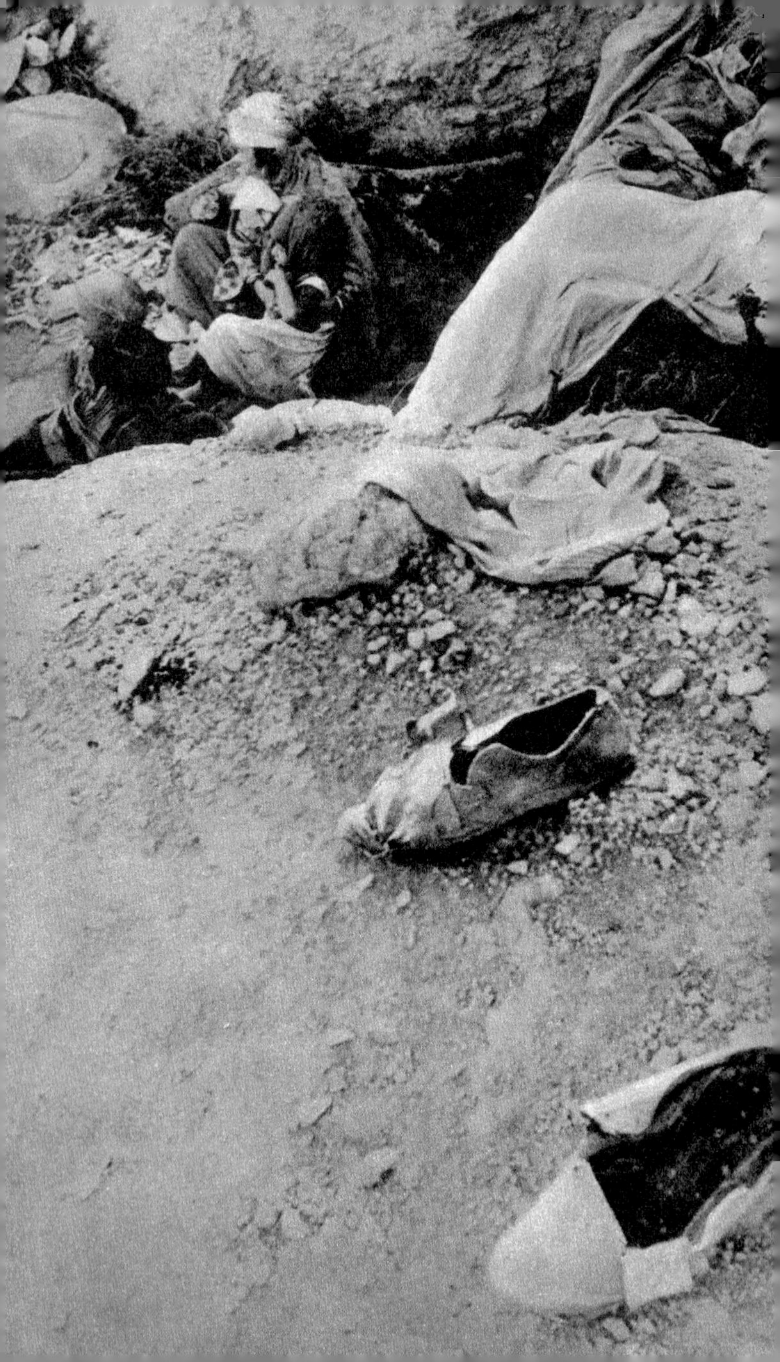

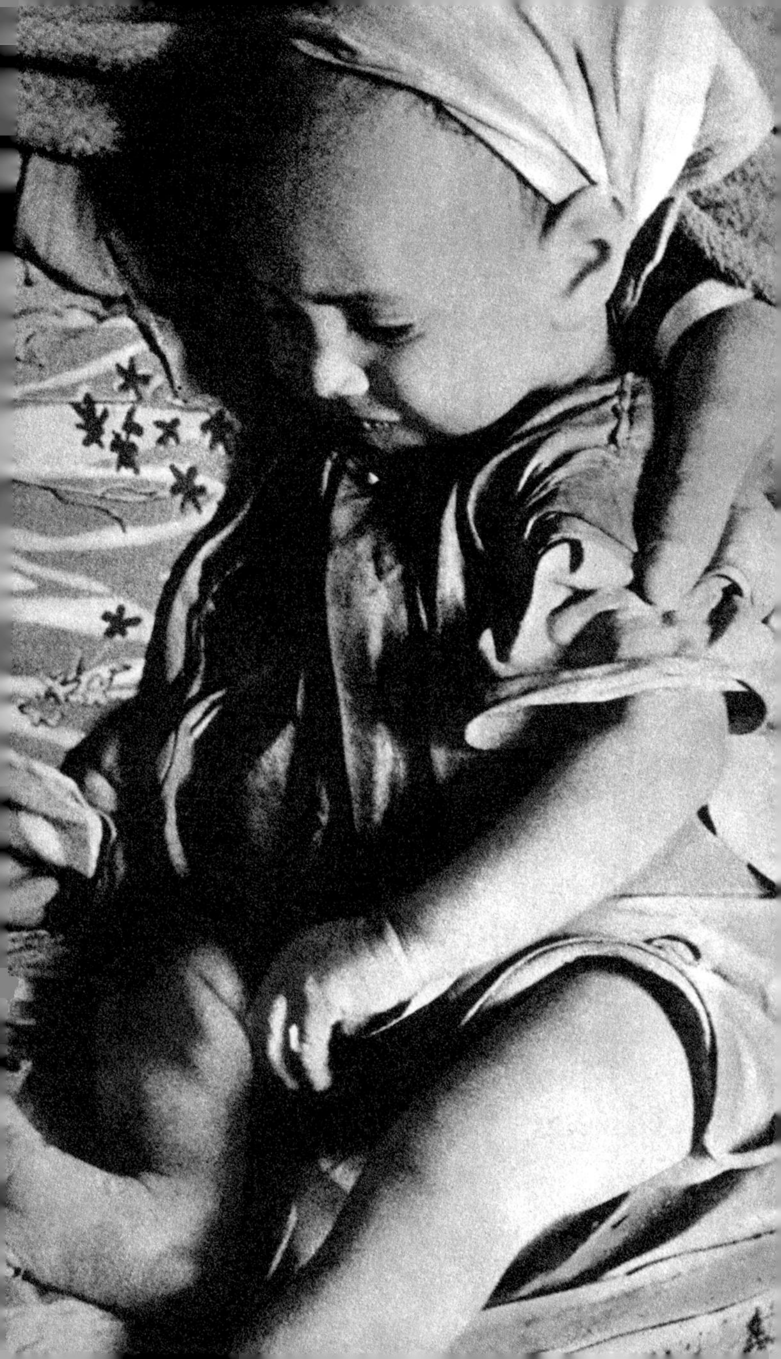

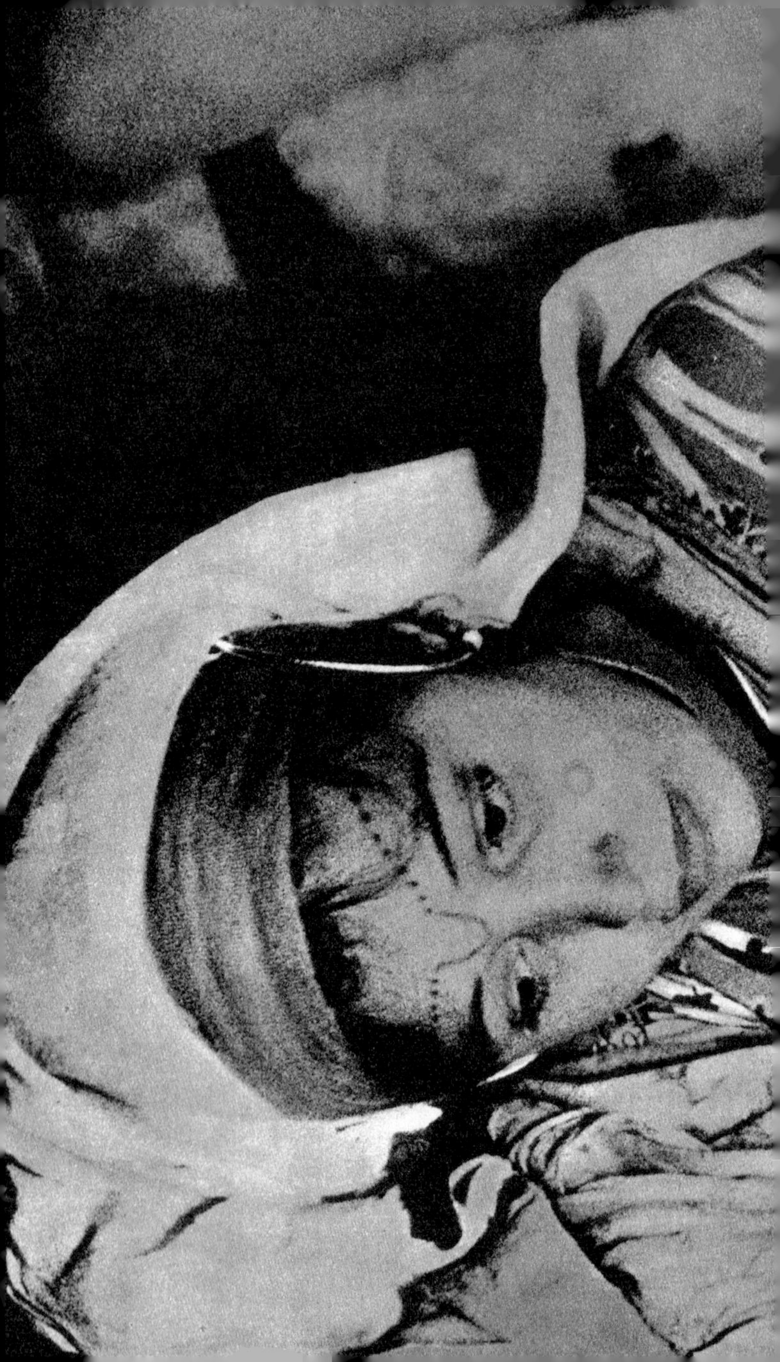

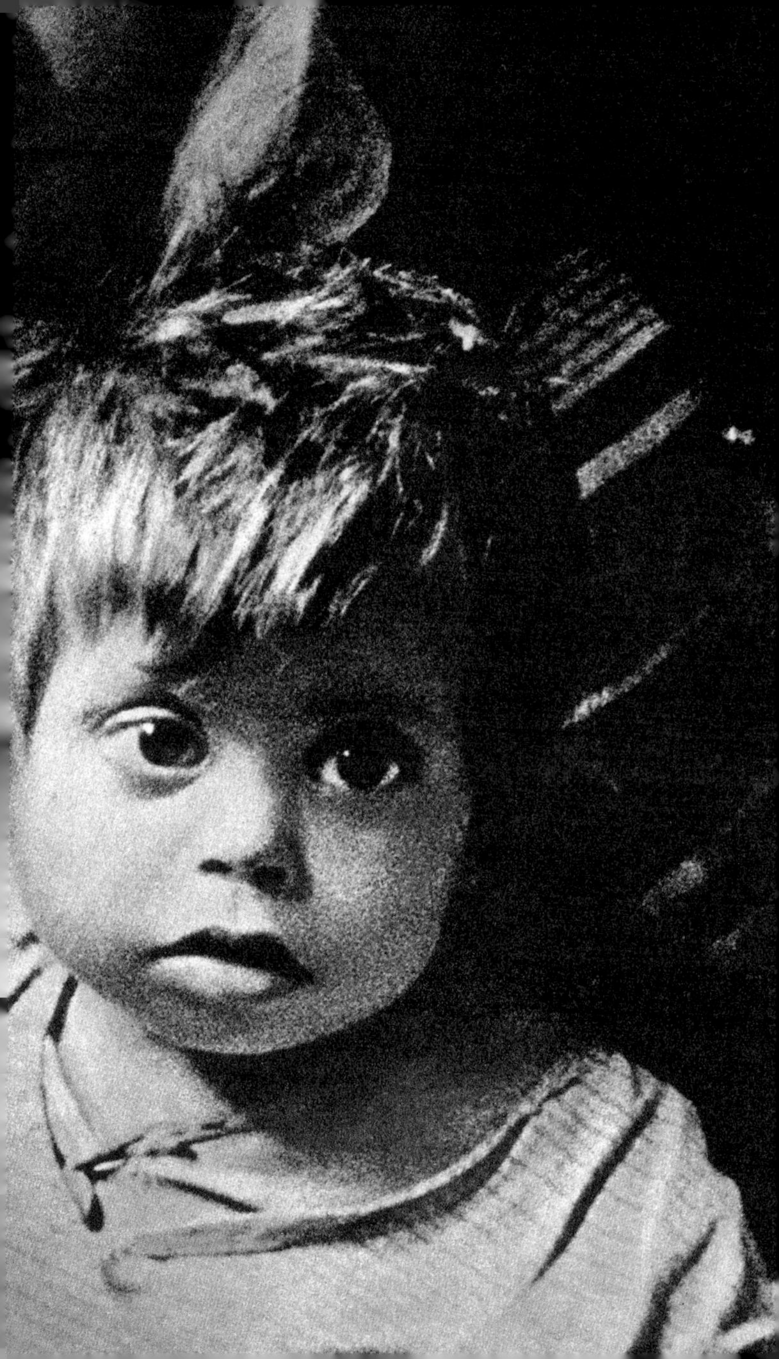

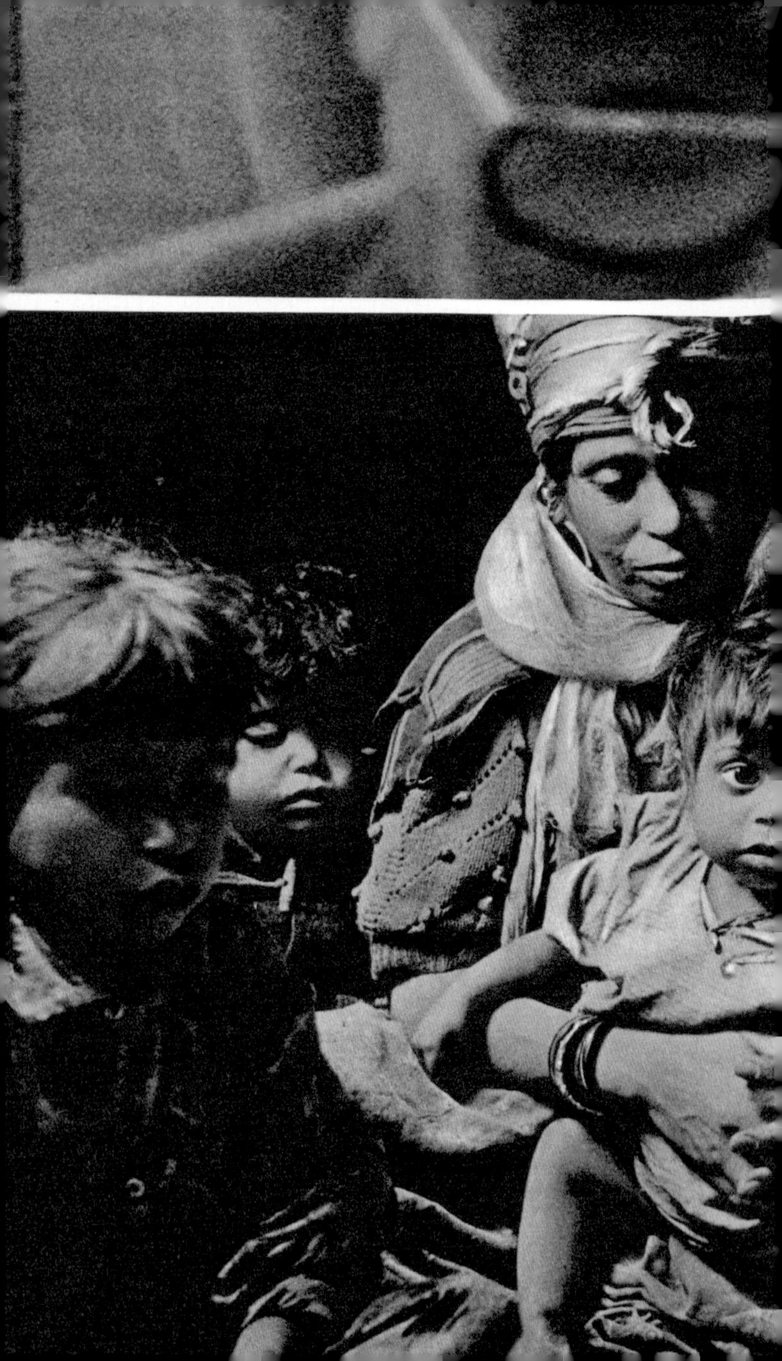

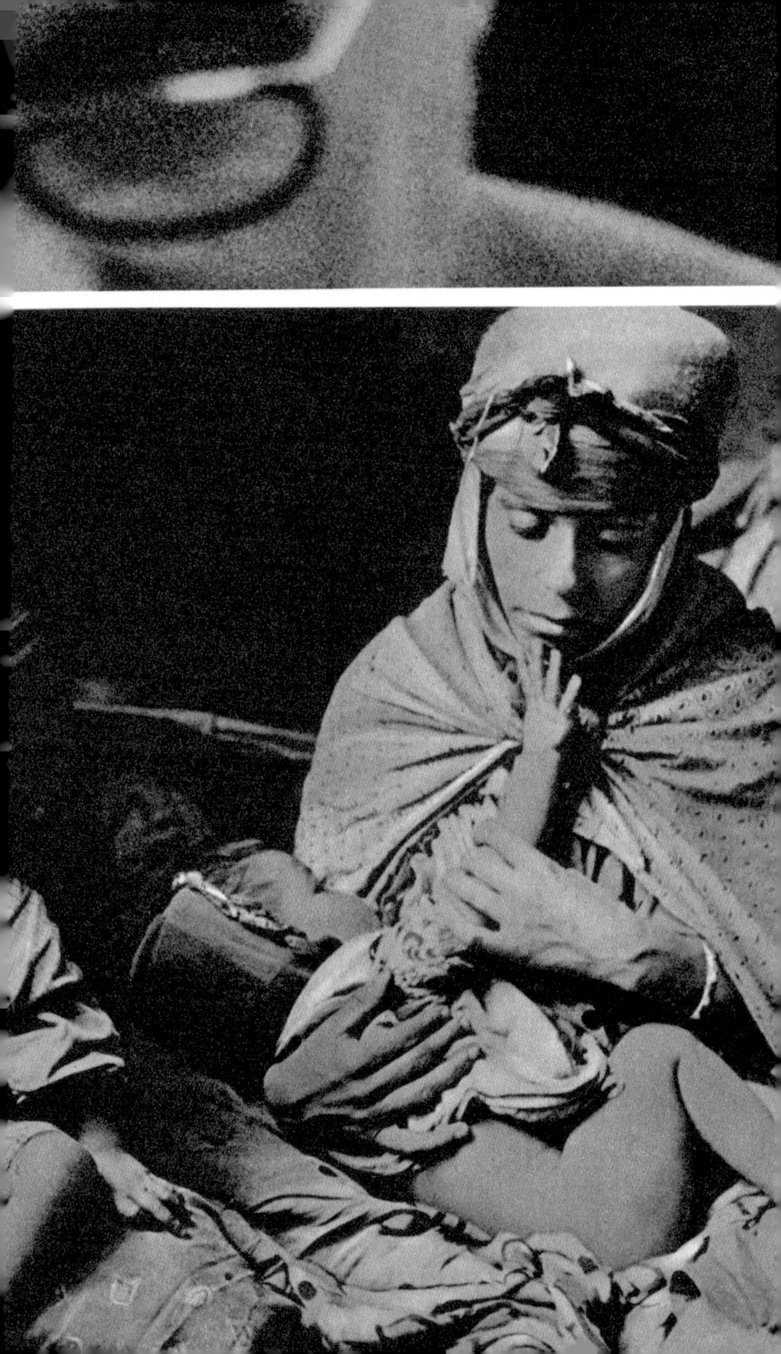

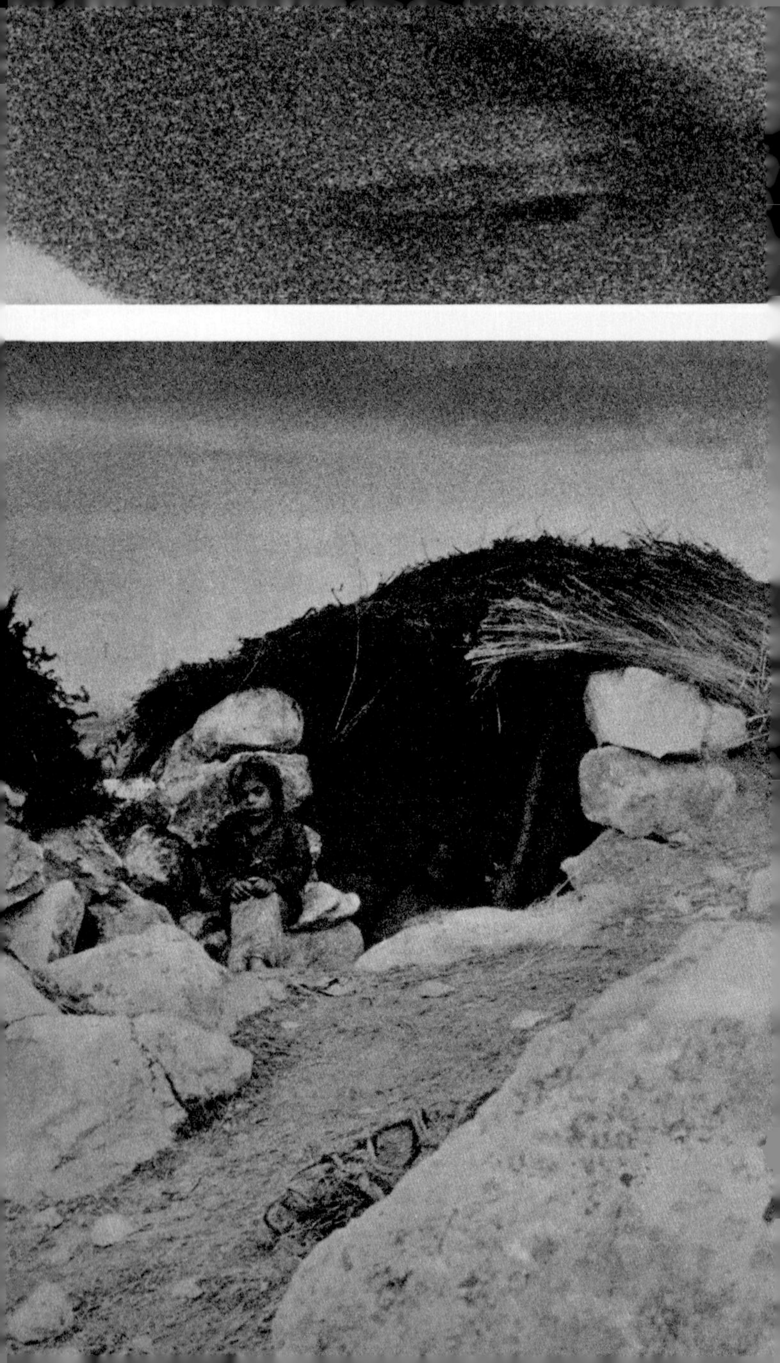

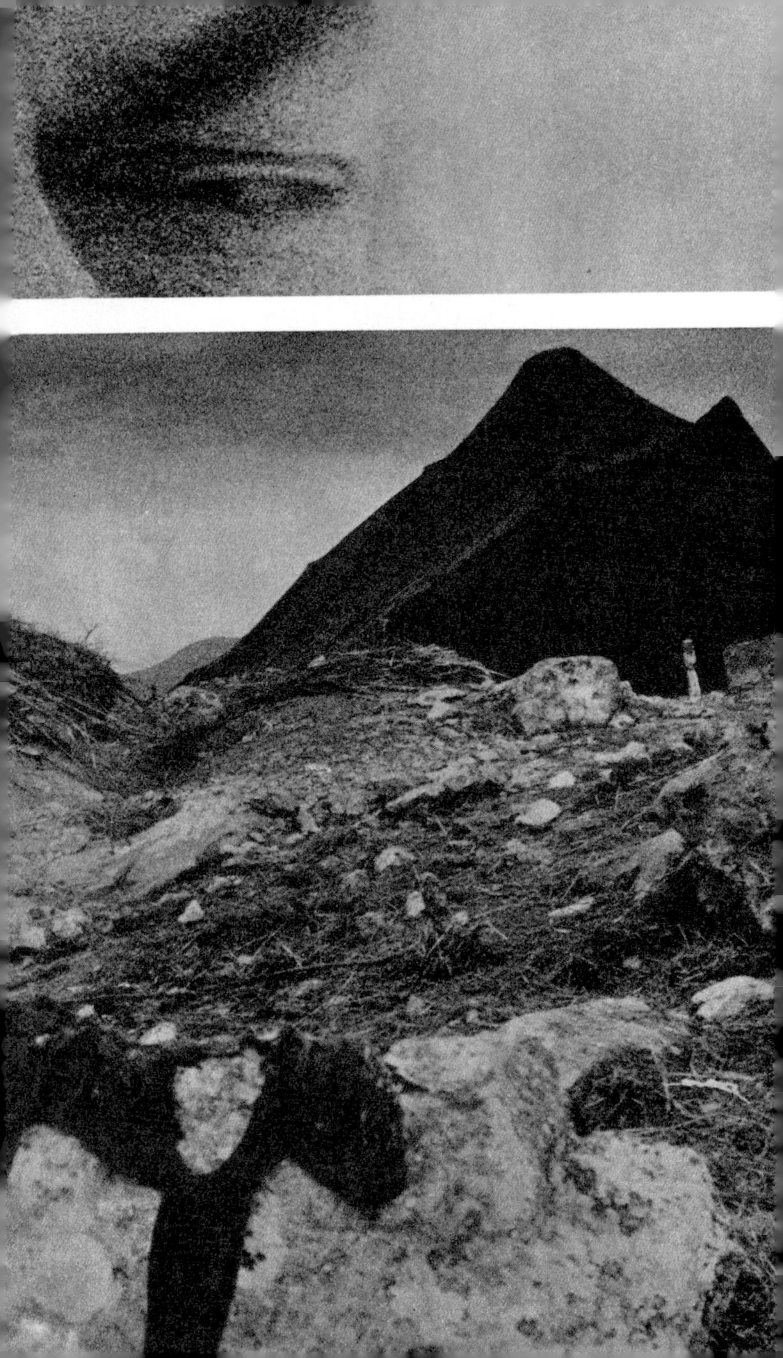

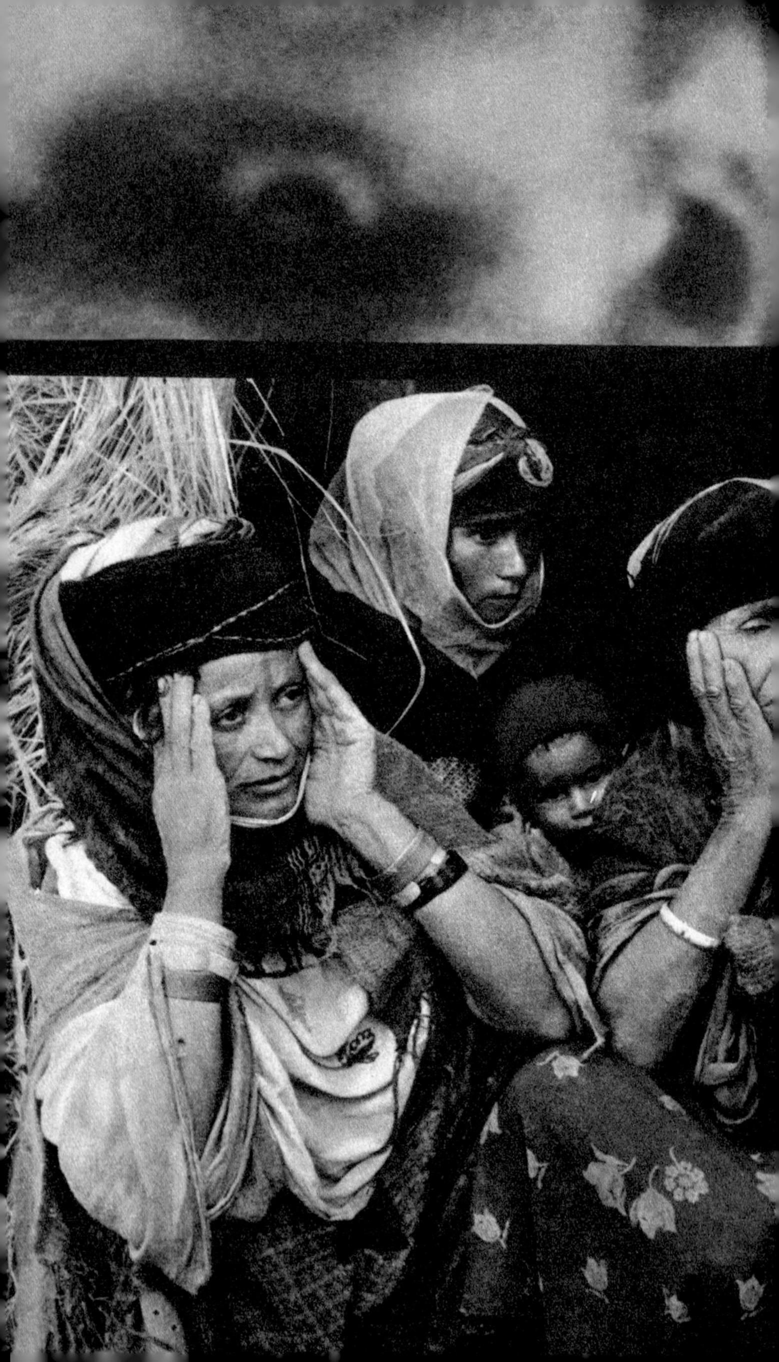

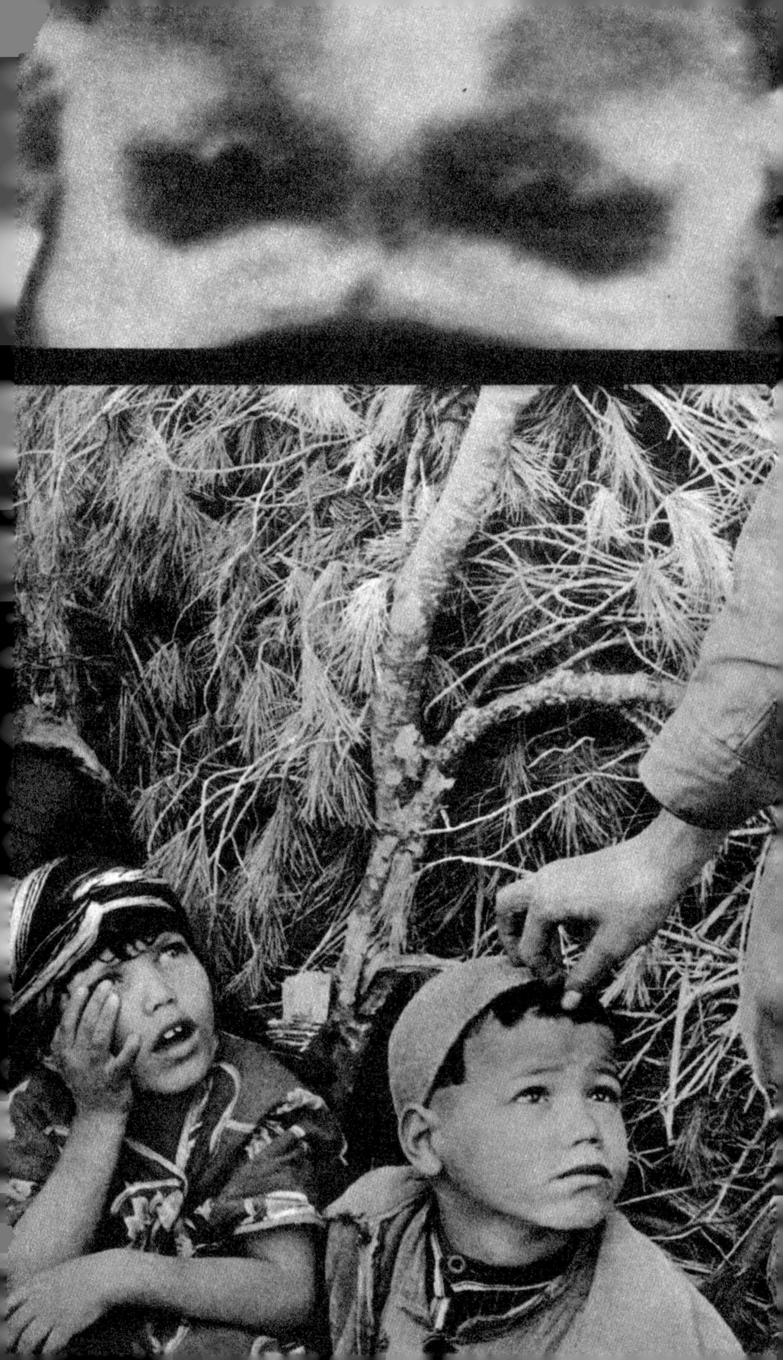

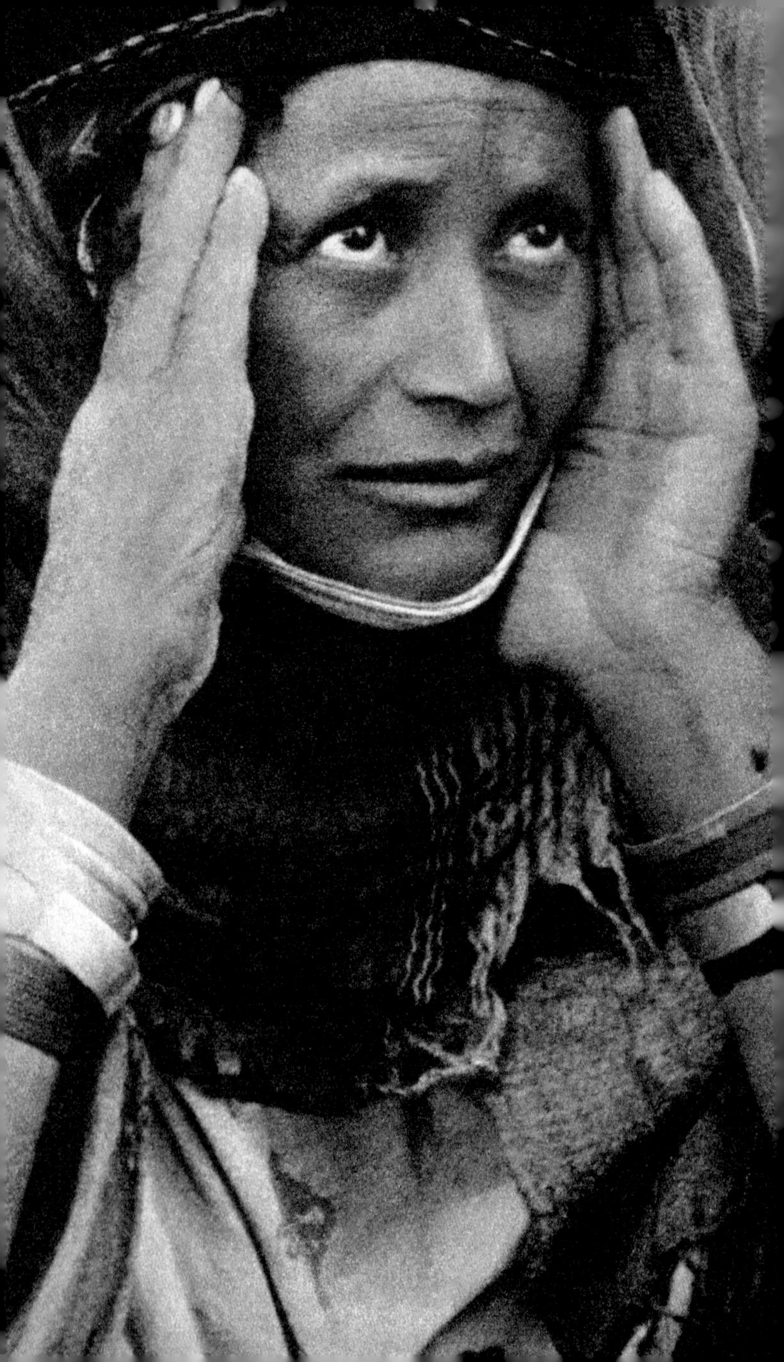

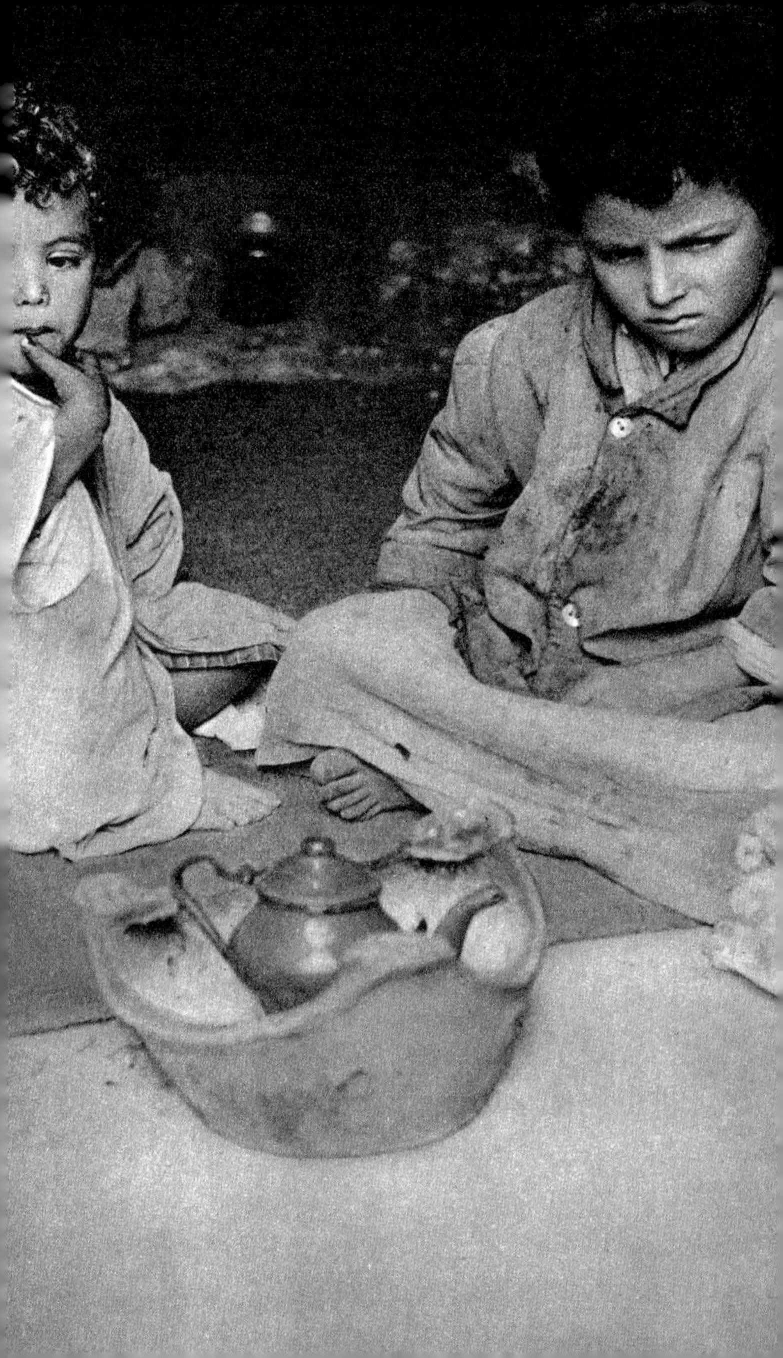

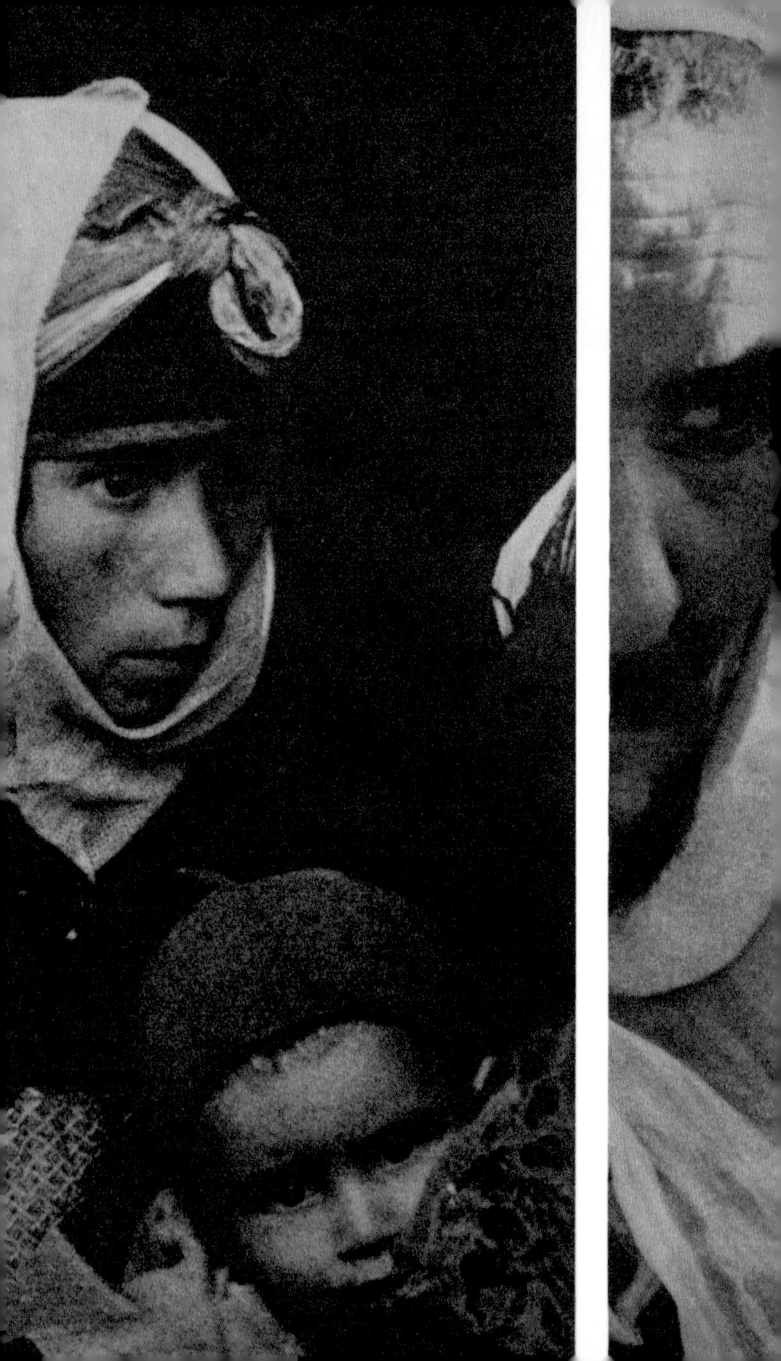

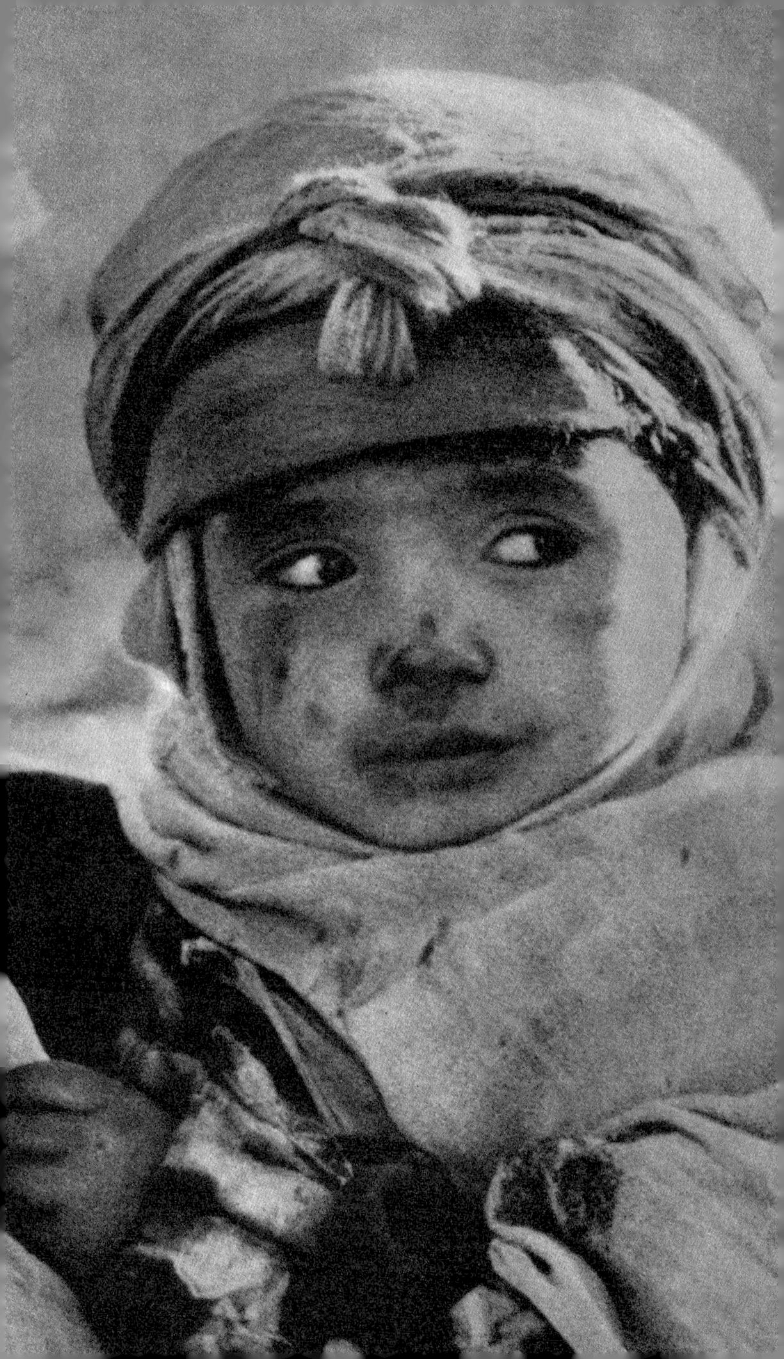

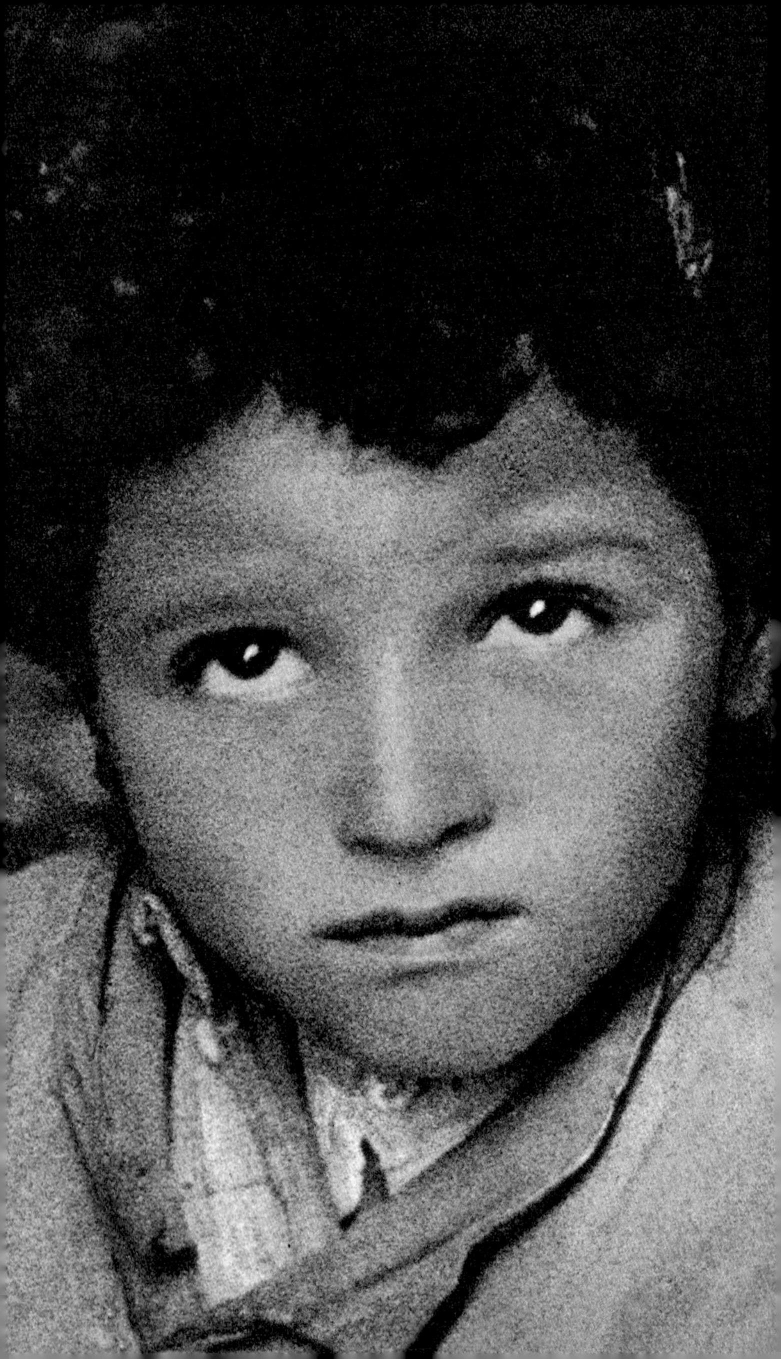

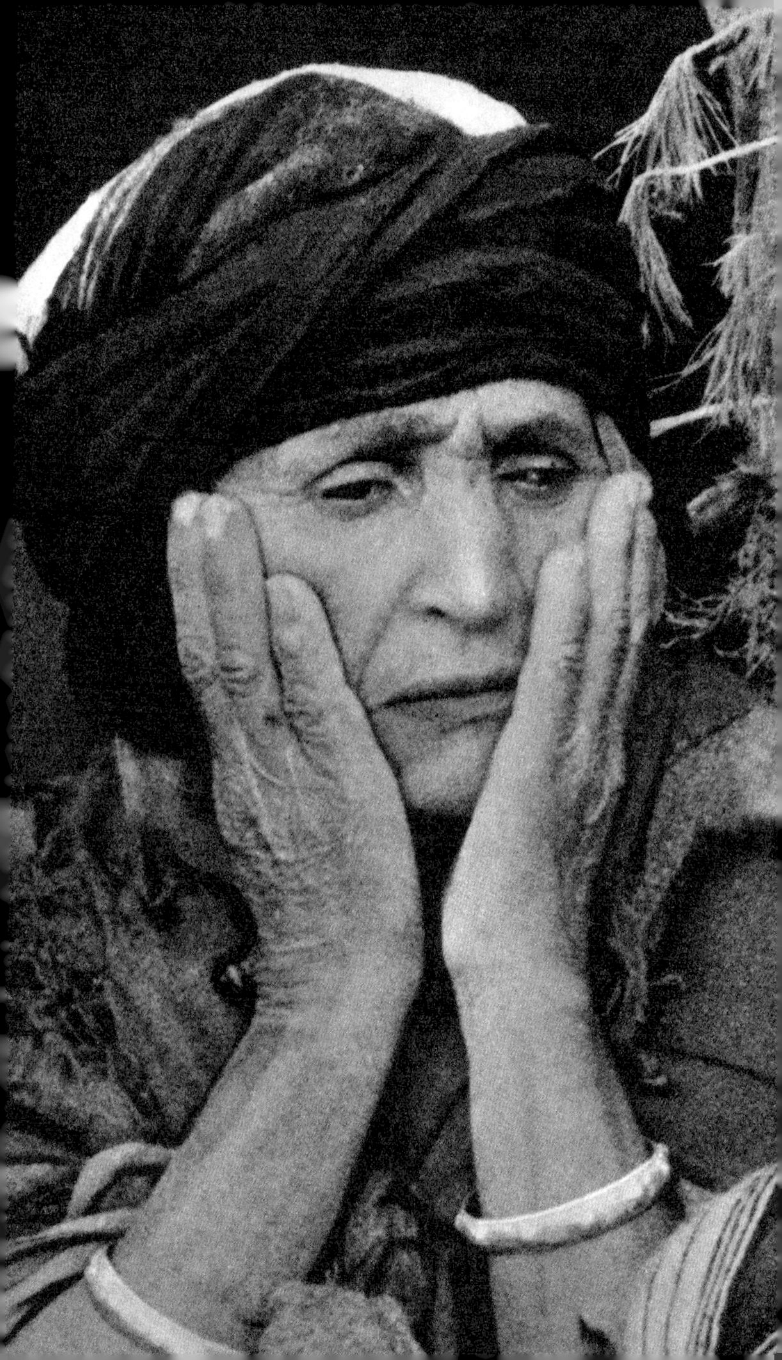

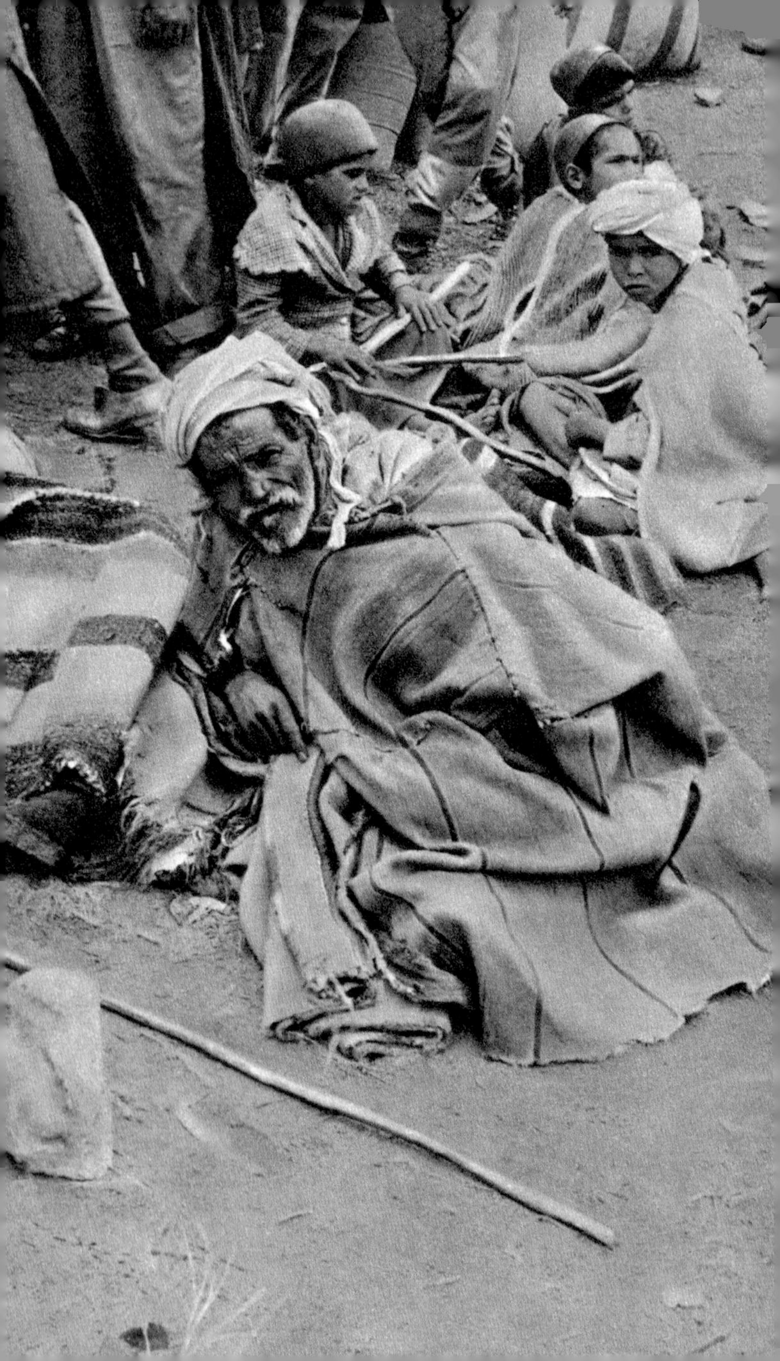

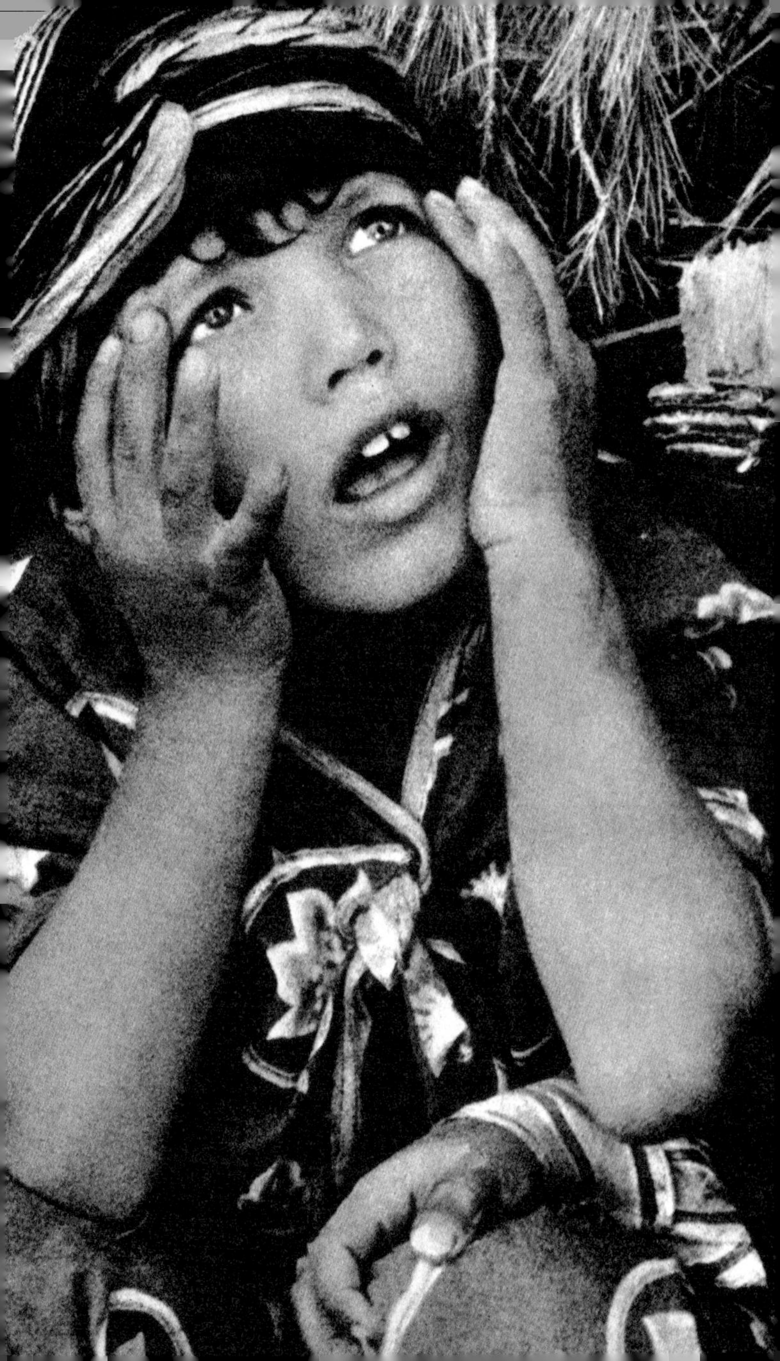

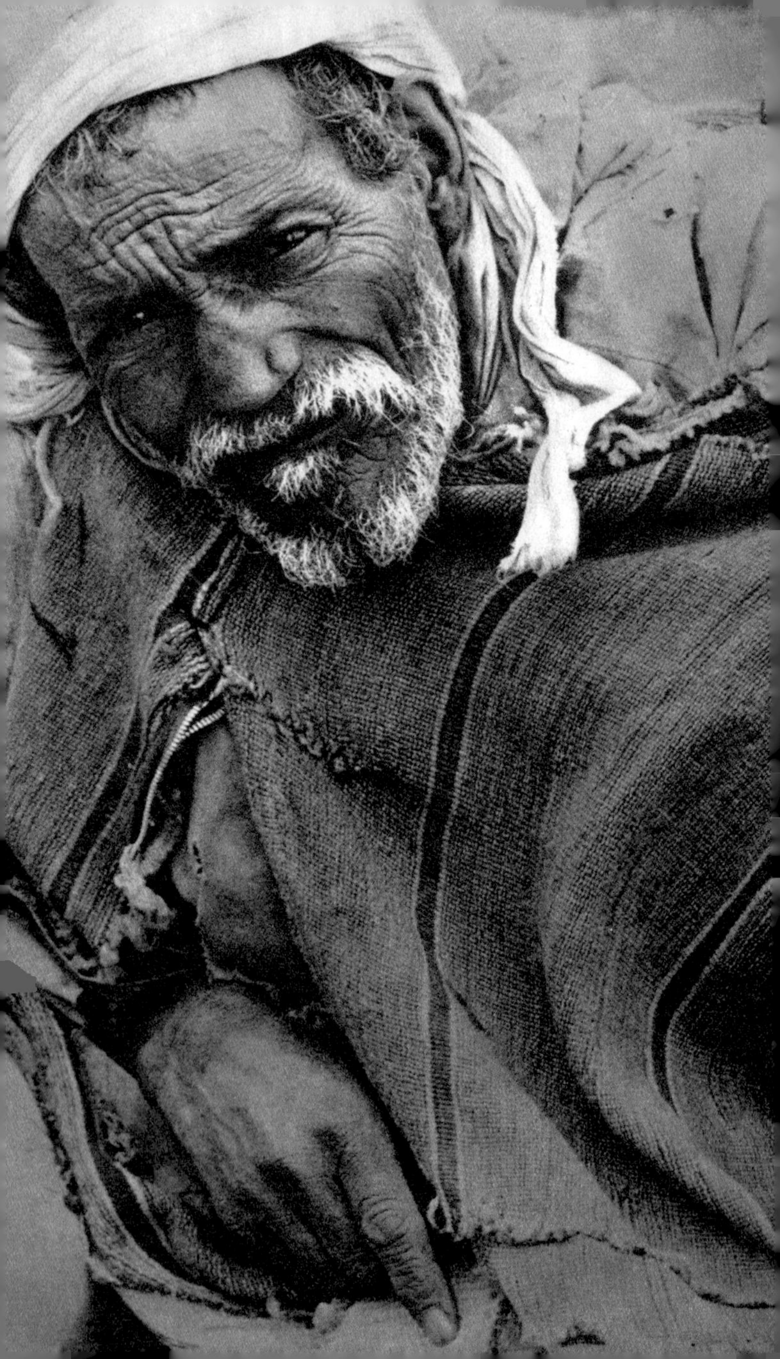

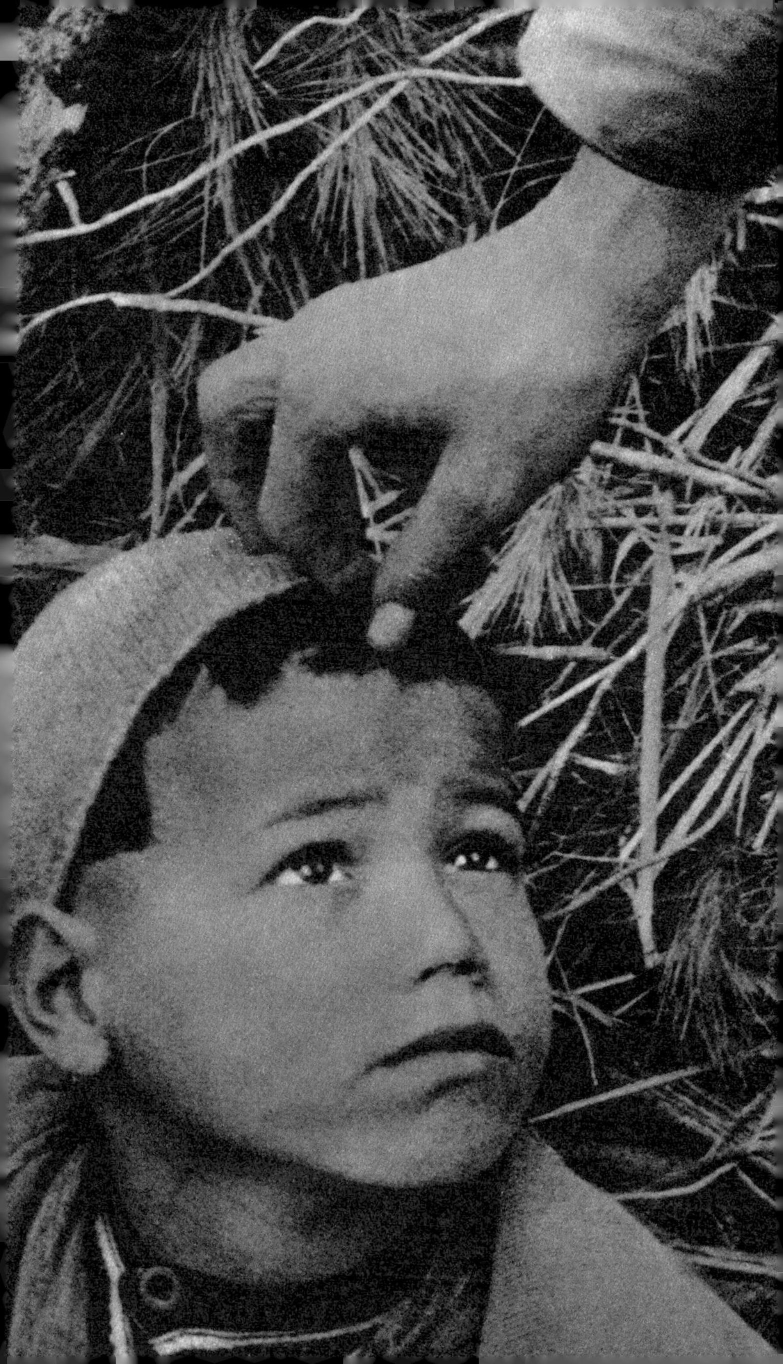

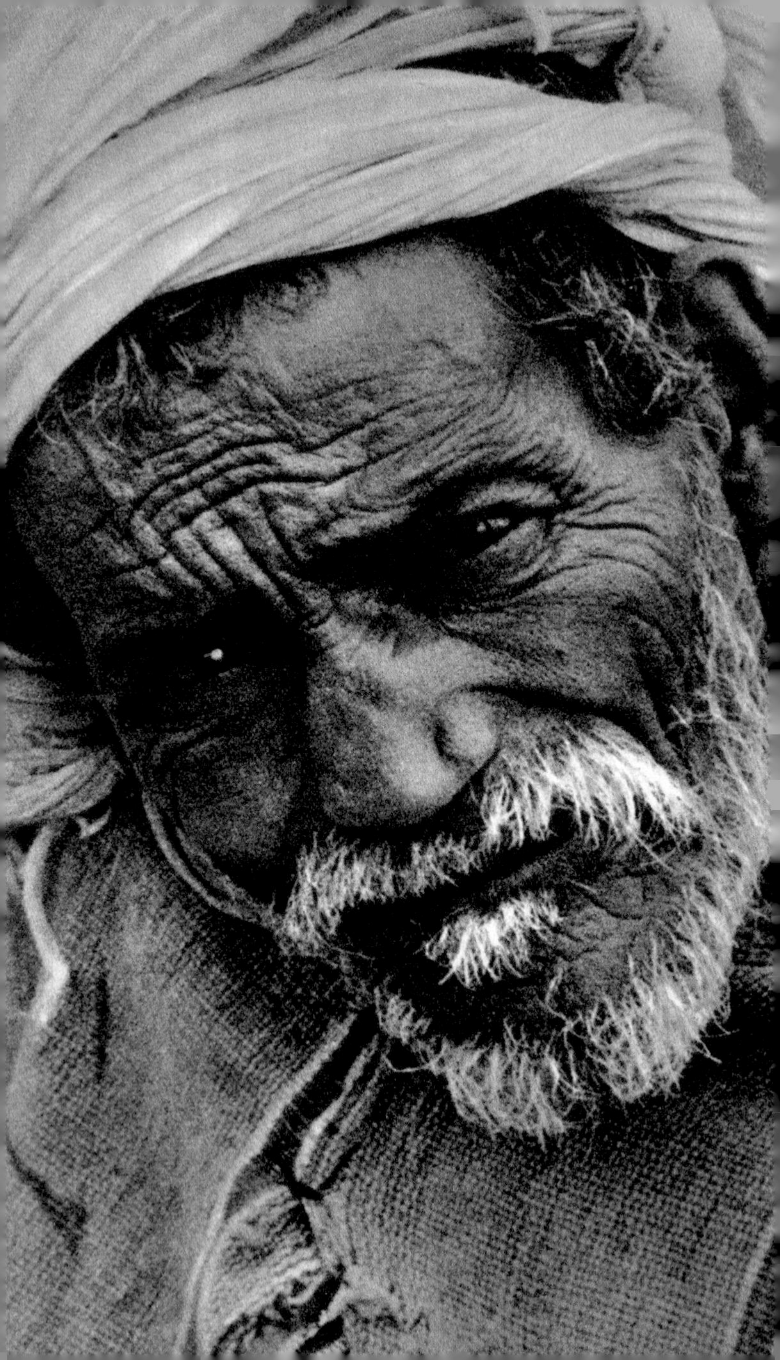

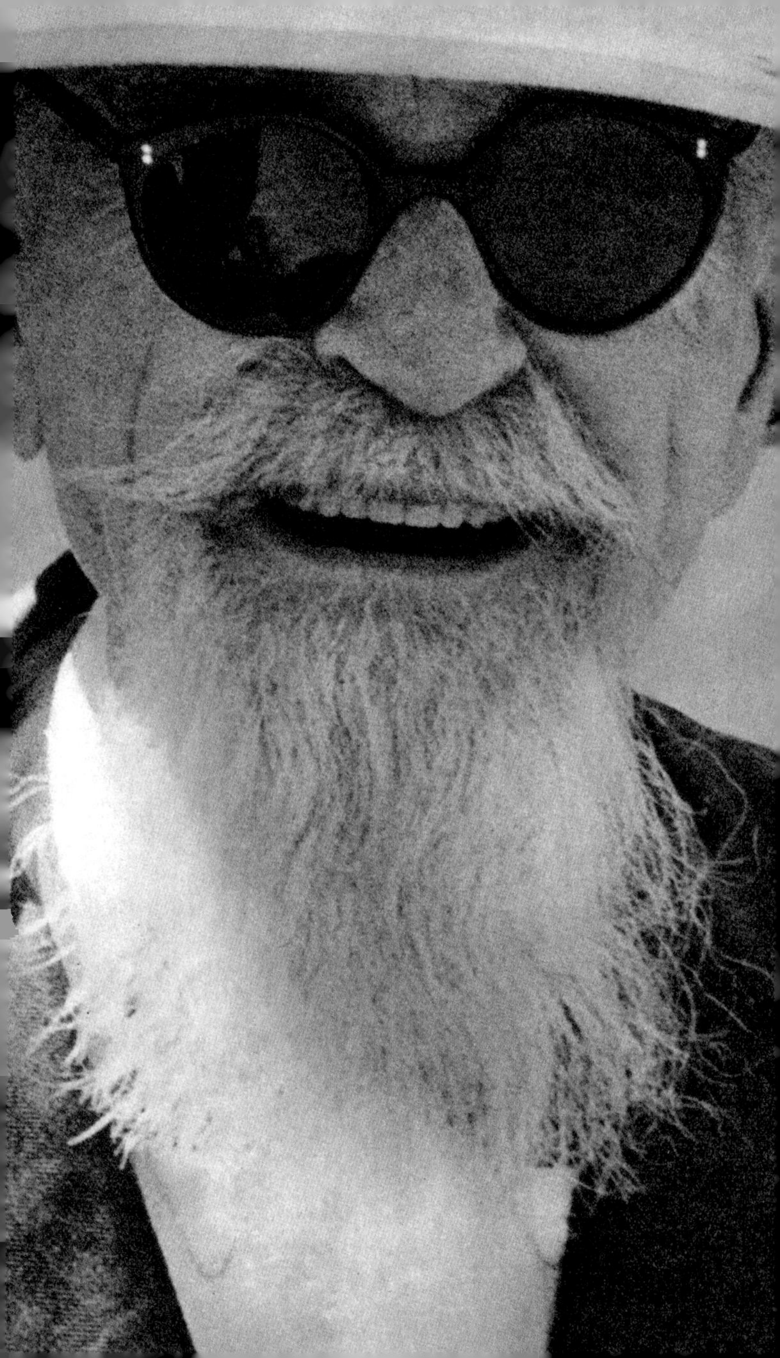

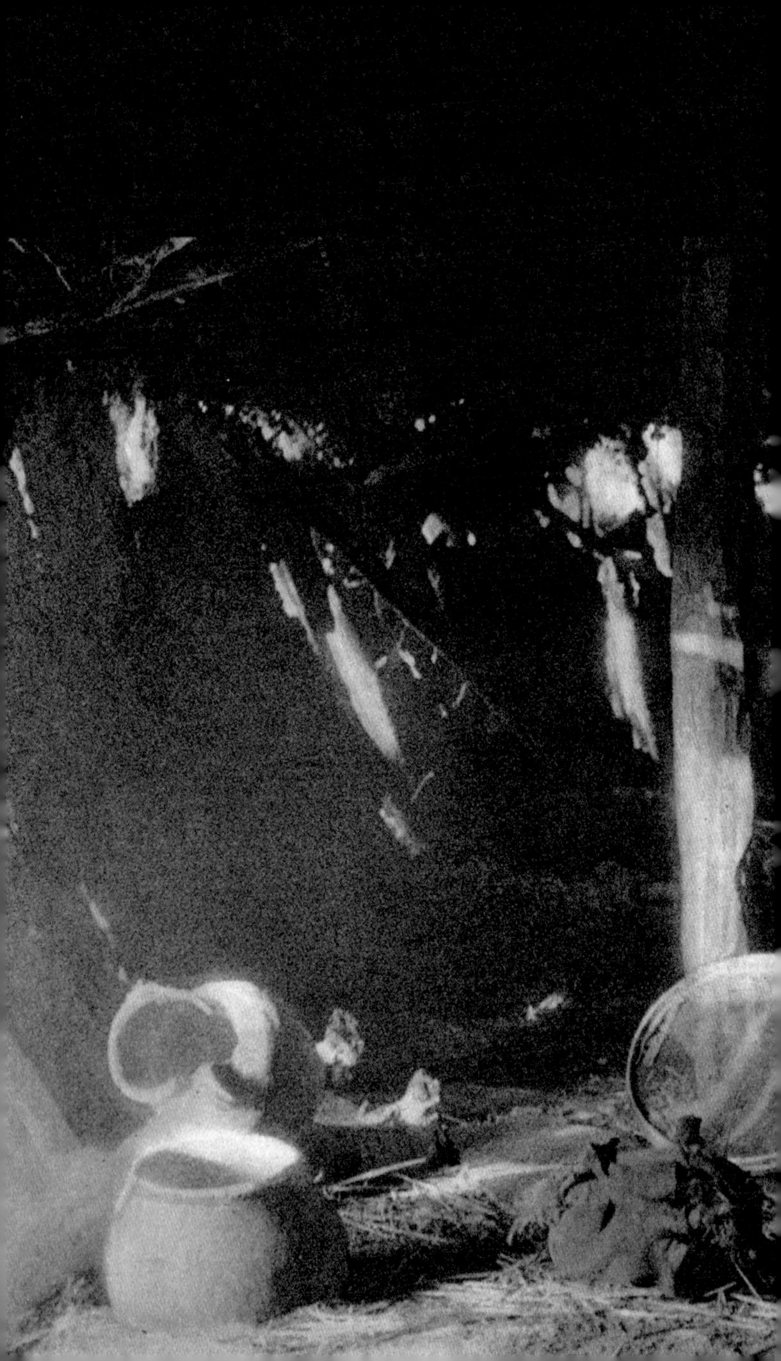

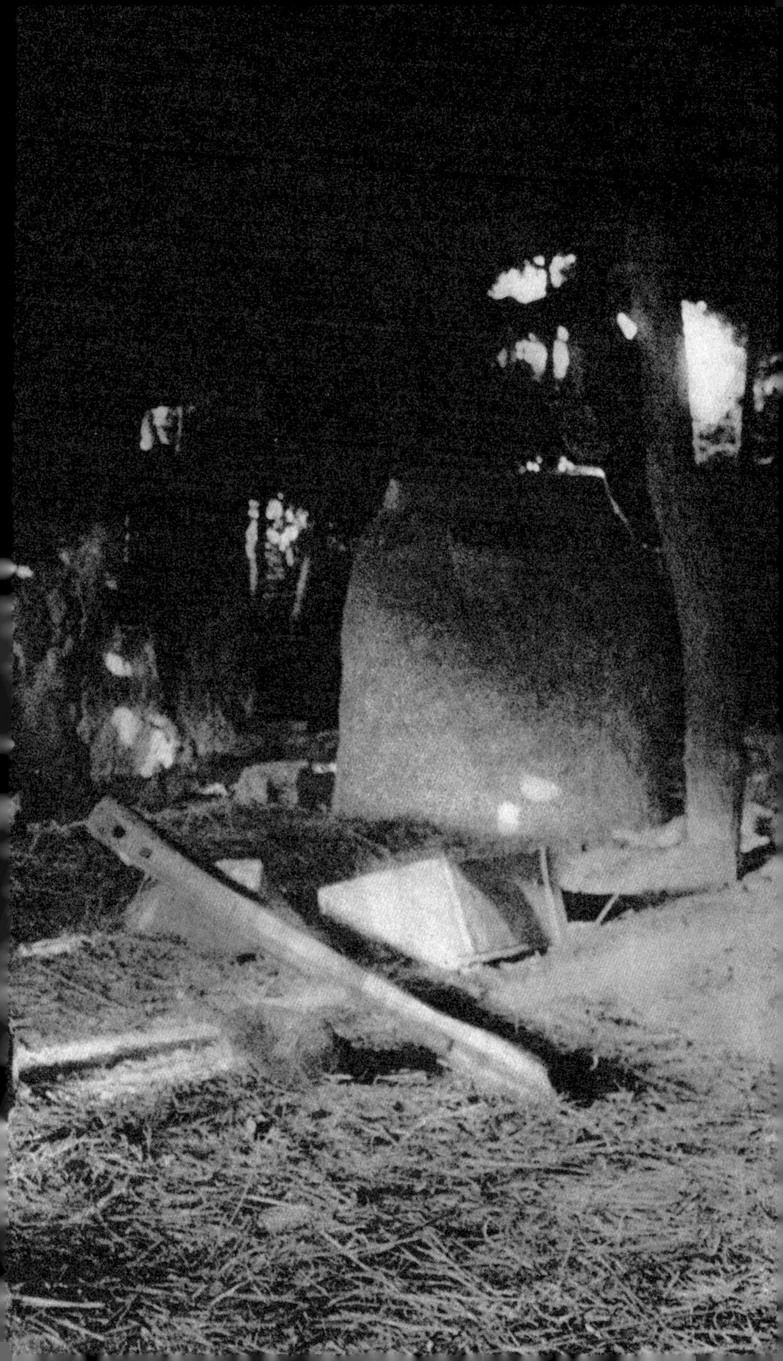

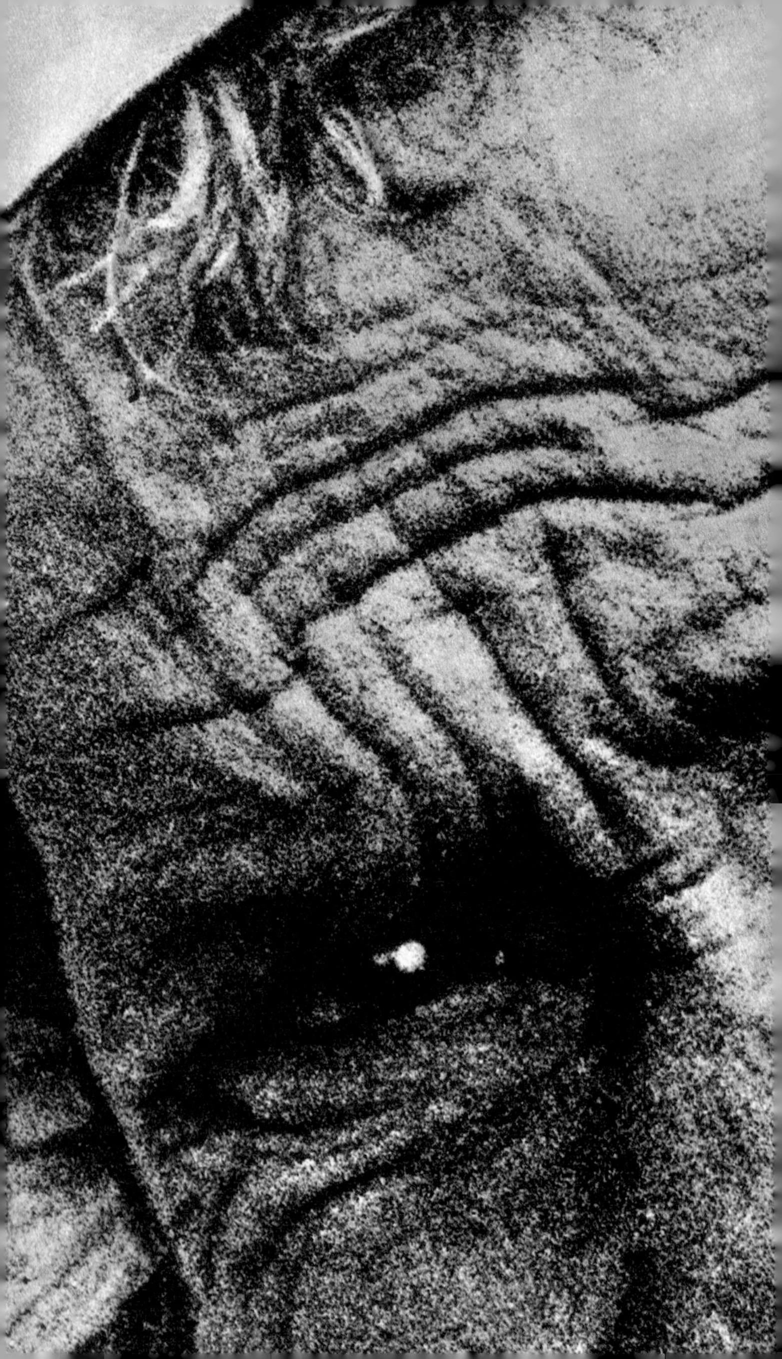

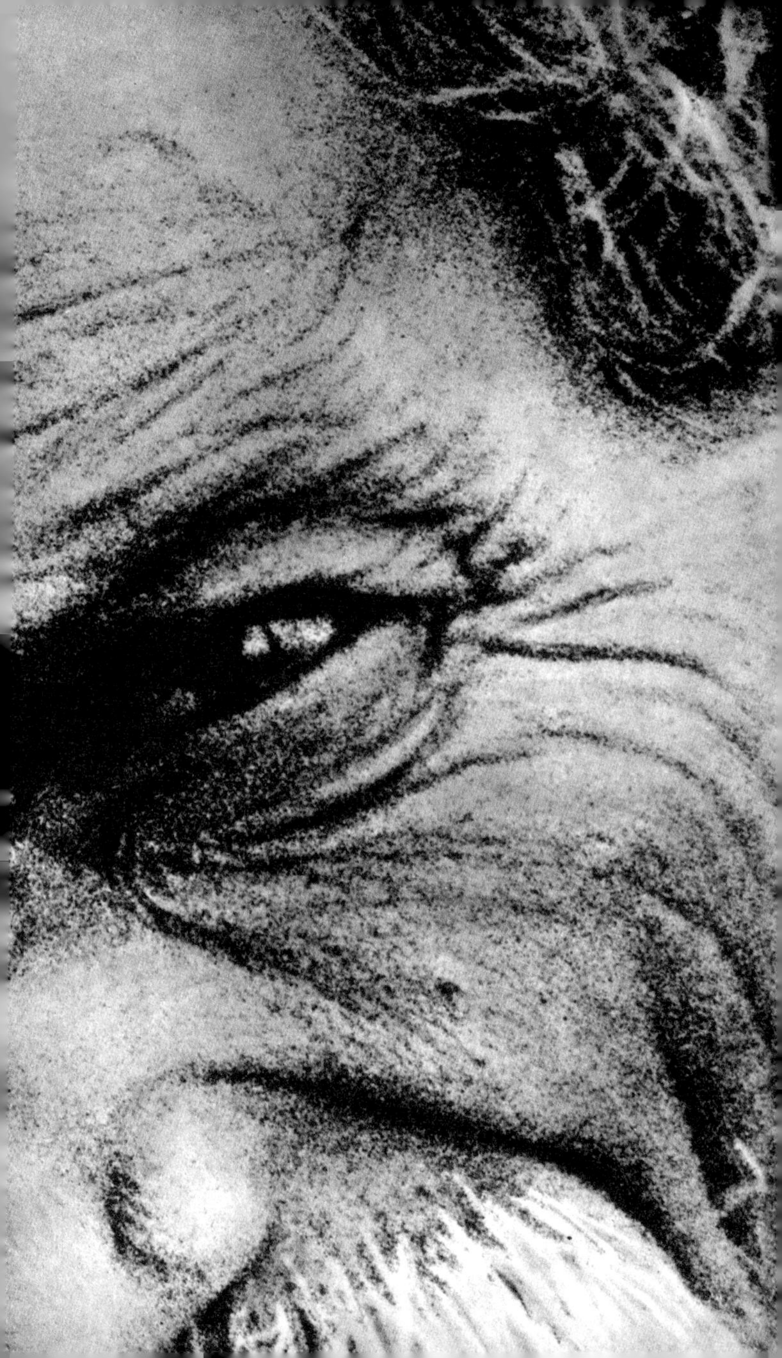

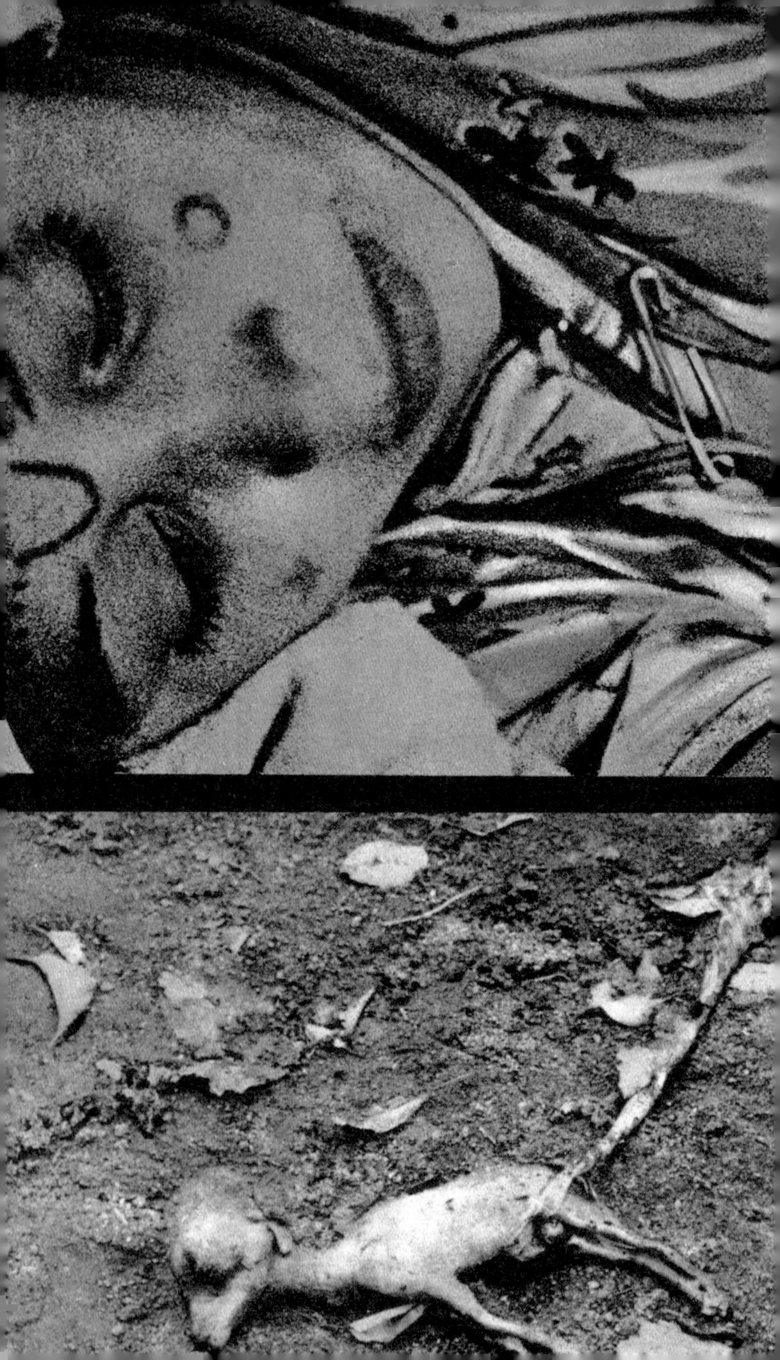

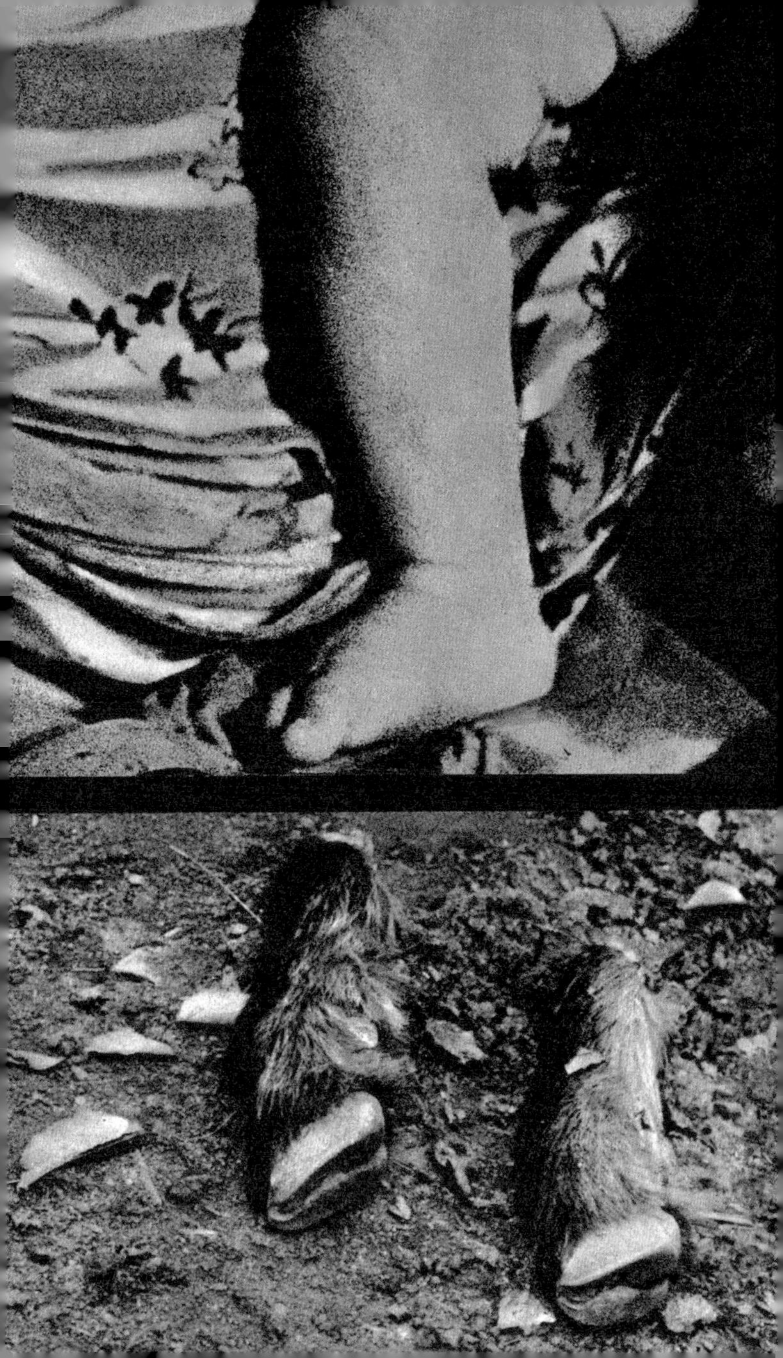

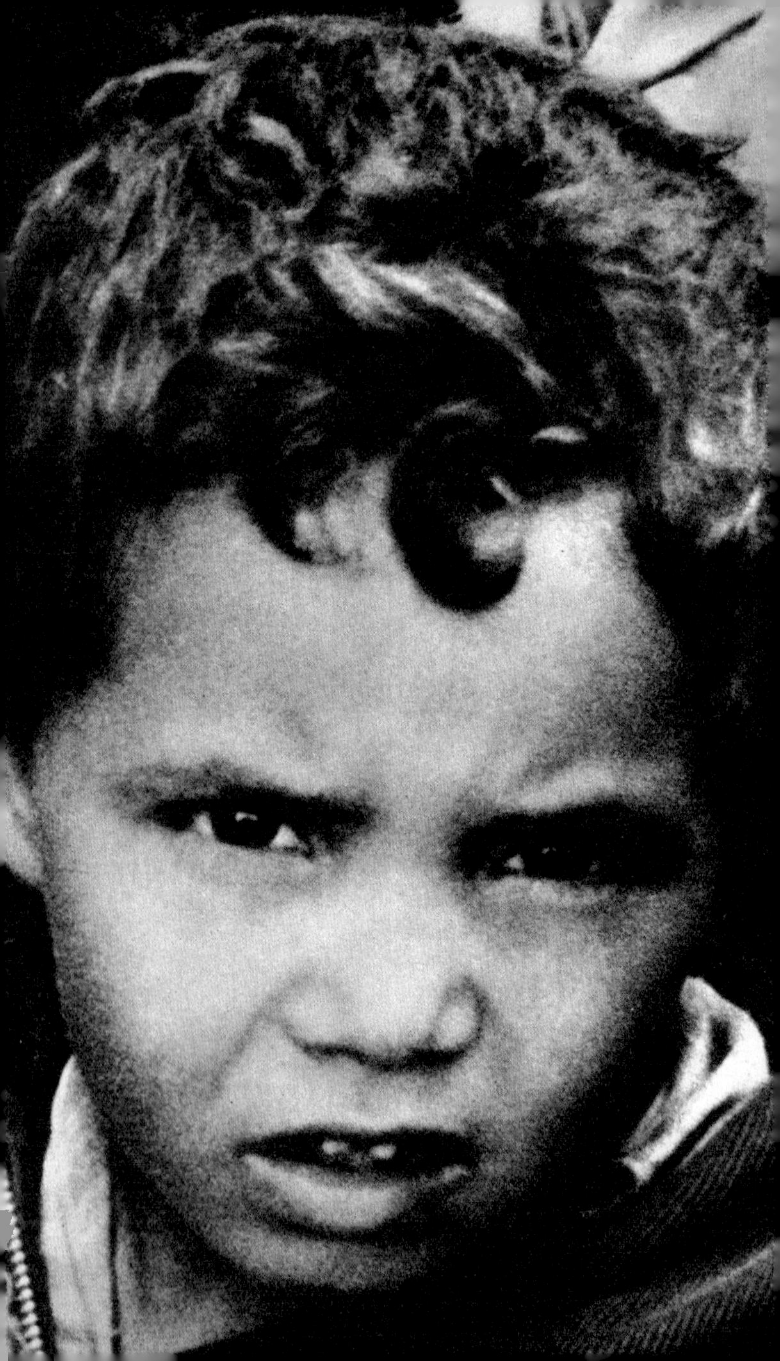

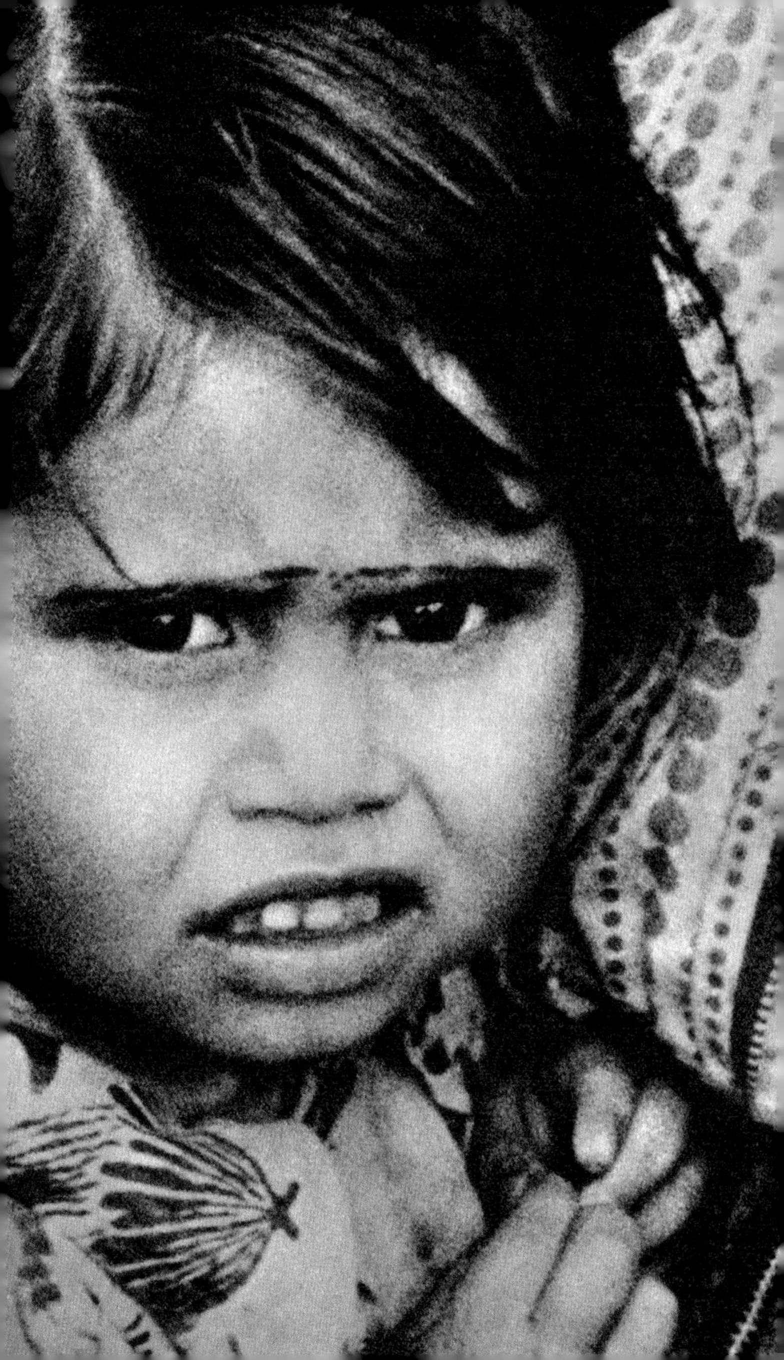

4.

"… an organised revolution and not an anarchistic revolt."

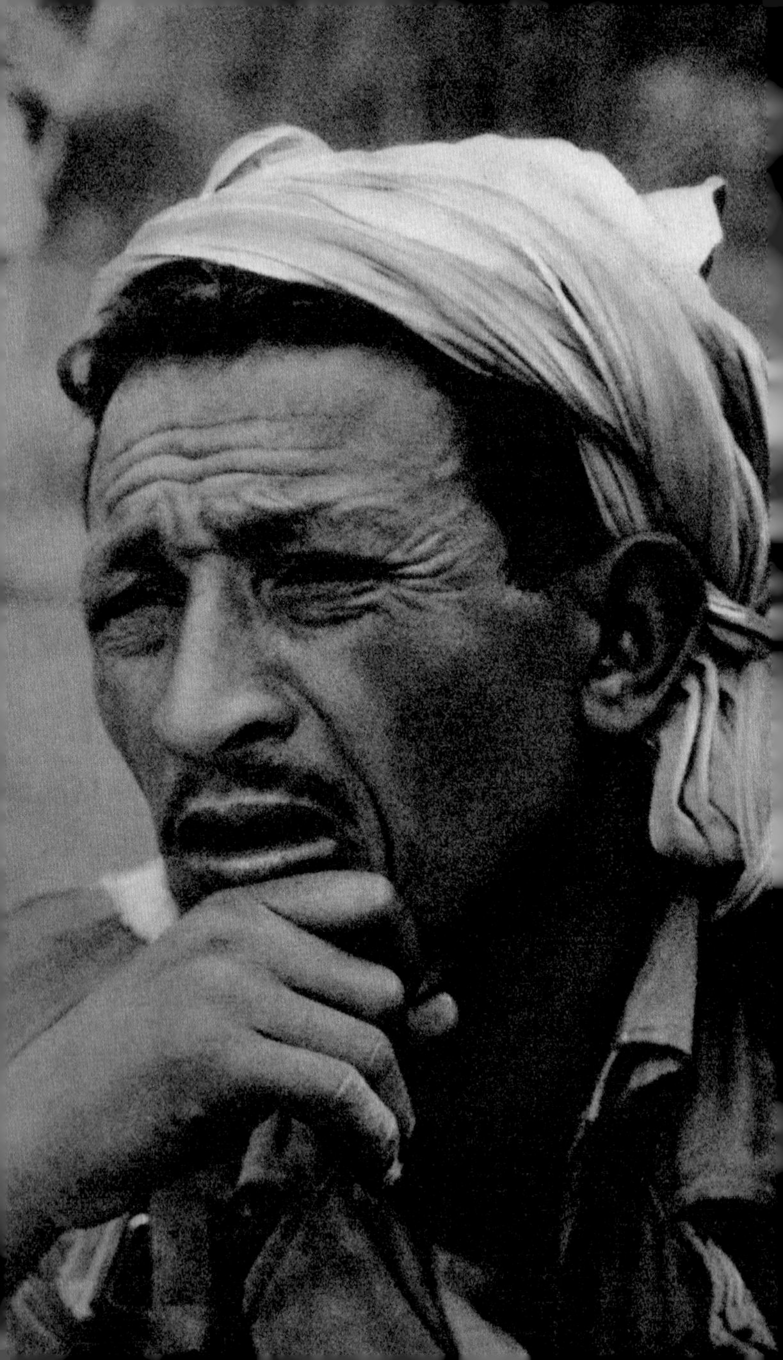

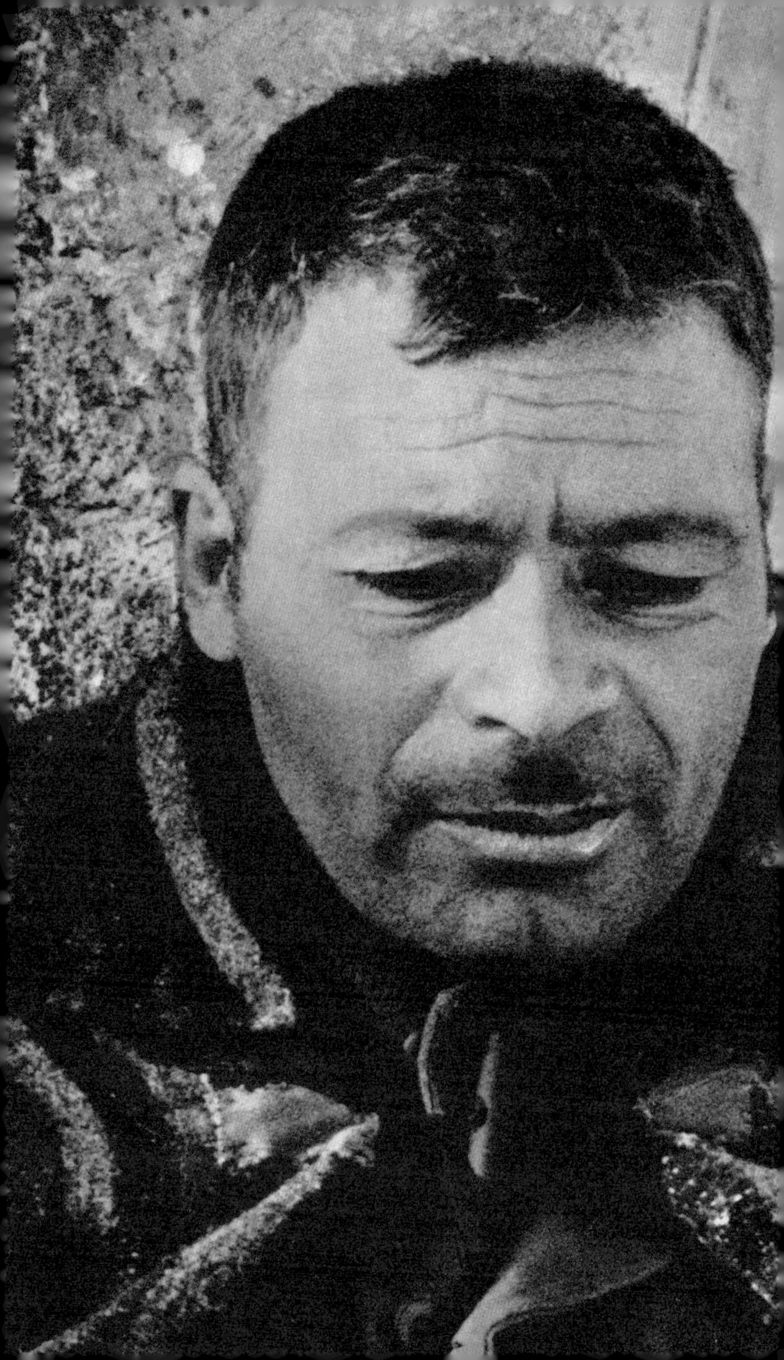

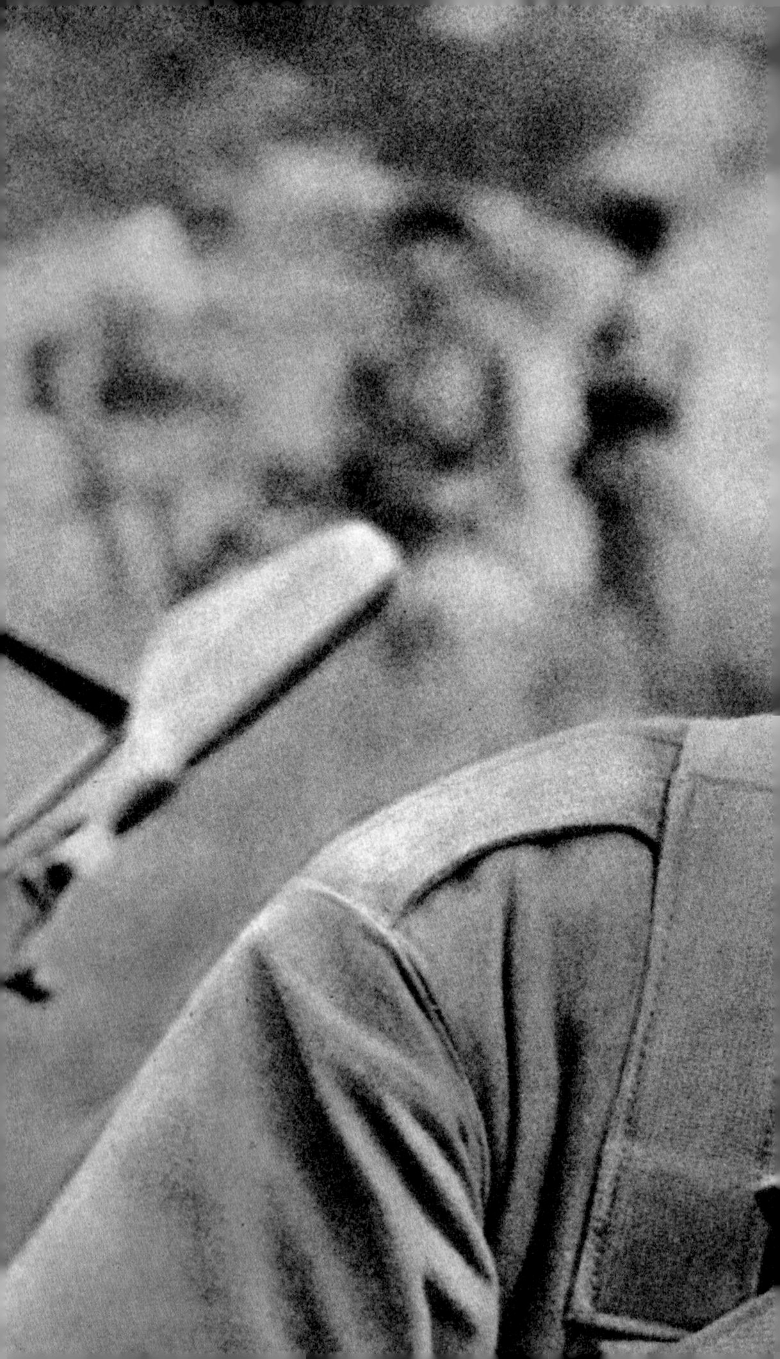

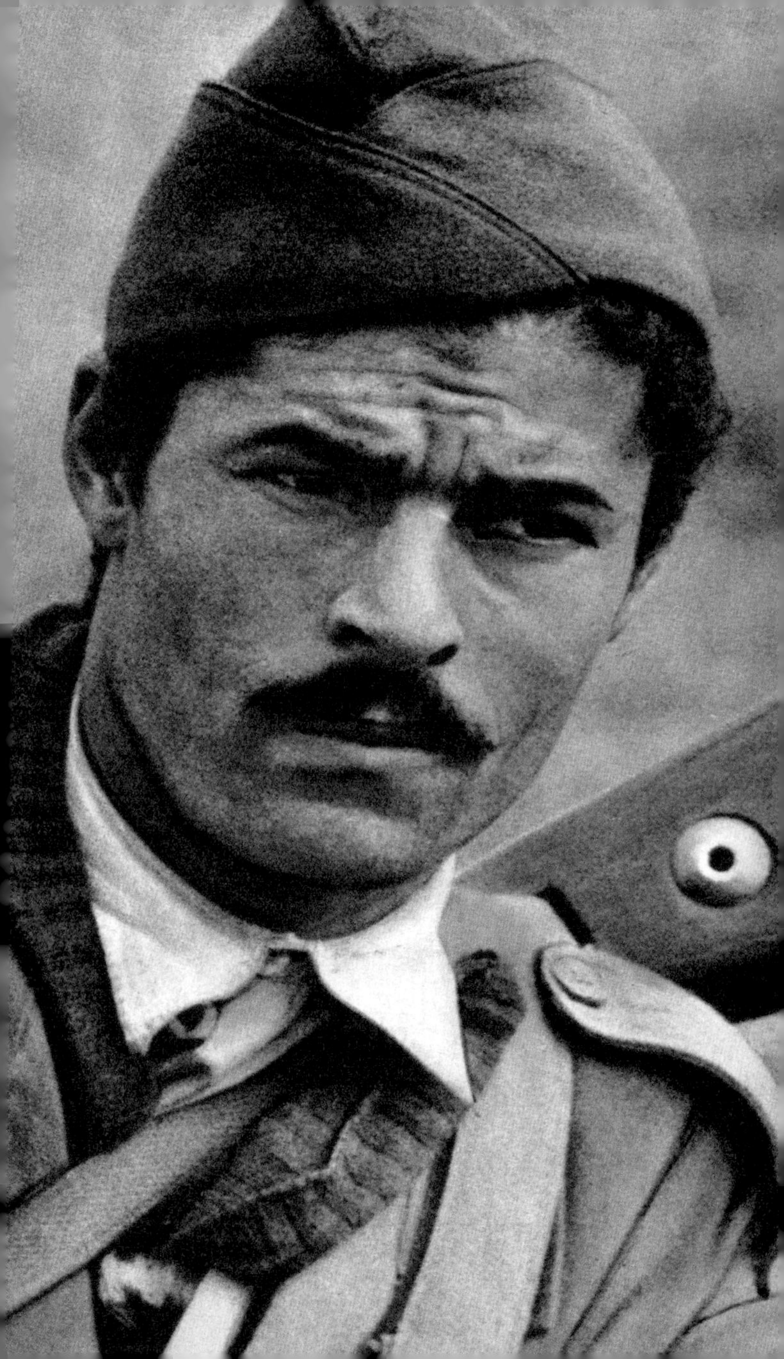

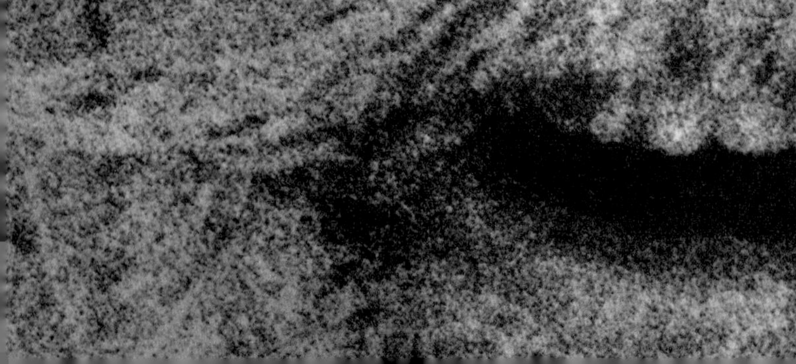

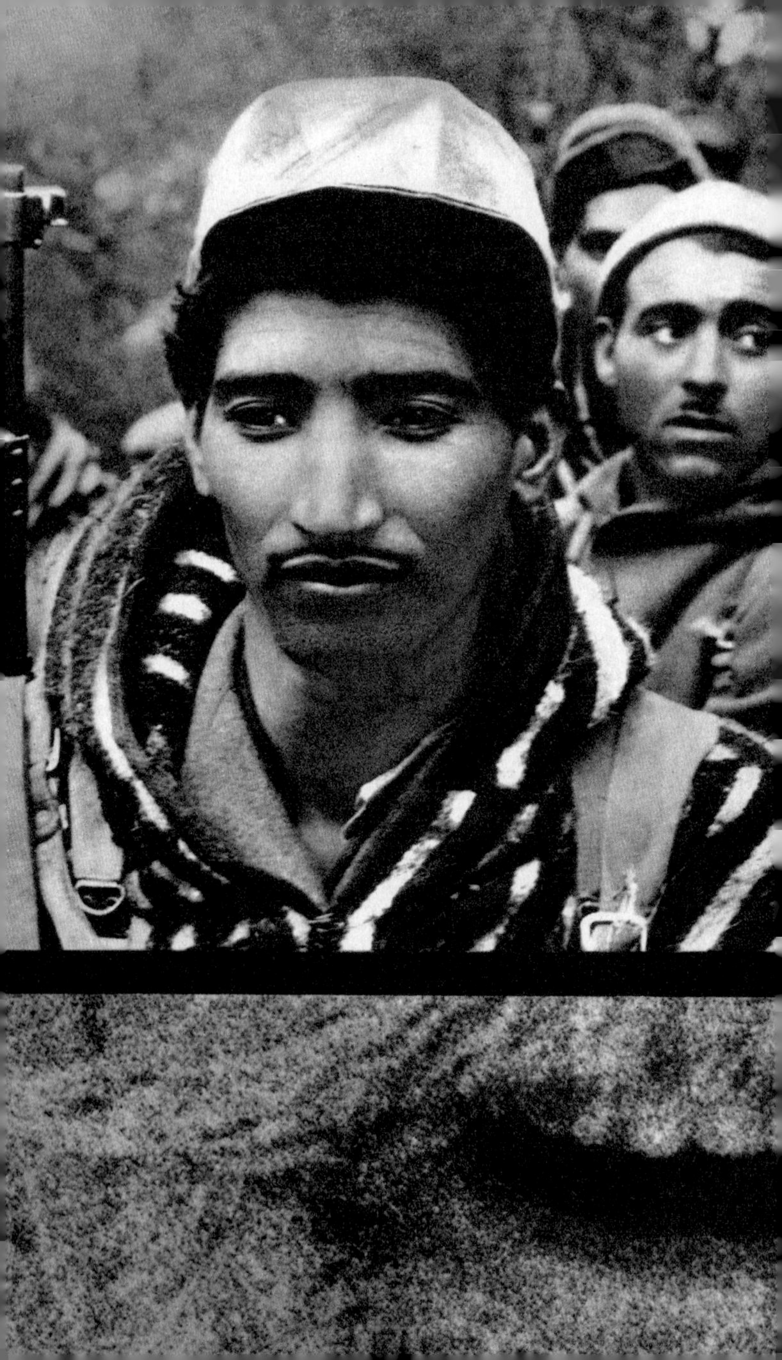

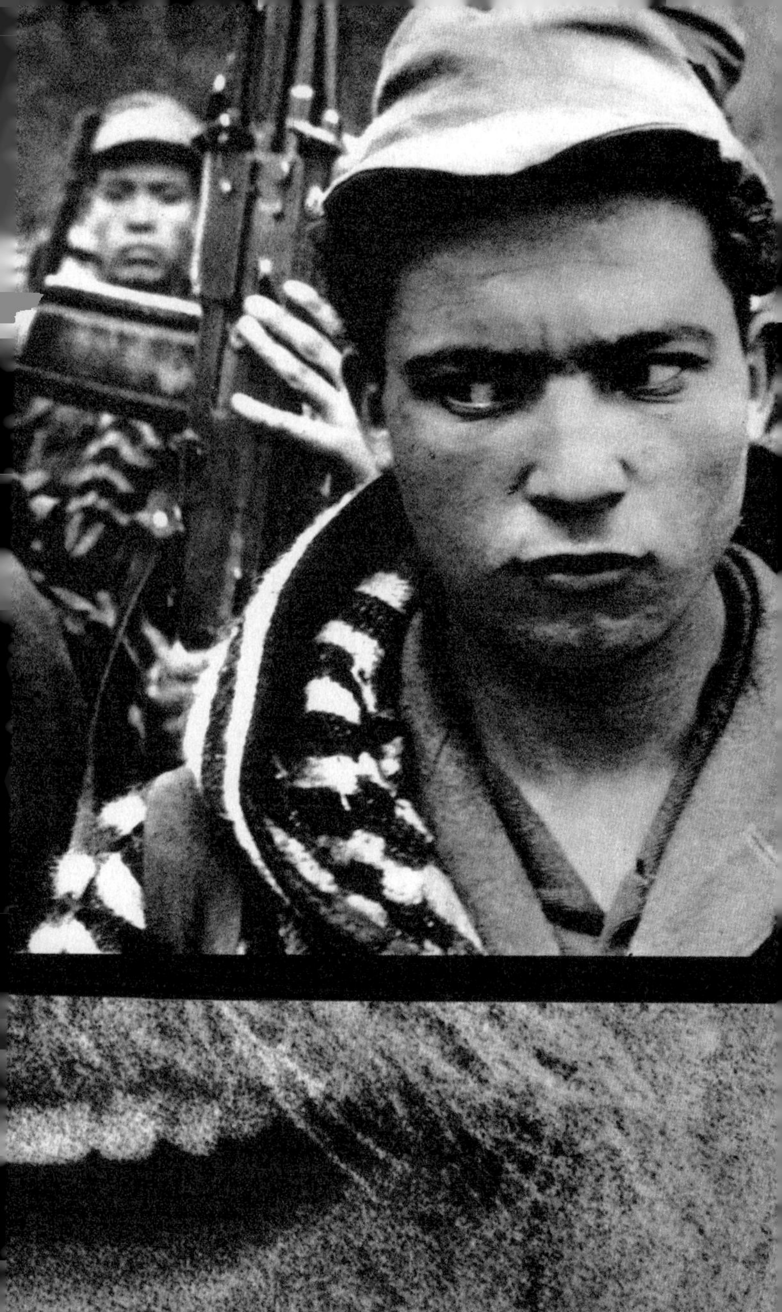

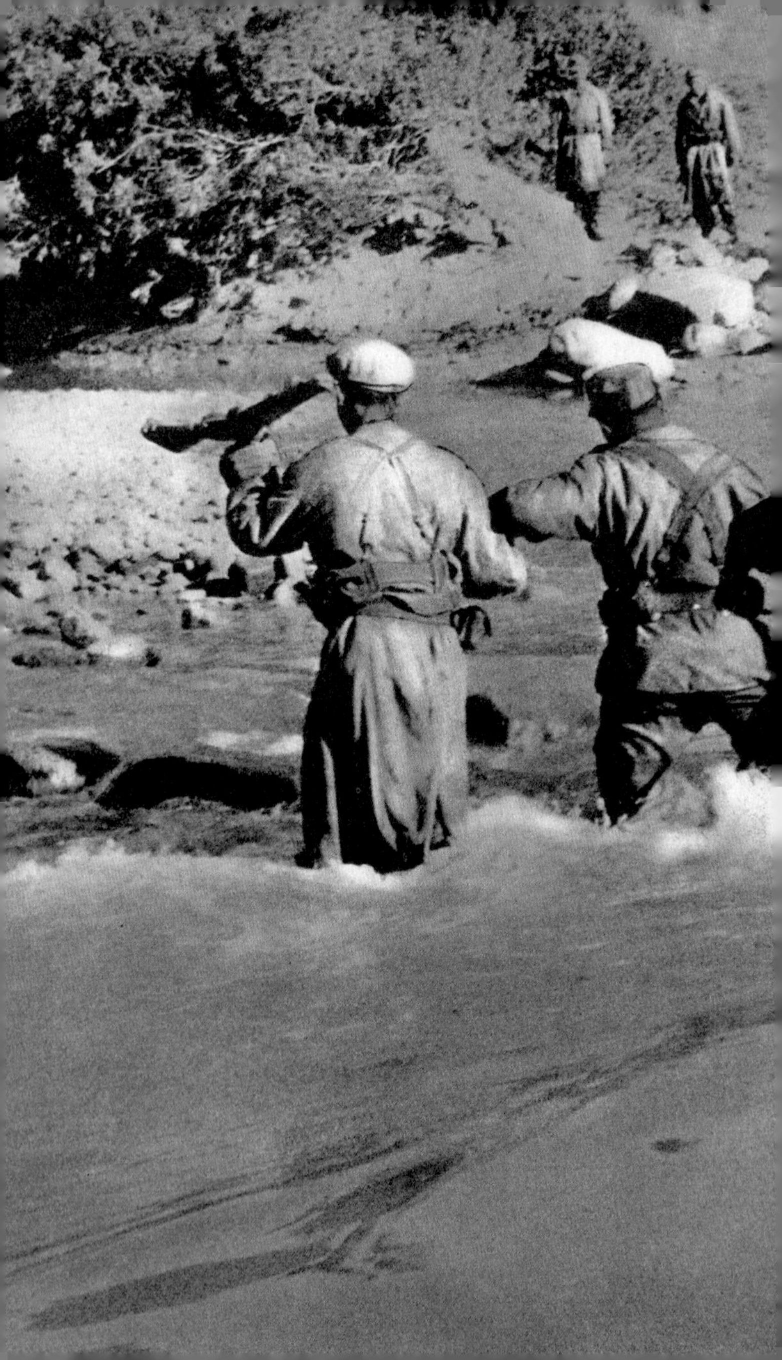

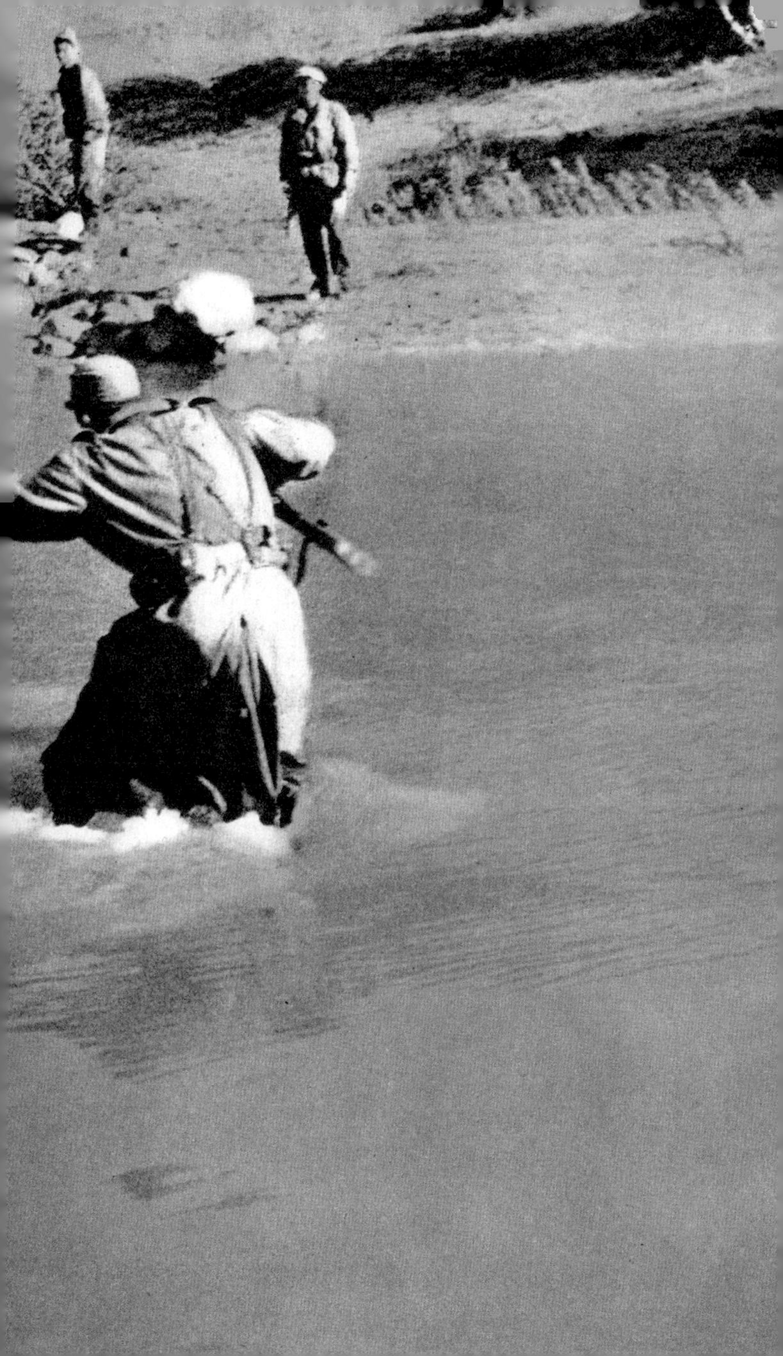

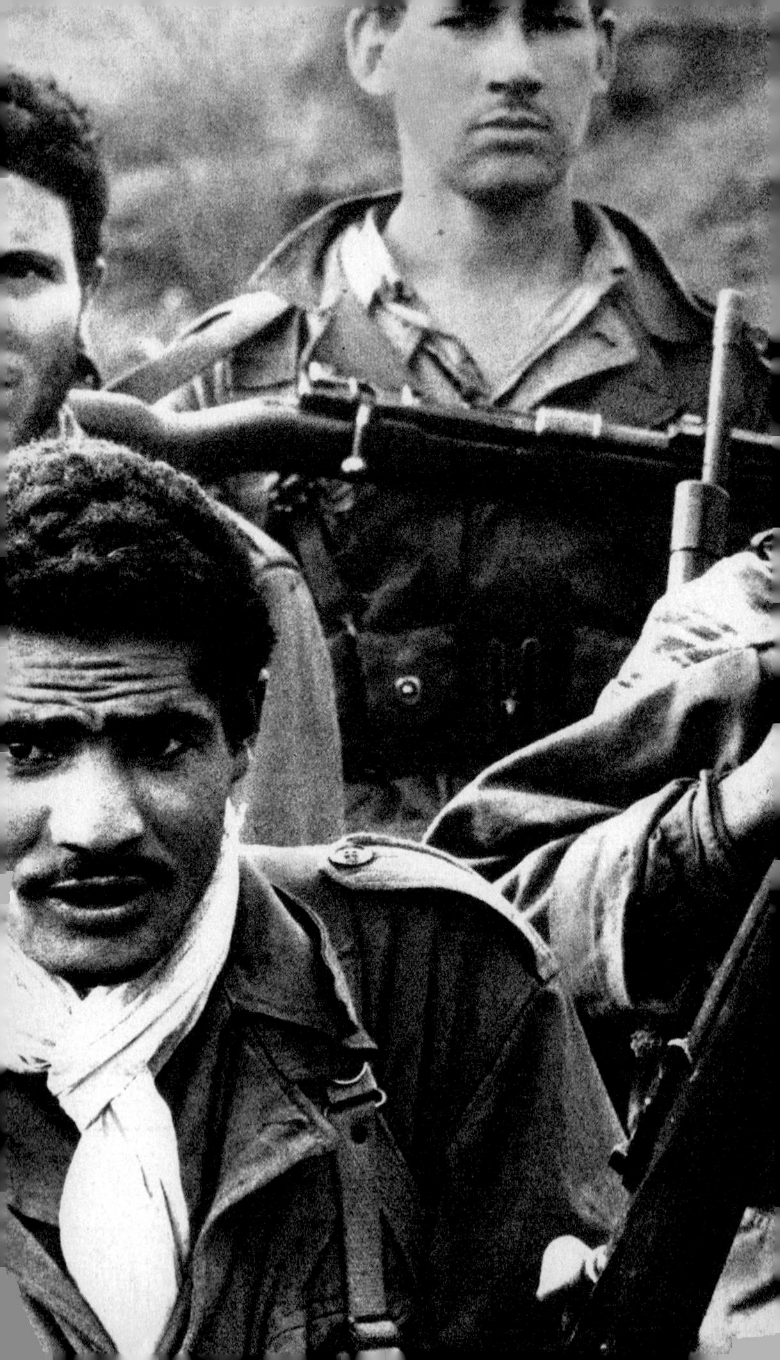

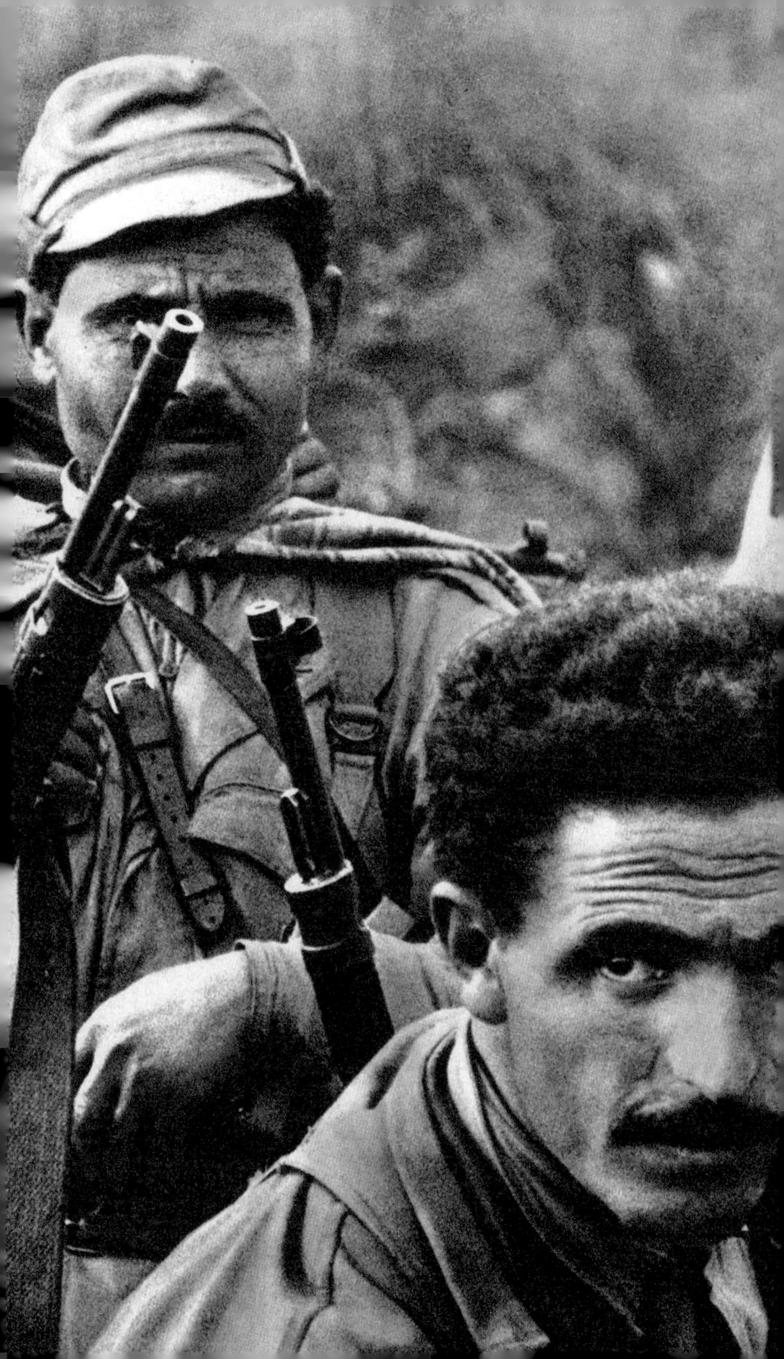

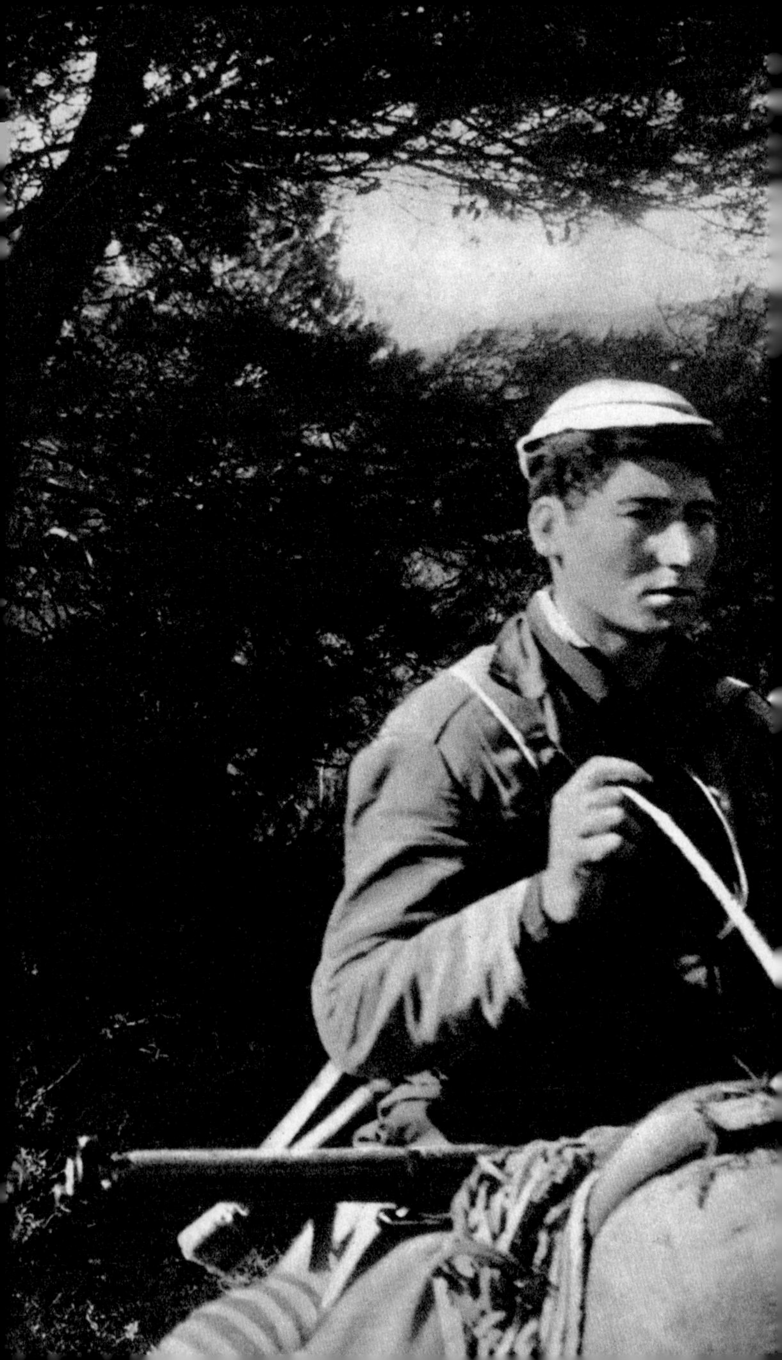

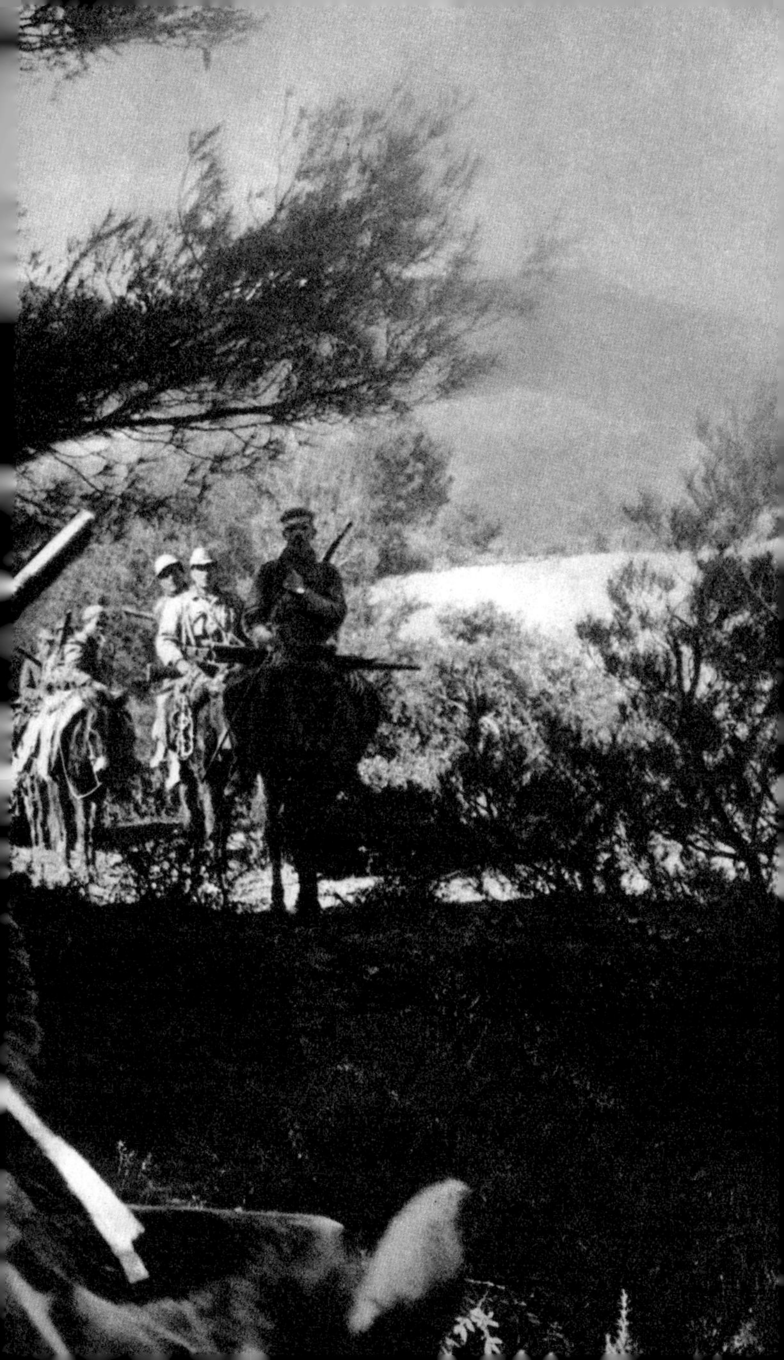

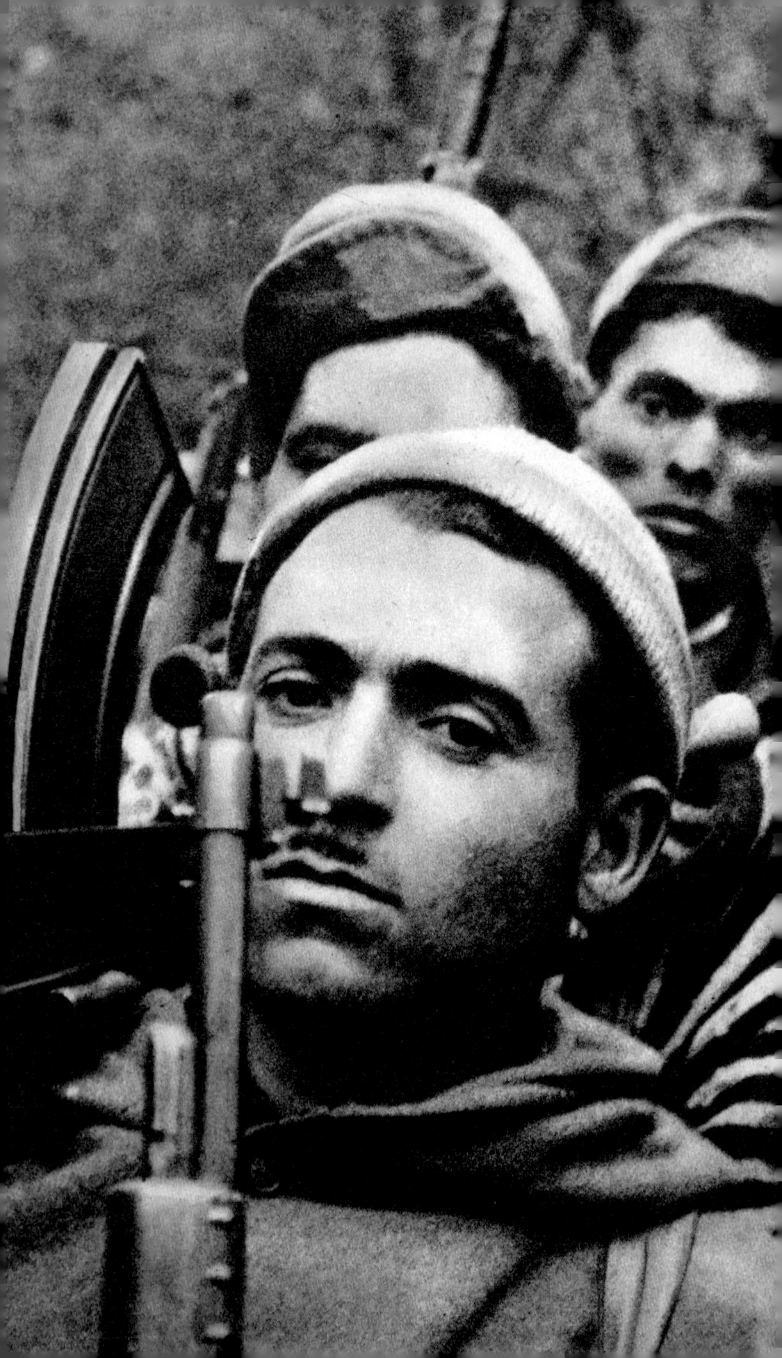

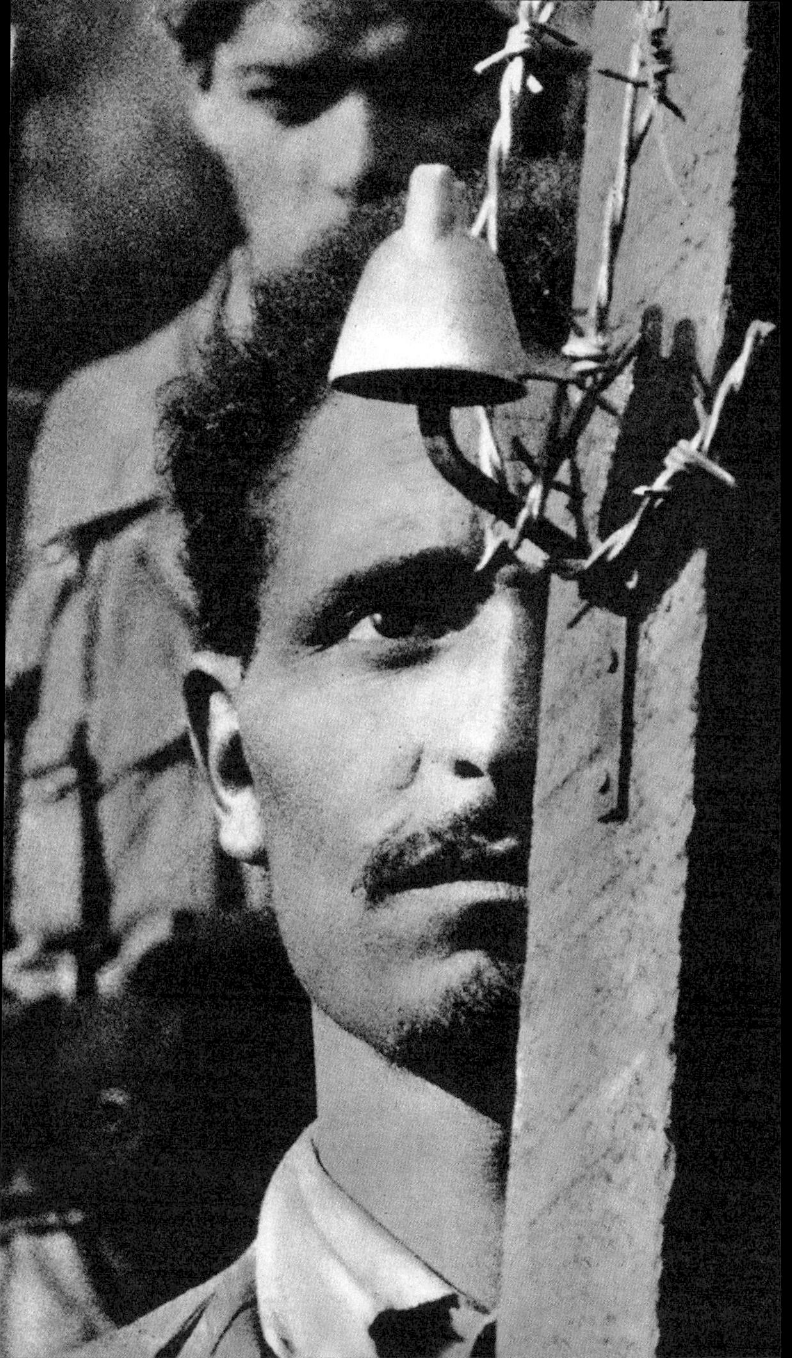

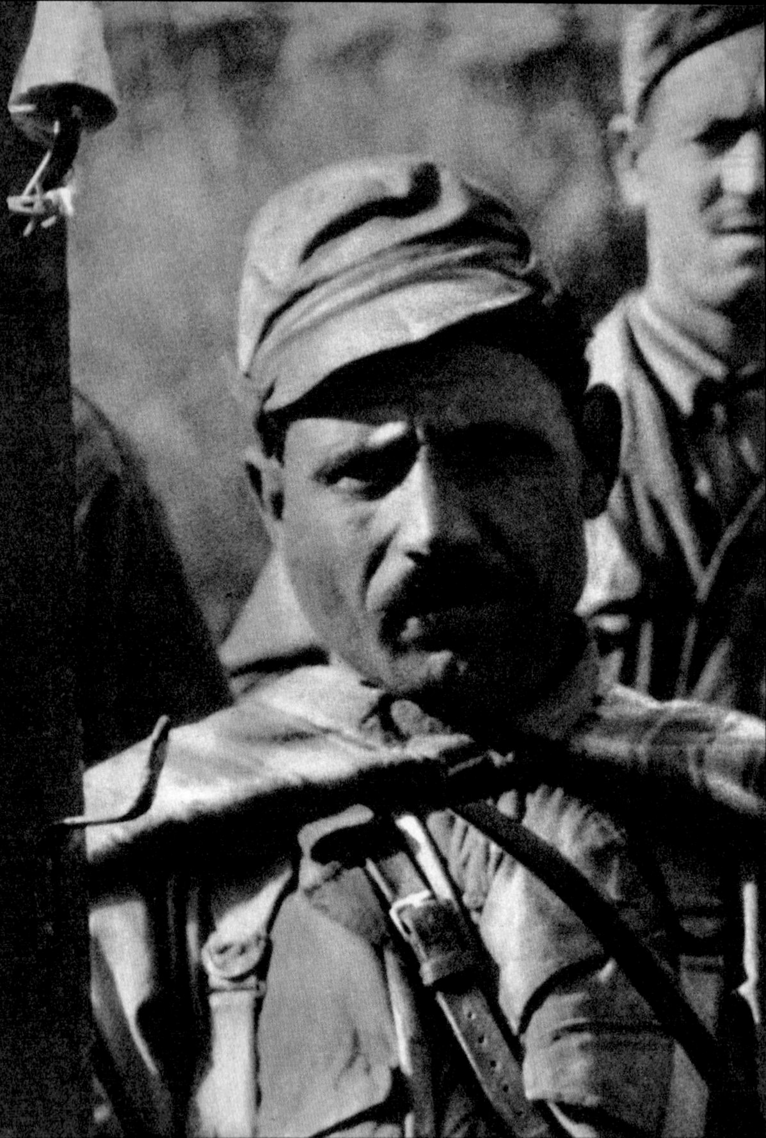

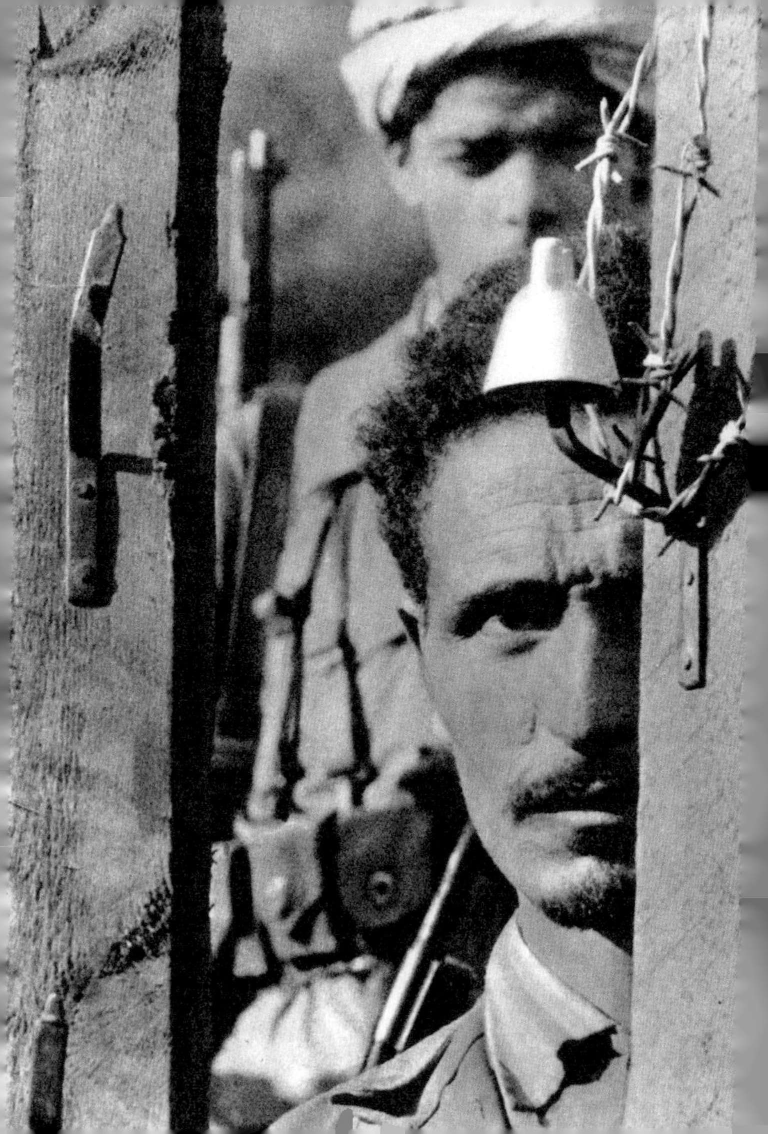

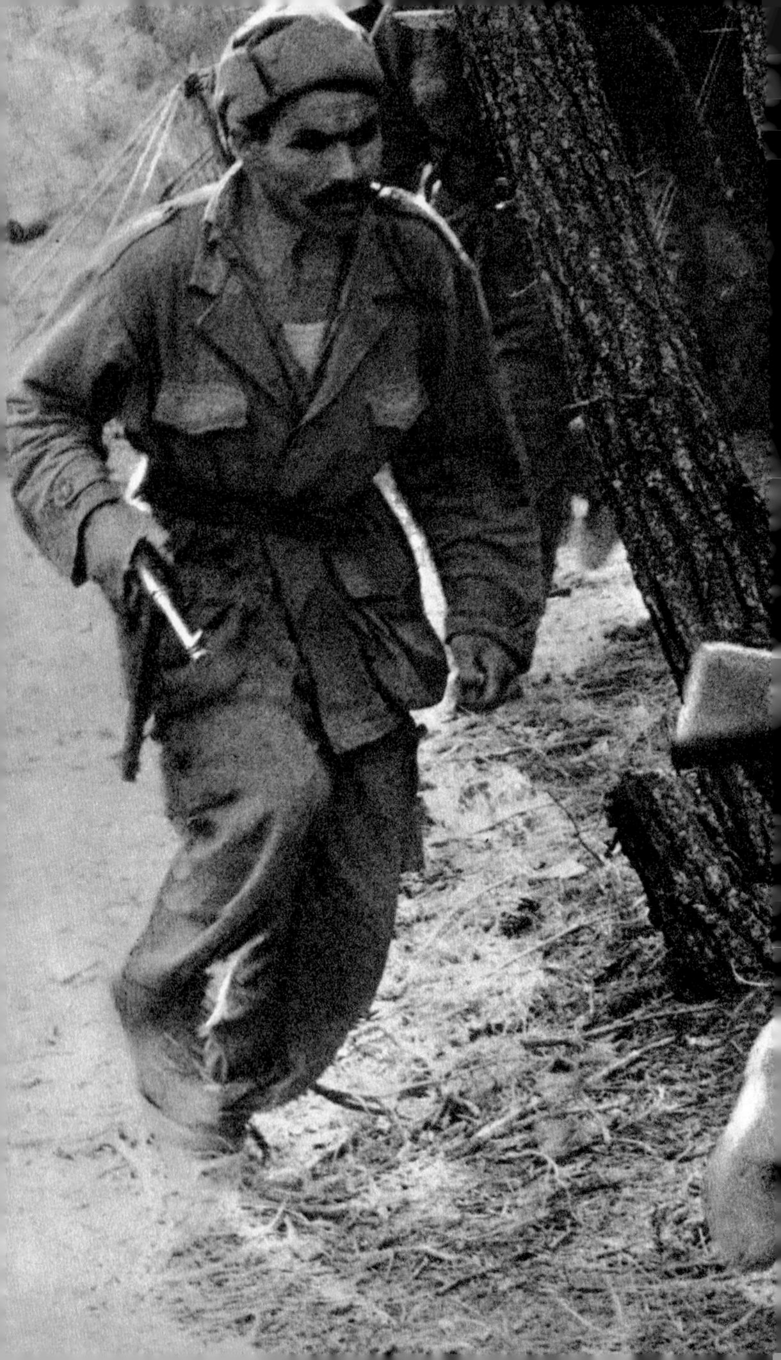

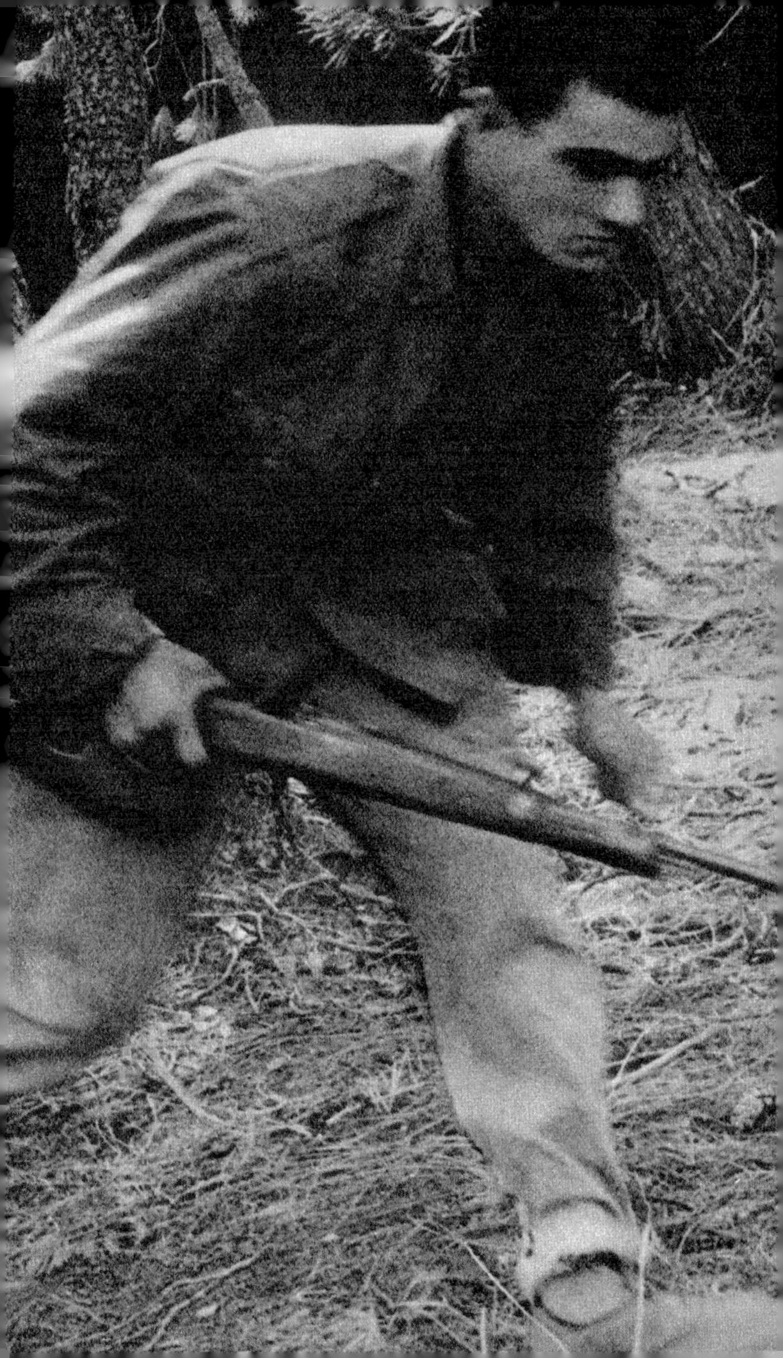

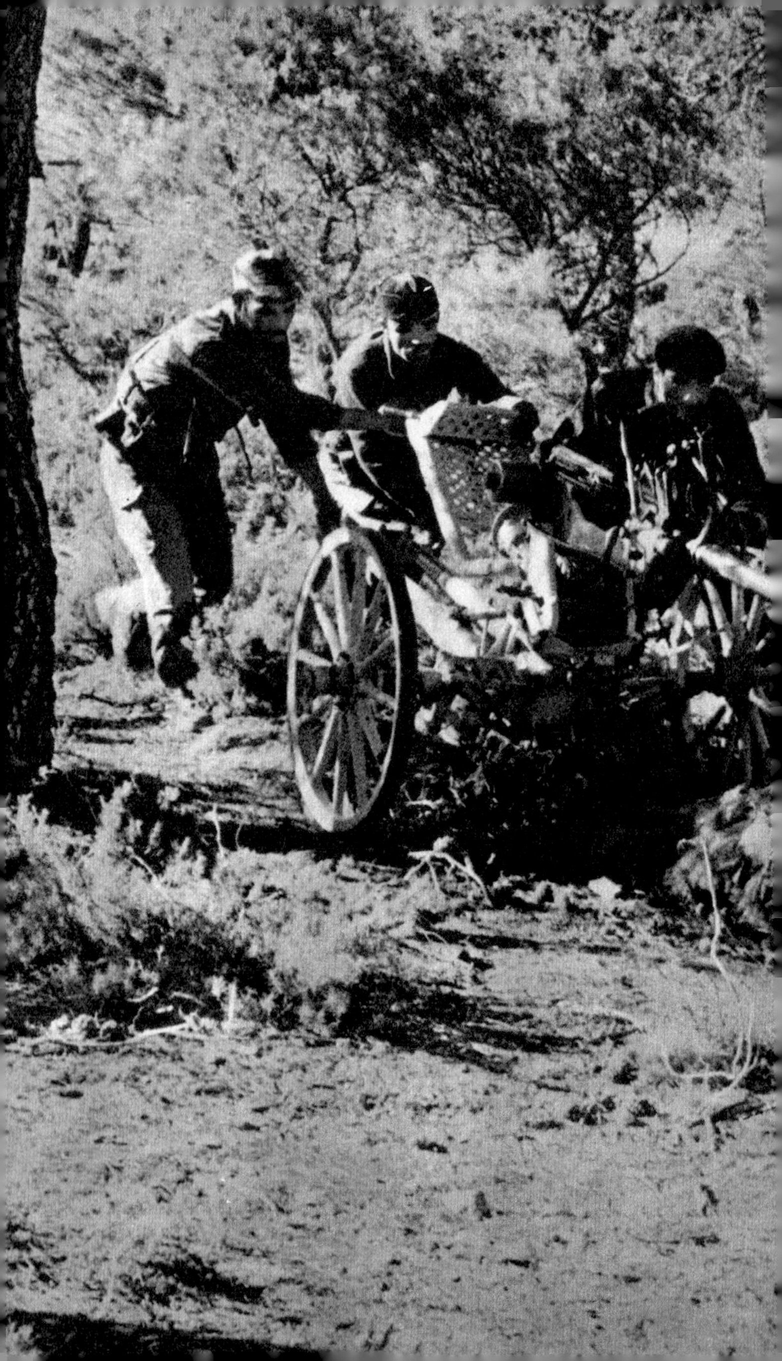

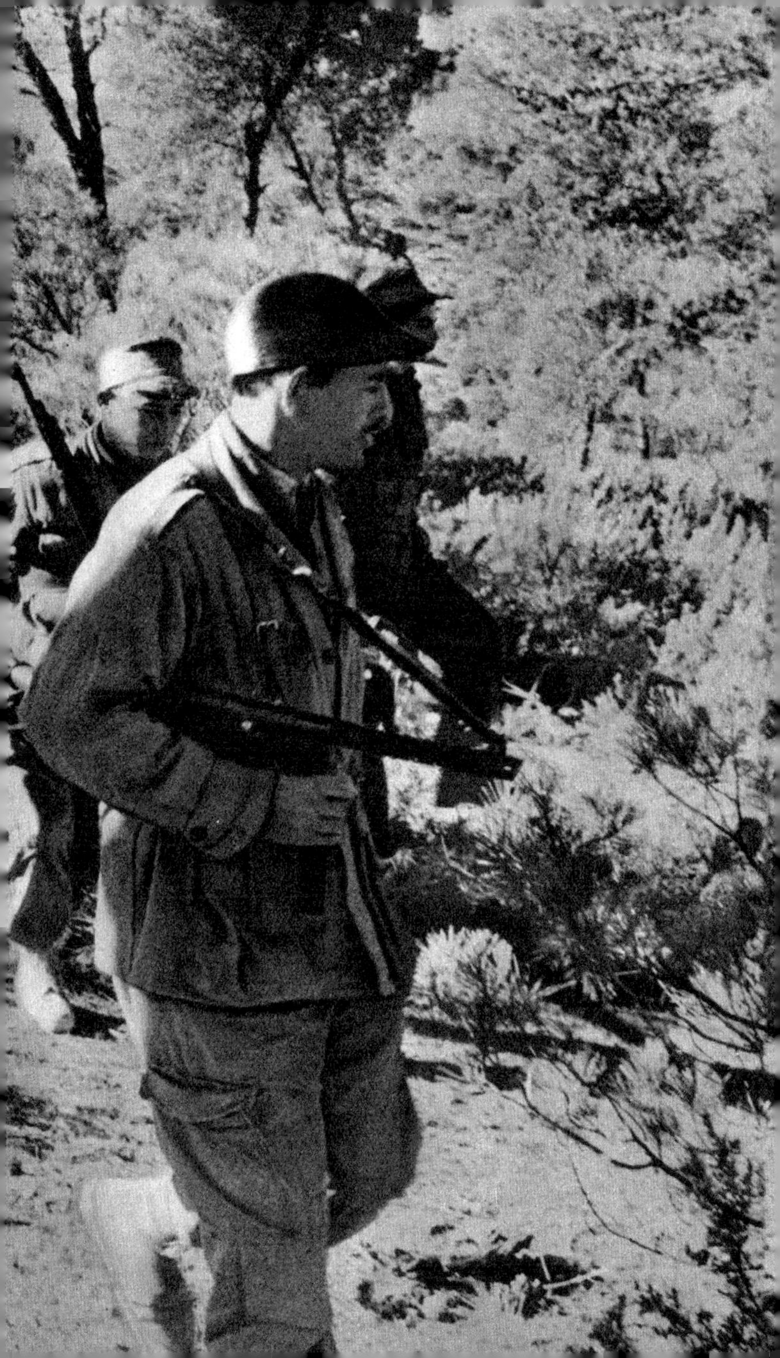

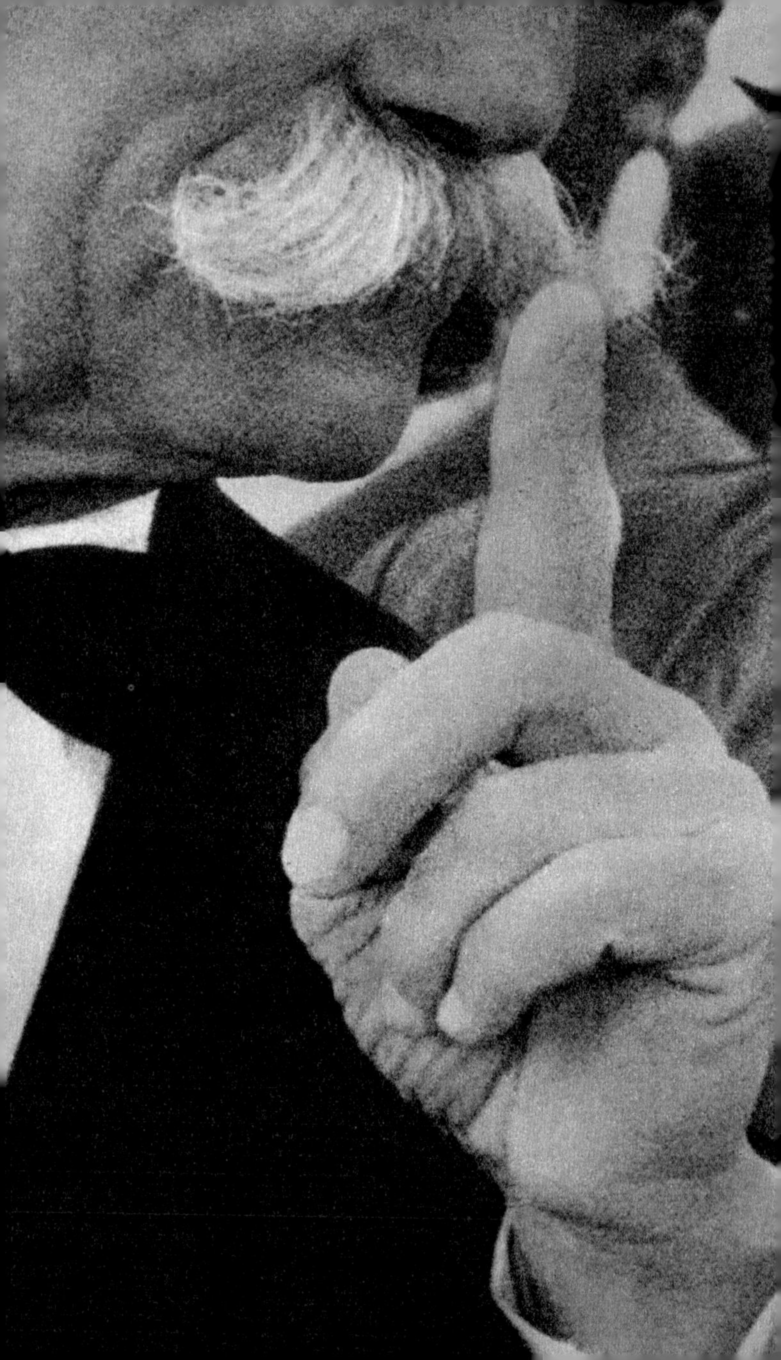

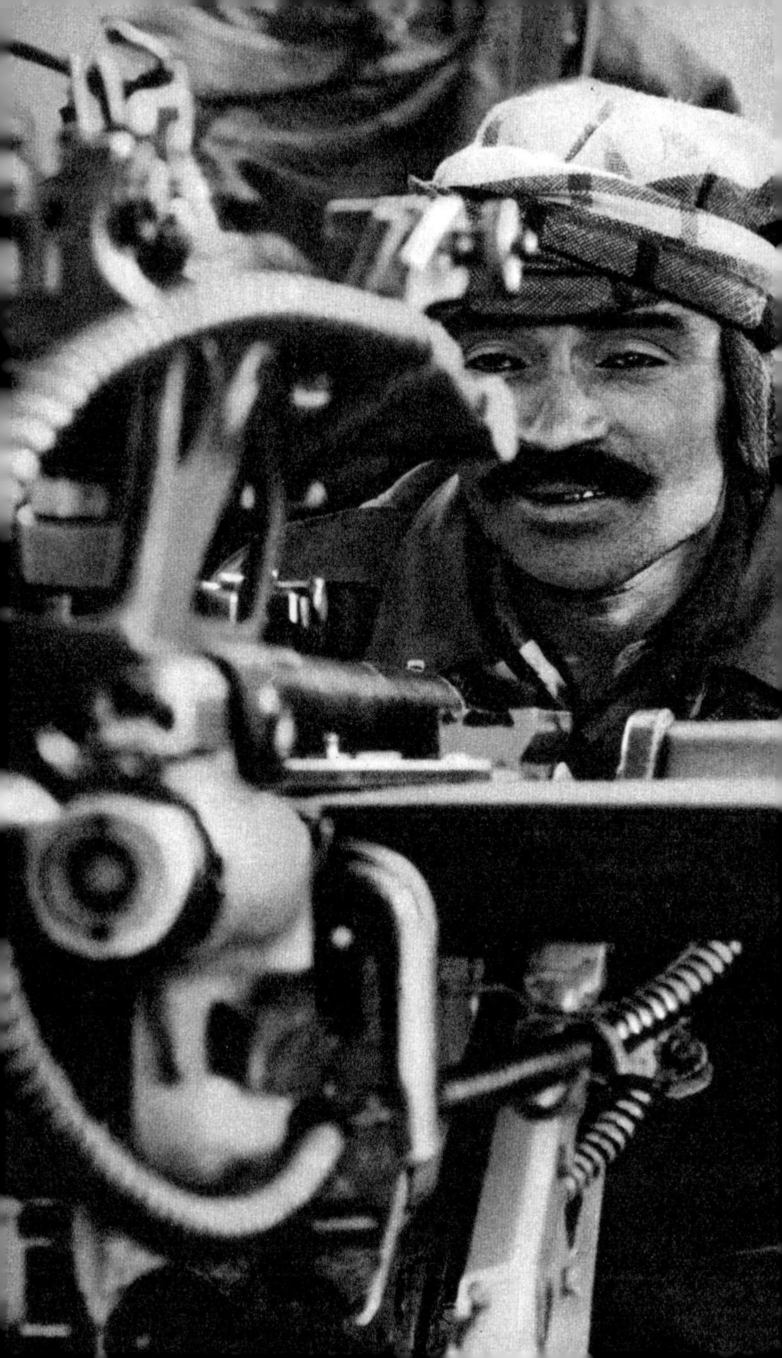

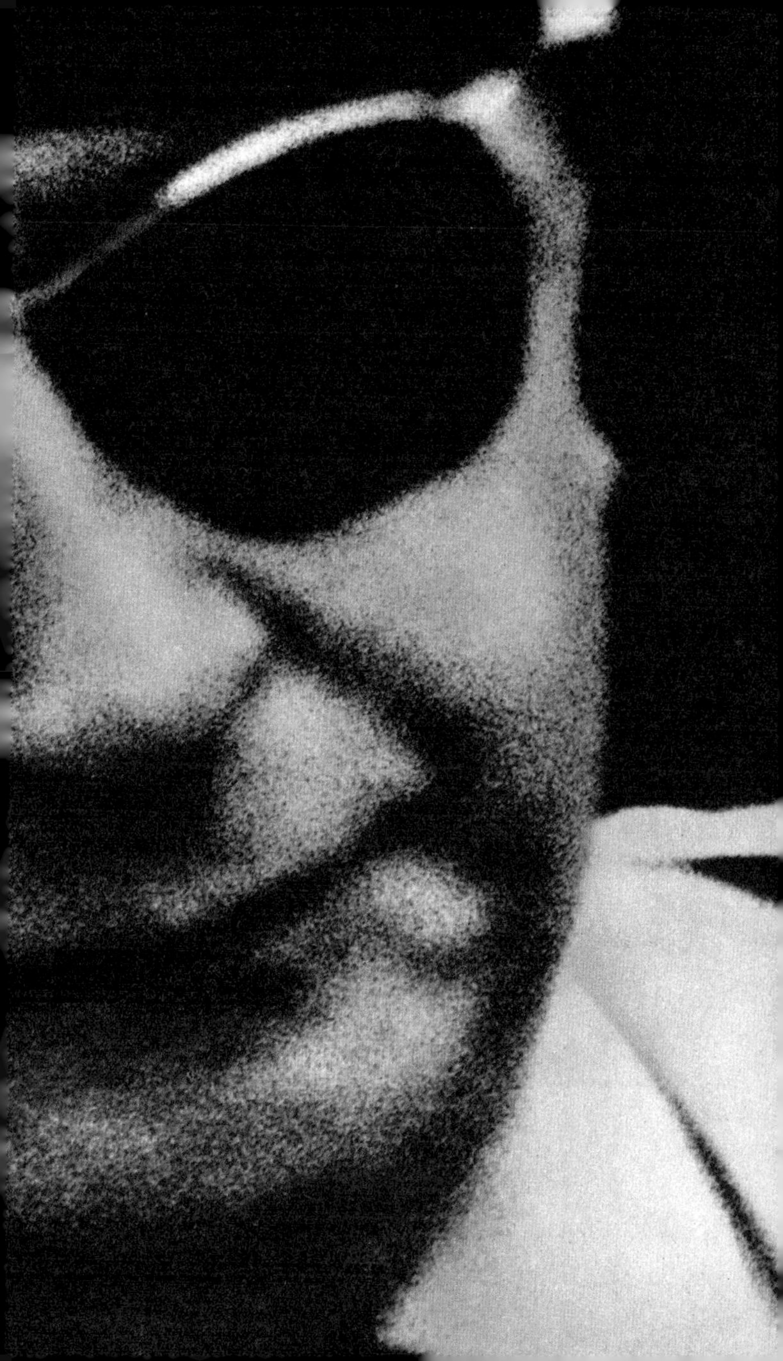

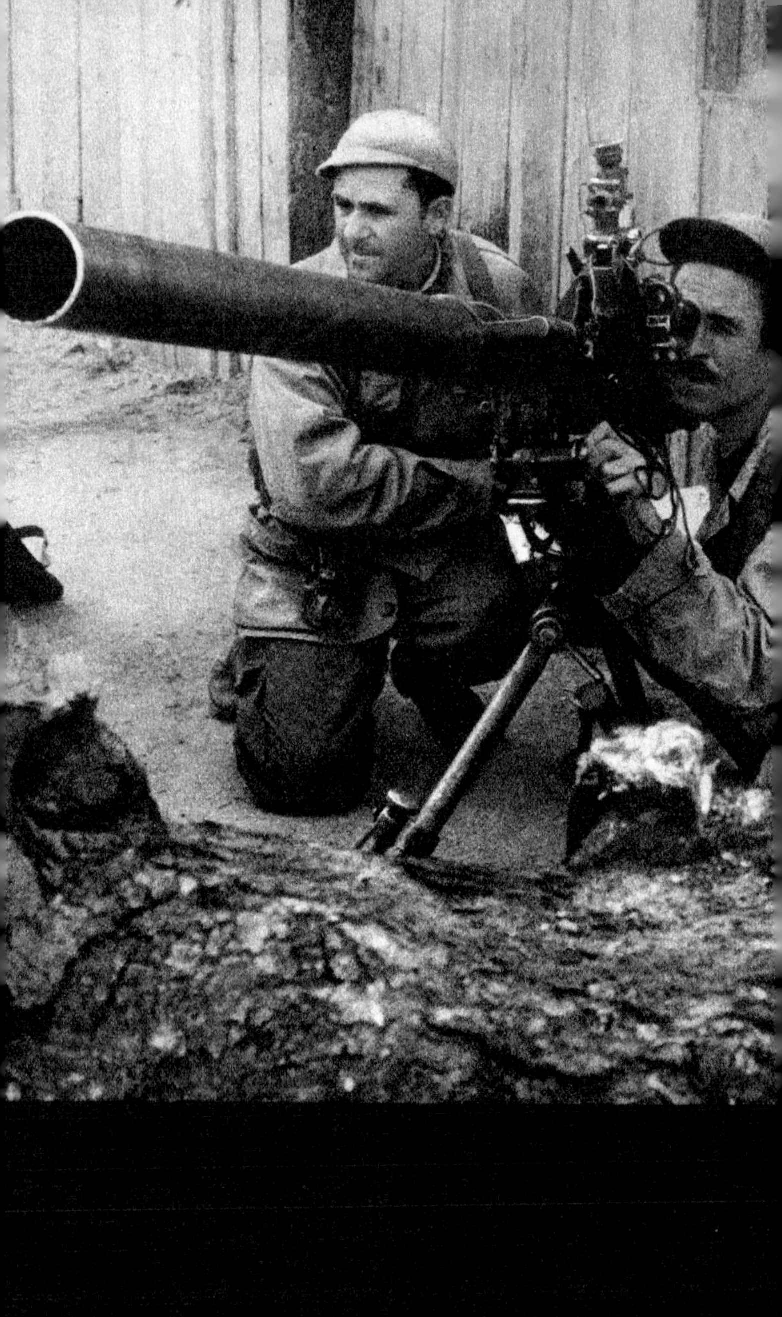

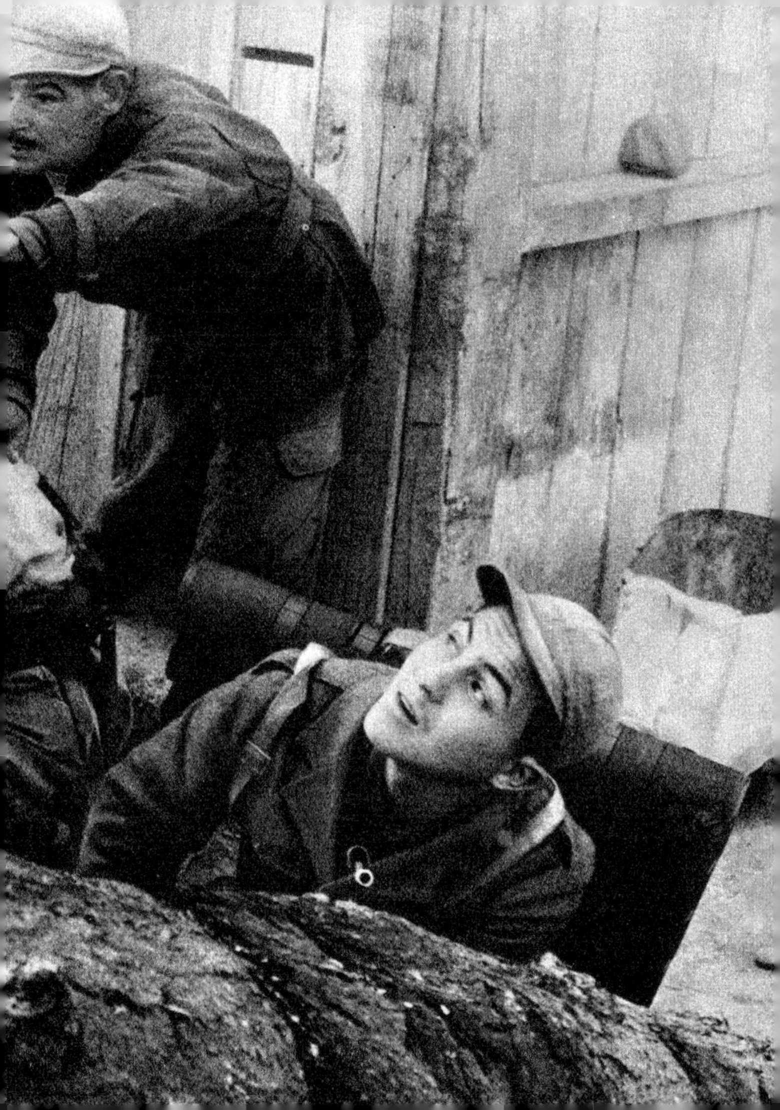

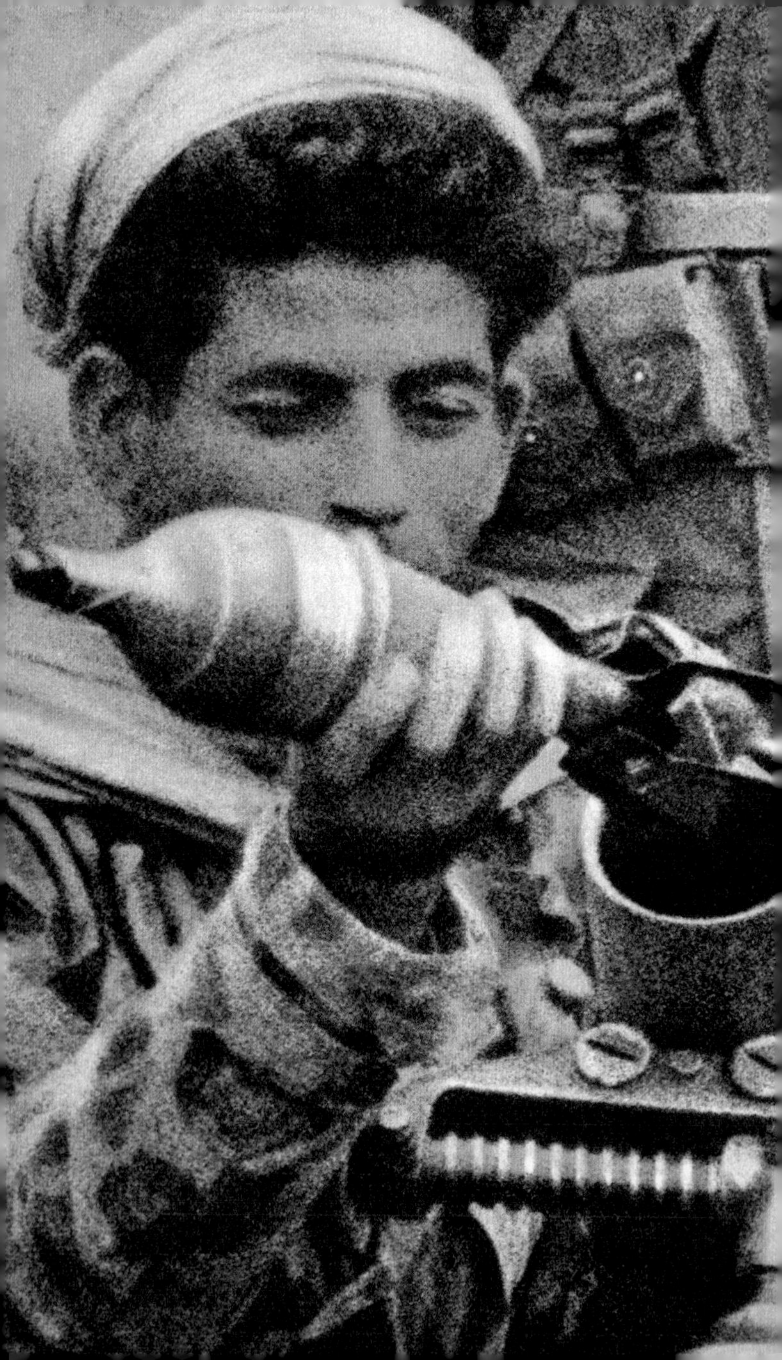

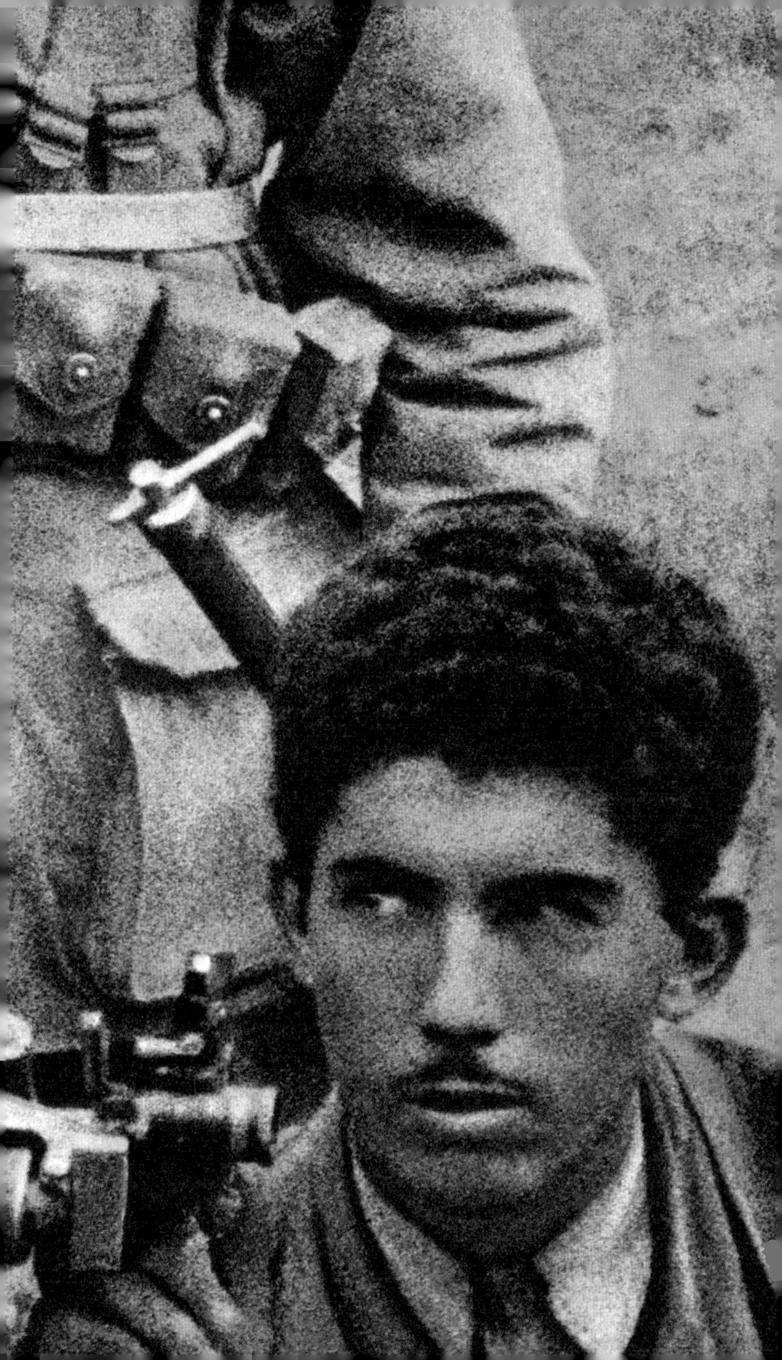

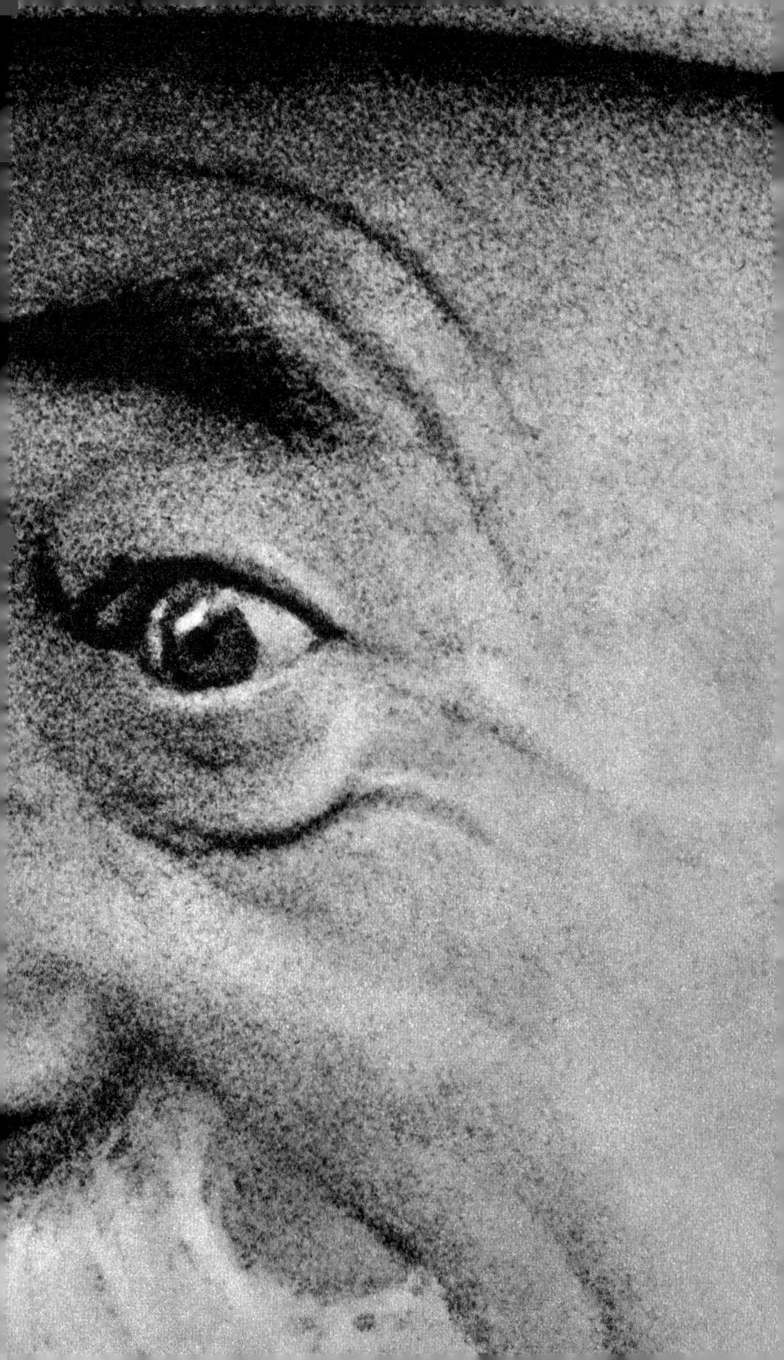

5.

"The liberation of Algeria will be the shared achievement of all Algerians ..."

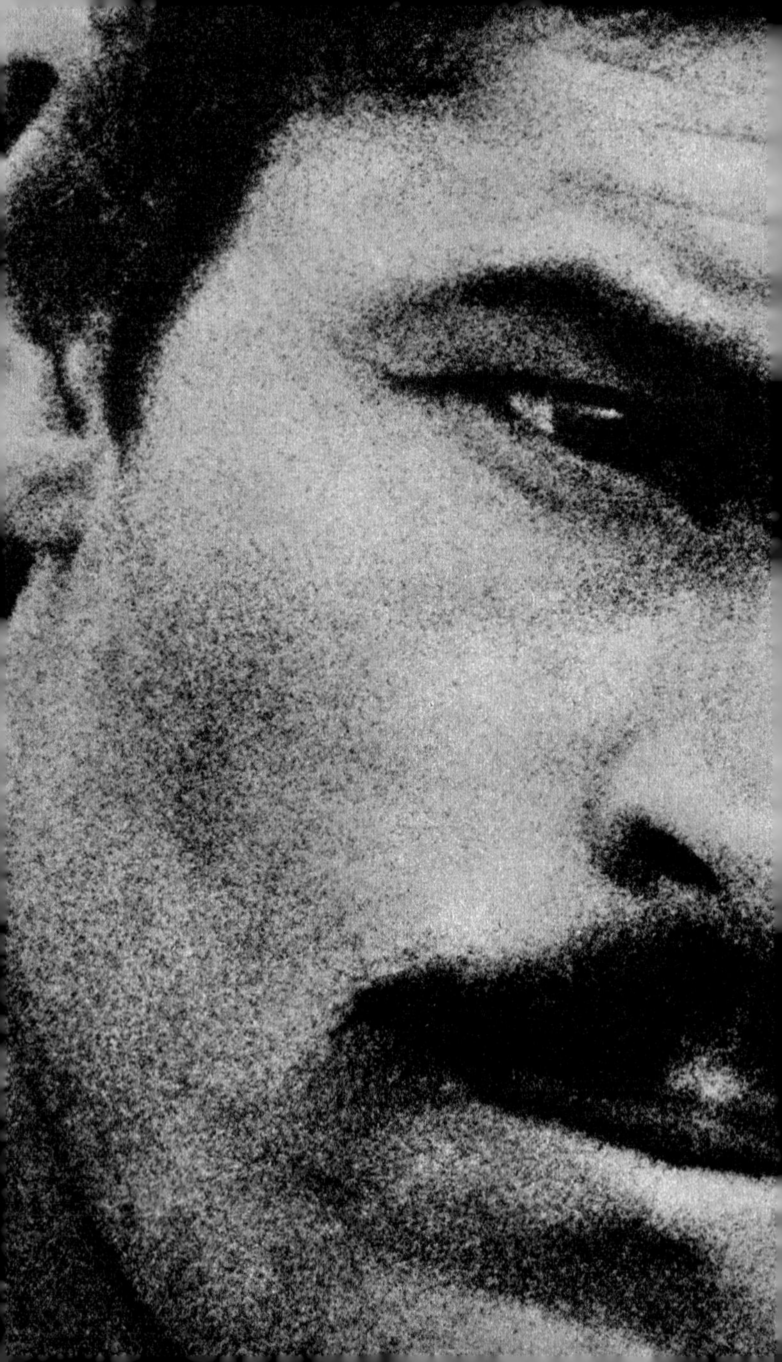

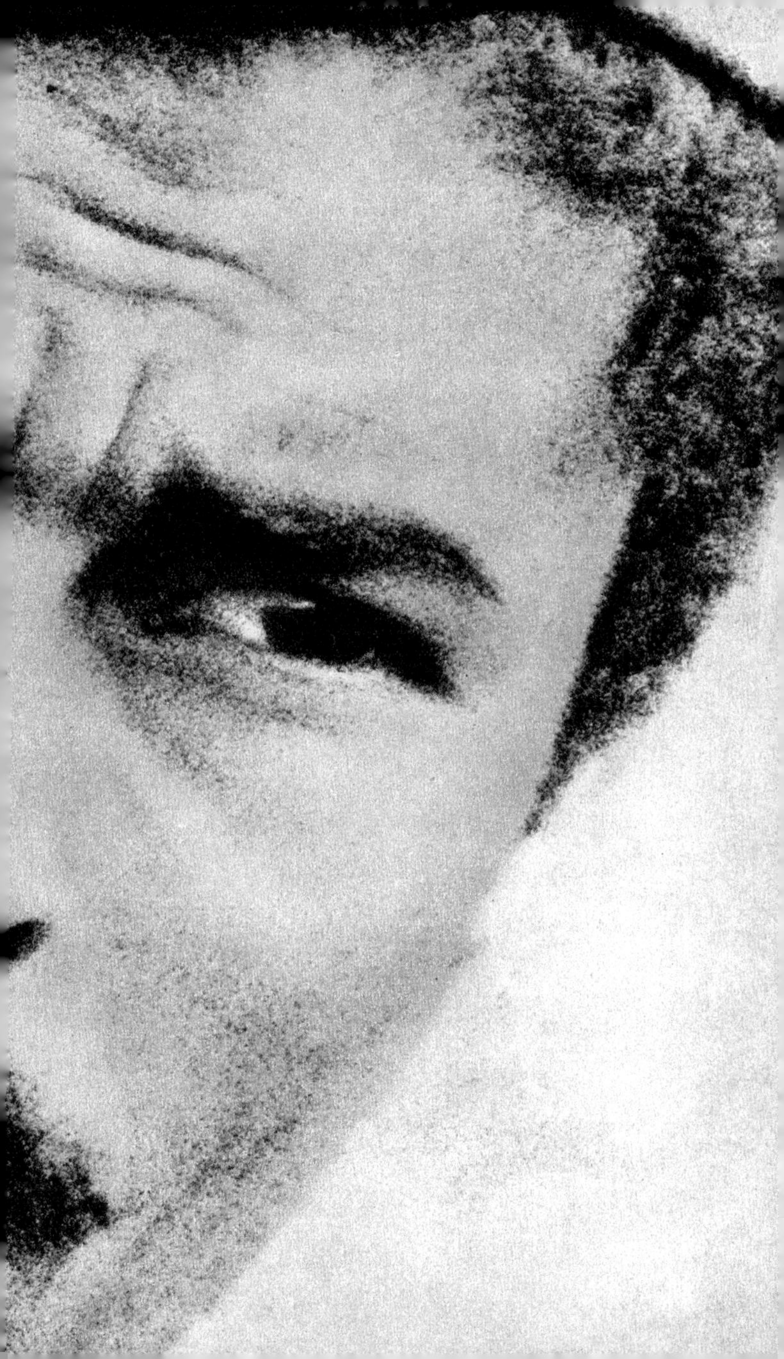

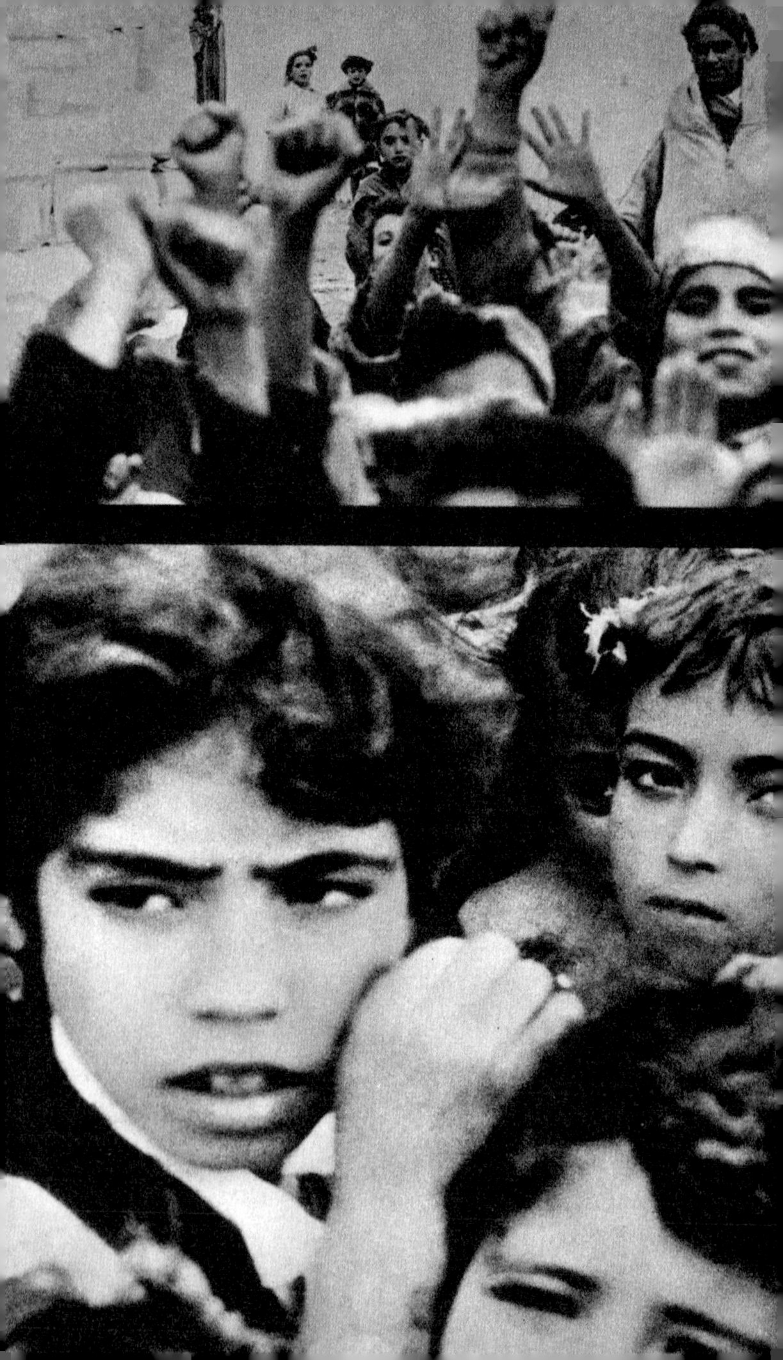

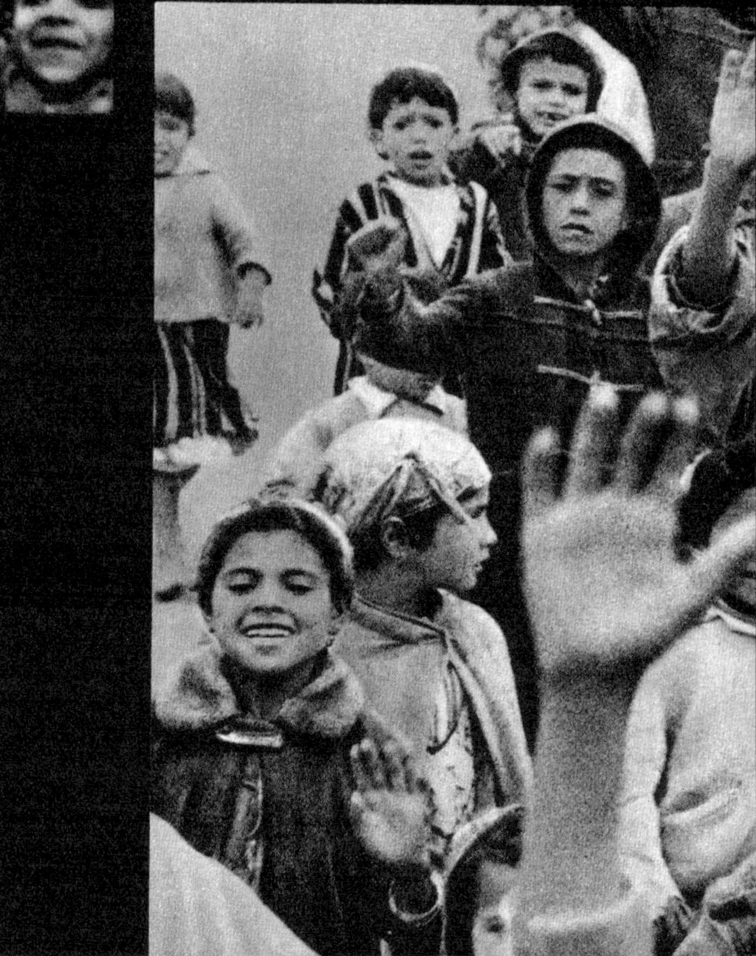

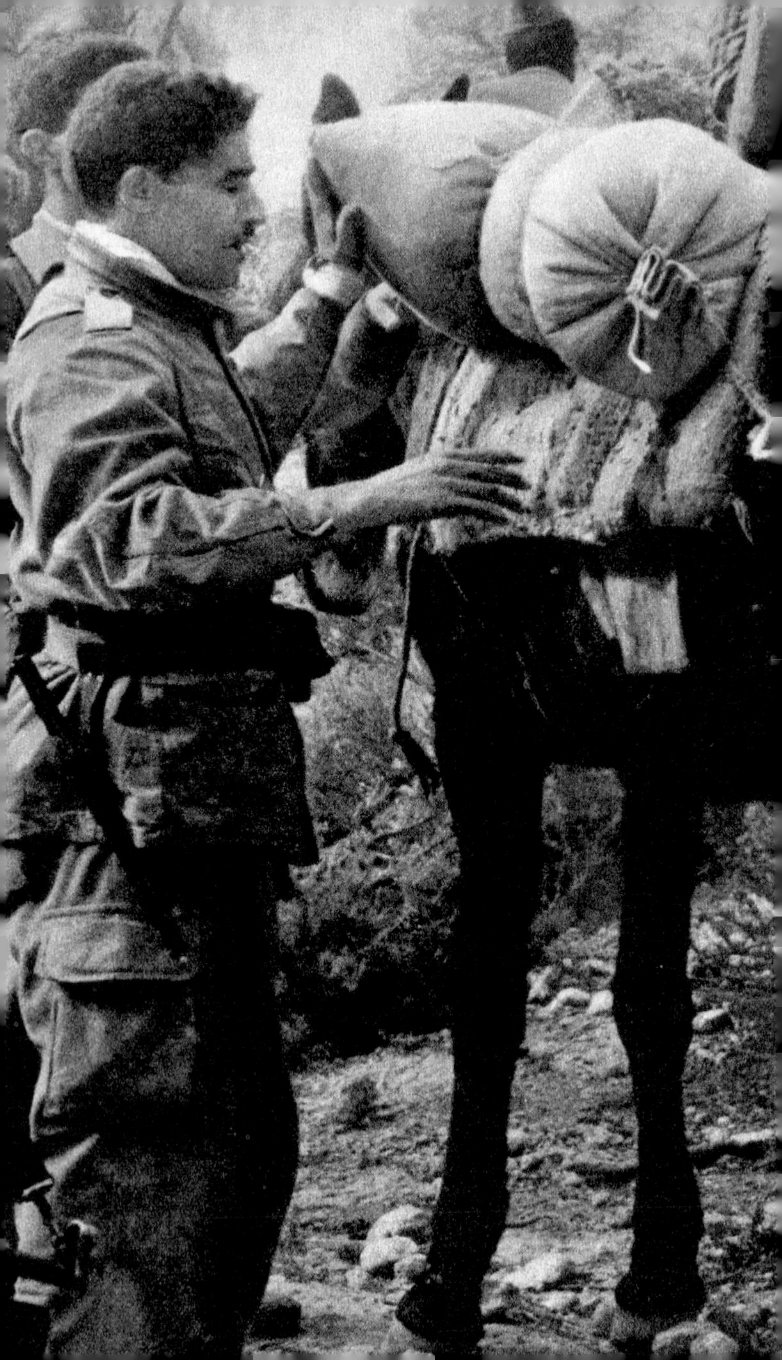

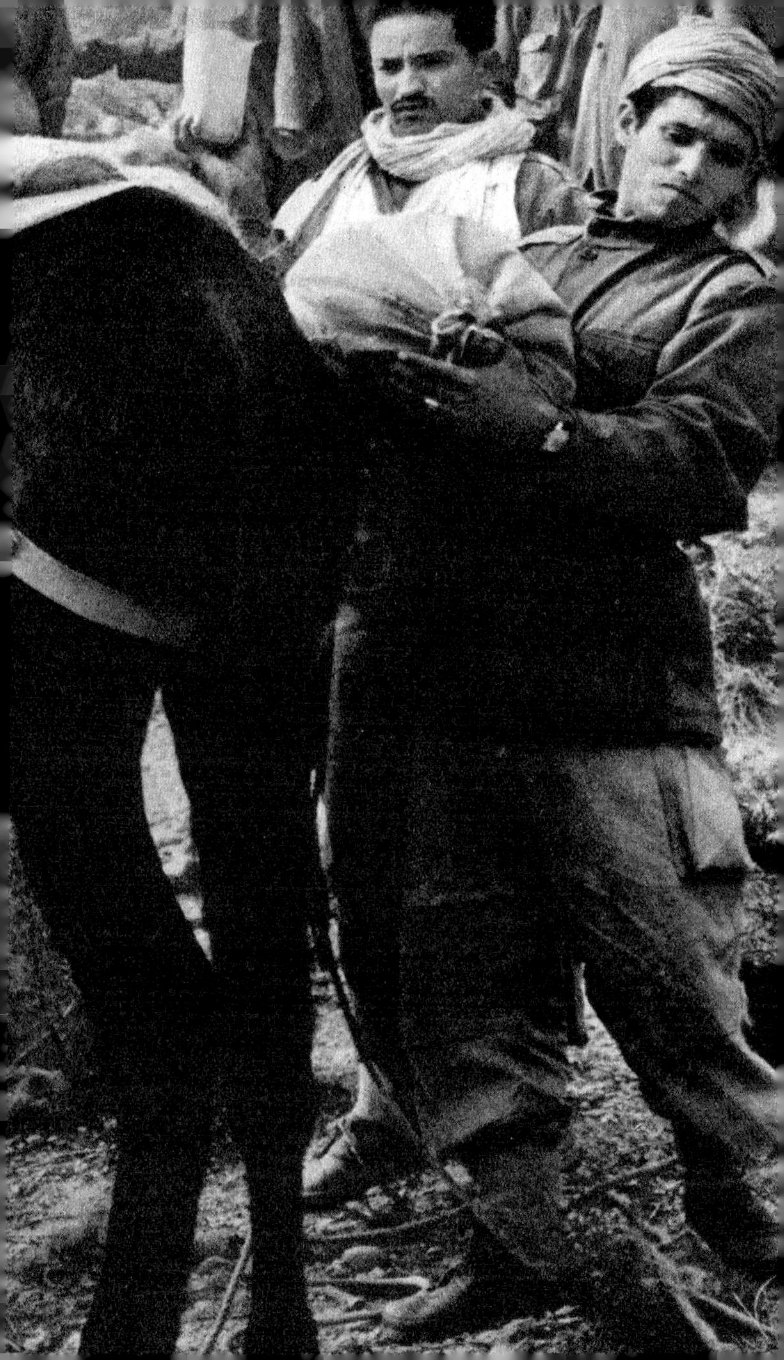

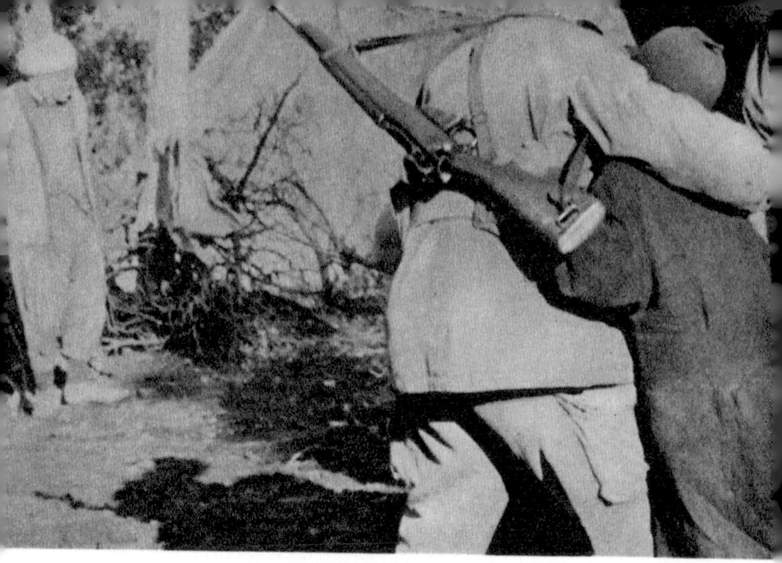

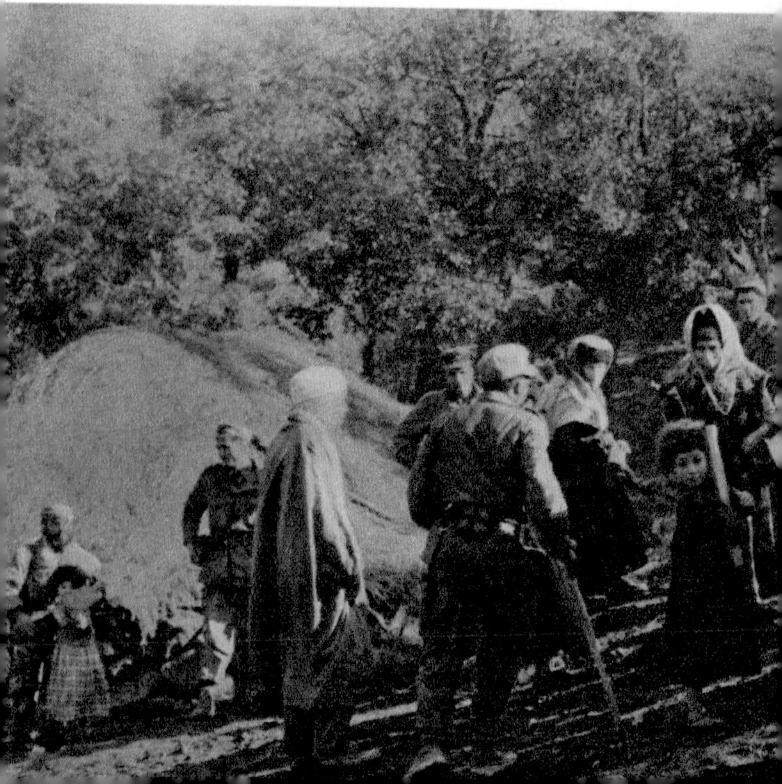

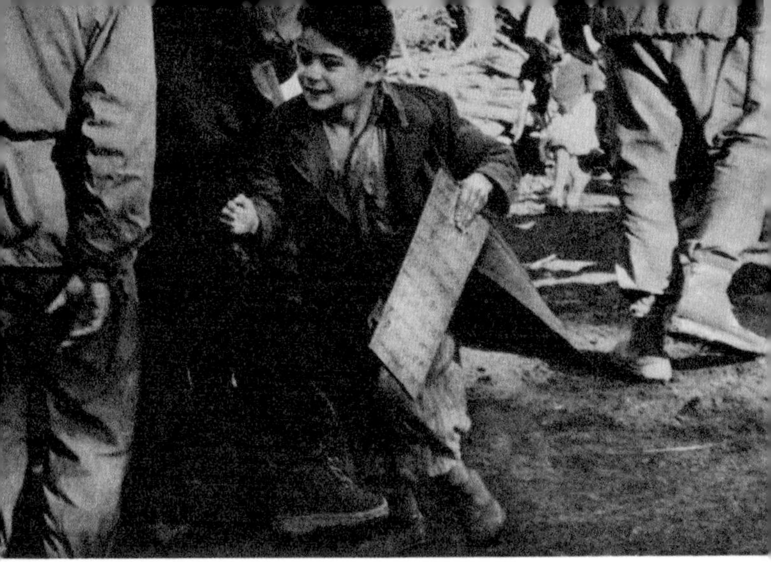

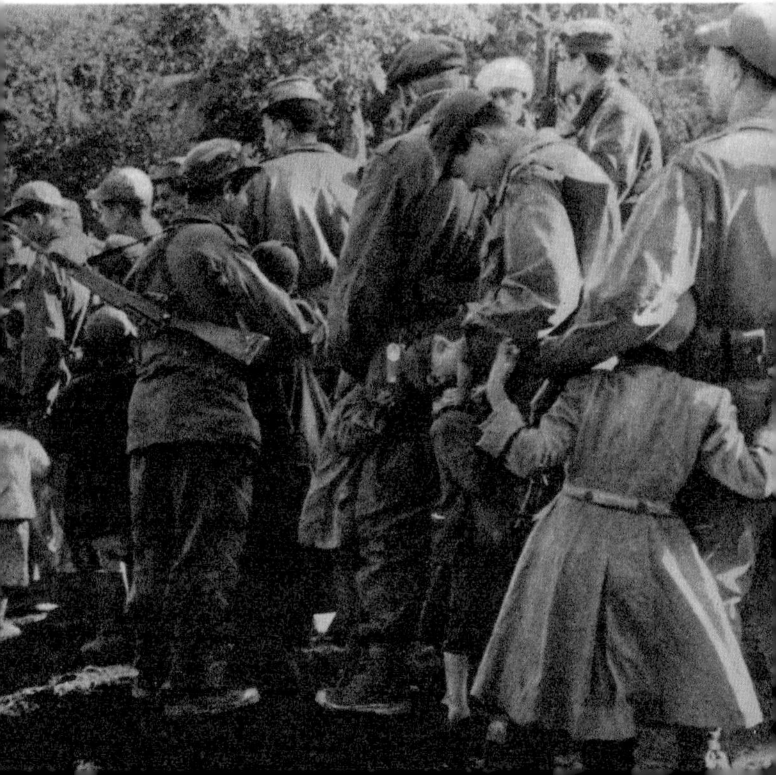

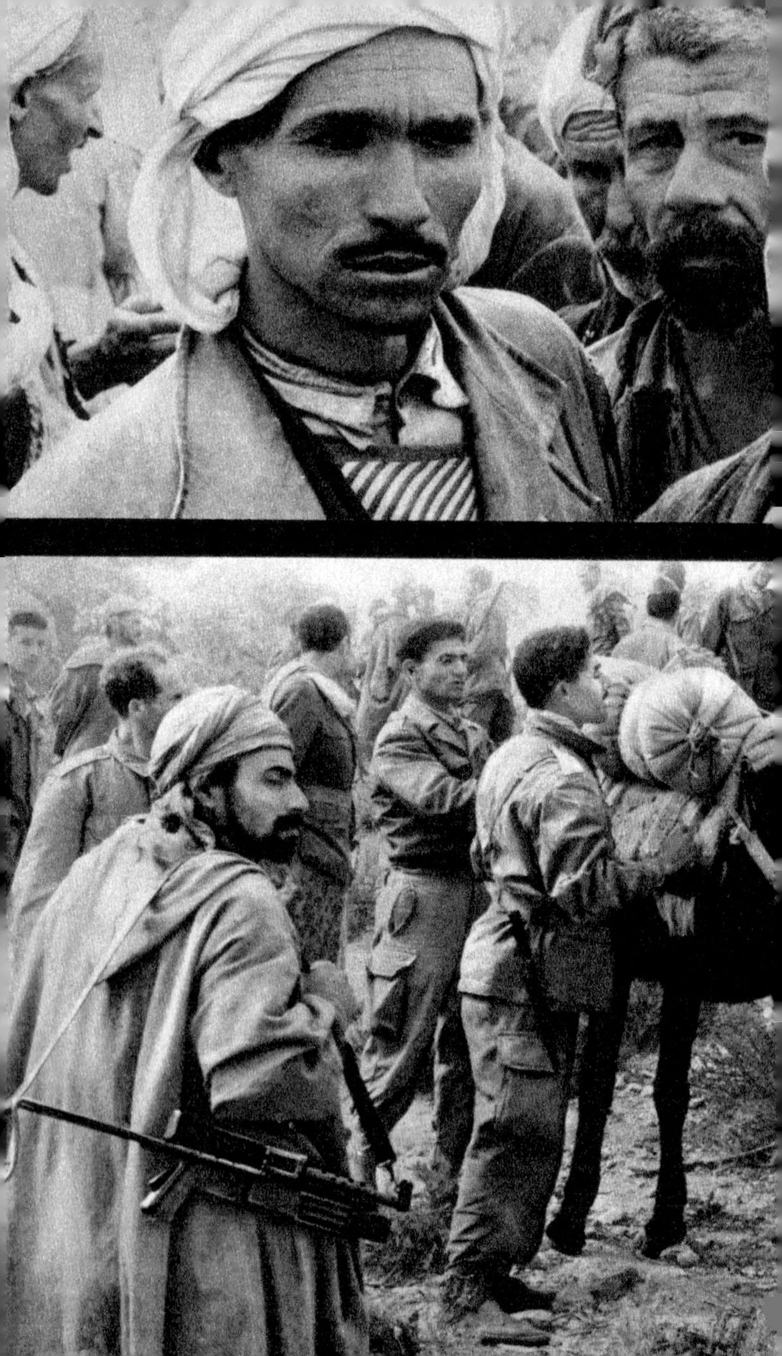

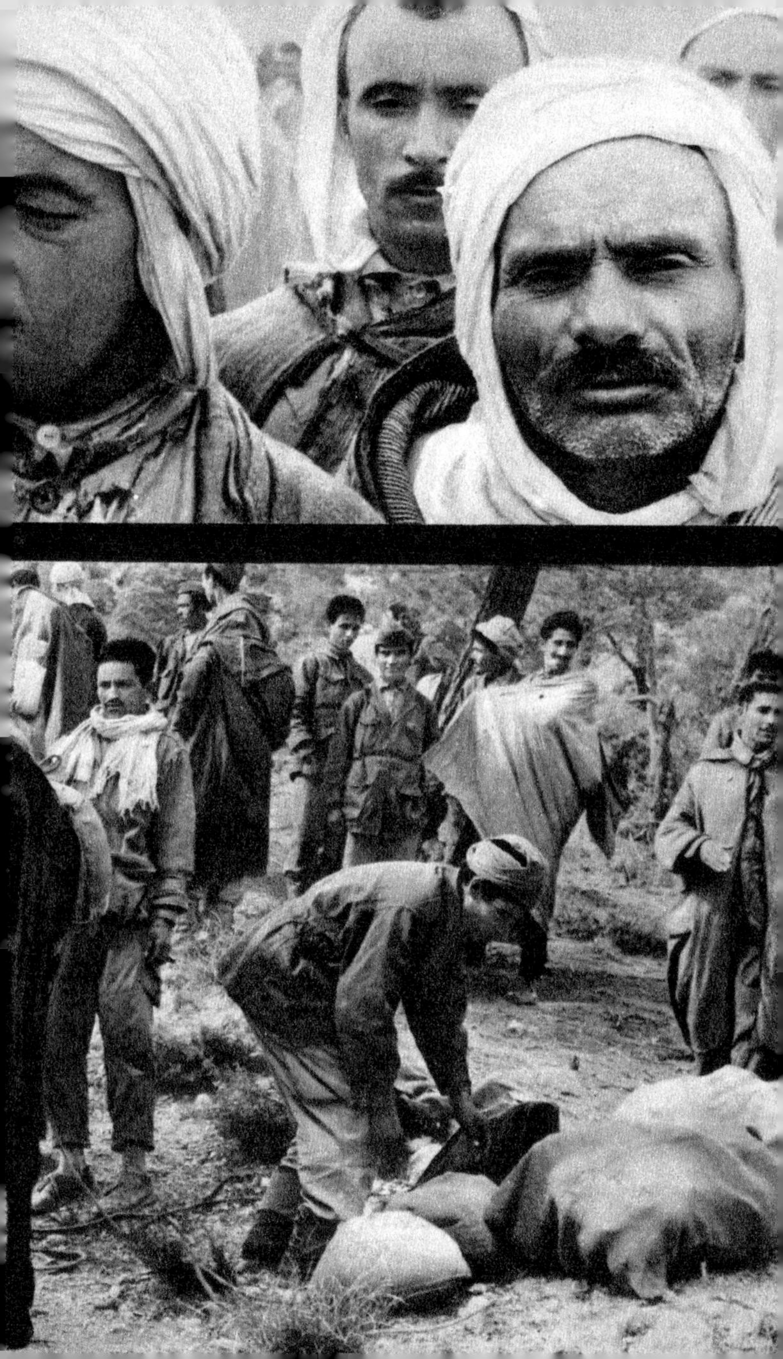

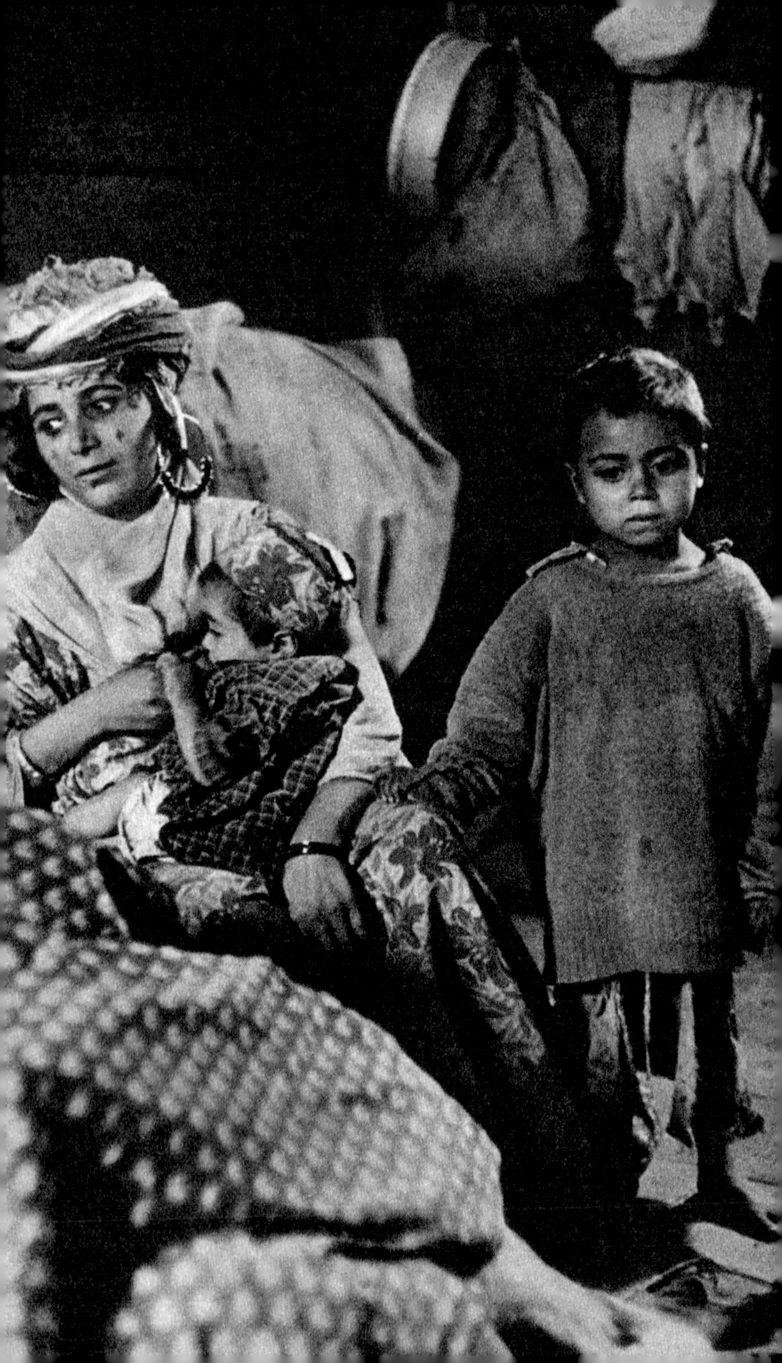

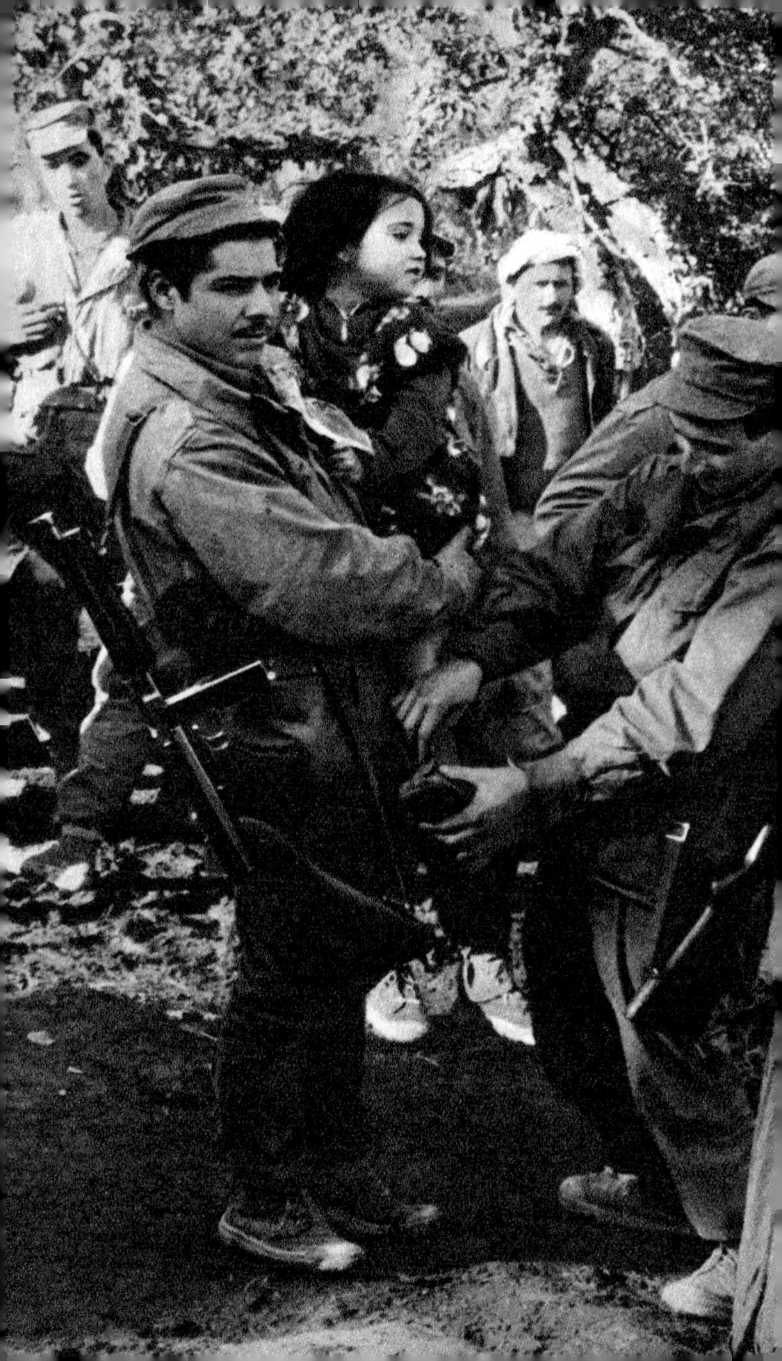

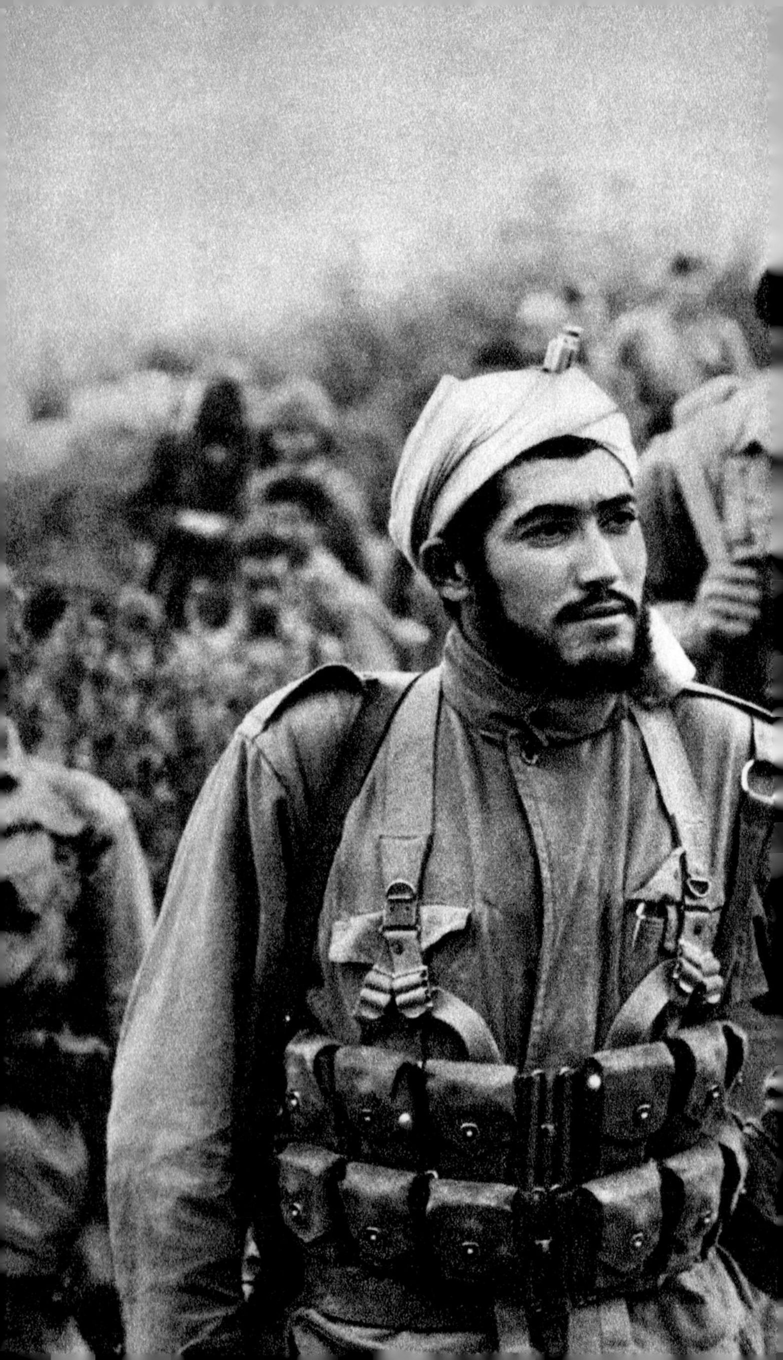

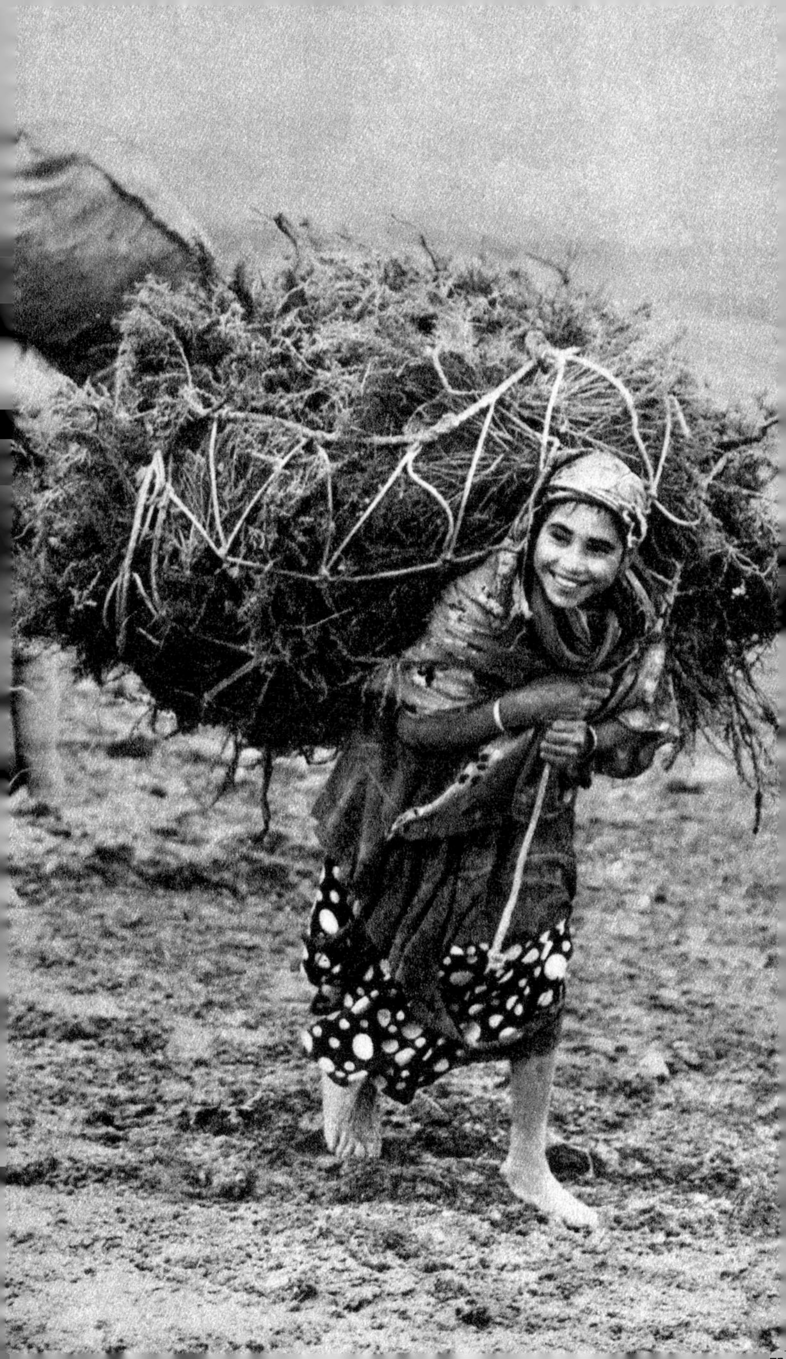

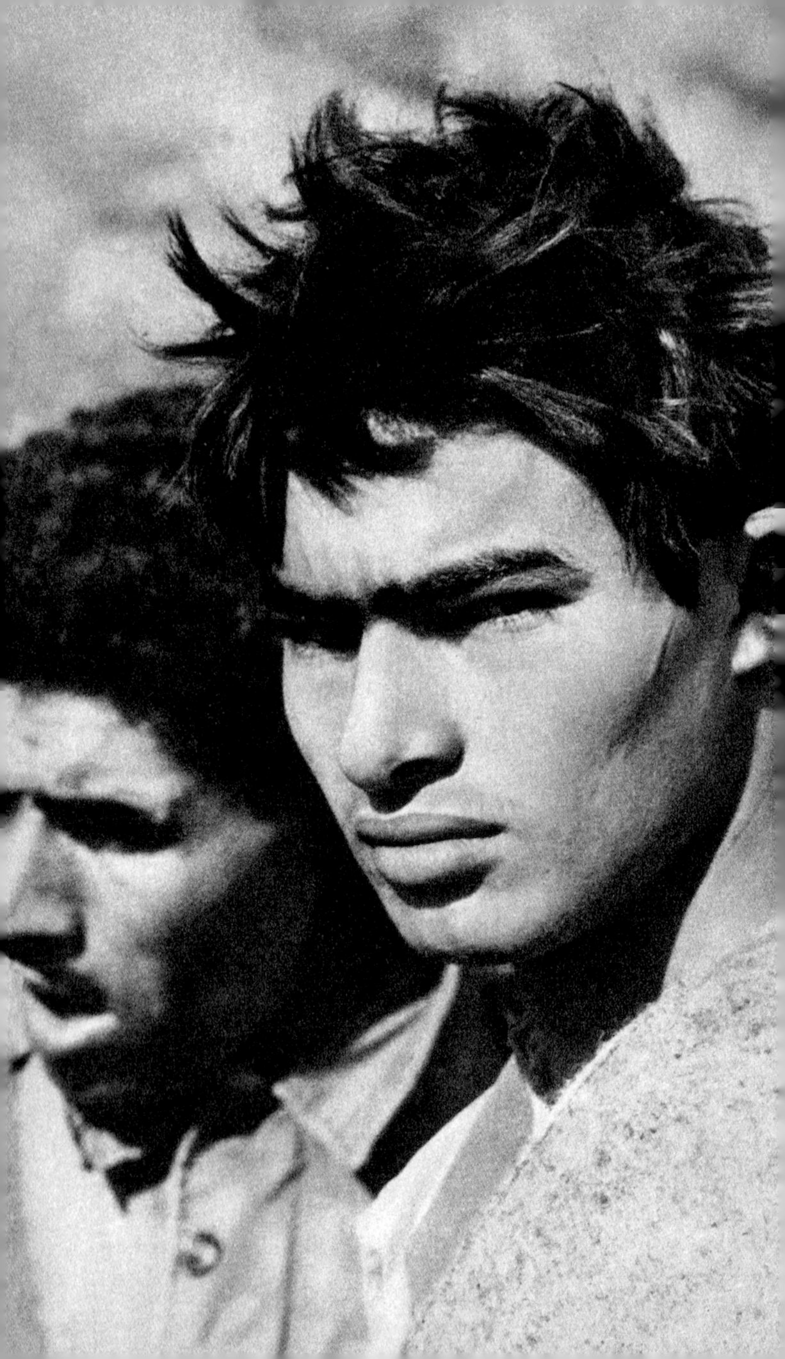

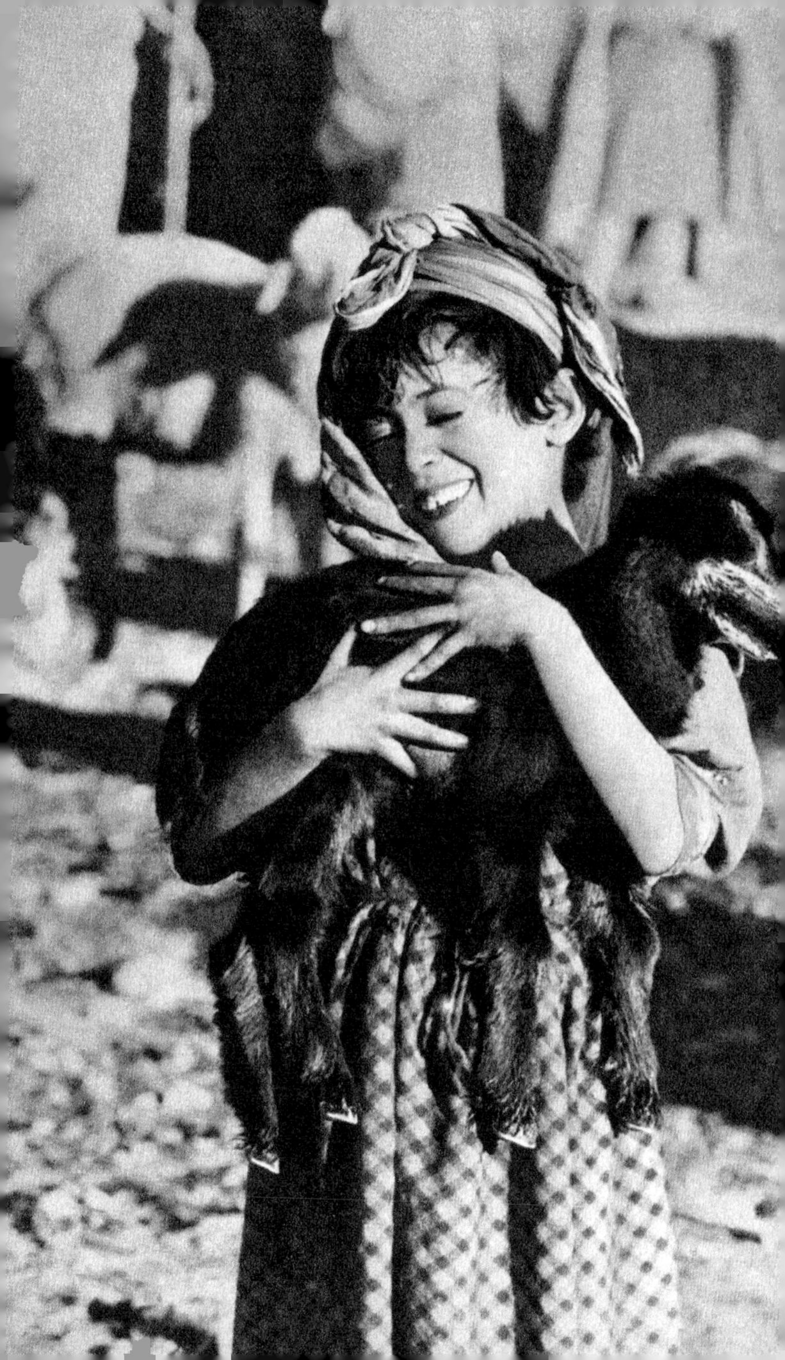

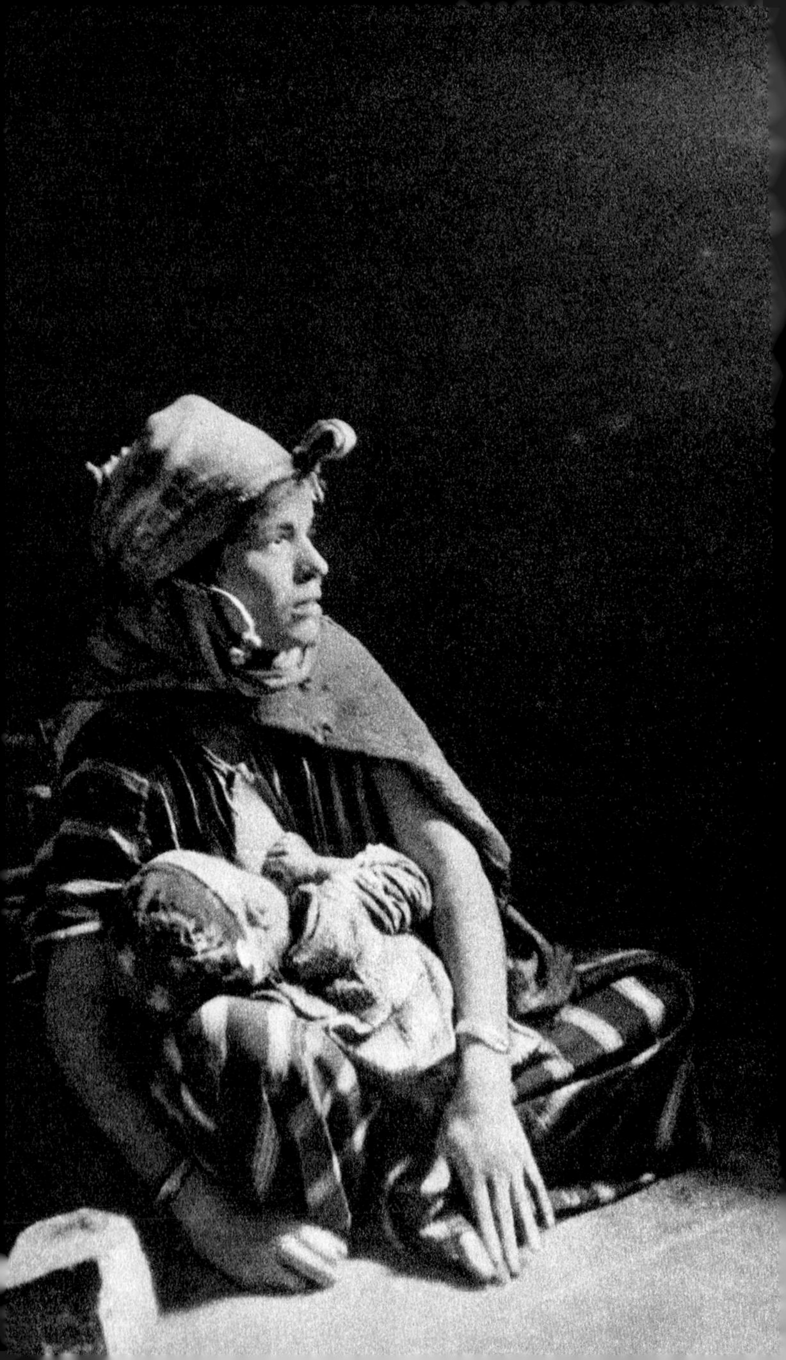

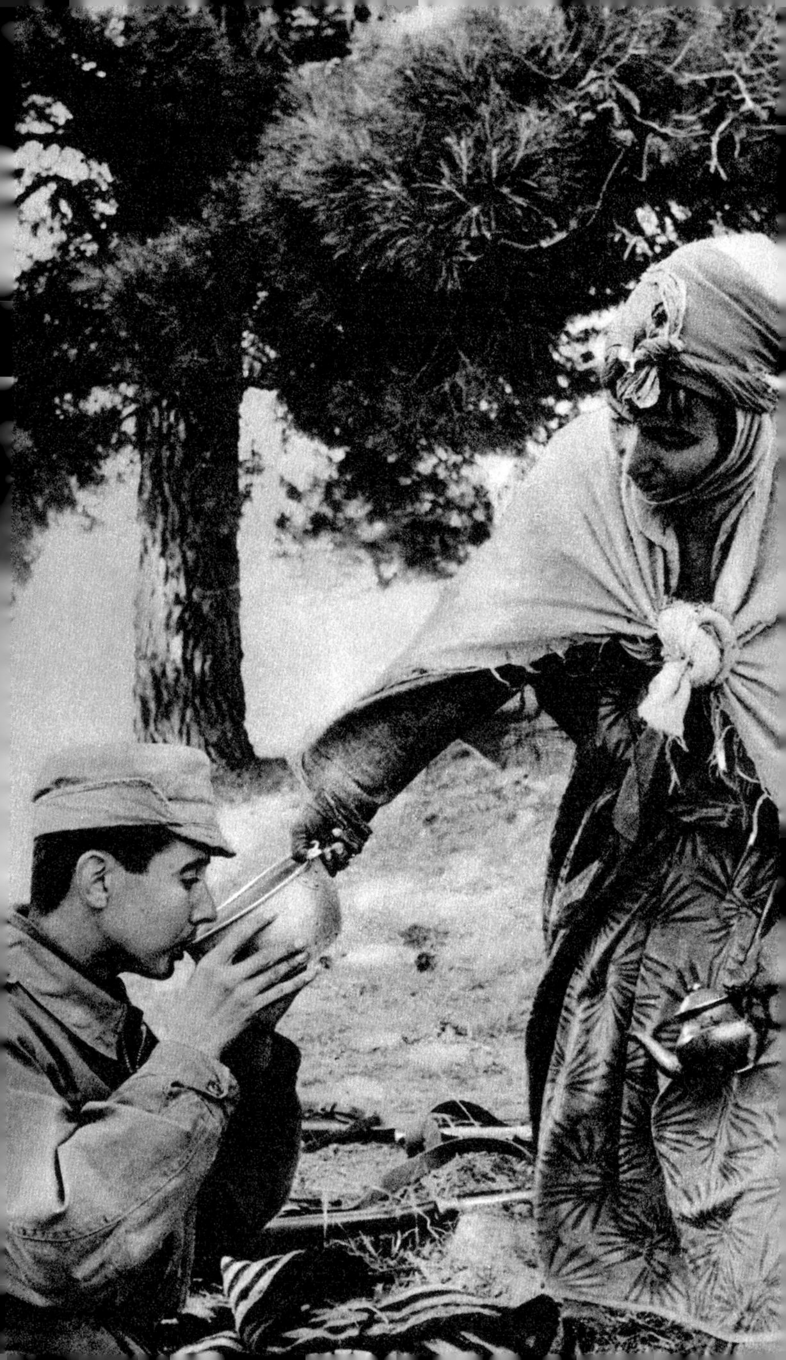

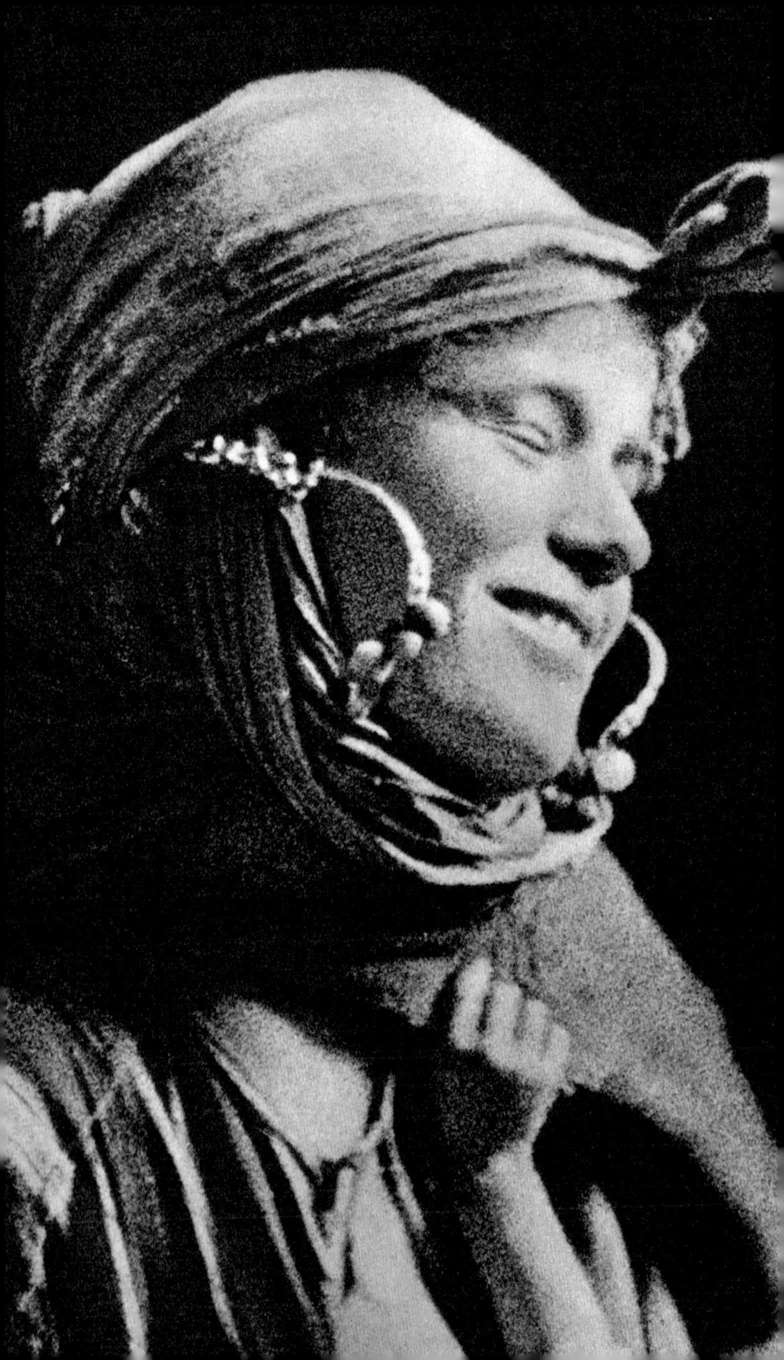

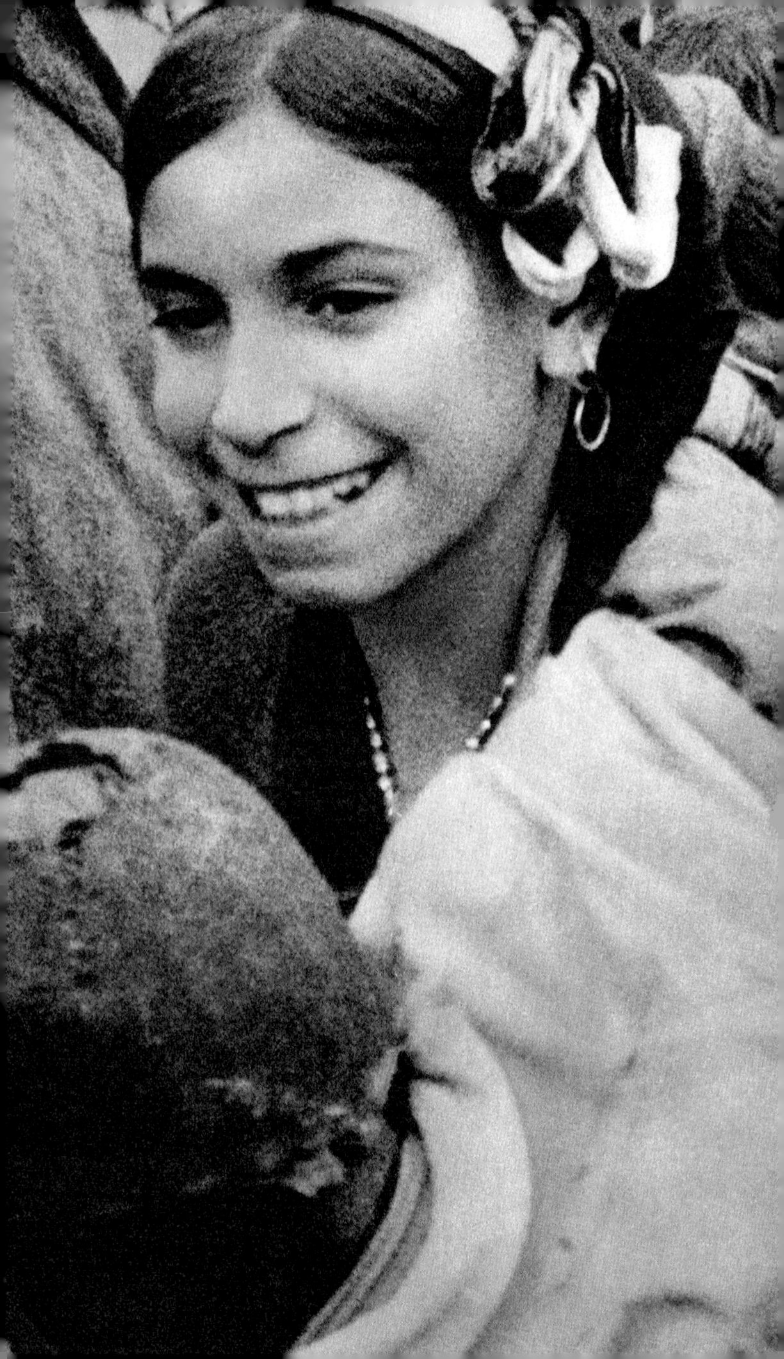

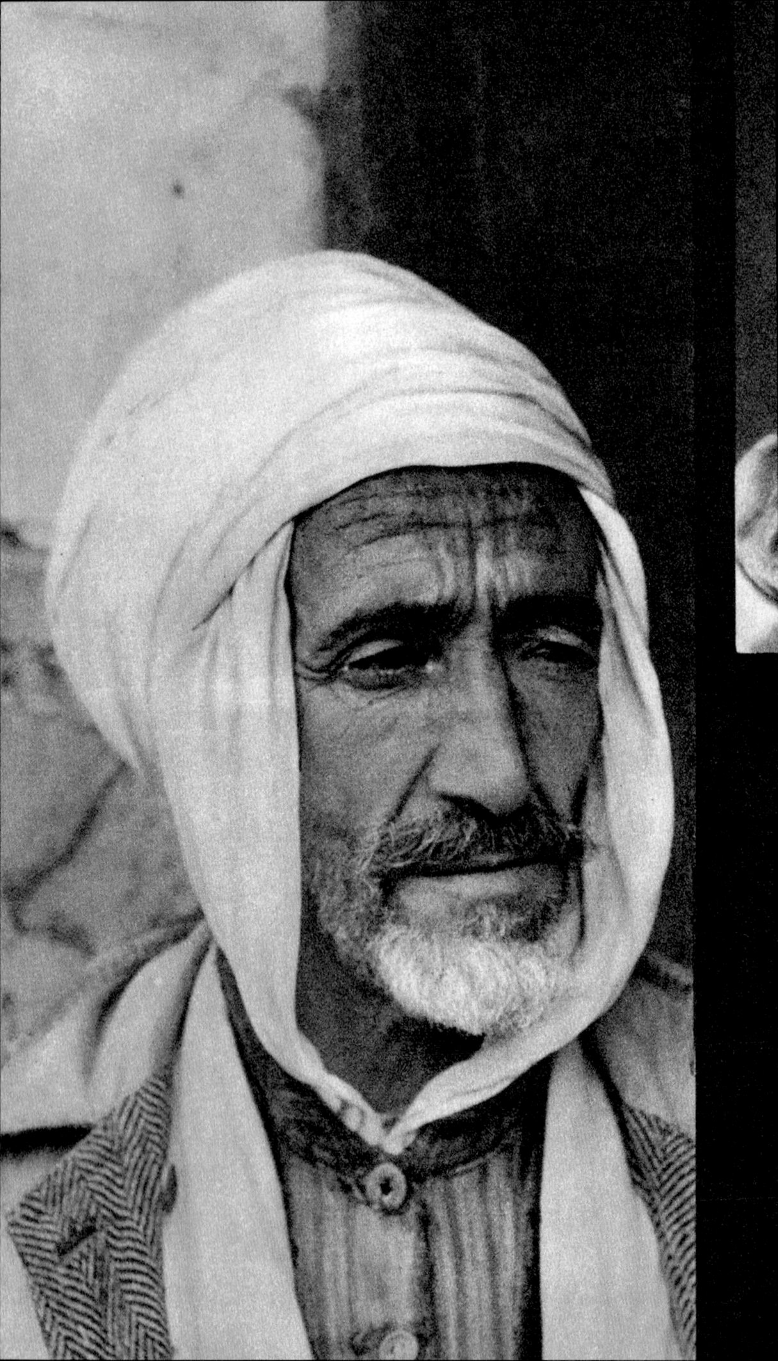

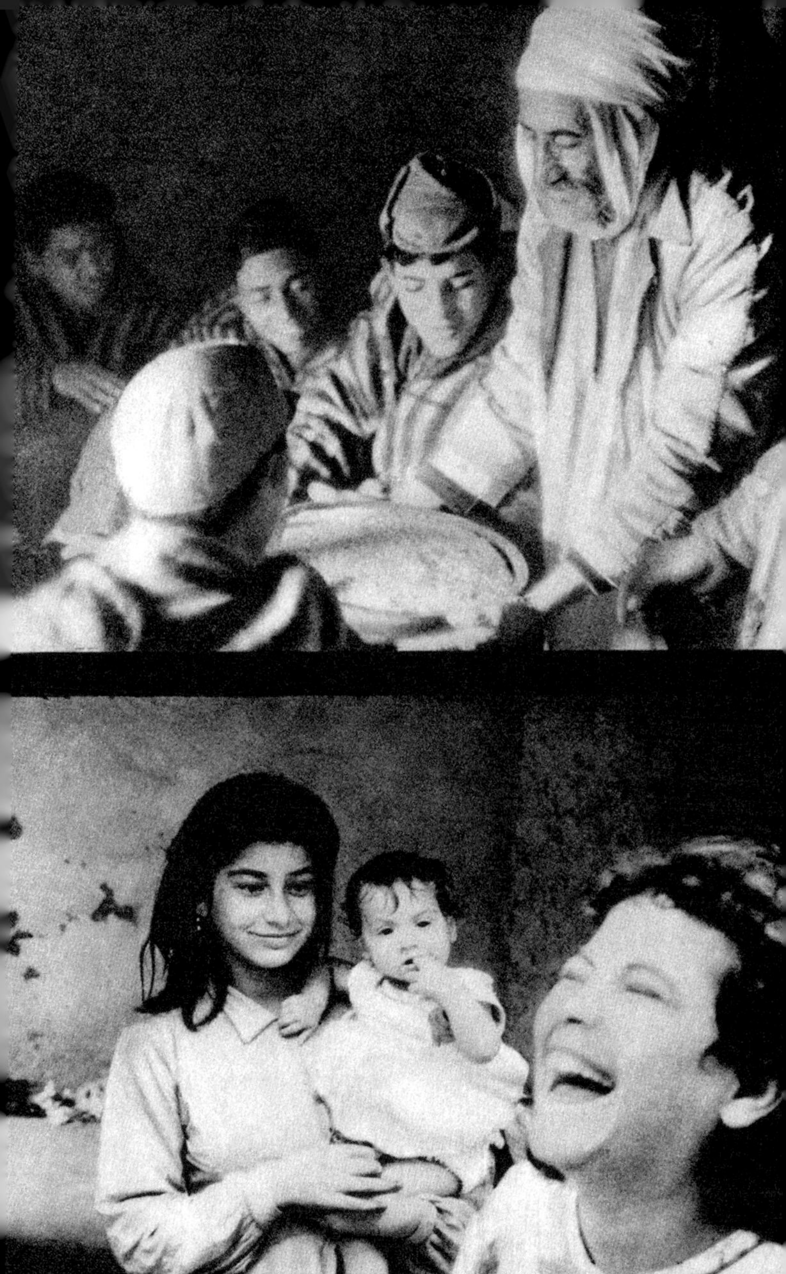

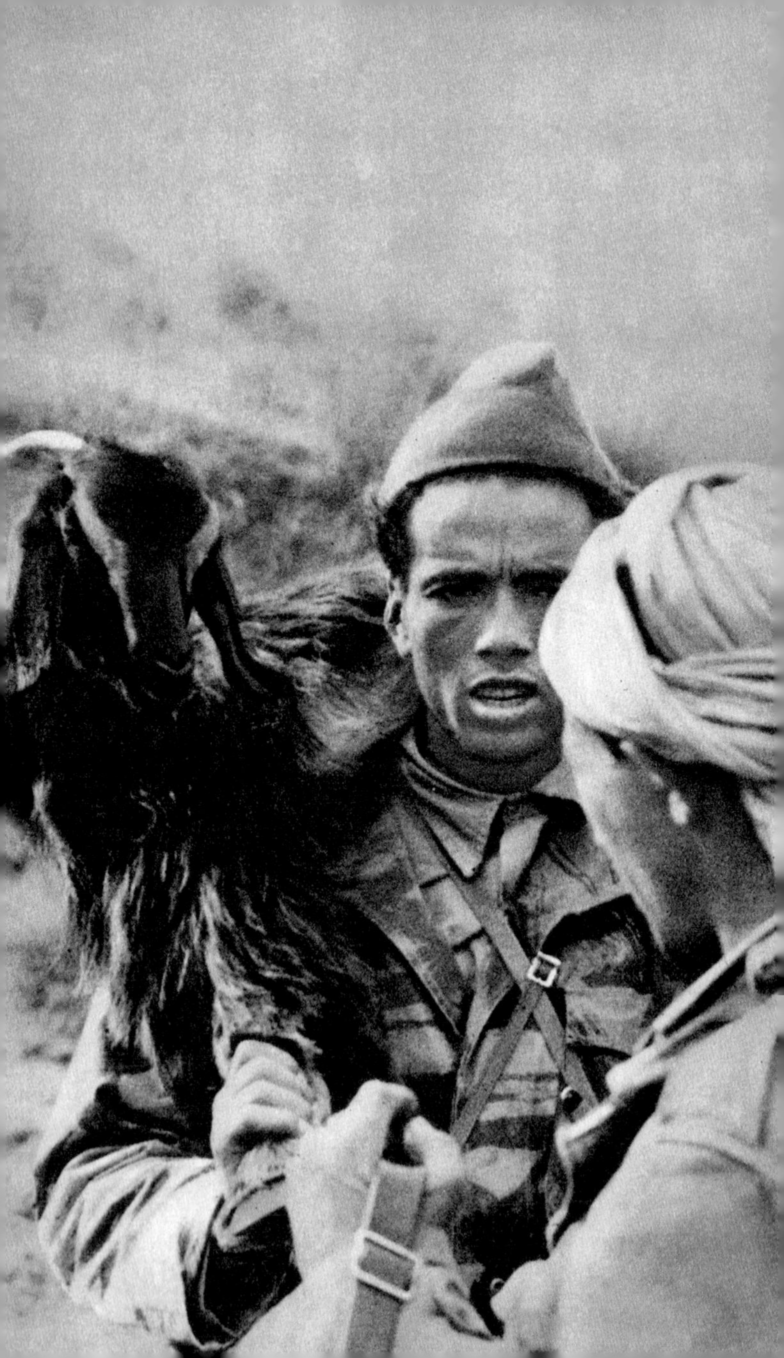

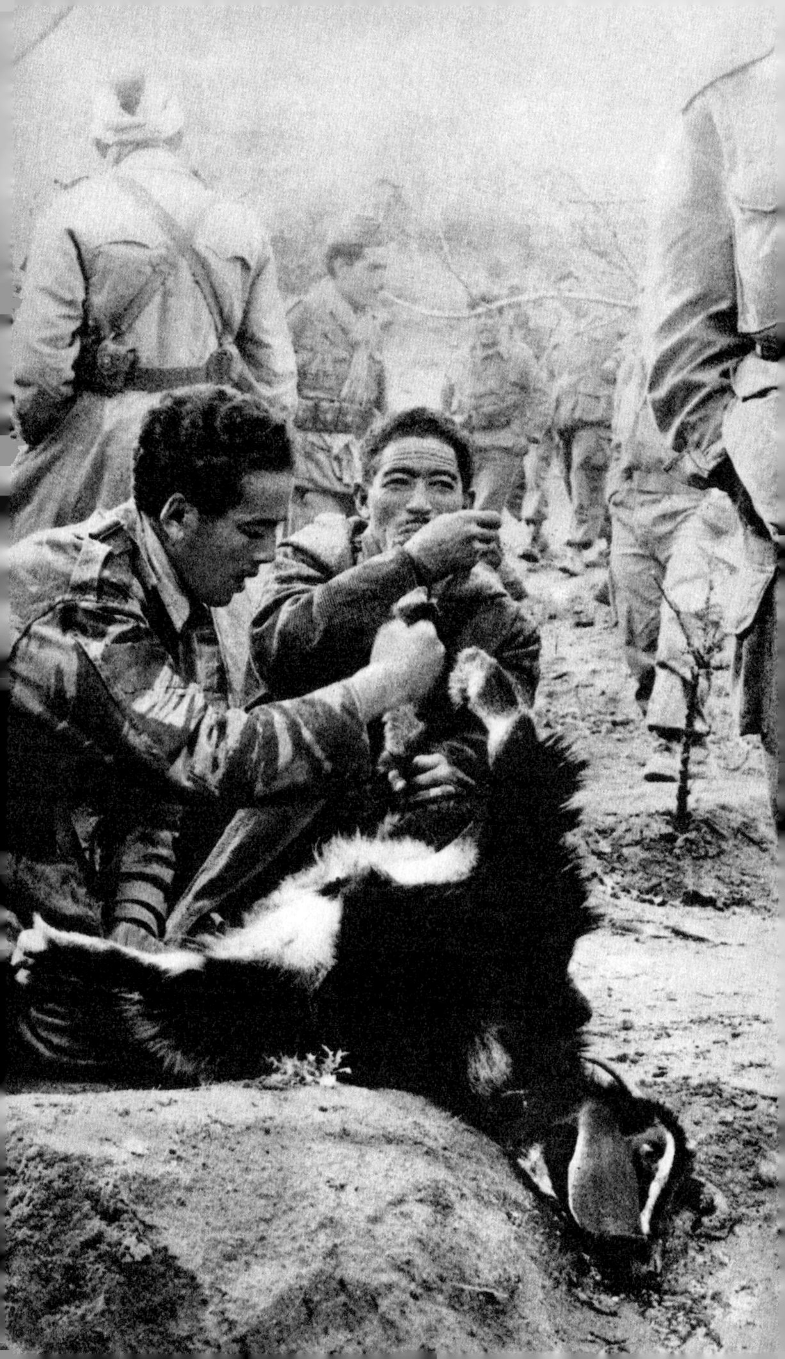

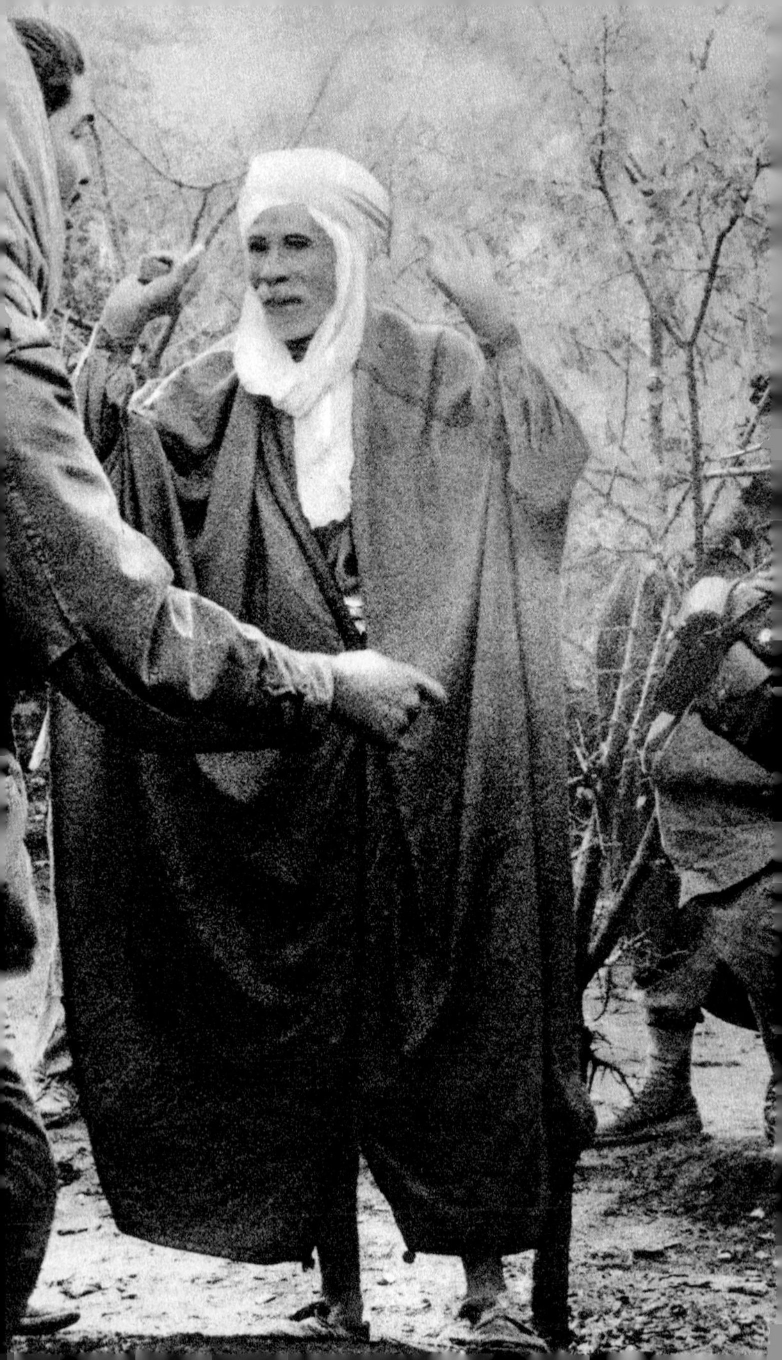

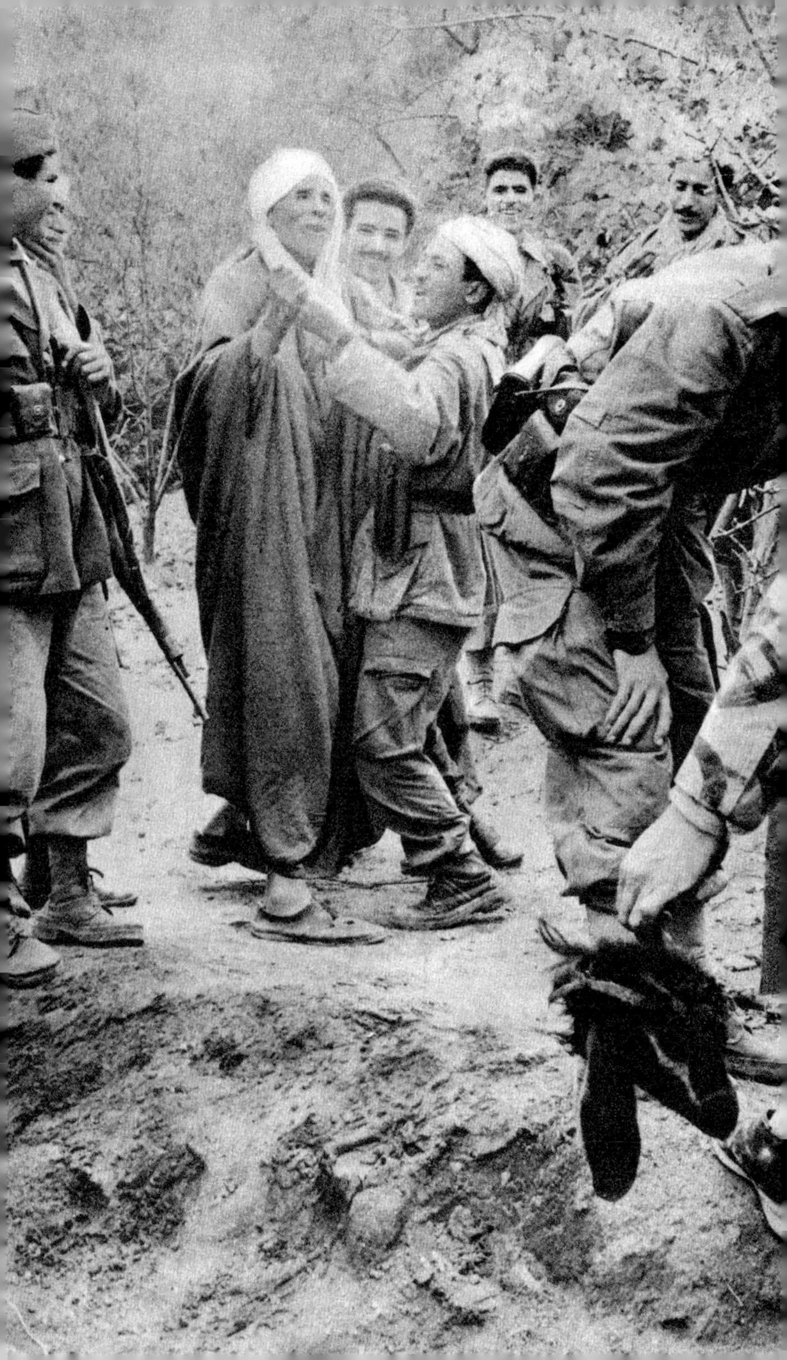

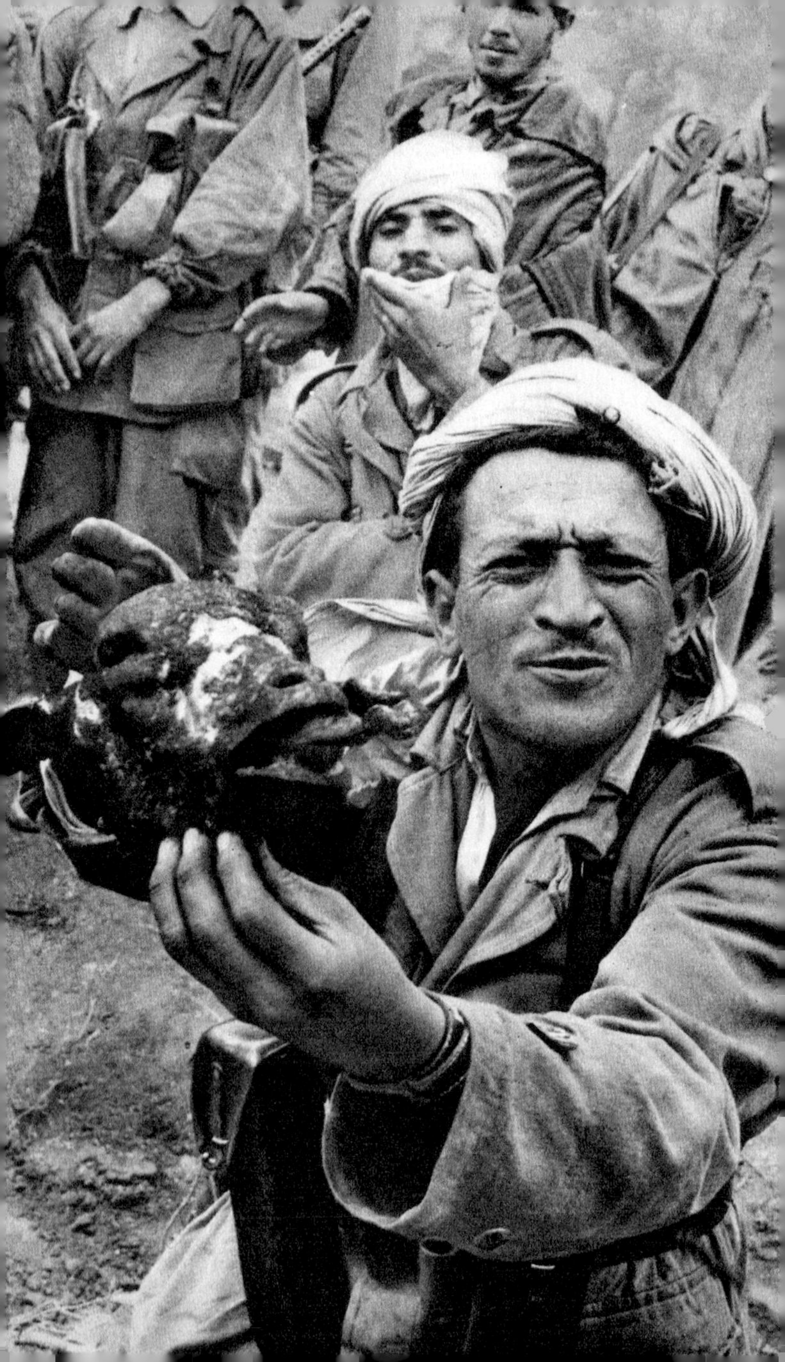

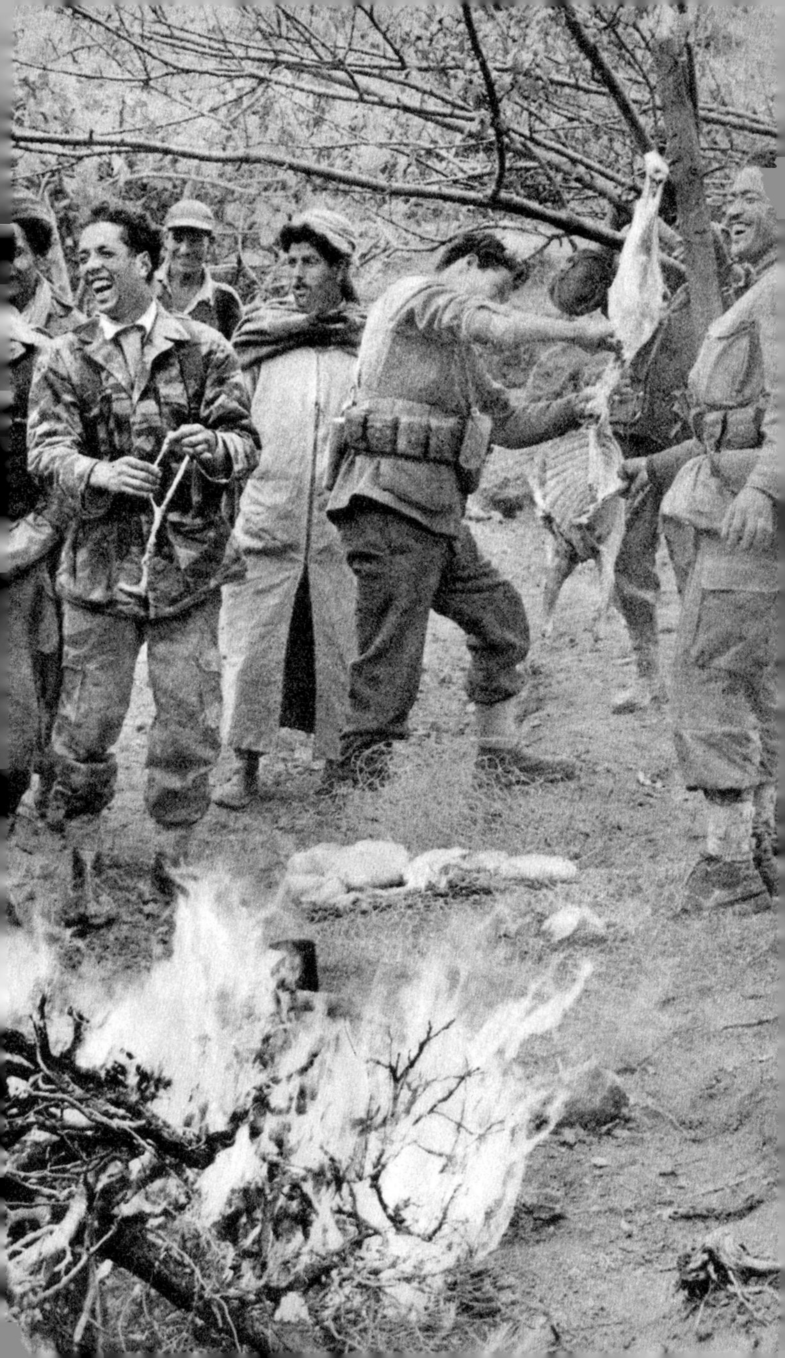

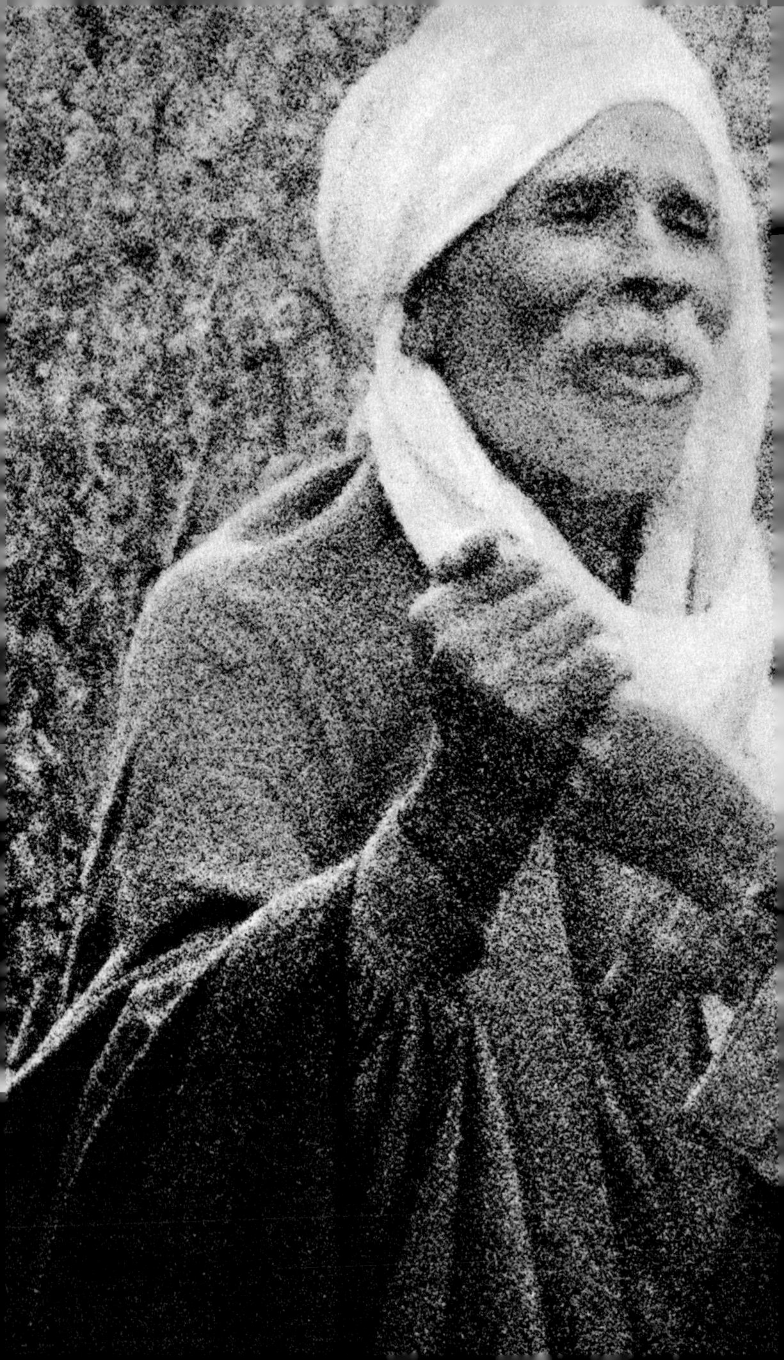

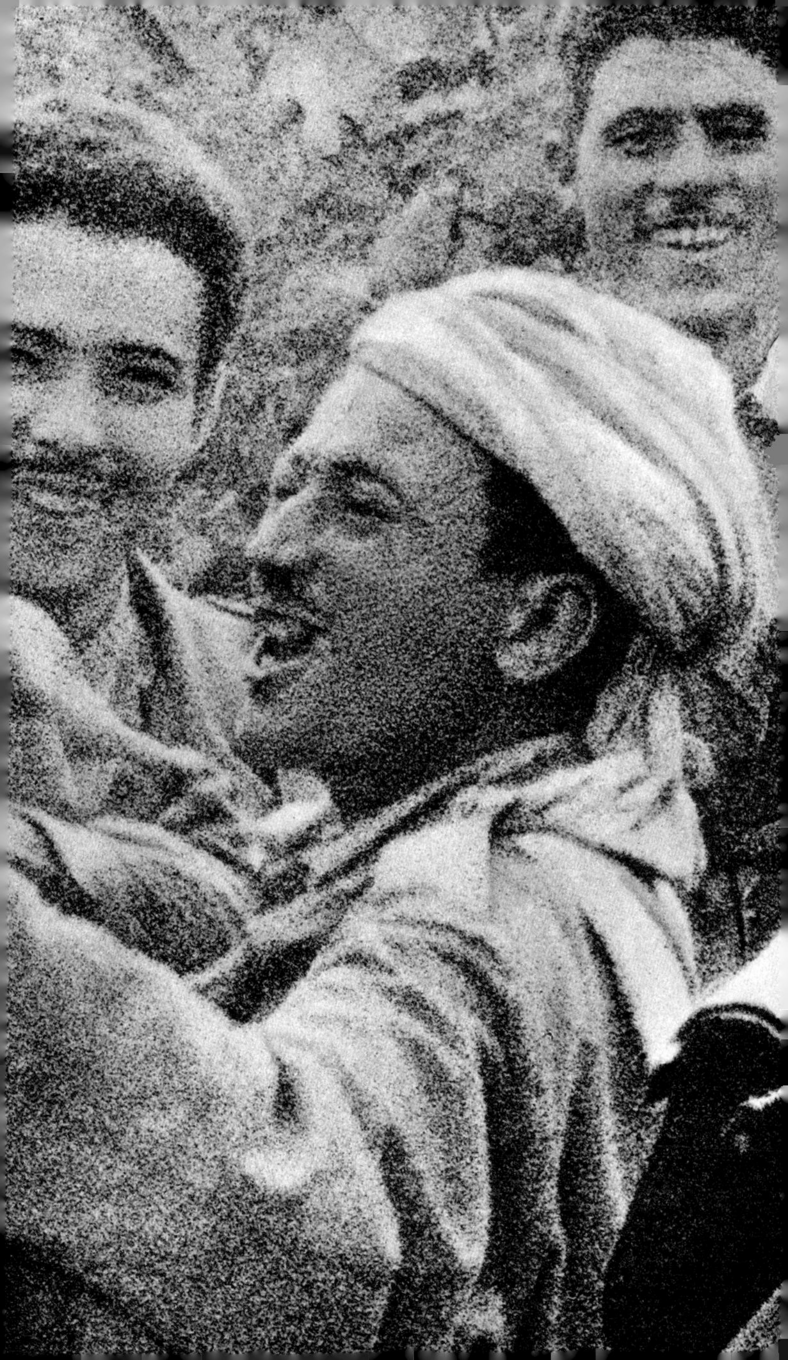

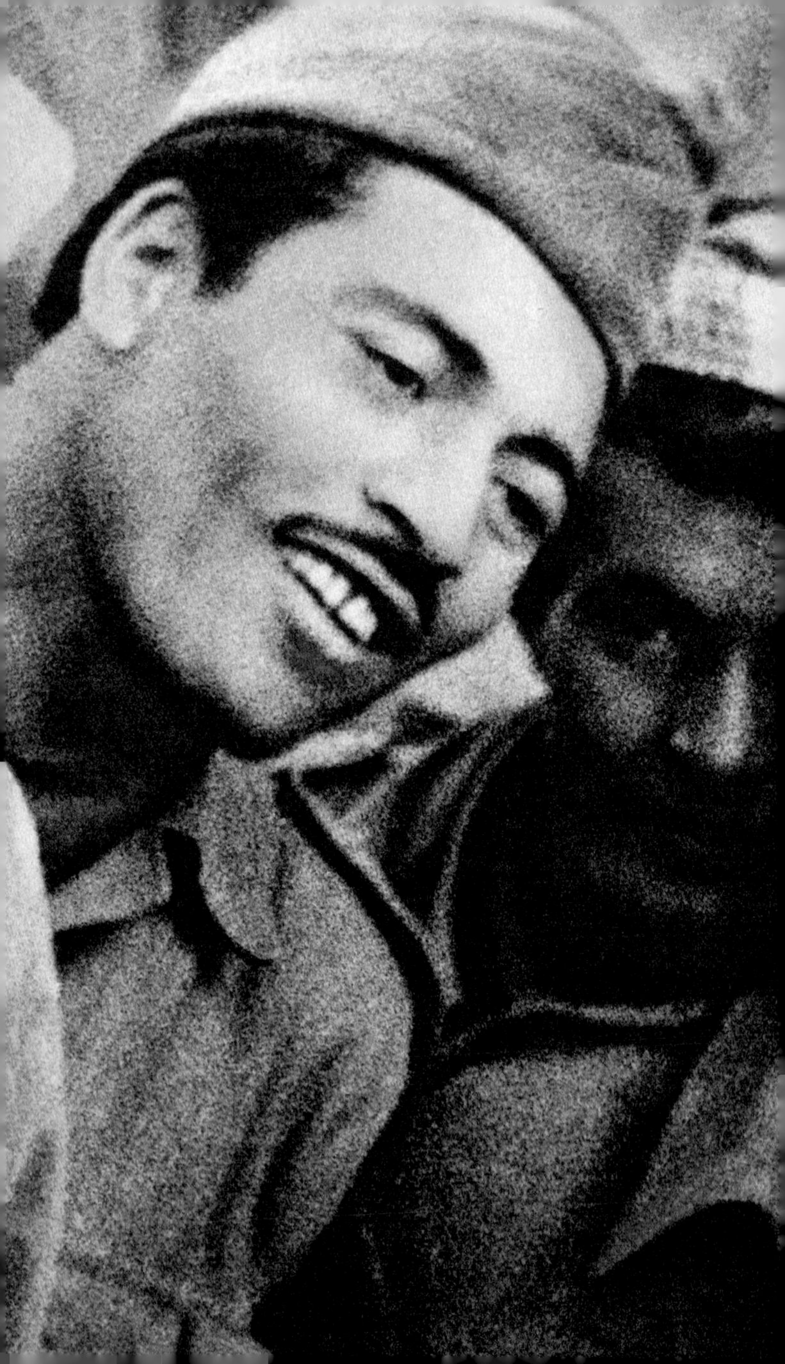

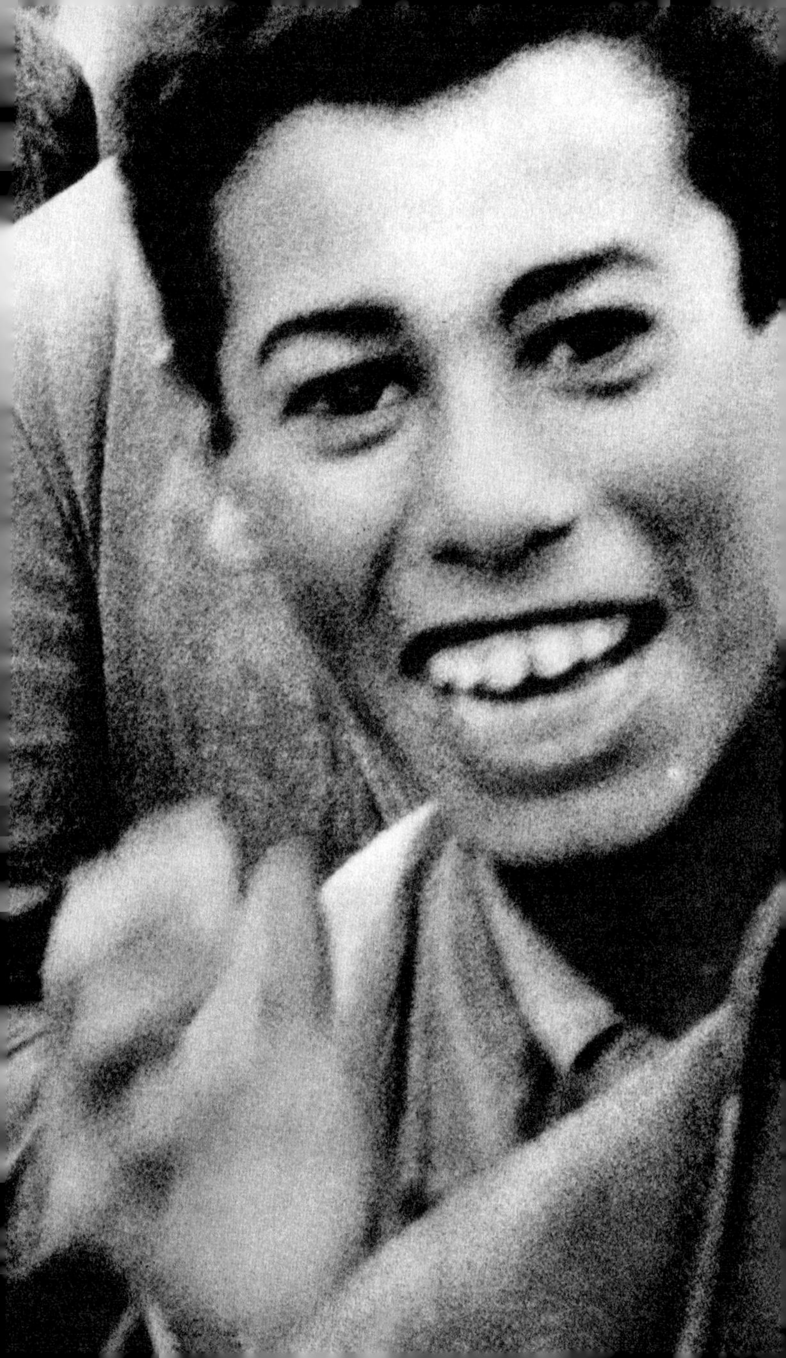

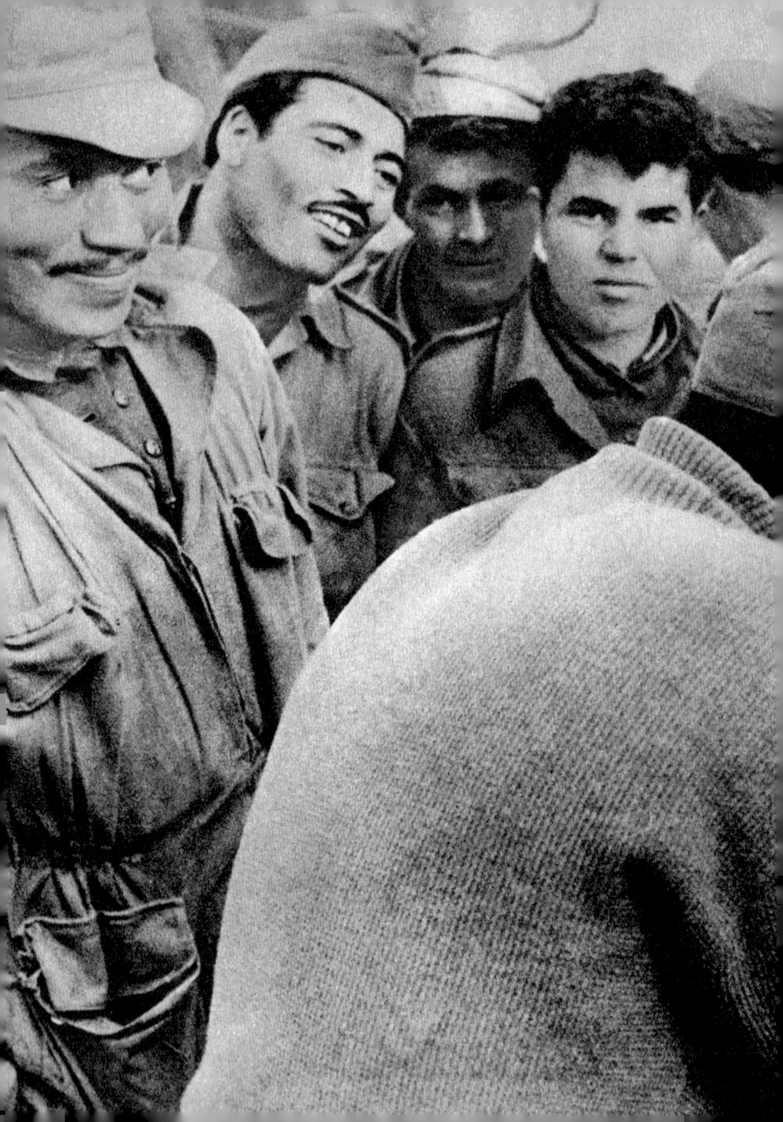

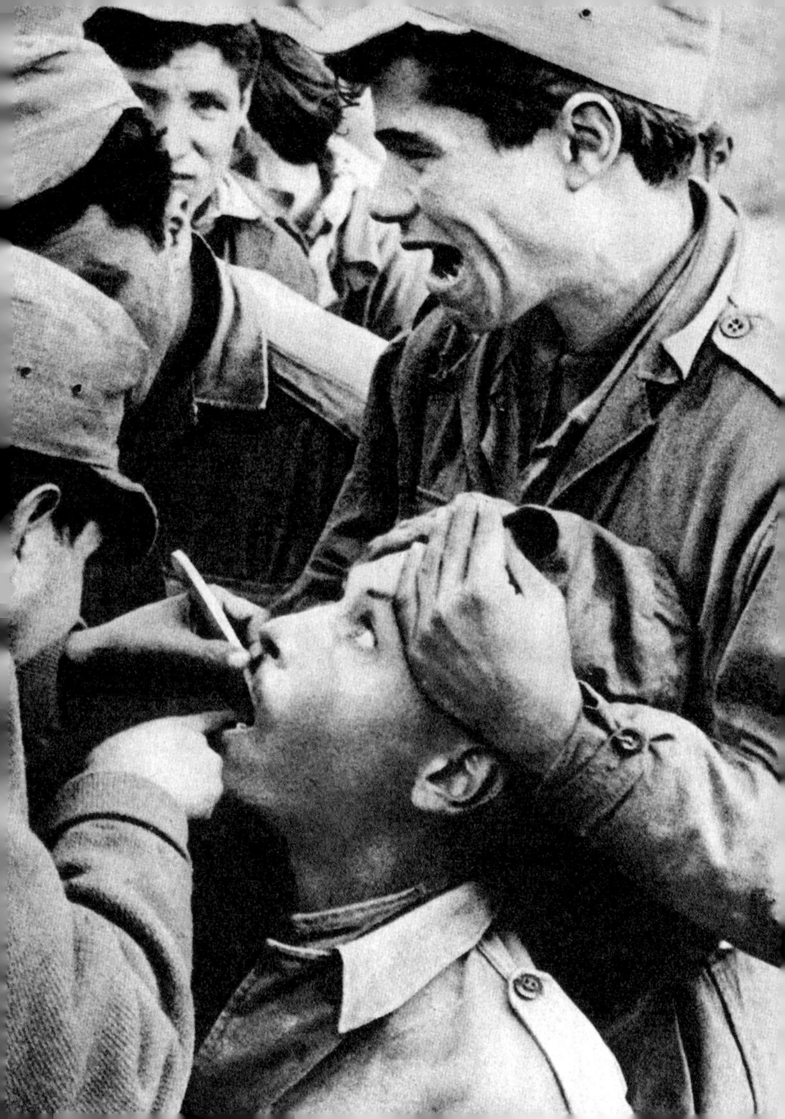

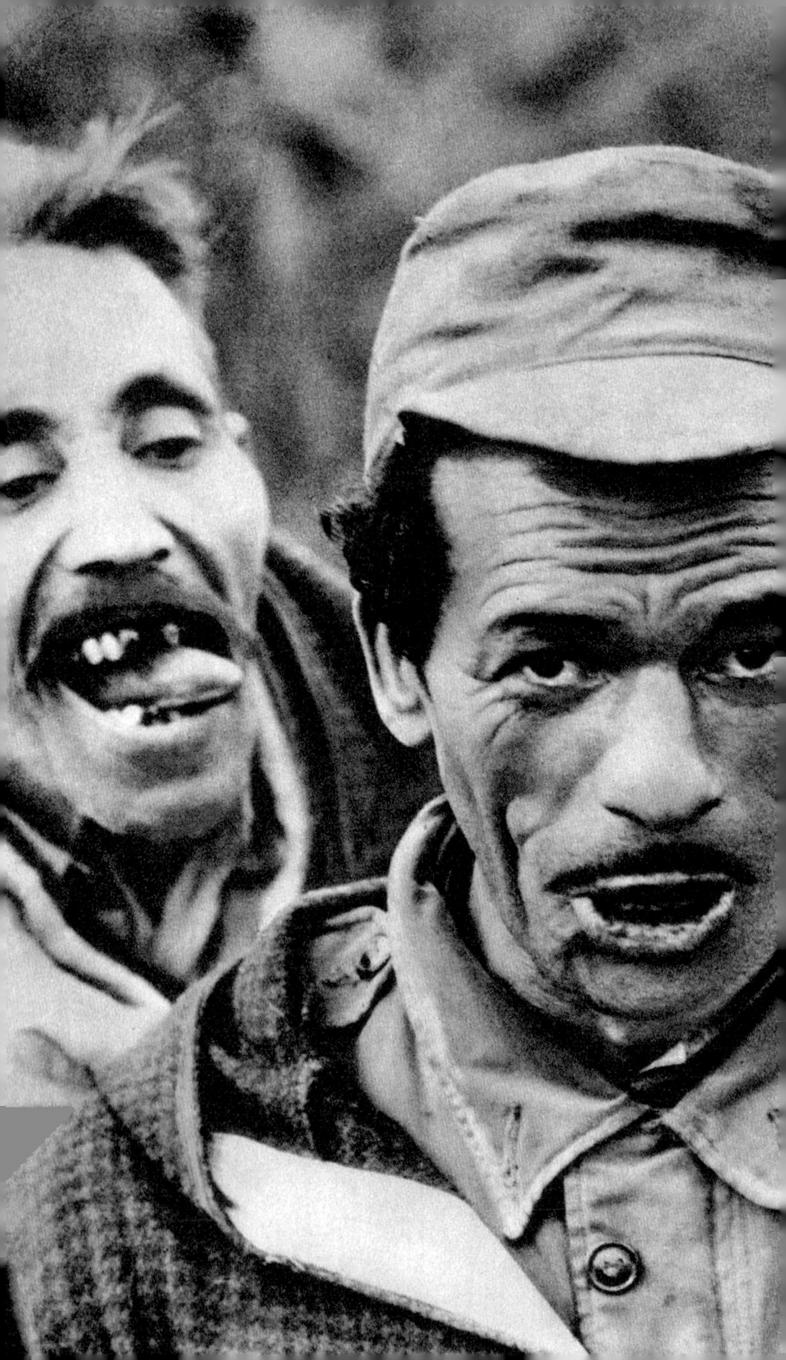

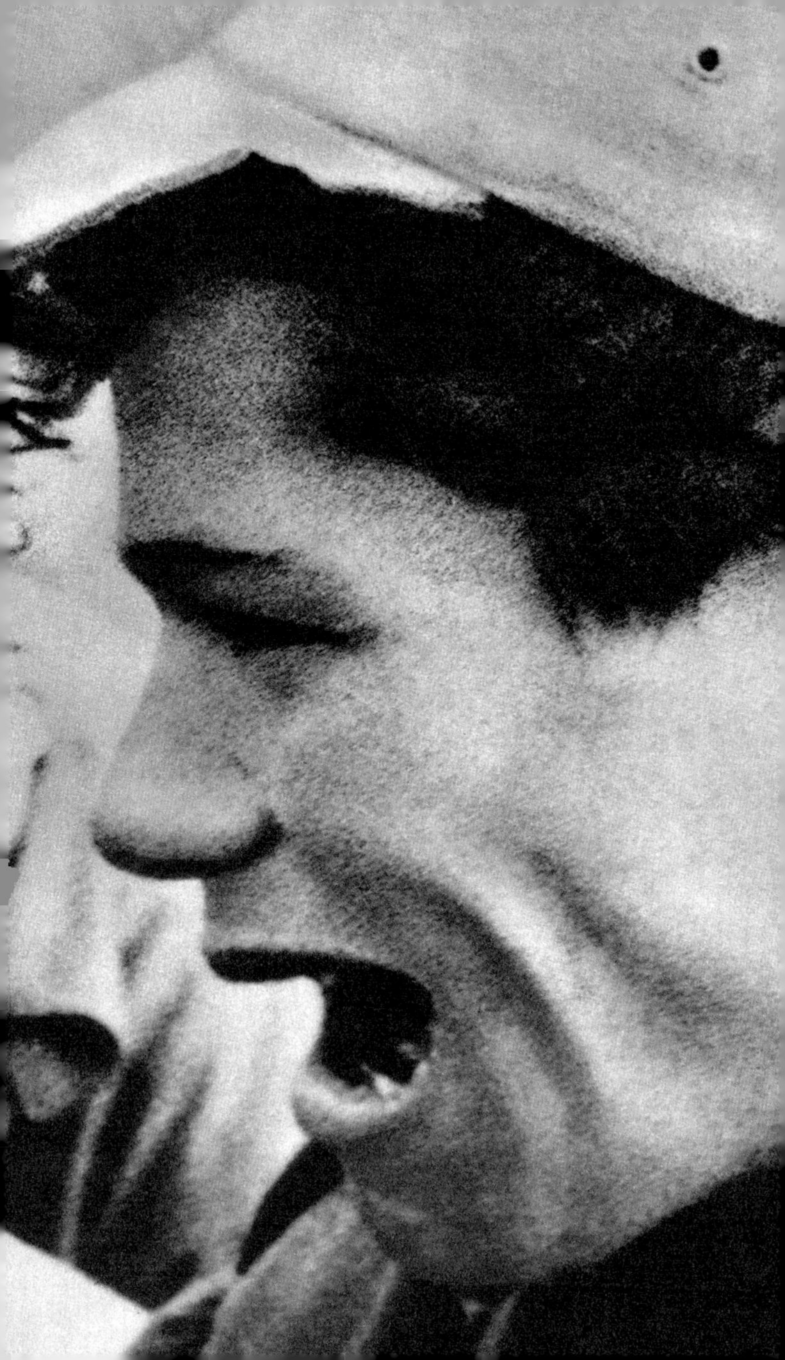

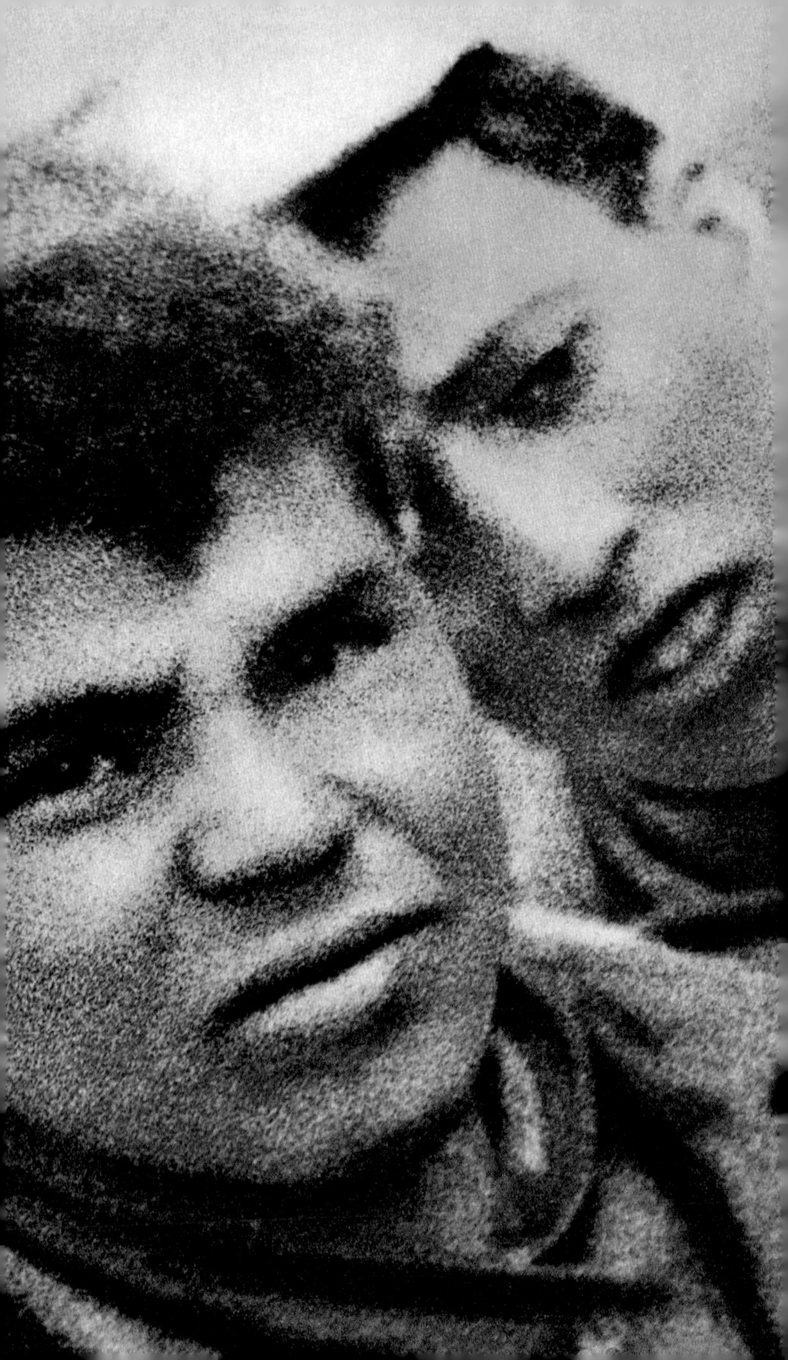

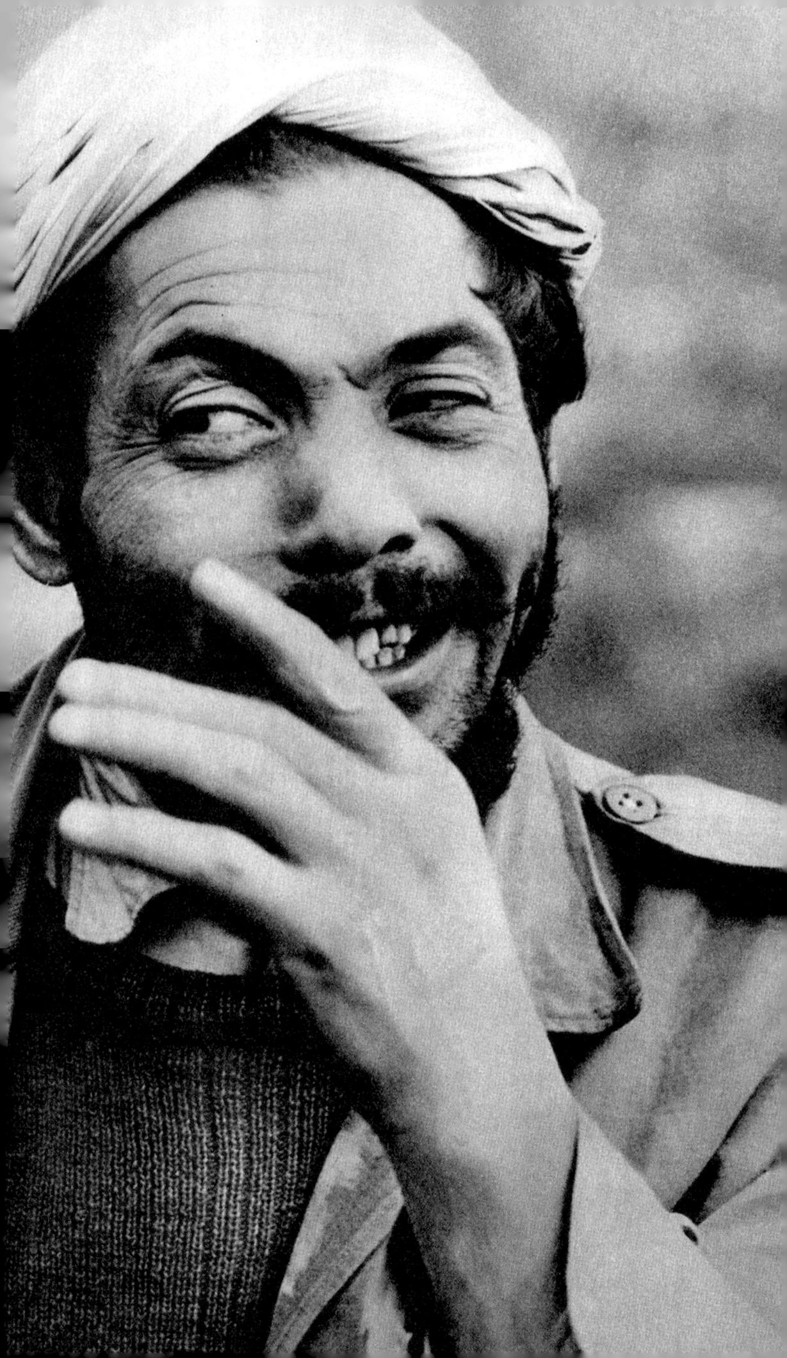

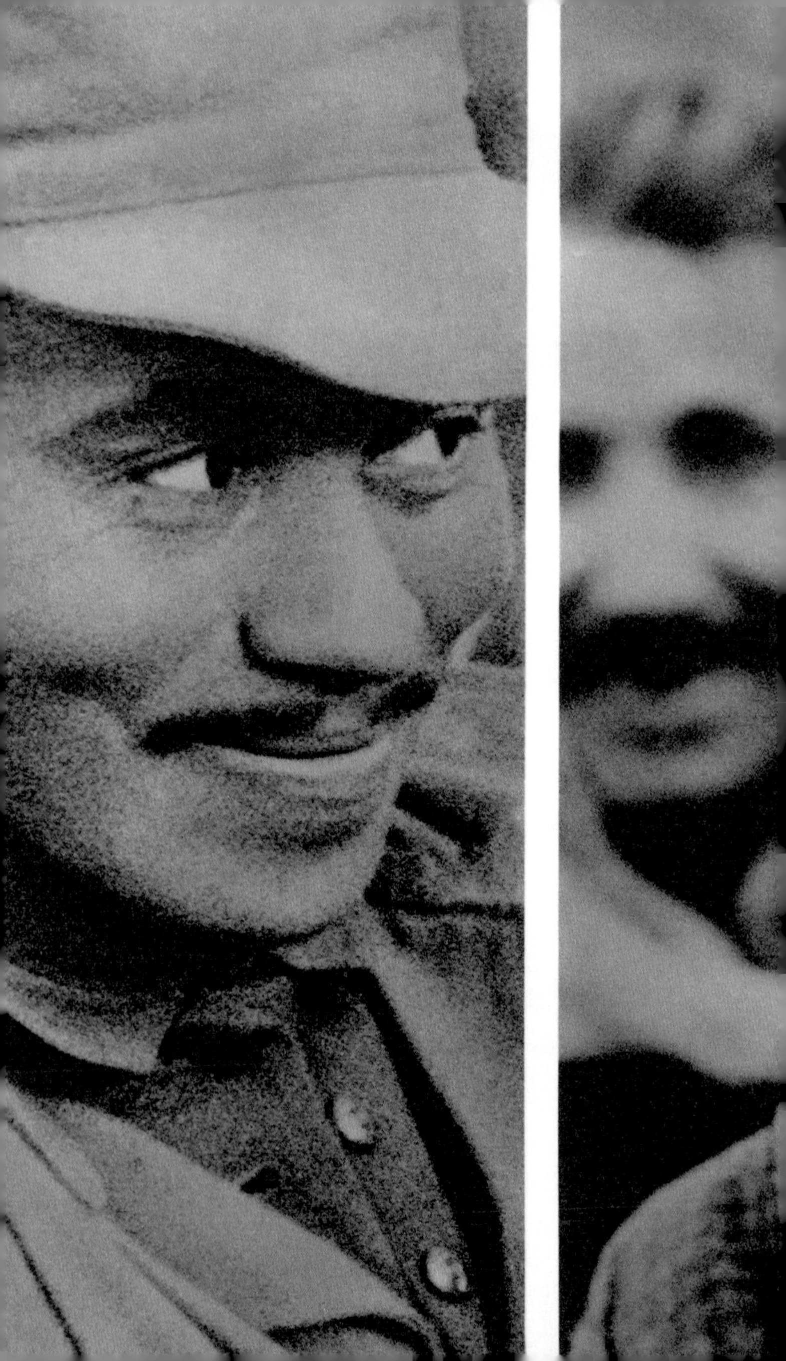

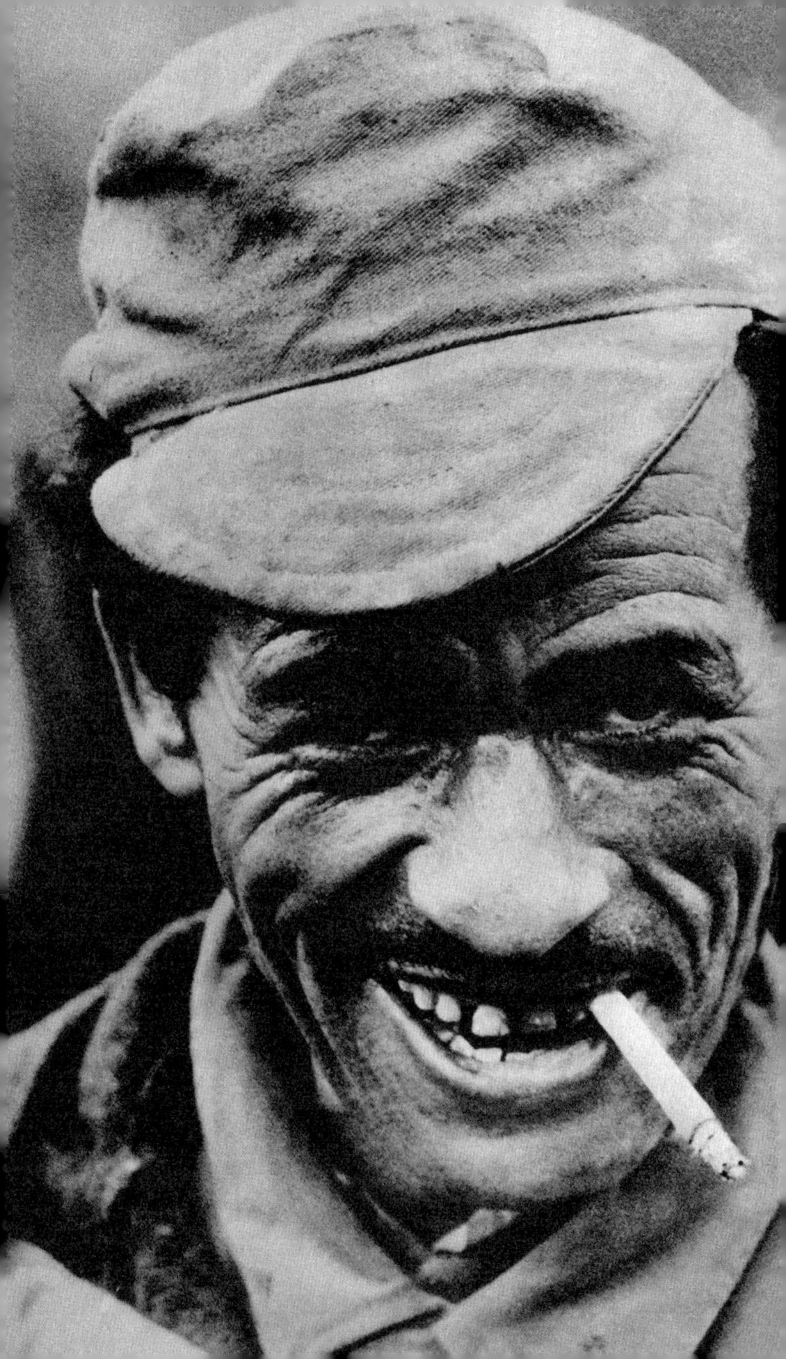

6.

" … **by the people and for the people."**

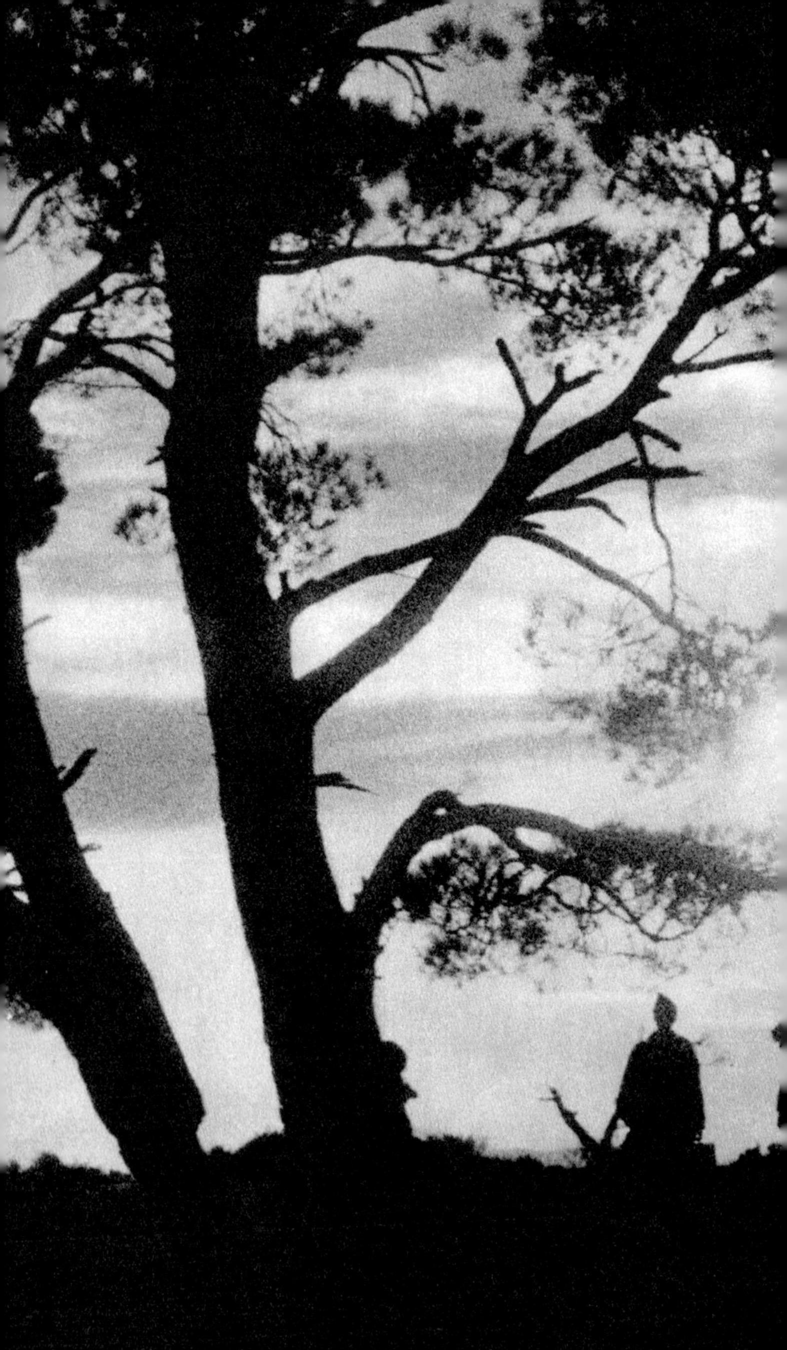

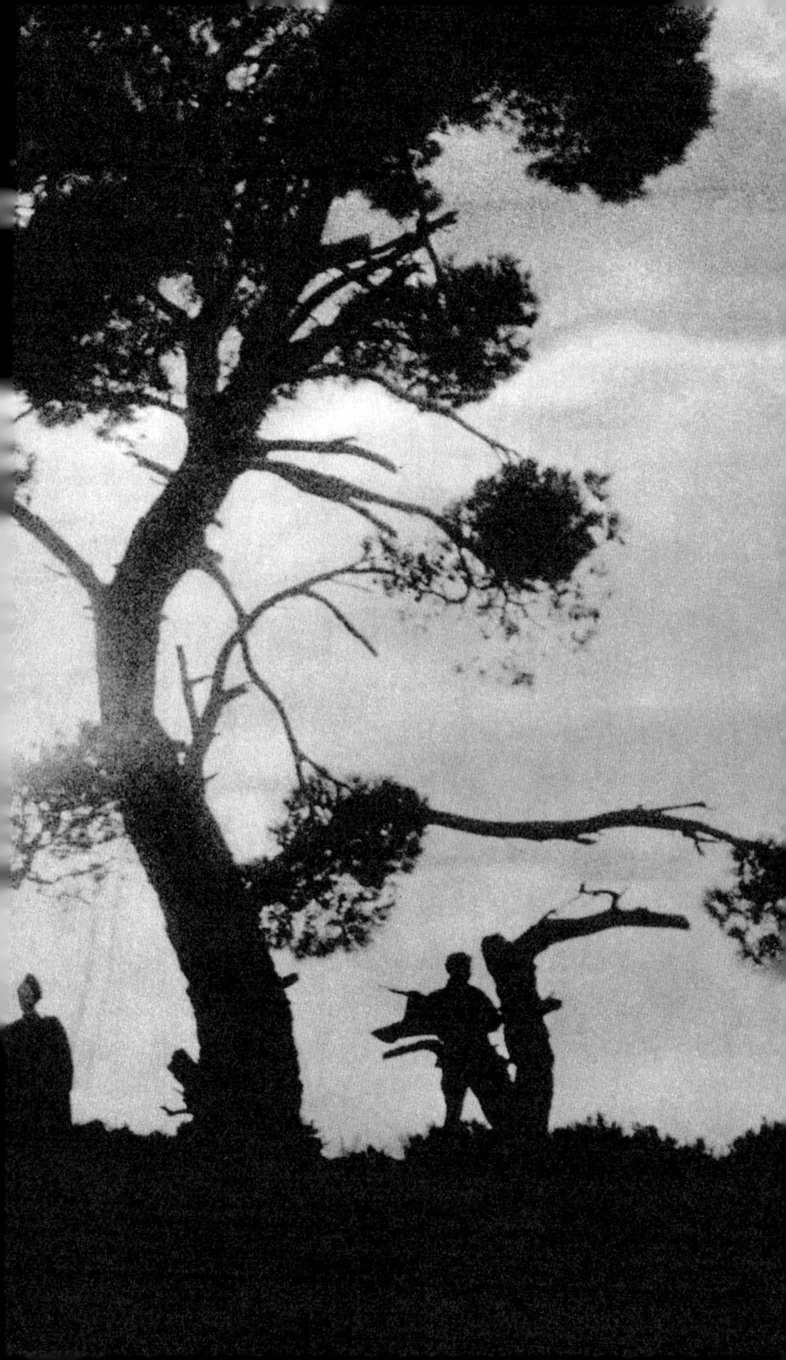

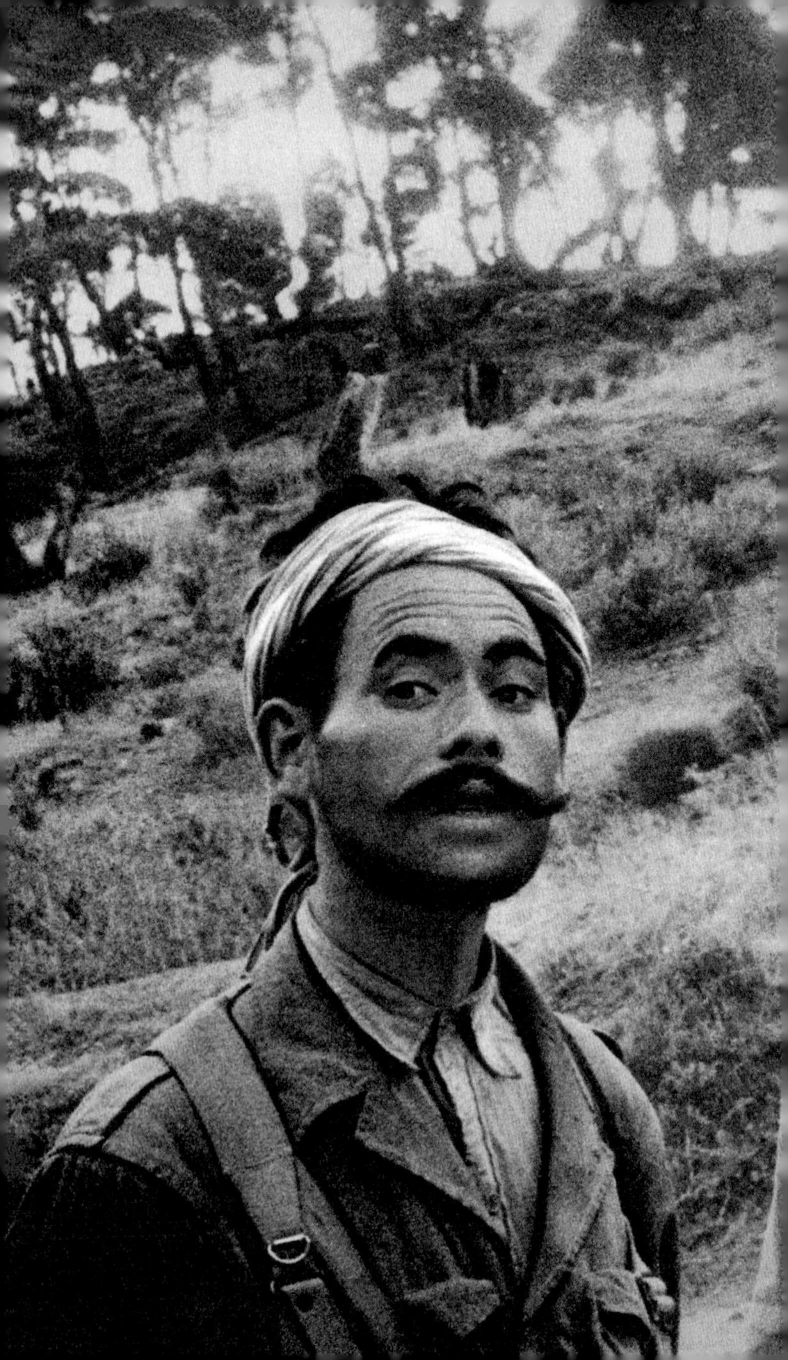

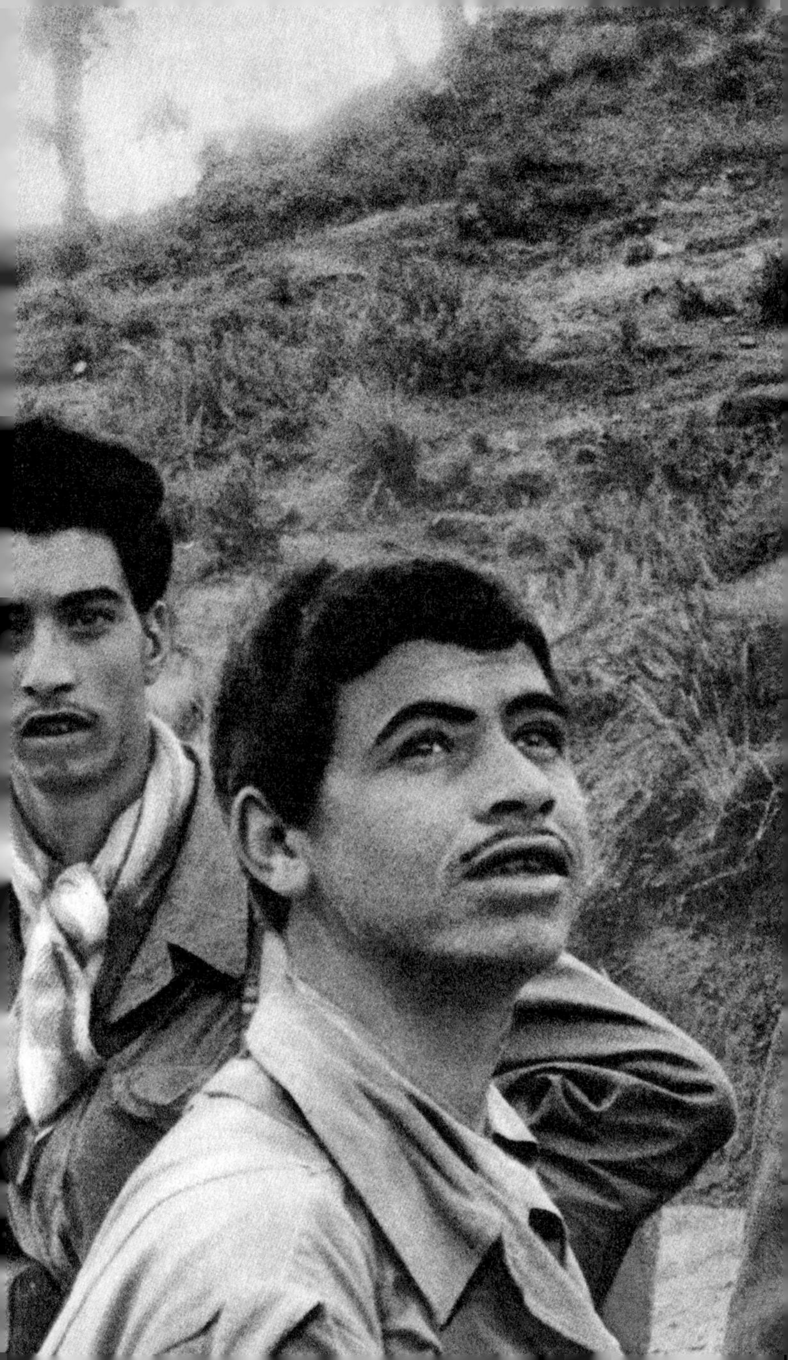

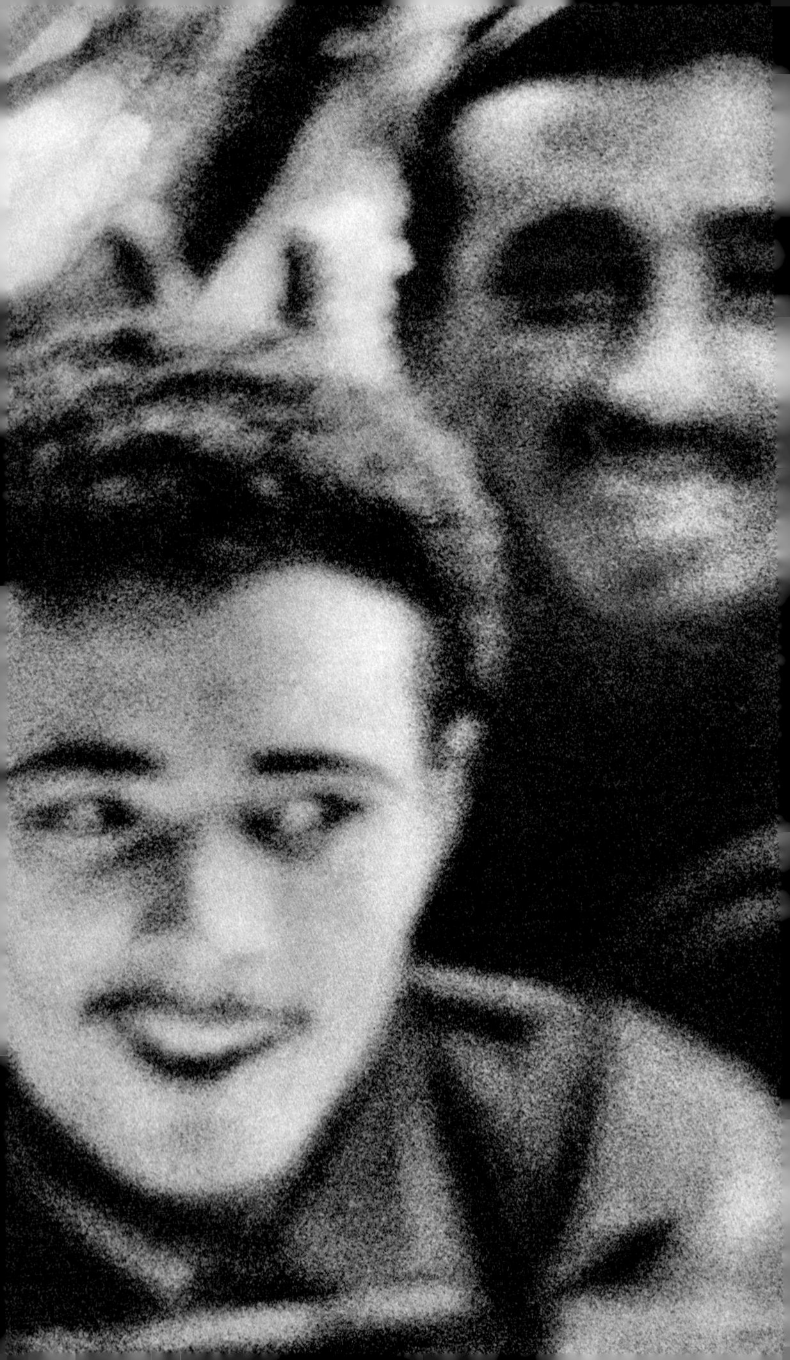

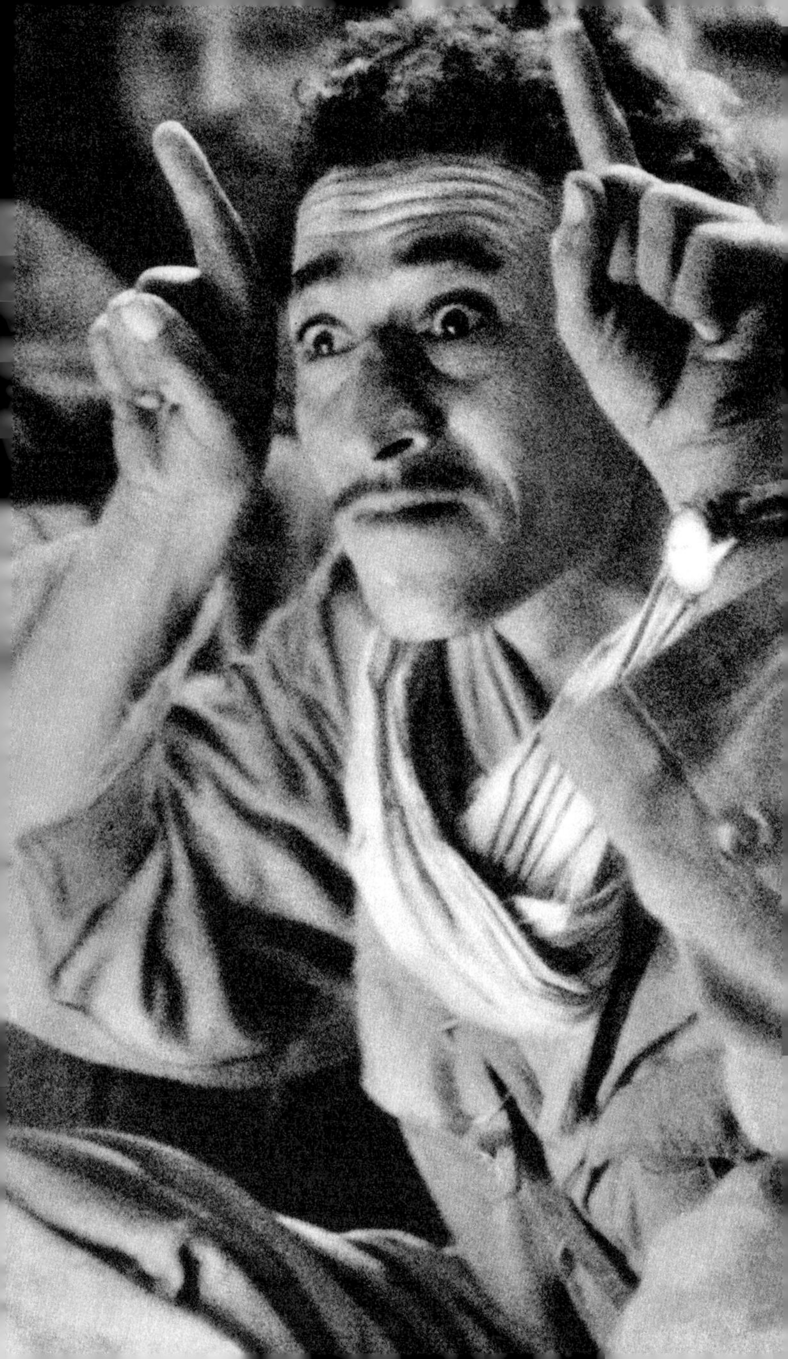

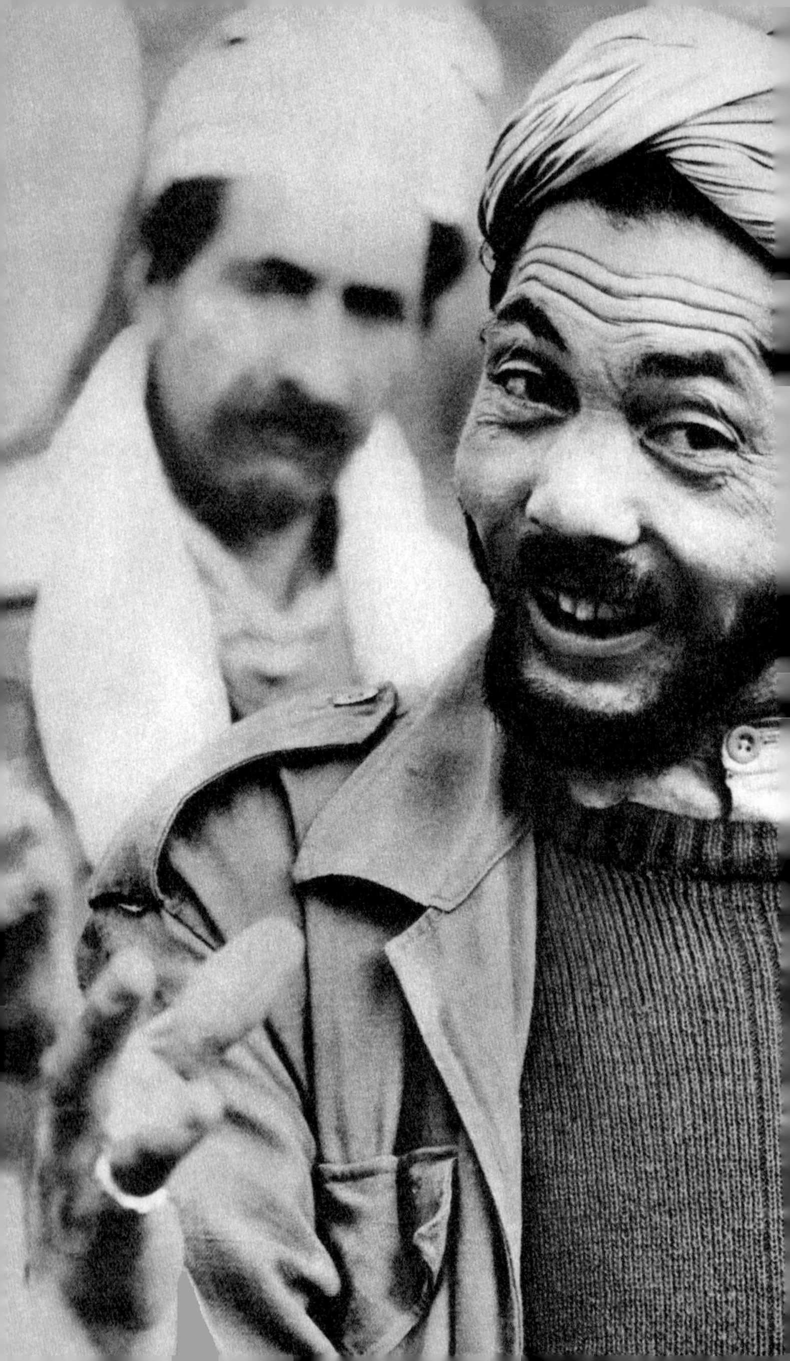

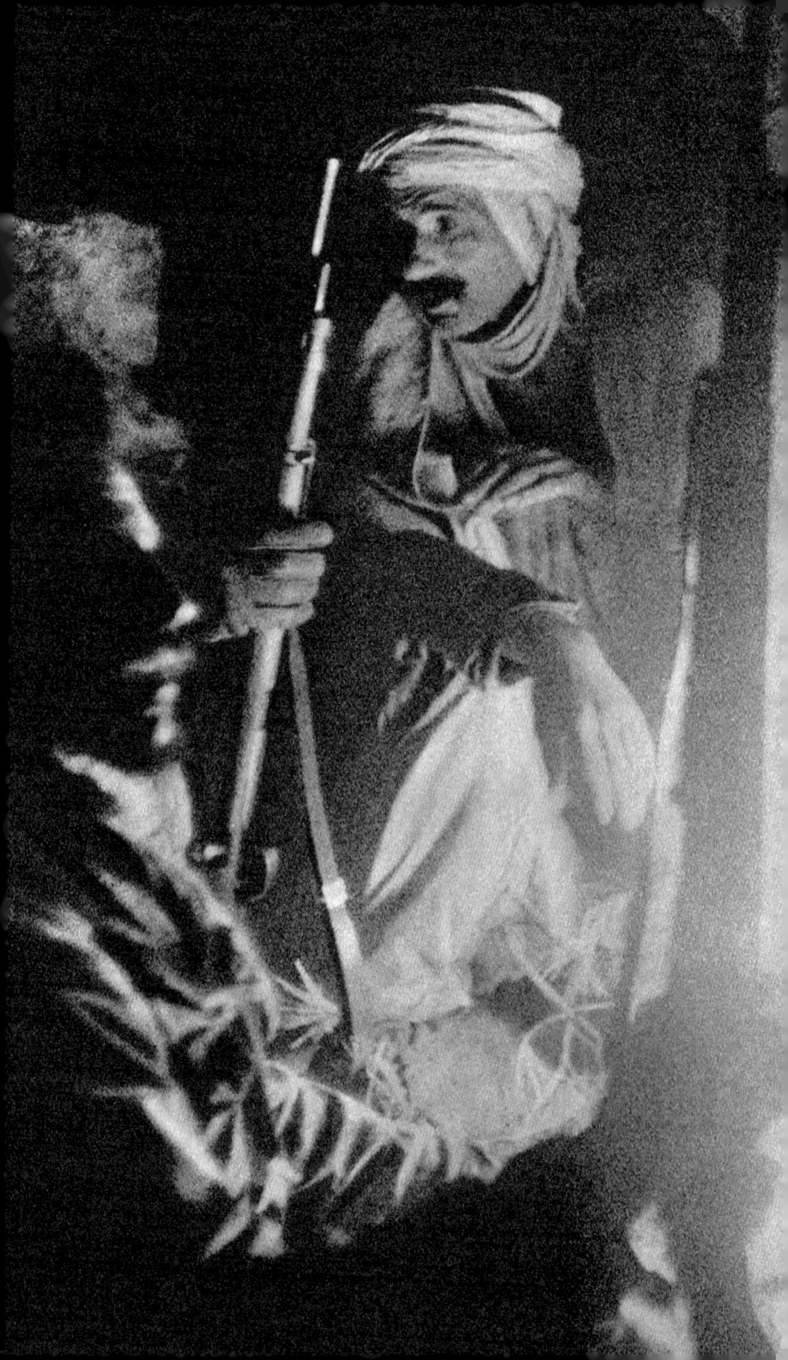

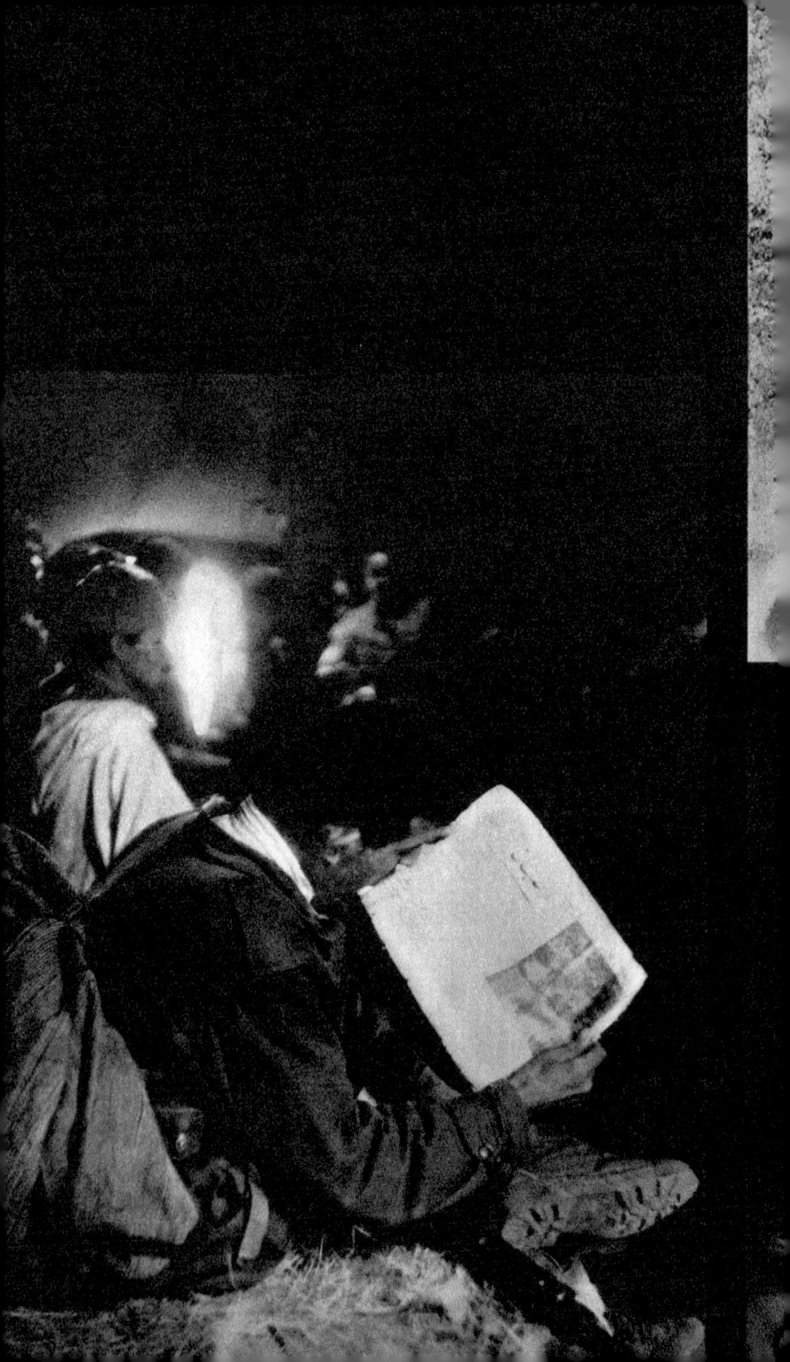

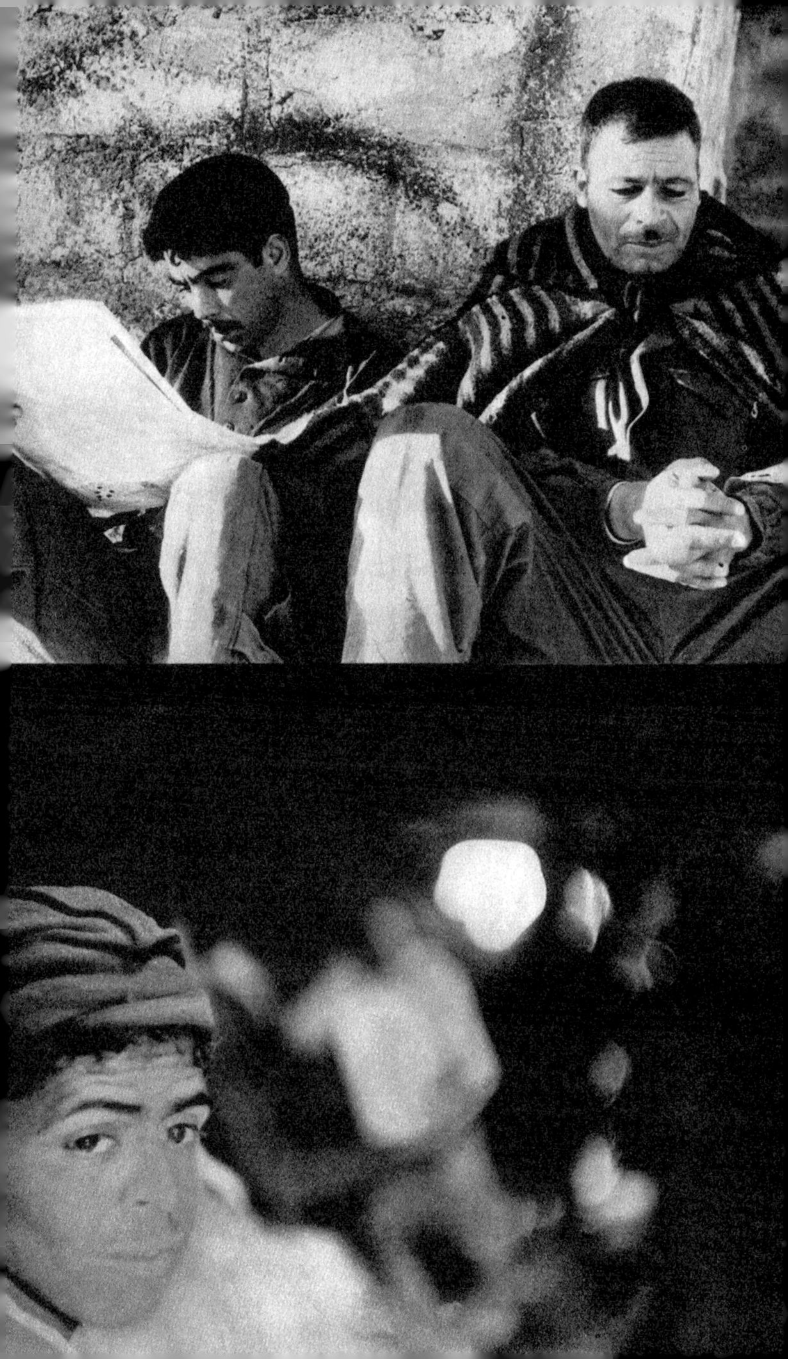

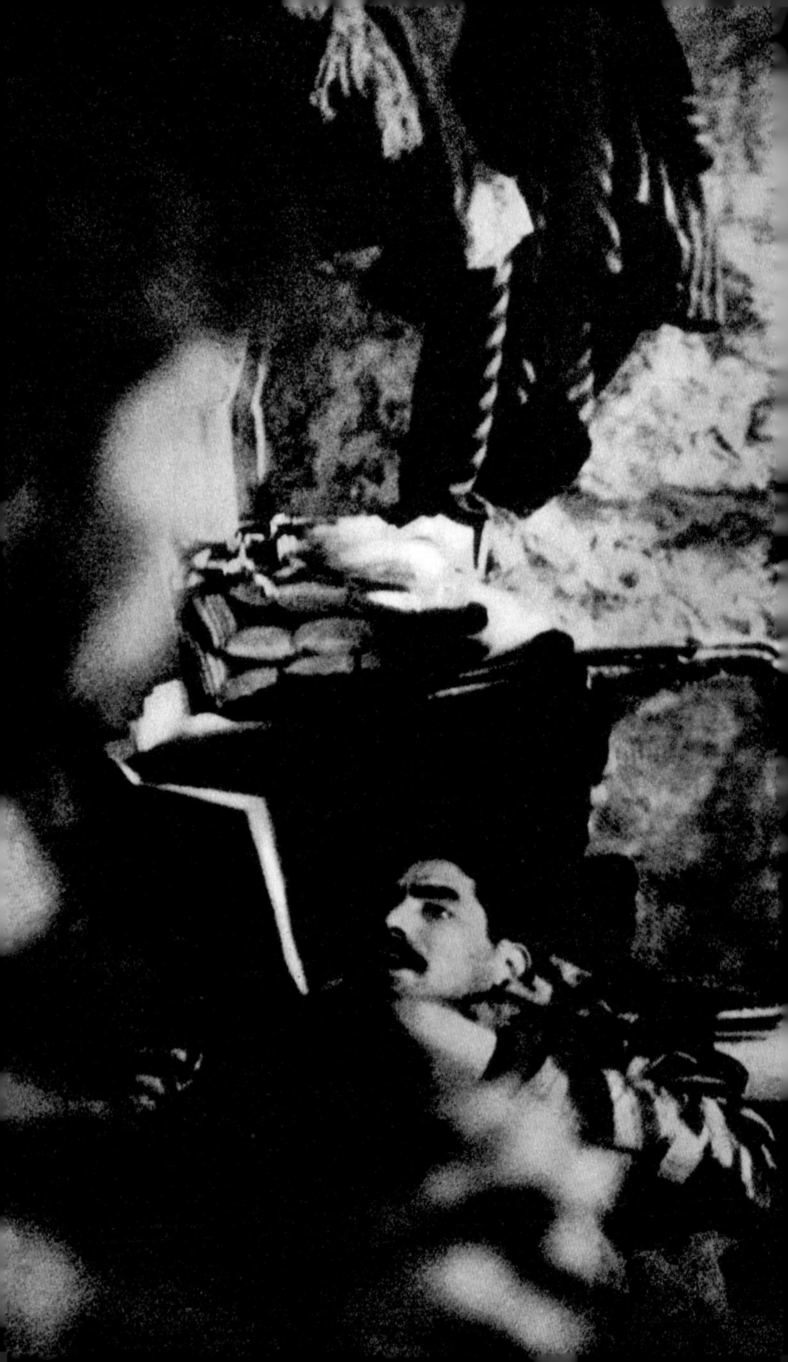

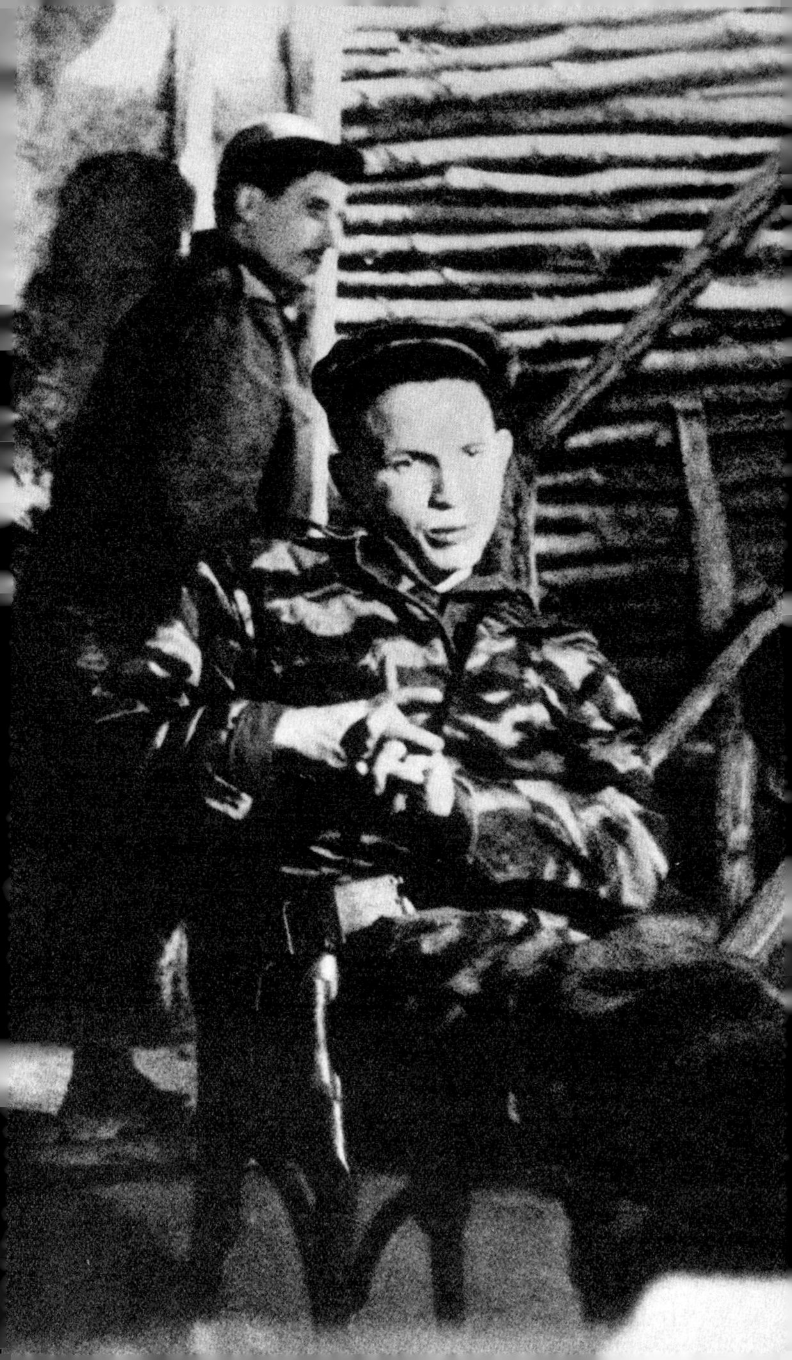

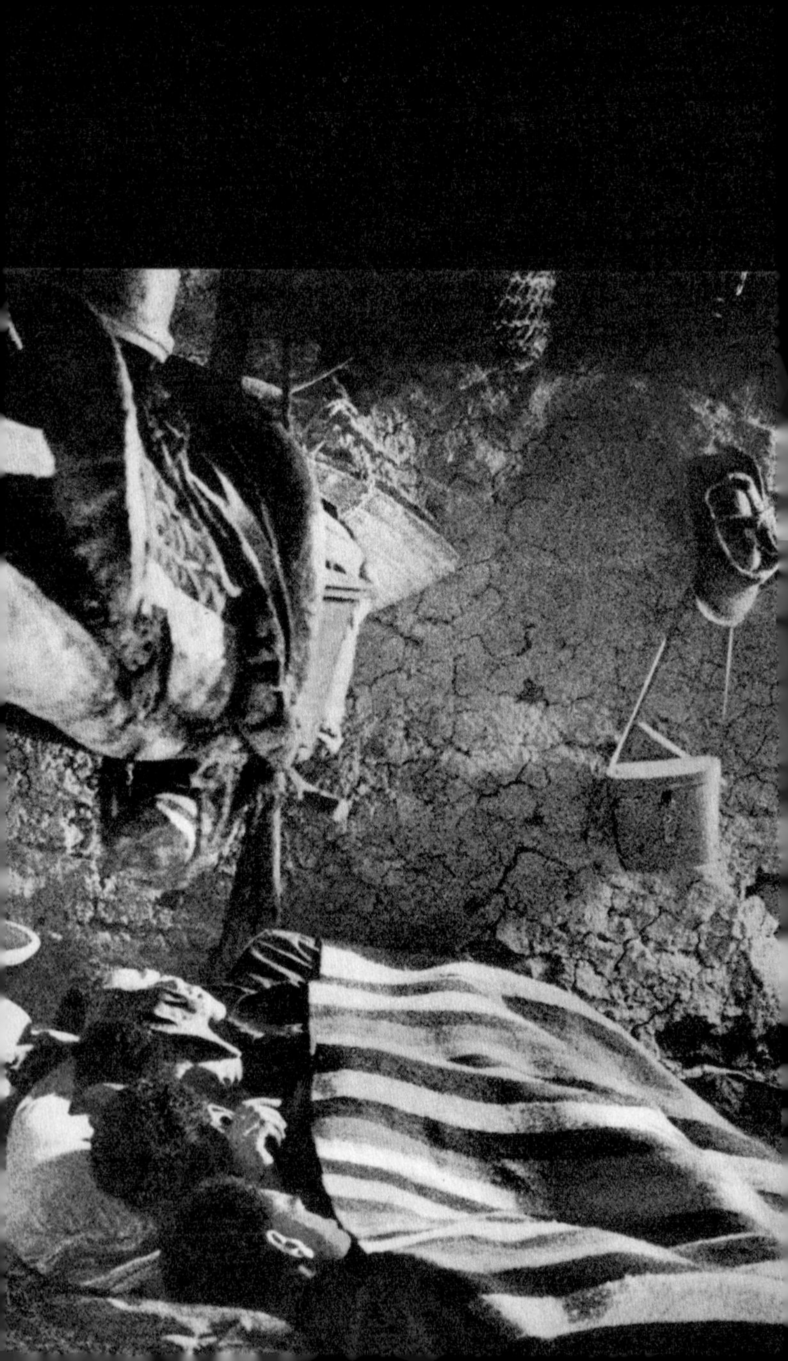

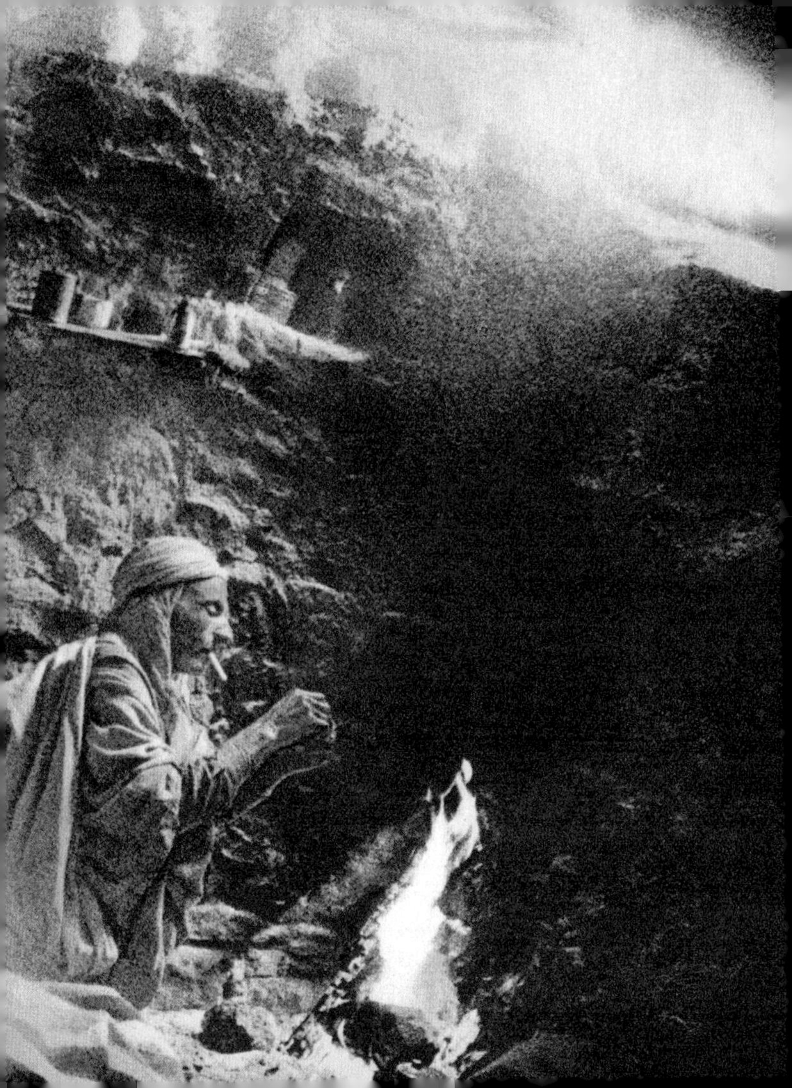

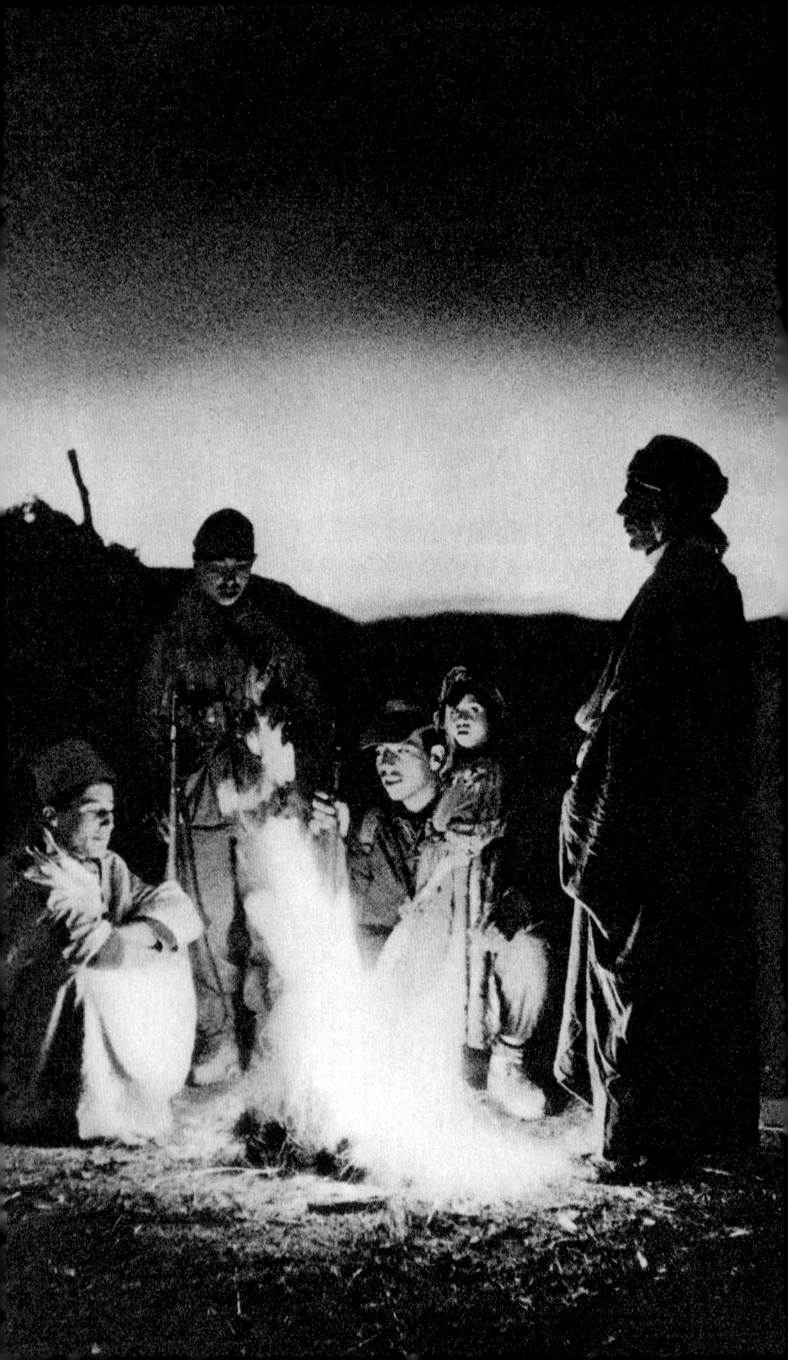

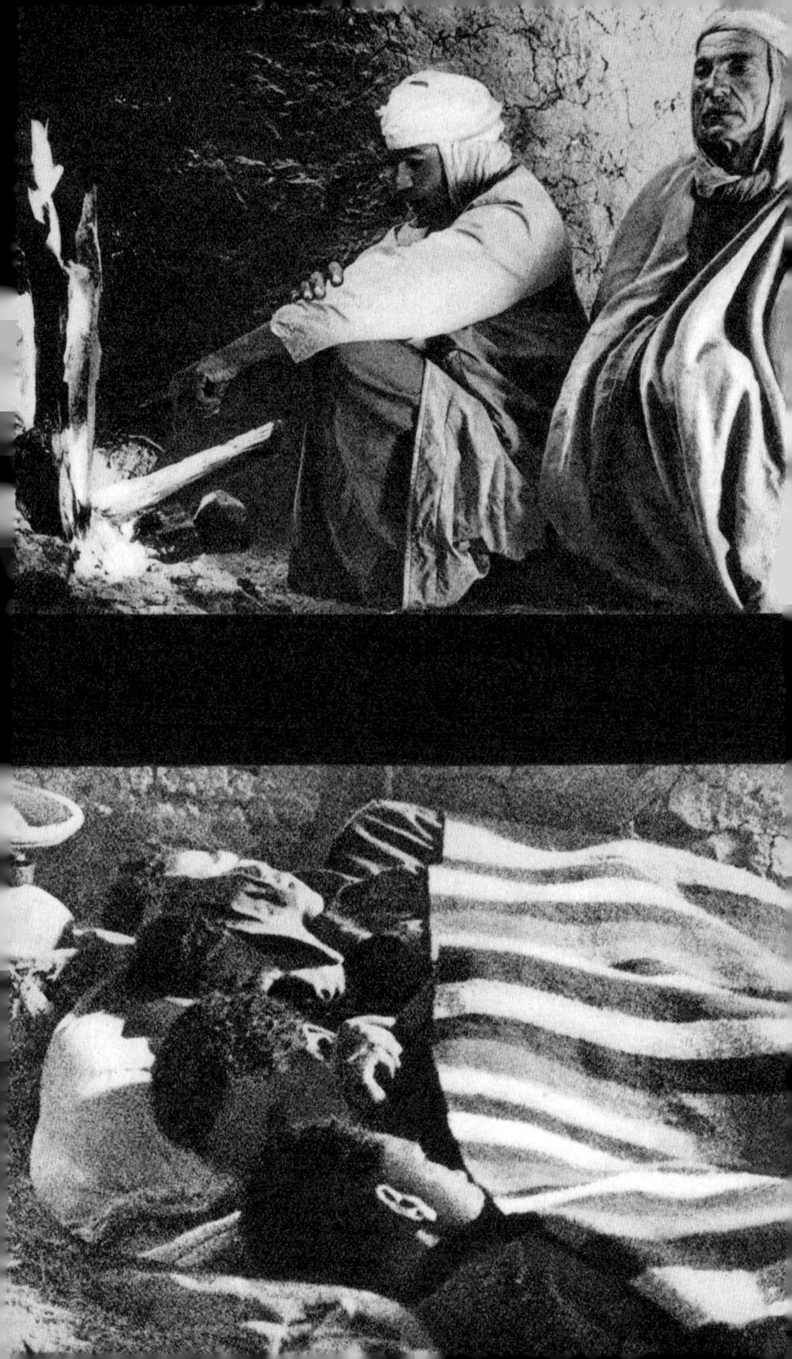

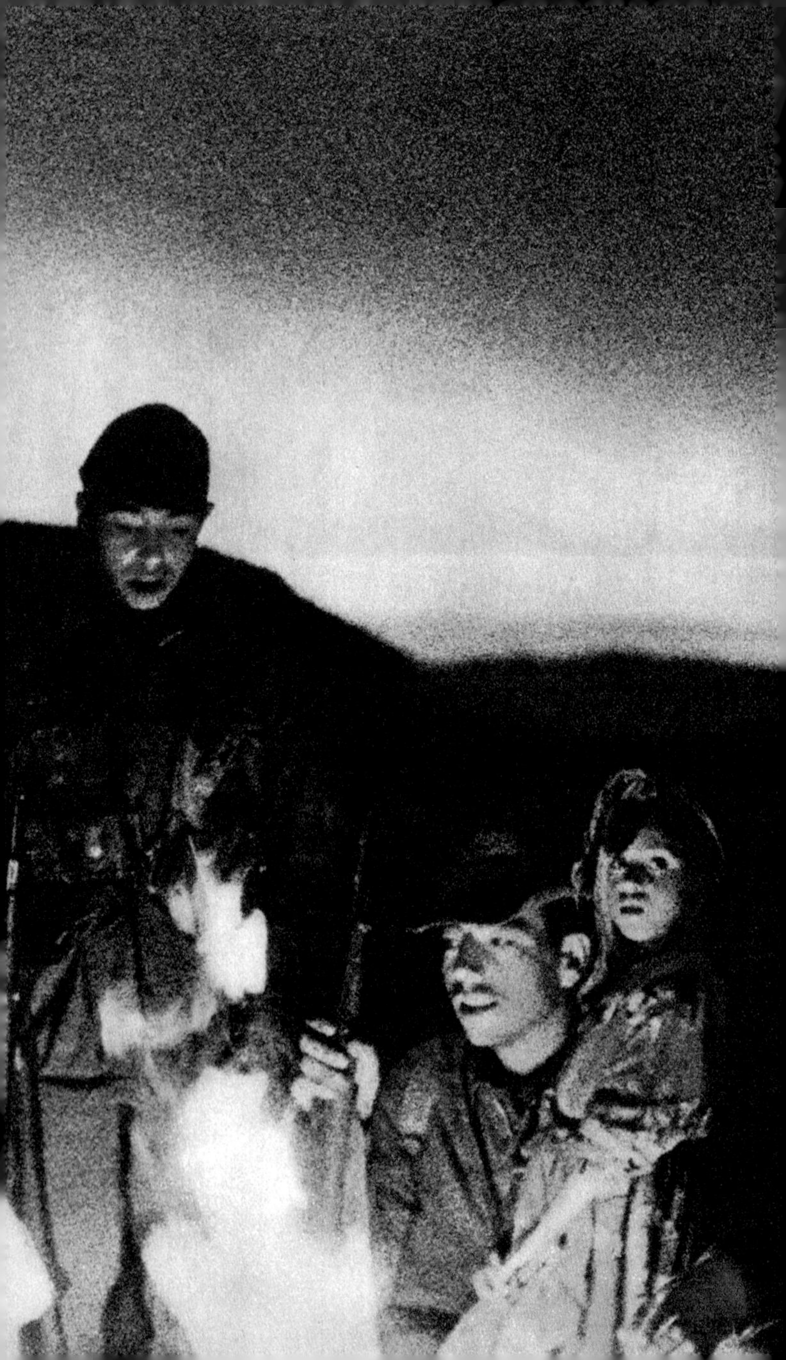

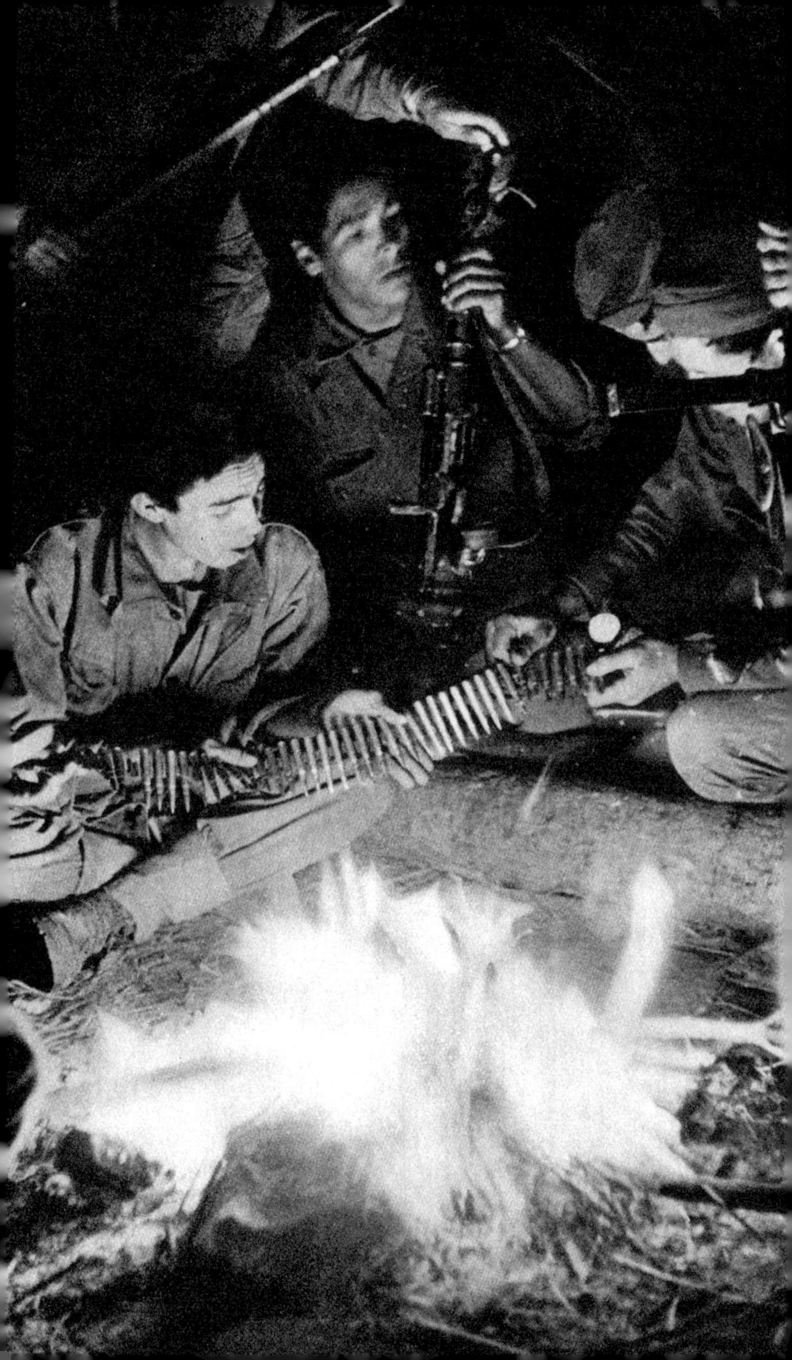

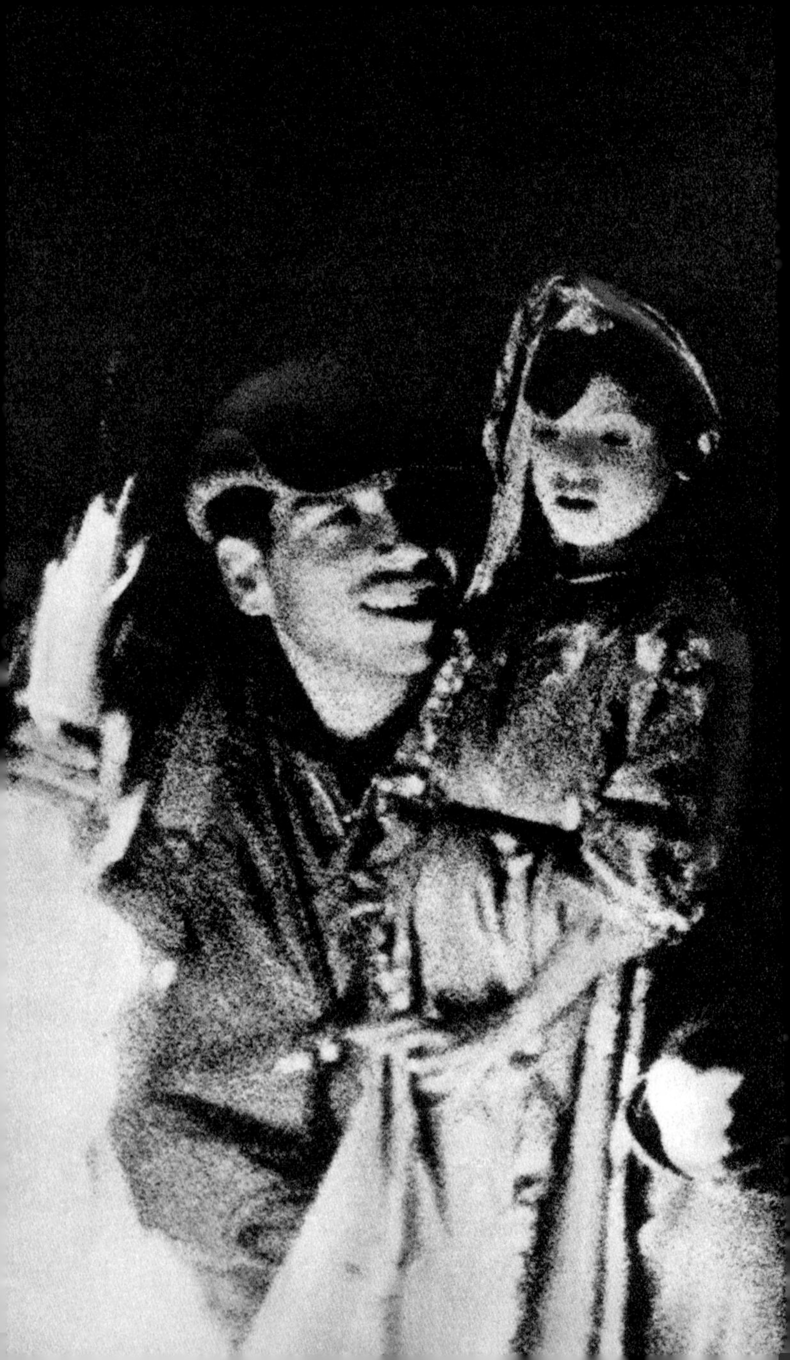

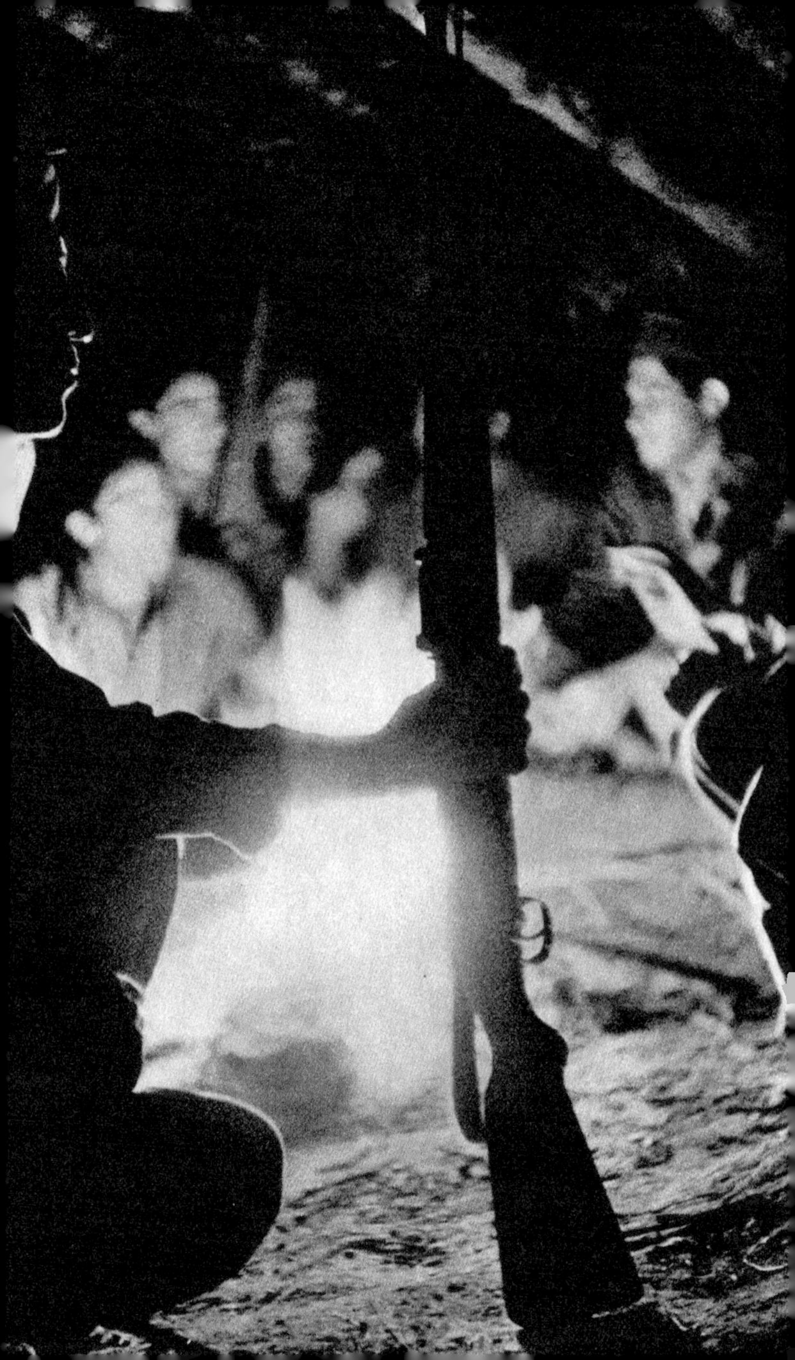

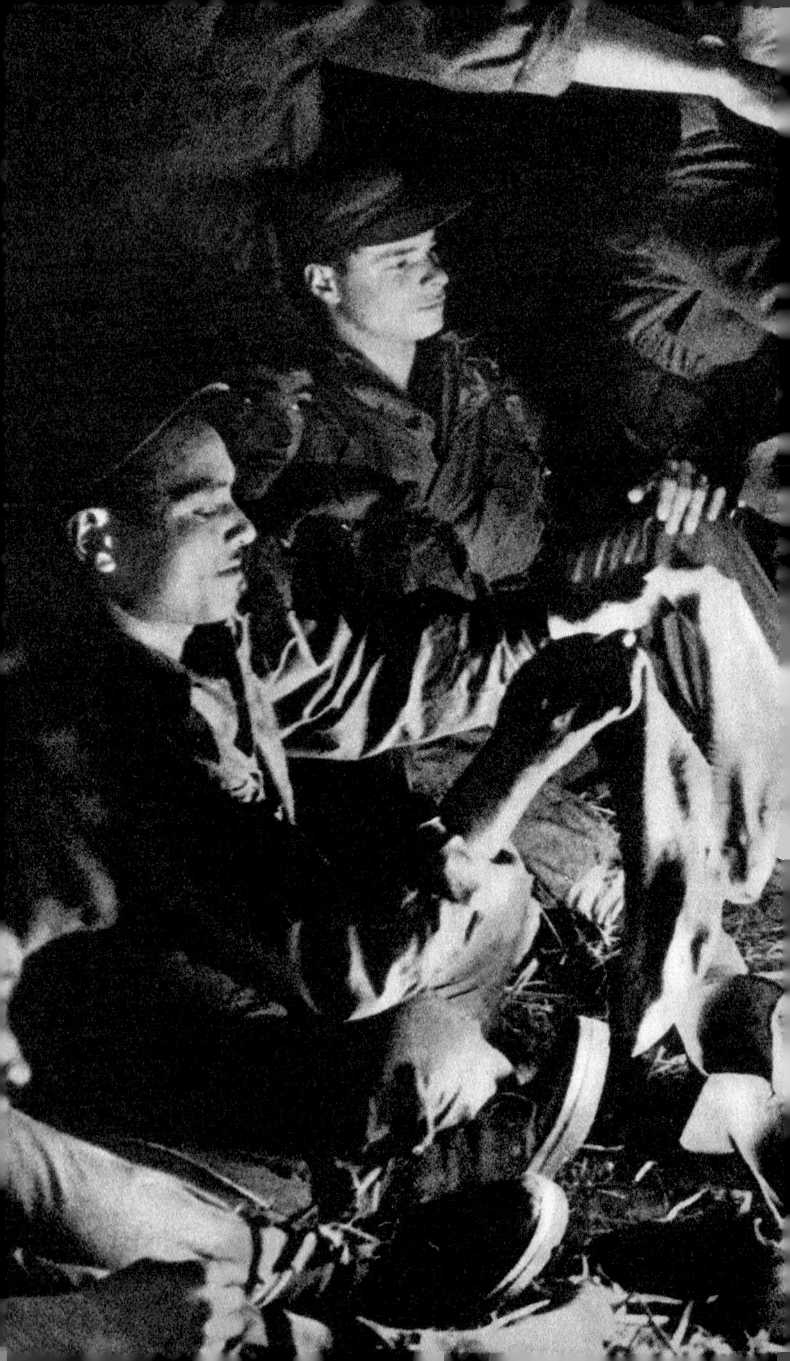

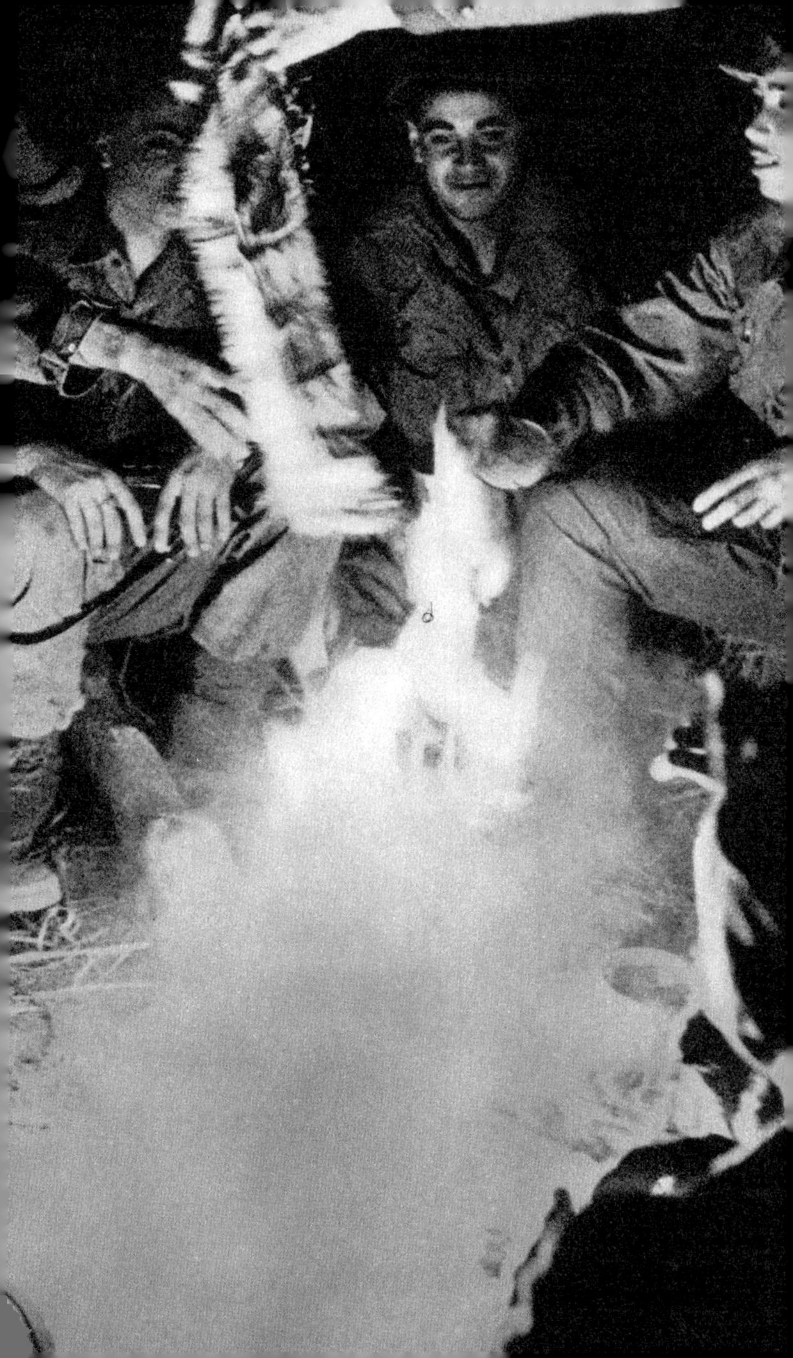

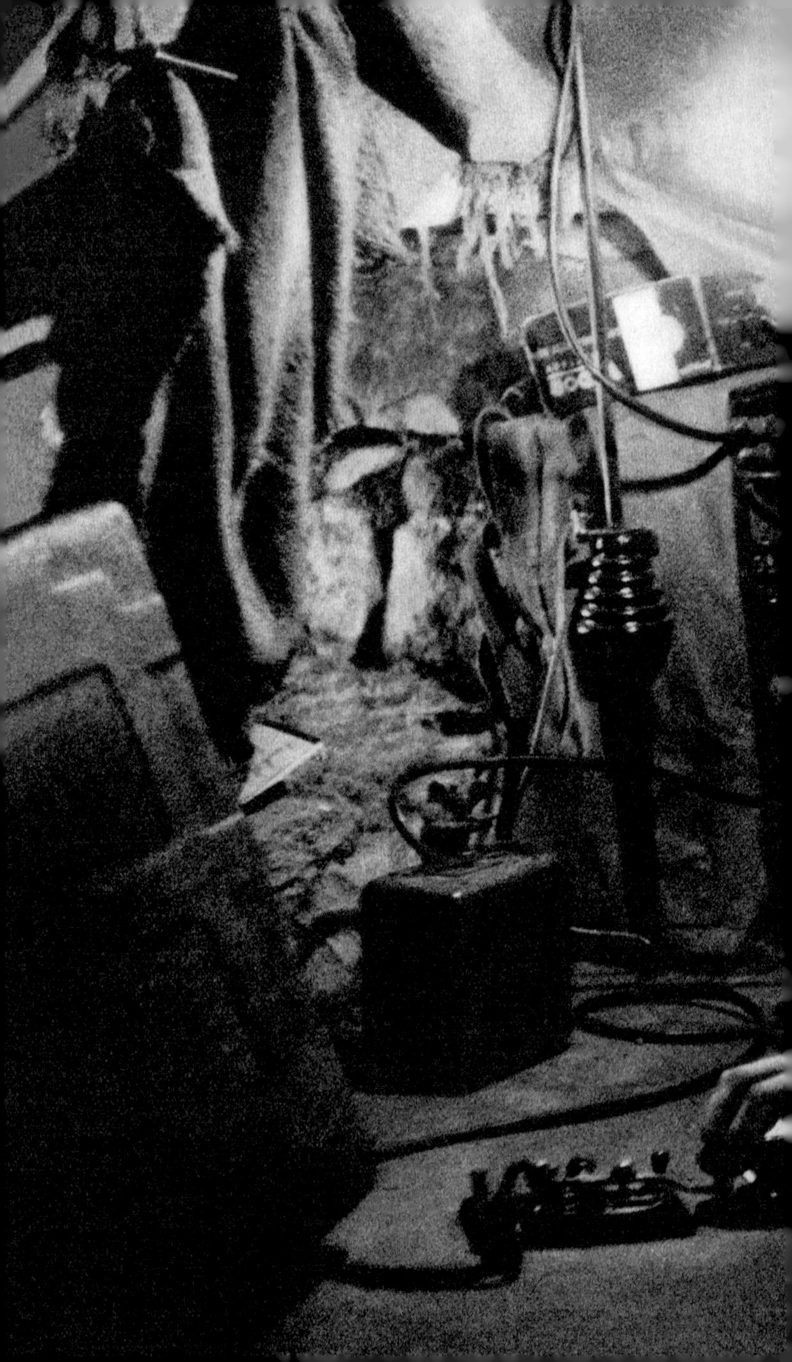

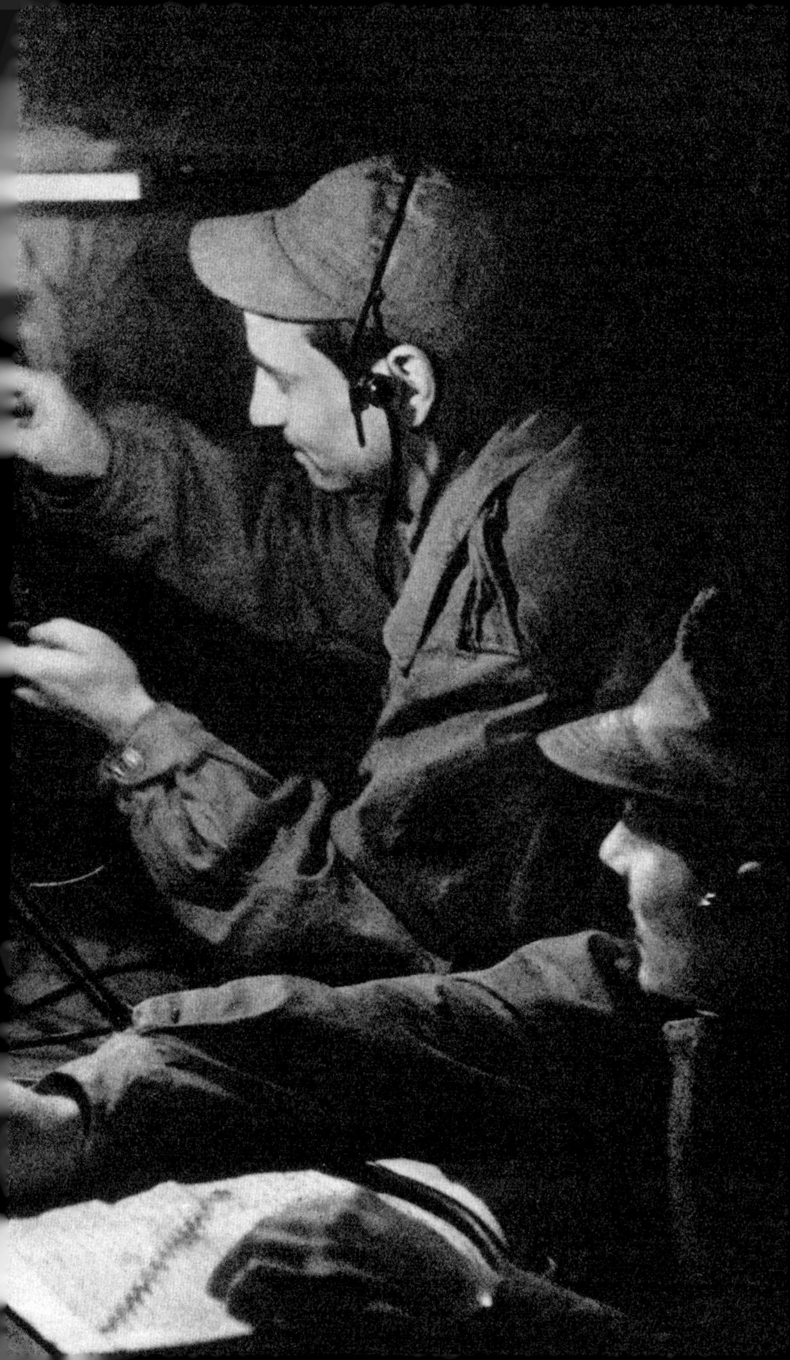

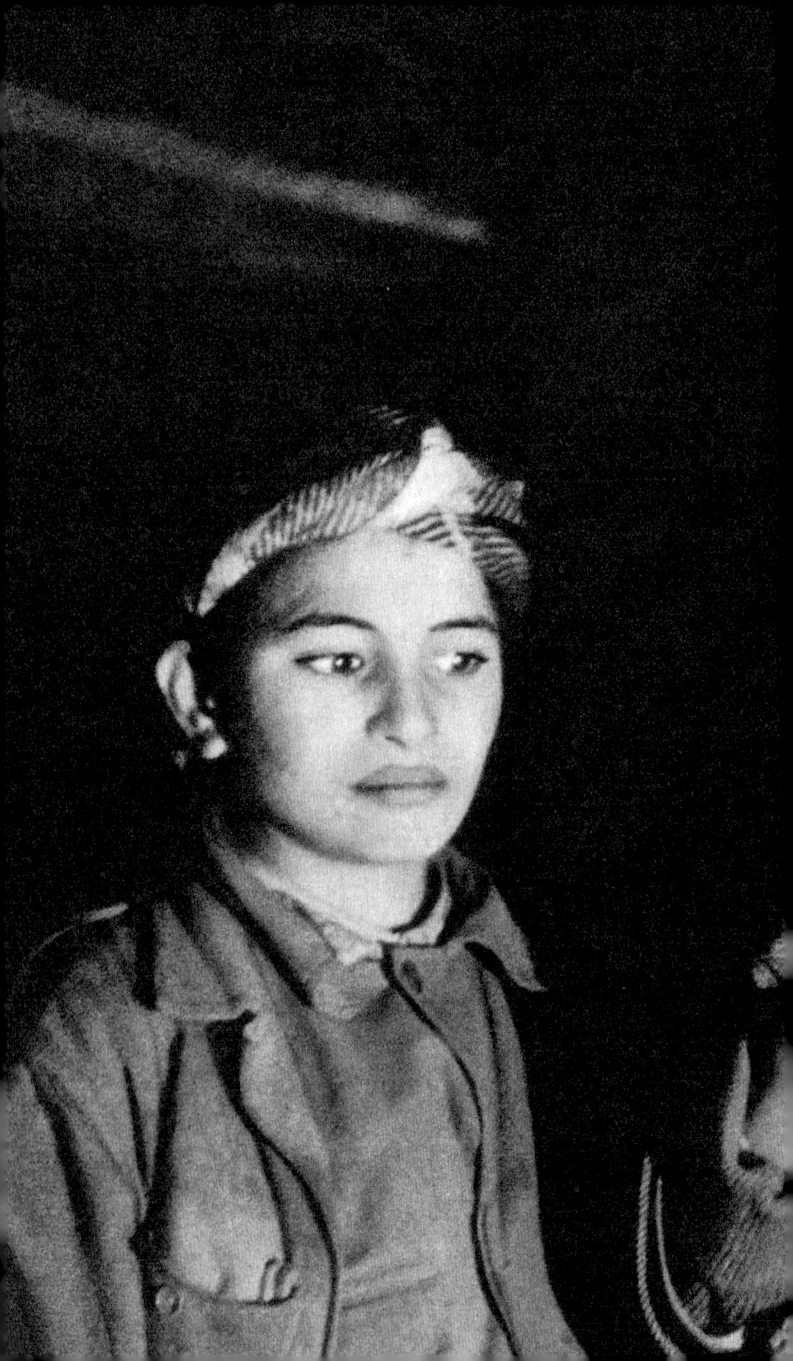

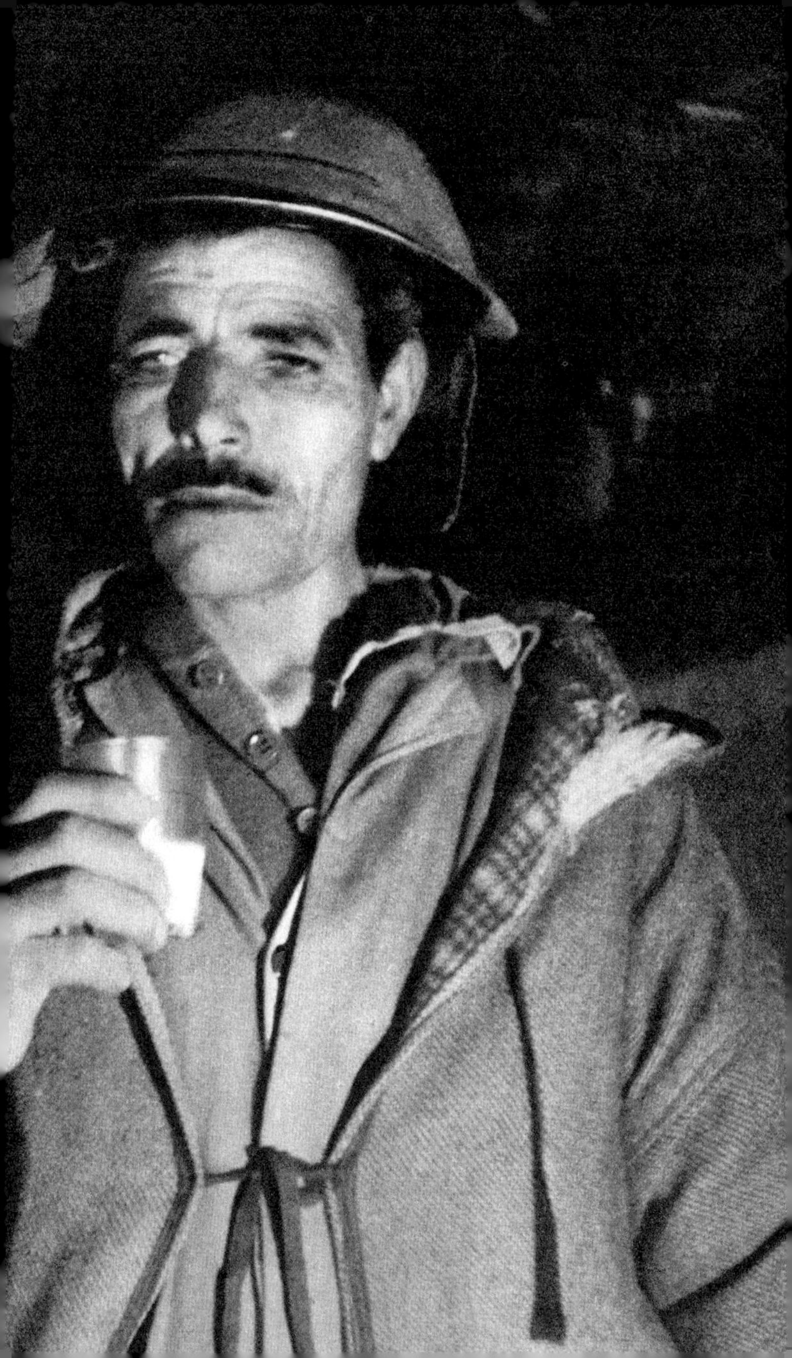

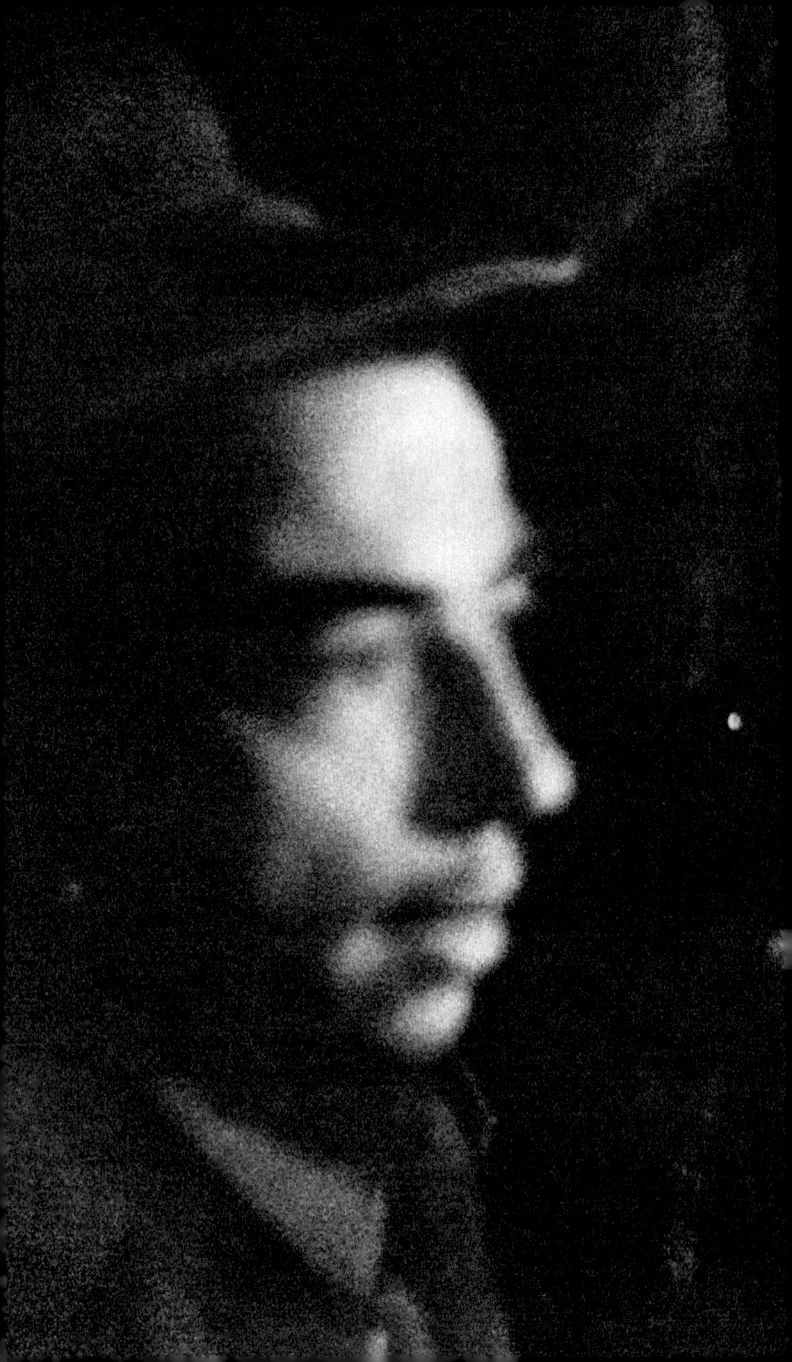

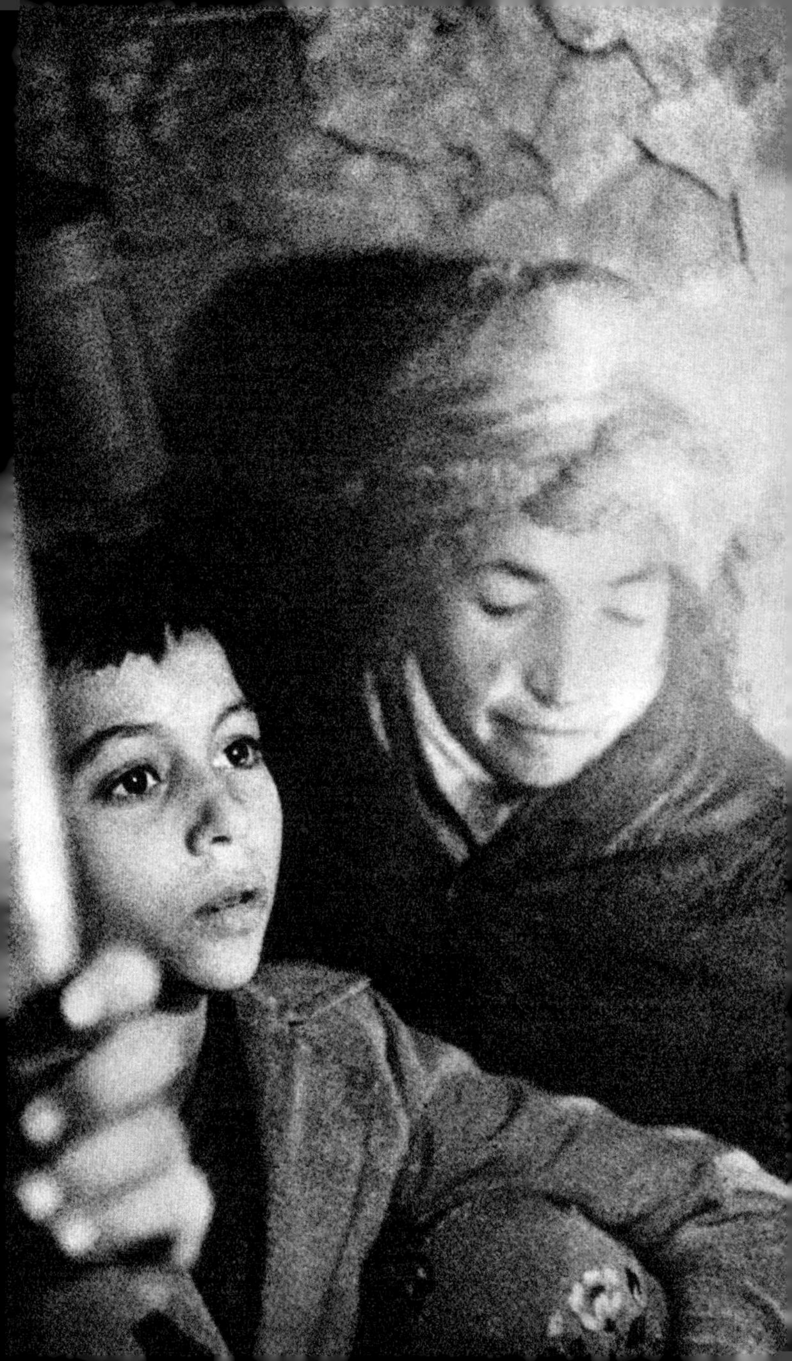

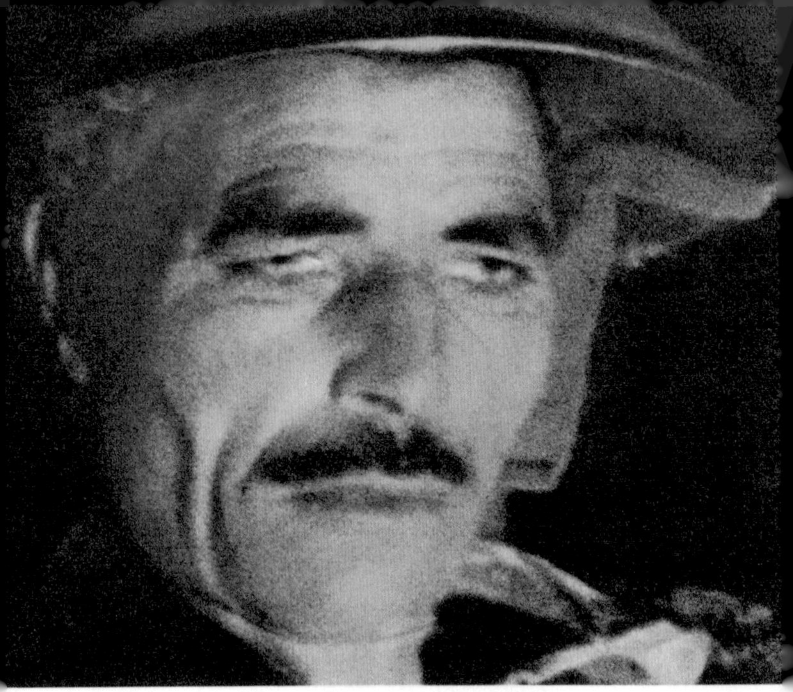

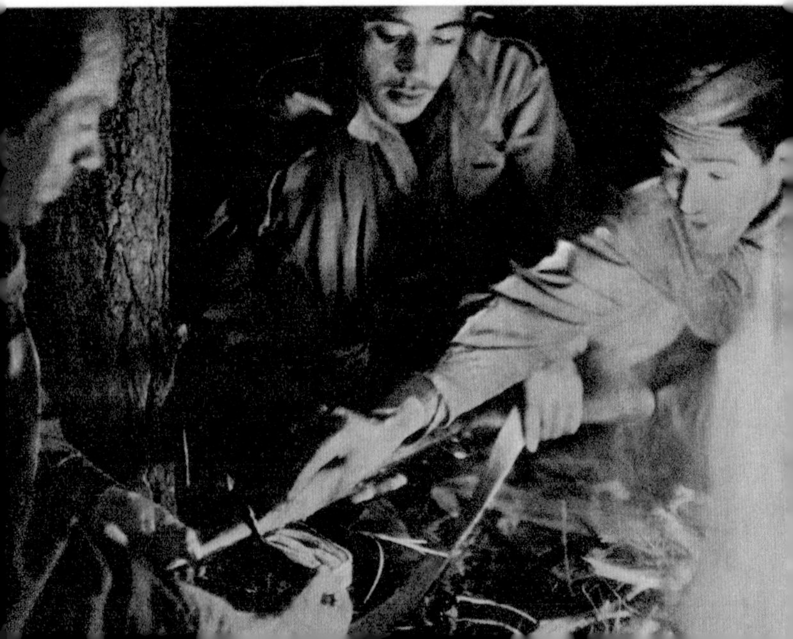

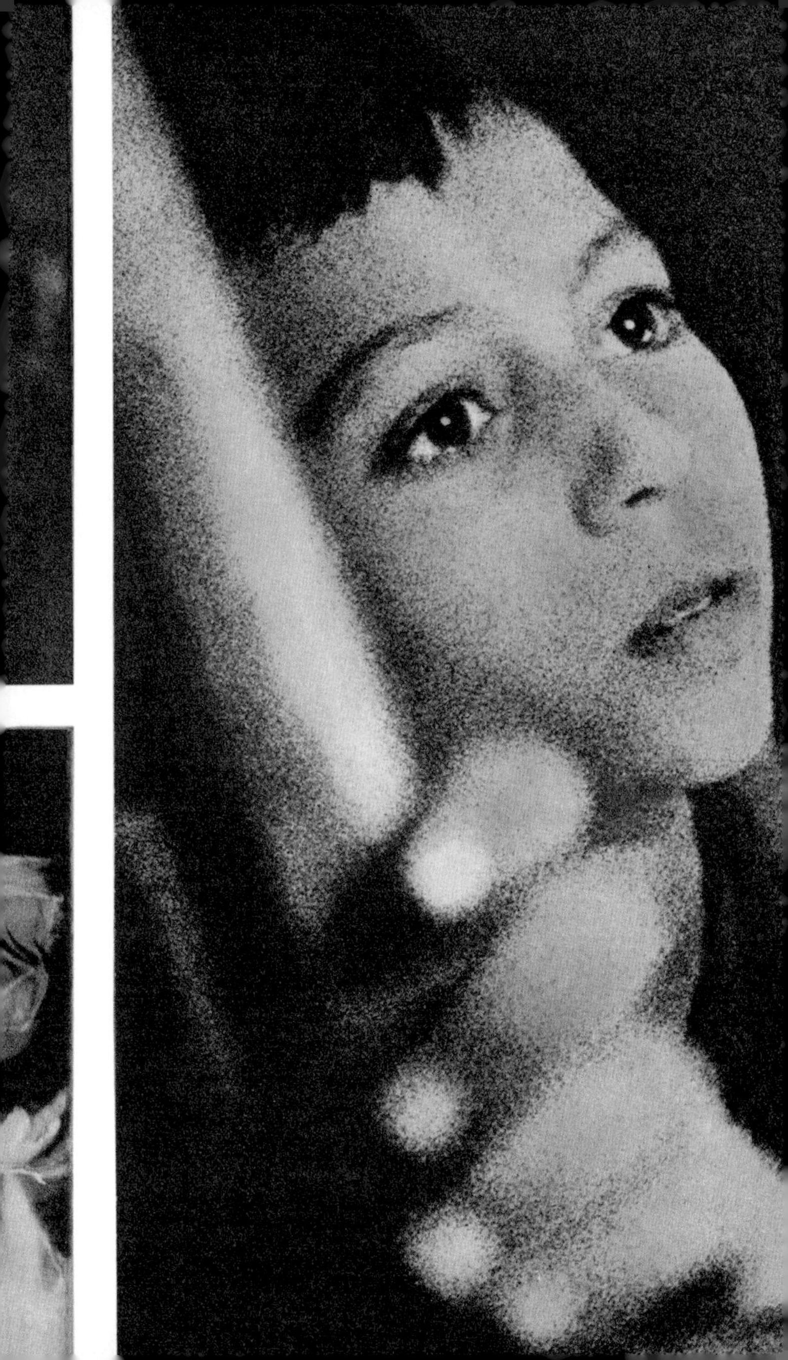

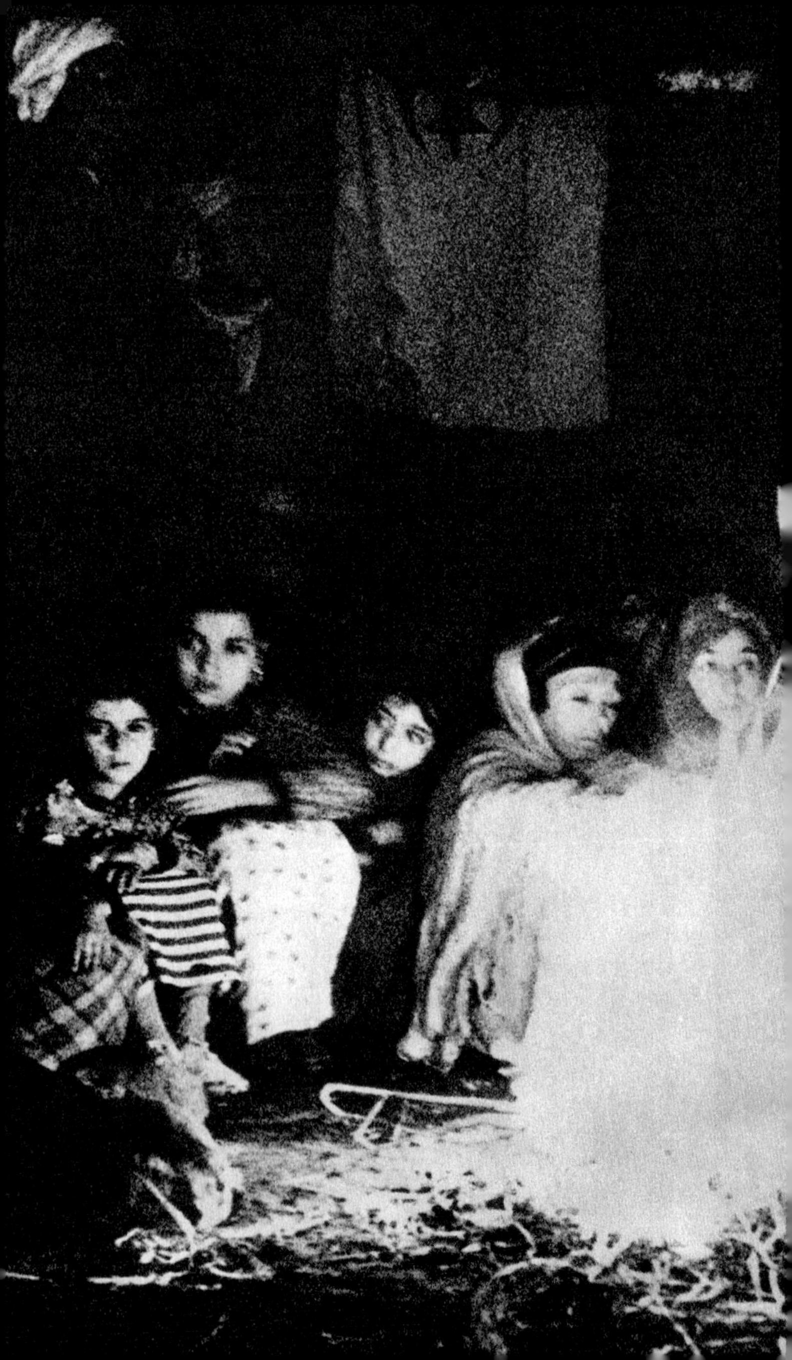

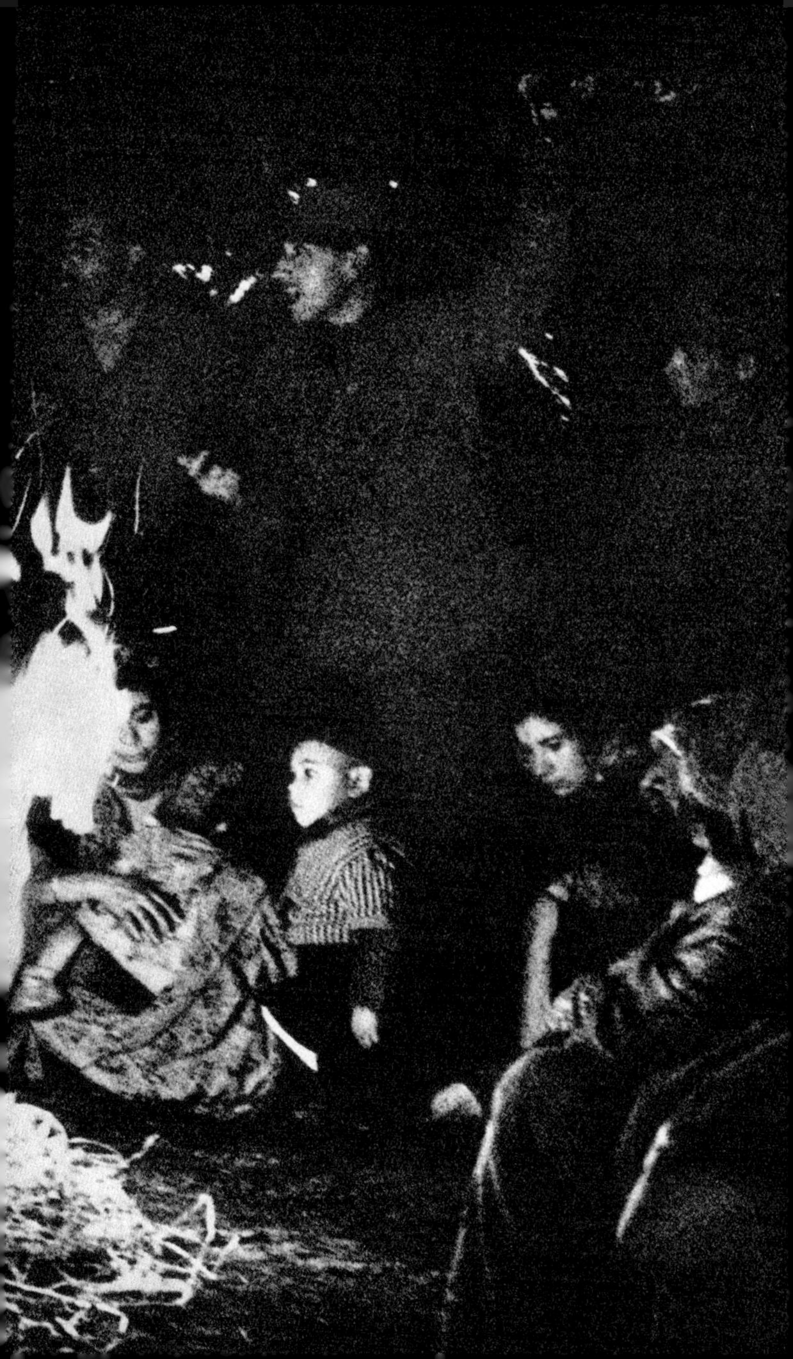

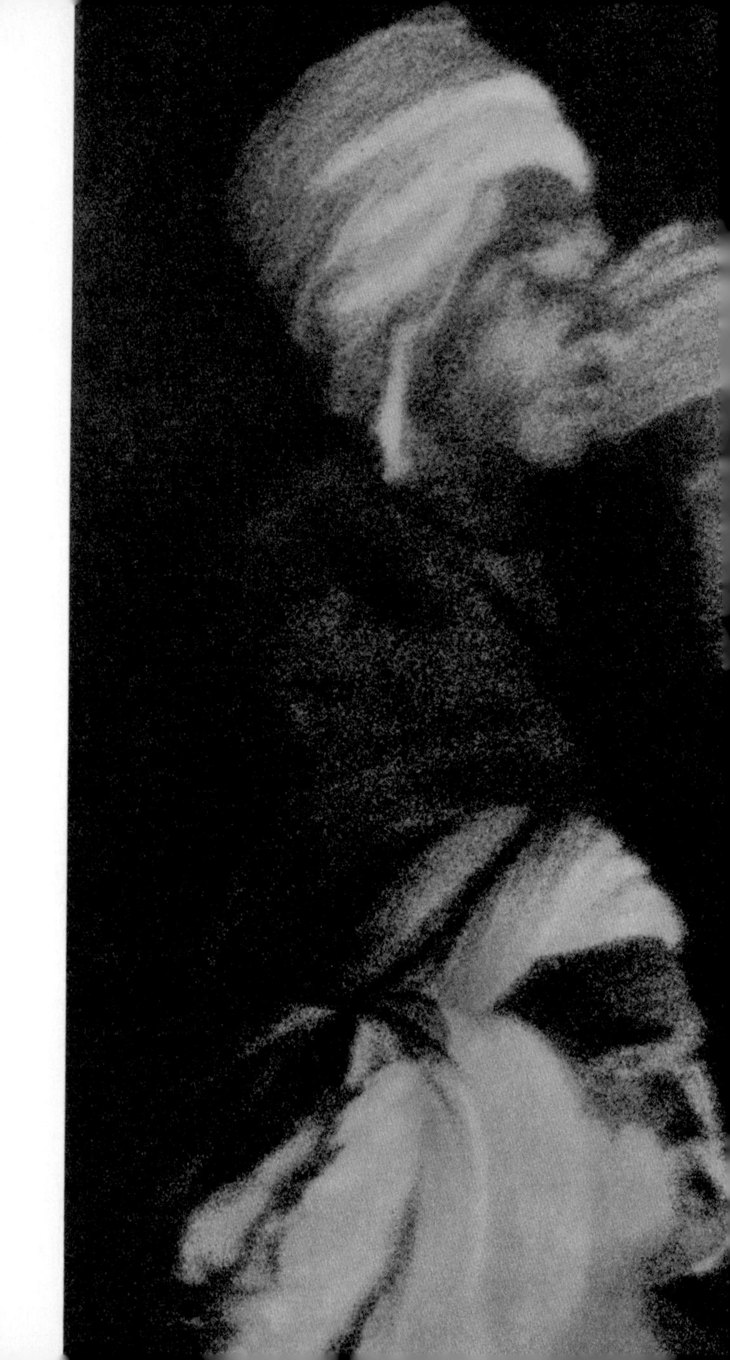

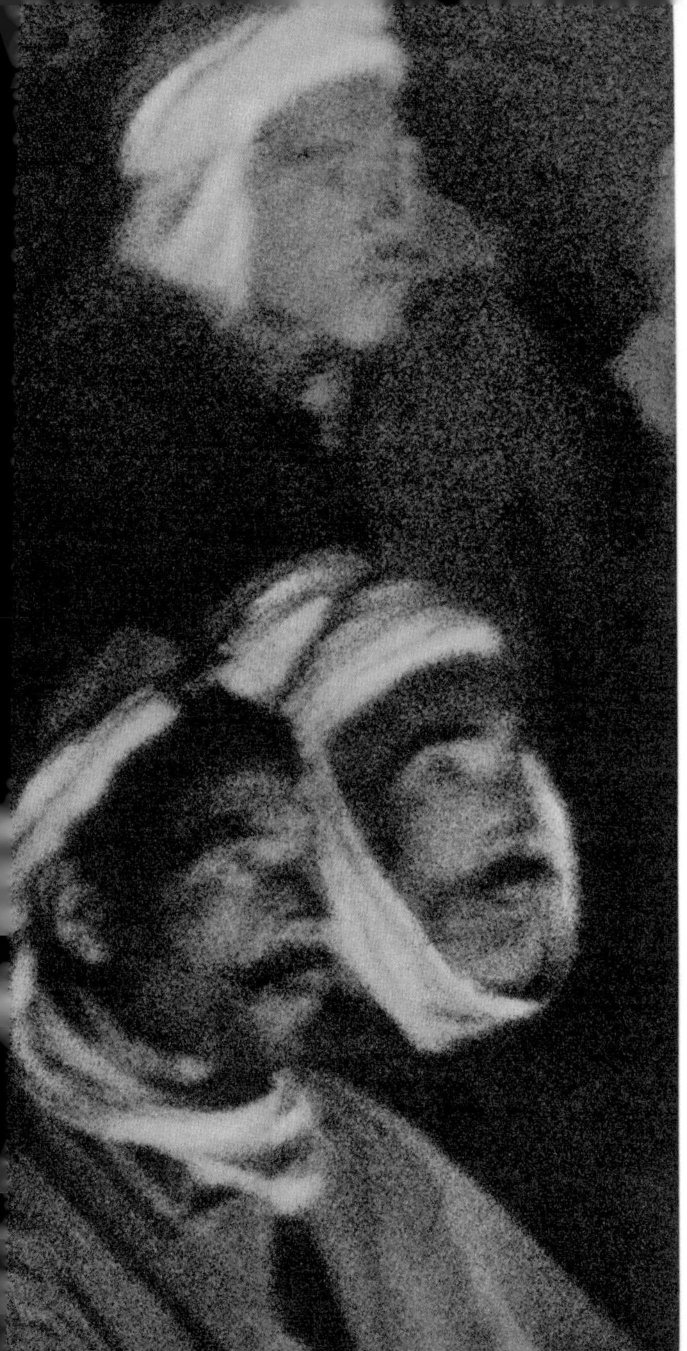

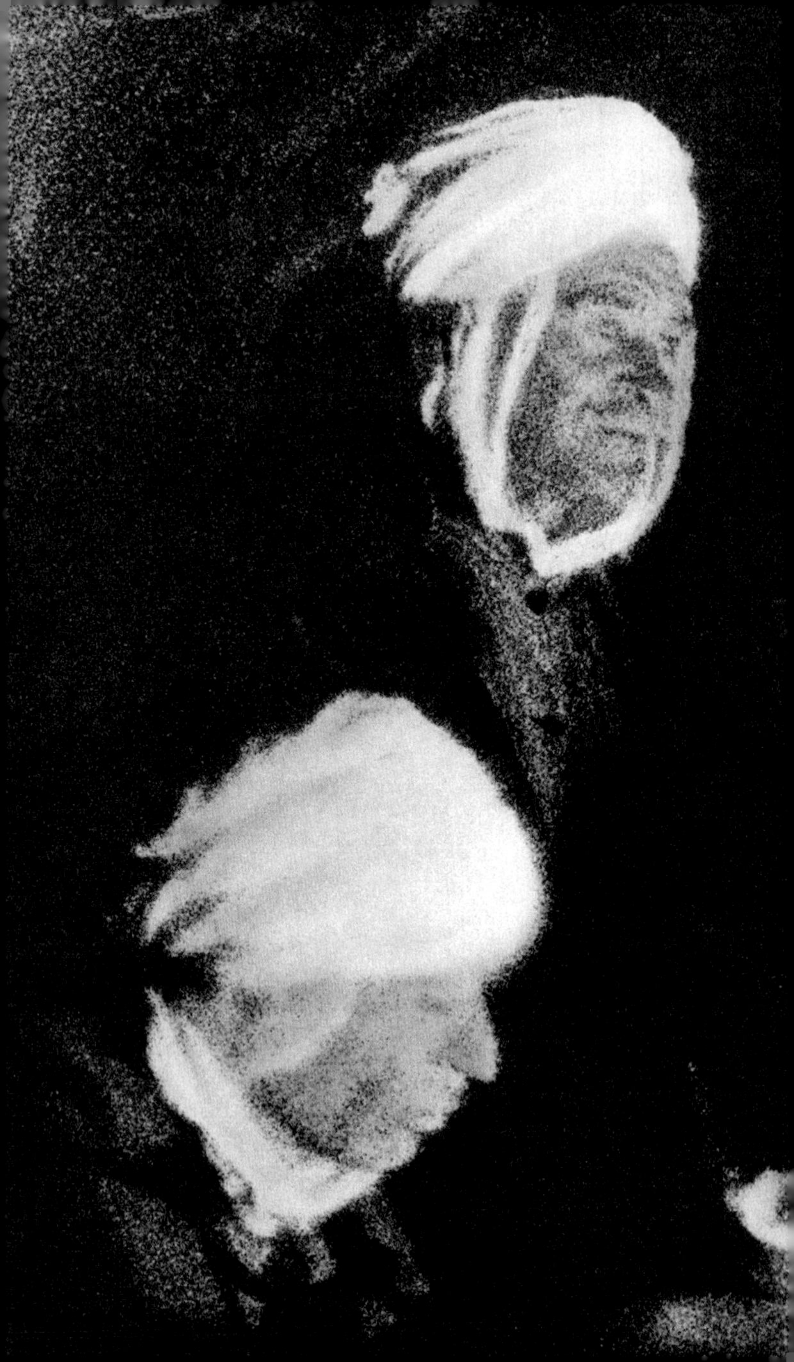

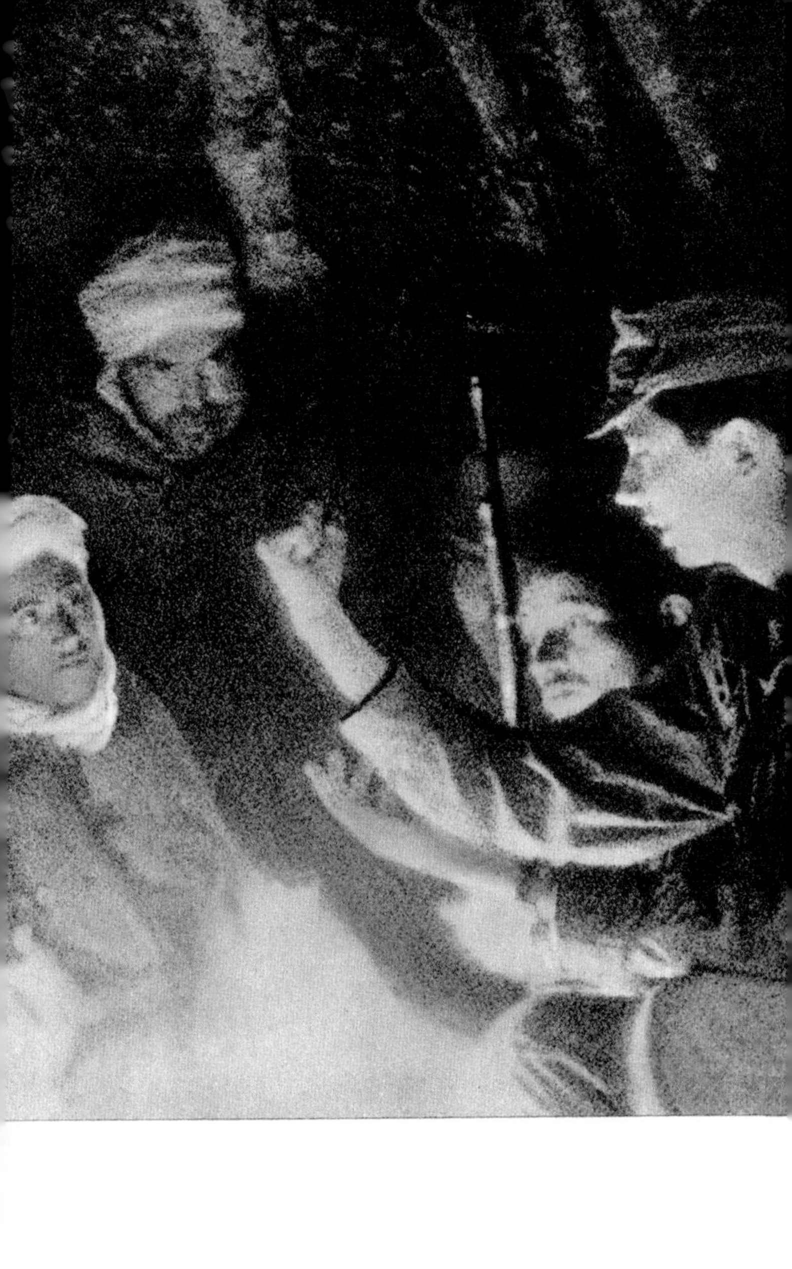

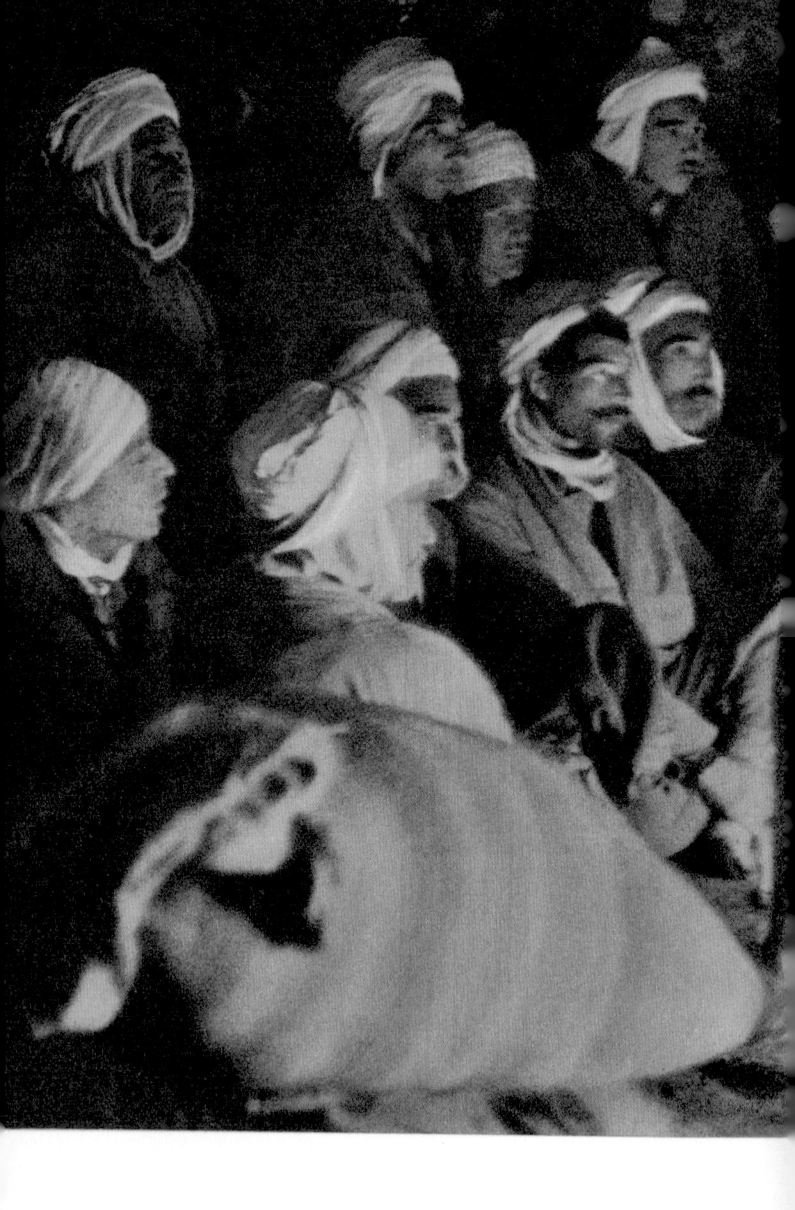